The Earth Belongs
to Everyone

Articles & Essays
by
Alanna Hartzok

The Institute for Economic Democracy Press
& Earth Rights Institute

Published by: the Institute for Economic Democracy Press
313 Seventh Ave., Radford, VA 24141, USA
888.533.1020 / www.ied.info / ied@ied.info

In Cooperation with Earth Rights Institute
717.264.0957 / www.earthrights.net / earthrts@pa.net

Library of Congress Cataloging-in-Publication Data

Hartzok, Alanna., 1948 -
  The earth belongs to everyone : articles & essays / by Alanna Hartzok
    p. cm.
  Includes bibliographical references and index.
  ISBN 978-1-933567-04-4 (pbk : alk. paper) -- ISBN 978-1-933567-05-1 (hbk : alk. paper)
1. Land tenure. 2. Natural resources. 3. Democracy. 4. Economic policy.
I. Title.
  HD1251.H37 2008
333.7--dc22
                    2008018115

Library of Congress provided the above.
5. Earth Rights Democracy 6. Reclaiming the Commons 7. Land Value Capture/Tax
8. Economic Democracy 9. Henry George 10. Green Taxes 11. Peace Studies 12. Land
Rights 13. Another World is Possible 14. Resource Rent for Public Revenue 15. Women
and Land 16. Prout 17. Financing Sustainable Development 18. New Economics

Book cover designed by Abel Robinson
This book is printed on acid free paper.

Table of Contents

Acknowledgements

To my generous mom and dad, Ruth and Lee Hartzok, and my wonderful children Abram Hartzok and Athena Azevedo.

To my dear and gracious friend and colleague Patricia Aller, with a special thank you for the many times you fed and sheltered me during my trips to New York City.

Thank you to J.W. Smith for mentoring me through the book preparation process and to Helen Snively for expert editing of the introduction.

Heartfelt appreciation to many other women friends and colleagues who have shared with me at various ages and stages the joys and challenges of this life: Anne Goeke, LaRue Brandt, Heather Remoff, Tatiana Roshkoshnaya, Joan Sage, Sue Walton, Marjorie Goldman, Rosemary Sullivan, Louise Morgan, Wendy Yost Adams, Aloma Handshu, Leslie Shanti Morjani, Shirley-Anne Hardy, Malka Brandzel, Judy Yetter, Norie Huddle, Diane Perlman, Carolyn George, Harriet Diller, Alison Mellotti Cormack, and mentors who have crossed over, Lucy Sylva, Lucile Green and Mildred Loomis.

Earth/People cover image created by El Salvador women's cooperative, courtesy of Marta Benavides. Cover page photos left to right: Eberi Koripamo-Eson, Rob Wheeler, Anne Goeke, Gordon Abiama, Alanna Hartzok, Judy Yetter, Francis Udisi, Tatiana Roskoshnaya, Father Jean-claude Atumaseo.

Introduction, Overview and Article Summaries

Reading through these essays and articles, written over the course of more than two decades, has led me unexpectedly to experience both mental integration and spiritual urgency. The integration came as my own work mirrored back my lifelong journey to both understand what is so wrong in our world today and to discover how we can begin to heal the enormous "person/planet pain." I was a young woman with very big questions when I left home. I wanted to understand the root causes of poverty and war, the basis of true happiness, the big picture of the meaning and purpose of life in general, and of my life in particular. I tenaciously held these questions in my heart, soul and mind, determined to find their answers.

During the course of a 25-year vision quest I traveled far and wide, touching down on four continents and many major cities. I worked with children of migrant workers in rural Pennsylvania, with impoverished African Americans in Atlanta, and in a coal-mining village in Appalachia. After studying at the Institute of European Studies in Vienna I traveled to Beirut and taught in a school for Palestinian refugees. During trips behind the "iron curtain" I met the "enemy." Once we saw each other as flesh-and-blood humans we quickly became friends.

I meandered the alleyways through the favelas of Santo Domingo. The slums of Nairobi looked much the same. Lagos was a living hell. I bore two children in San Francisco, and then endured a period of personal poverty and homelessness in that city of the Golden Gate. I had attained a Master's Degree in psychology but was unable to find employment sufficient to pay the rent. I came back home to Chambersburg, Pennsylvania – a town that was burned to the ground during the Civil War. Why, oh why, my heart and soul cried out, is there poverty and war on this beautiful and amazing planet?

I gathered answers one by one, like items on a treasure hunt. The articles and essays in this book are a result of my long journey through the social and political movements of our times. Published in diverse outlets, they explore root causes of economic injustice and put forth emerging solutions to the needless material deprivation that so many suffer in a world that has plenty for all. Assembled and published together now for the first time, these writings are my treasure chest. I am happy to share it with you.

Herein you will find a way forward to a possible future of peace and abundance for all, a future that Franklin D. Roosevelt glimpsed when he put forth his Four Freedoms: freedom of expression, freedom of religion, freedom from want, and freedom from fear. These writings propose a deep reorientation of our social contract, meaning the rules by which humanity agrees to live and let live. The essence of the new contract is the acknowledgement in principle and policy of the birthright of humanity to the planet, and thus, equal rights for all to the gifts of nature.

My vision quest gave me a clarity of thought and understanding, but with it has come a greater sense of responsibility – "ability to respond" – and thus the urgency I feel right now to strongly partner with others in order to implement the "earth rights" policies described in this book. Words on paper can be powerful intellectually, but they are merely words unless we put them into action. We live in a time of crisis and chaos, in a world on a precipice. Ahead lies catastrophe unless humanity can act together in global cooperation. Ahead lies increasing and relentless warfare, unless humanity can respond quickly through awareness that we are all one human family on one small planet. We are all in this together. Warfare or earthshare? That is the question.

This book is also an invitation to you the reader. If you like what you learn here, please link up with our work at Earth Rights Institute. Together we can build a world that works for each and every one of us.

Overview

These articles and essays are roughly clustered by theme. The first three articles set forth the vision and ethical foundation for a new form of democracy, which I call Earth Rights Democracy. In such a democracy, the contract between people and their government contains three primary components:

1. The equal right to land and natural resources is a fundamental human right.
2. The earth and all her life forms have a right to biological and ecological integrity and well-being.
3. Taxation and other economic, social and political principles and policies should be based on these rights.

Earth Rights Democracy establishes political democracy on the firm foundation of human rights to the planet as a birthright and is a key to securing other economic human rights. Earth Rights Democracy is an essential ethical framework for creating a world of peace and plenty for all.

The next three describe how the earth rights ethic can be linked to governance through fundamental reforms in public finance policy. Articles on "green taxes" and the "tax shift agenda" combine two trains of thought: public finance programs of "land rent for the people" as advocated by Thomas Paine, Henry George and other classical economic thinkers and more recent movements for ecological, polluter-pay type taxes.

The seventh article is an example of this worldview as applied to current social and economic realities in West Virginia, presented in a public dialog format in a letter to the editor of the *Charleston Gazette*.

Number eight shows how earth rights ethics and policies are integrally aligned with the original Biblical teachings on land rights and social justice and how these teachings have been obscured and neglected by most mainstream religious institutions. The tragic results are persistently increasing human suffering and environmental degradation.

The next four articles, 9 through 12, place these ideas into an integrated local-to-global framework that balances the need for global cooperation with that for both decentralized and bioregionally based economics. Those involved with current movements for global governance and world democracy will discover the essential importance of a proposed new global institution that would collect and distribute economic rent from transnational and common heritage resources. – A Global Resource Agency.

Articles 13 through 16 build on this framework by highlighting current and proposed governmental institutions that collect taxes and economic rent on land and natural resources and then distribute a portion of these funds as direct citizen dividends. It is crucial to have participatory democratic input into the ways that land and resource rent is distributed. Such "earth dividends" or "earthshare" options should be included in "people's budget" decision-making processes.

My speech at the Harvard Club of New York (Article 17) summarizes my experiences at the global UN HABITAT II conference convened in Istanbul in 1996. "Sharing Our Common Heritage via the Tax Shift Agenda" (Article 18), the keynote speech I gave at the Council of Georgist Organizations conference in 1998, is a wide-ranging overview of actual and potential arenas of action for building an earth rights democracy.

The three Pennsylvania articles, numbers 19 through 21, focus on (1) my home state, where several cities are successfully implementing earth rights democracy policies via local tax reform; (2) the details of a state campaign that passed enabling legislation to expand this tax policy option; and (3) the potential effects of land value taxation on large and small farming operations.

Articles 22 through 26 are about the work I do, which cannot be conveyed by a simple job title, career niche, or organizational affiliation. They are slice-of-life stories and interviews, sketches and vignettes of my life as an earth rights democracy activist. Each year, each month, and each day is different from all others in this never boring and always interesting adventure through a meaningful and purpose-ful life.

The last four articles focus on earth rights democracy and the quest for peace on earth during these past several years of the Iraq War. Number 30, "Economics of War and Peace," is my most recent article. It is an expansive four-part paper that I presented on the Economists for Peace and Security panel at the Eastern Economics Association Annual Conference in New York on February 23, 2007.

I suggest that you begin this book by looking at the articles and essays that initially seem most interesting. While several are brief and could be read at one sitting, some longer ones contain substantial information and new ideas that might take some time to digest. After living with this book for a few weeks and gradually absorbing the information, you will have gained an important new worldview with profound possibilities for transformational action. At that point, I invite you to call or email me and we can discuss ways that we can work together to build earth rights democracy wherever you live. Our network is worldwide and we can build an effective partnership for this work. Contact information is at the very end of the book.

To continue this introduction here is a brief summary of each article, along with some of the context in which I came to write them.

Articles, Summaries and Background

1. Democracy, Earth Rights and the Next Economy. This article occupies the prime space in this collection as it puts forward a sweeping, though highly condensed, perspective on the evolution of Western politics and economics over the past 700 years. Beginning with the first phase of Enclosures which privatized common lands and ending with Vision 2020 "full spectrum dominance" policies of the US nation state, this 2001 E. F. Schumacher Lecture describes the land problem and sets forth the concept of Earth Rights Democracy. Pithy quotes from several land rights thinkers and activists are sprinkled throughout the lecture, which was nearly ninety minutes long and is also available on audiocassette. In the last part I outline several specific policy approaches based on an ethic of equal rights to earth for all. This lecture, edited by Hildegarde Hannum, was published as an E. F. Schumacher lecture series booklet.

In one of the great honors of my life, the esteemed social visionary and peace activist Robert Swann urged the Schumacher board to invite me to be one of the three lecturers that year, the other two being Amory Lovins, Chairman and Chief Scientist of the Rocky Mountain Institute, and John Todd, the ecological design and "living machines" bioneer. Both are foremost thinkers and innovators in sustainable energy systems and policies. It was also a joy to meet with Bob the day after the lecture, which was our last time together. His legacy lives on through the innovative work of his partner, Susan Witt, the current executive director of the E.F. Schumacher Society, who introduced me that October day of 2001 in Johnson Chapel at Amherst College.

2. Who Owns the Earth? Here I ask a "first principle" question, an outside-of-the-box question. It is one of my earlier essays, first published in 1987. In nearly every country, about 5% of the people own at least 90% of the privately owned land. So this question aims to understand who SHOULD own the earth and even what it means to "own" the earth. As such, "Who owns the earth?" is a profound ethical and spiritual question that functions rather like a Zen koan. The question cannot be answered in the same mindset from which it is asked. The answer lies beyond the concept of "ownership" and goes to the heart of the matter: that all life is interconnected.

In other words, how we hold the earth is how we hold each other. This essay shows how we can move beyond the politics of right versus left into a new ethical, economic, and political realm where we can hold each other and the earth in love, respect, and profound appreciation.

3. Land for People, Not for Profit. I wrote this piece after several years of participating in sessions at the United Nations. In 1993 Pat Aller and I were appointed United Nations Non-Governmental Representatives for the International Union for Land Value Taxation and Free Trade, founded in London in 1933. This is a long name for an organization and I usually drop the Free Trade part, but not just because the name is a mouthful. In many of the networks I interact with, free trade has a bad reputation. Currently most progressives advocate "fair trade" as opposed to the monopoly capitalist Washington consensus version of free trade. But the IULVT & FT (the IU for short) is rooted in the brilliant perspective elucidated by Henry George in his book *Protection and Free Trade*, first published in 1886. He analyzed the problematic trade issue that was rooted in the land problem: trade can be neither free nor fair when so few own such a disproportionately large share of natural resources, surface land, and land value.

The IU is formally affiliated with the United Nations through both the Department of Public Information and ECOSOC (Economic and Social Council). While the IU supports fair free trade it does so primarily through its core mission of achieving socially just land tenure and a fair distribution of wealth via fundamental taxation policy reform. Our goal is to remove the burden of taxes from the backs of working people, which includes everyone producing needed goods and socially useful services, and to shift the tax base to the "rental value" of land and natural resources. For the common good, we advocate full collection of the earth's economic rent – that is, its surplus value – from land and natural resources that have some monetized (money used in exchange) value. In brief, tax land not labor.

Pay for what you take from the earth, not what you make with your work. If all land and resources were used fairly, efficiently, and in an environmentally sensitive way, all human beings now on earth and those yet to come could meet their basic needs and live in dignity and purpose.

As a representative of a UN NGO I participated in HABITAT II, one of several major global conferences organized by various UN agencies during the 1990s. In 1996, the UN Center for Human Settlements (Habitat) organized and sponsored HABITAT II, a two- weeklong session in Istanbul. I carefully observed several of the official proceedings, paying particular attention to the section on Land Access. Along with more than 15,000 others, I also participated in sessions of the HABITAT II NGO Forum. I also organized and led six NGO Forum events that focused primarily on land tenure and tax policy.

I was very pleased with the results of the UN HABITAT II Action Agenda section on Land Access. This section describes land access as key to eliminating poverty and environmental degradation and calls for land value capture, land-based taxes, proper land cadastres (maps and records), and other elements essential to implementing the fundamental taxation policy reform that we advocate.

Some time after the Istanbul conference, however, I read a post by UNCHS intern Anna-Karin Jatfors on the Global Campaign for Secure Tenure section of the Habitat website; she encouraged using land as an investment and speculation commodity. At that point I recognized how confused many people are about how to proceed towards a truly just system of land tenure. My intention in writing "Land for People, Not for Profit" was to articulate the benefits and drawbacks of private property in land and to articulate a clear way forward towards equitable land rights and poverty eradication.

4. Green Economics: A Decentralist, Bioregionalist, Global Agenda. This one was published in *Land and Liberty* in August 1985. It is the oldest article in the book. It draws on many influences, among them PROUT (Progressive Utilization Theory), Ralph Borsodi, founder of the School of Living, American bioregionalists Peter Berg and David Haenke, and the great 19th century economic philosopher Henry George. It puts forth a People's New World Order vision, if you will, that many of us yearn to see made real. Were this future vision to become manifest, all people would have their basic needs met and be as self-reliant as possible within the opportunities and constraints of a biologically defined region. Meanwhile, workers in flourishing local-based cooperatives would enjoy the meaning and value of right livelihood. New institutions would provide the minimum basic requirements for global peacekeeping and environmental restoration and protection. This people/planet-centered approach would take us beyond the artificially (most often militarily) drawn lines of the nation state to a world where each individual and place is uniquely valued as part of the planetary whole.

Reading this article again, 22 years later, I am rather amazed that I still hold this same vision today. Like so many millions of us, I am greatly distressed by our nation's current political and economic conditions and its military and foreign policy engagements. Our federal tax system no longer effectively supports the welfare of the people on any level. Our constitutional rights have been eroded decade after decade until we can hardly distinguish the power of the president from that of a dictator. The power mongers in Washington, DC live nearby ever-increasing numbers of downtrodden and impoverished citizens. It is one thing to respect, and be committed to, the values of life, liberty, and the pursuit of happiness, and freedom of worship and expression, production and exchange. Blind adherence to a fossilized and exploitative political order is quite another.

5. Restructuring Economic Relationships. This is an essay published in the Winter 1988 edition of my short-lived newsletter, *Geodata*. It simply and succinctly traces the maldistribution of wealth to the exploitation inherent – and apparent -- in our systems of land tenure, capital ownership, financial and monetary policy. I call on us all to rethink the whole area of work, jobs and wages and to thoroughly analyze the economic structures of our own communities, beginning with a list of five questions.

6. Earth Rights Democracy – Land Ethics and Public Finance Policy as if People and Planet Mattered. The subtitle of this article draws on E. F. Schumacher's classic, *Small is Beautiful: Economics as if People Mattered.* I presented it at the Richard Alsina Fulton Conference on Sustainability and the Environment held March 26 – 27, 2004 at Wilson College, located in my hometown of Chambersburg, Pennsylvania. It was a rare and valued opportunity to present my ideas at a local venue. Dr. Inno Onwueme, then a professor at Wilson and director of the Fulton Center, organized the conference. Inno was born and grew up in the Niger Delta region of Nigeria. A brilliant professor who writes both academic papers and short stories, Inno is an agricultural economist whose special focus on the African yam has taken him to many countries.

During the few years that Inno lived in Chambersburg we met for several stimulating conversations over dinner at my Aradhana ecological homestead. As Earth Rights Institute is beginning an ecovillage development project in Bayelsa State in the Niger Delta, I was particularly interested in Inno's profound and personal experiences growing up in this region. I was especially pleased that he invited me to present this paper at this conference.

In 2005, Trent Schroyer, Professor of Sociology-Philosophy at Ramapo College and President of The Other Economic Summit (TOES), asked if I had any recent papers appropriate for the anthology that he and Thomas Golodik were putting together; this one seemed a good fit. Trent and Tom did a great job editing this Wilson College paper for *Creating a Sustainable World: Past Experiences/Future Struggles*, published by Apex Press in 2006. I strongly recommend their book; as Professor Jeff Boyer says, it is "an important tool for international activists and educators working to democratize economic, technological, and environmental resources."

7. Forget the Old Tax Fights: All Should Enjoy the Profits from Nature's Gifts. One day early in February 2007 I received a call from my friend Art Rybeck, a land value tax activist and dentist in Wheeling, West Virginia. Art said that several particularly interesting opinion pieces had been recently published in the Views section of the *Charleston Gazette*, one of the state's major newspapers. He urged me to read them and respond with an article that would touch upon those writers' concerns and then bring them into a focus on the land problem and the land value taxation policy approach. The editorial page editor, Dawn Miller, replied to my submission by saying, "It is a joy to have such attentive readers." I wrote a mix of philosophy and fundamental economics and appealed to readers to rise above the pessimism of past corruption. My article appeared on April 16. Dawn gave it the terrific title.

8. Public Finance Based on Judeo-Christian Teachings. Appearing one day among my many emails was an invitation to present a paper at the Christianity and Human Rights Conference at Samford University in Birmingham, Alabama. This invitation was an excellent opportunity to put together materials I had collected over the years on Judeo-Christian land ethics and their relevance to the economic justice paradigm set forth by Henry George in *Progress and Poverty* and his other works. The paper also held a deep personal meaning to me. I was born into a fundamentalist Christian family in the rural Cumberland Valley in Pennsylvania. Mom and Dad made sure that my brother, sister and I went to Sunday school and church every week and Bible School for two weeks in the summer. At age ten I had the "born again" experience of giving my life to Jesus.

But by age twelve, I was seriously troubled by my mother's statement concerning our pediatrician which went something like this: "It's too bad that Dr. Schapiro will not go to heaven; he's such a good doctor." Well, it seemed too bad to me, too, and somehow just plain unfair. How could it be that those who have a non-Christian religious belief system were condemned to an eternity of hell? And what about the people in other parts of the world who live and die, never having heard the story of Jesus? After all, in Sunday School we sang "red and yellow, black and white, they are precious in his sight." Something just did not compute! I became an agnostic.

In college and on into my twenties I explored and experienced every major religion. I sat in Zen Buddhist meditation, whirled with the Sufis, and listened to the wisdom of Islamic mysticism with Pir Vilayat Khan. I delved into the broadminded

Judaic teachings of rabbis Zalman Schachter Shalomi and Schlomo Carlbach and participated in Jewish holy days with the Aquarian Minyon in the San Francisco Bay Area.

I studied and experienced psychic phenomena and the further reaches of human potential attaining a master's degree in psychology at West Georgia College (now the University of West Georgia), followed by four years of training at the Canadian Institute of Psychosynthesis in Montreal.

This long search for spiritual truth greatly expanded my worldview. Essentially, I have come to know that we all have equal value as human beings and an equal right to exist in this amazing universe. Our existence on this plane totally depends upon the primal elements of earth, air, fire and water. As beings that are equal in value and totally dependent on nature, it follows that just political and economic rules and structures must be based upon equal rights to the earth. In this paper I make a case for a new form of democracy based on the human birthright to the earth. Showing that this ethic is foundational within the Judeo-Christian tradition of jubilee justice and both Old and New Testament teachings, I present a practical policy approach of tax fairness based on this stance. Although I focus on the Judeo-Christian tradition, I set forth a broad, ethical humanist worldview compatible with the truth of all the major religions.

While living in Atlanta I learned specific methods of yoga and meditation from instructors at the Ananda Marga Yoga Society founded by P.R. Sarkar, whose spiritual name was Anandamurti, meaning "embodiment of bliss" in Sanskrit. I remember being moved to tears upon hearing my first PROUT (Progressive Utilization Theory) lecture, which set forth a high-minded purpose and vision for humanity worldwide. Securing a better, brighter planetary social order was the Ananda Marga mission and I was happy to sign up.

In 1973 I moved from Atlanta to Montreal where I lived and helped run the Ananda Marga jagriti, or small ashram, for a couple years while I trained in psychosynthesis with Martha Crampton. PROUT teachings say "time, place, and person" will determine the specific policies that will build a political economy beyond both communism and capitalism (Anandamurti predicted the collapse of both these systems).

I had my antennas out for those specific transformative policies when I moved to San Francisco in 1979. Not learning much that was new to me in the Ph.D. program in which I was enrolled, I noticed a posting for a free class in economics. My next intellectual breakthrough in understanding the root causes of poverty and social injustice came through this non-credit adult education class at the Henry George School of Social Science of Northern California. Within five weeks I received answers to questions I had been asking for years, and answers to other important questions I had never even thought to ask.

Shortly after what I now call my "economic enlightenment," I dropped out of the Ph.D. program in psychology and headed off on a new path as educator and activist for the Henry George School and the "Georgist" movement. Over the past 25 years I became ever more appreciative of how this great Philadelphia-born seer of political economy had articulated for his times that golden thread of economic wisdom teachings of the ages. Many of us think of Henry George as a prophet. He preached the doom of systems of social injustice that resulted in the suffering of masses of people and showed how those systems could be uprooted so that humanity as a whole could move forward to a state of mental and spiritual expansion.

9. Financing Local to Global Public Goods: An Integrated Green Tax-Shift Perspective. Green tax-shift policy is a rapidly emerging new perspective on tax reform that emphasizes the incentive capacity inherent in public finance policy. From this vantage point, taxation not only raises the money necessary to fund governmental services; it also reflects the overall value system of a given society, rewarding some activities while punishing others. If we are to have global stability and human security we must re-think the logic of globalization, including the best ways to finance public goods such as health, education, infrastructure, environmental sustainability, and efforts towards peace and conflict resolution. A coherent, integrated and ethically based local-to-global tax system can evolve out of the current public finance hodge-podge of the world's more than 180 nation states.

I presented this paper at the Global Institute for Taxation Conference on Fundamental Tax Reform sponsored by Price Waterhouse Coopers and St. John's University, New York, on September 30, 1999. It was published in *Taxation Alternatives for the 21st Century*, the proceedings of that conference. In it I describe several successful practices and works-in-progress on green tax shift policies that harness incentives to produce and distribute wealth in an efficient, equitable, and sustainable way. I site research that shows the impressive potential of green tax reform to help solve major social, economic and environmental problems. I also present an integrated local-to-global public finance framework based on green taxation principles and policies.

In researching and writing this paper I had the chance to pull together several crucial concerns including for wealth inequality, environmental degradation, and economic inefficiency and exploitation and use them as a context for an emerging integrated worldview of property rights, human rights, and public finance policy. I describe several specific working examples of the new policy approach and present a local, regional and global perspective on implementation.

10. Financing Planet Management: Sovereignty, World Order, and the Earth Rights Imperative. In Pasadena, California, in 1979 I met two women who became important mentors to me, both on the same day at an International

Cooperation Council conference organized by Leland Stewart. I had recently been introduced to the economic justice work and writings of Henry George and was conducting my first workshop on the subject at the conference when a woman raised her hand and said, "We all know this. What are we going to do about it?" Mildred Loomis had already been working along these lines for more than forty years, and, along with Ralph Borsodi, had founded the School of Living community land trust movement. Though a staunch decentralist, Mildred agreed with Ralph on the need for new global institutions to solve problems that could not be addressed at local and regional levels.

That day I also met Dr. Lucile Green, a leader of movements for global governance that would empower individuals by giving them a voice via the World Citizens Assembly. Lucile encouraged me to participate in an amazing three-week-long journey in Japan, where people from more than forty countries discussed how to implement this idea. The bullet train took us from Tokyo to Kyoto and Osaka, ending in Hiroshima for the 35th anniversary of the dropping of the atomic bomb.

I well remember that rainy day as I sat between the Secretary of the Soviet Peace Committee, whose name I cannot recall, and Gennady Gerasimov, then a journalist for a Soviet magazine of the caliber of our *LIFE* magazine. Our hearts broke open, as we fully understood the enormity of the atomic bombing; we were especially concerned that all the Japanese people around us were shielded from the rain with umbrellas, hats or jackets. This of course was during the Cold War, when the Soviets were our enemies, and people of the Soviet Union rarely traveled out of their country. Some time later, while I sat in my parents' living room in Pennsylvania watching the evening news, Gennady appeared on the screen informing the world of what had happened at Chernobyl. He had become the chief foreign spokesman for the Soviet Union. I remembered us both in blue jeans with our arms linked together having our photo taken in Japan.

In ensuing years I gained greater knowledge of the various movements for global governance and United Nations reform. Dr. Harry Lerner, who had become my good friend during the Japan World Citizens traveling conference, invited me to speak in New York at several events he organized both inside and near the United Nations. While Harry strongly validated the points on economic democracy that I was making, the global governance movement as a whole sorely lacked any thorough analysis of the land problem, or of the importance of various incentives and disincentives of public finance policy.

After attending one too many UN reform and global governance conferences where people told me once again that all these economic issues would be addressed AFTER the world government was established, I had had enough of such sidestepping. The intention in this little paper with the big name was to put forth reasons why it was essential to solve the land problems and add issues of economic democracy and equitable tax policy in order to form effective and fair global governance structures. And, unless we were clear about these concerns we risked having a top-heavy world government that might unnecessarily limit the powers of individuals and local and regional authorities. Resource rent funds organized at local, regional and global levels would address the root causes of many problems the world government people were trying to address.

I received many responses agreeing with this paper (they can be found herein). The one that pleased me most came from Dr. Benjamin Ferencz, who had been a US prosecutor at the Nuremburg War Crimes Trial and at the time was teaching international law at Pace University. I was also quite pleased with a comment from Jack Yost, then the UN NGO Representative for the World Federalist Movement. He agreed with me "very much that world federalists and world governmentalists need to think through the fundamentals of economic justice." A few years later Jack moved back to Oregon and wrote *Planet Champions: Adventures in Saving the World*, which highlighted leaders of both the Georgist economic teachings and the world federalist work. Sadly, Jack died suddenly just before his planned book tour.

11. Acting As If the Second Assembly Already Exists. The same Harry Lerner mentioned above also mentored me into movements for global democracy. His special focus and contribution was the effort to build a Peoples' Assembly as a second house within the UN system. The UN Peoples' Assembly would be directly elected by the people of the world and would speak for the well-being of the world as a whole rather than for individual nation states as does the UN General Assembly.

Harry invited me to speak at a UN Reform conference that he and Jeffrey Segall held in New York in 1990. This talk was included in *Building a More Democratic United Nations - Proceedings of the First International Conference on a More Democratic UN*, edited by Frank Barnaby and published by Frank Cass in 1991, now available on the internet.

My ending statements are insights I still carry close to my heart: "How we hold the earth is how we hold each other. The needs of the person and the needs of the planet are one and the same."

12. Land Value Tax and Resource Rent Approach to Financing for Development. I wrote this policy paper with input from Pat Aller, my IU UN NGO colleague and good friend. We submitted it to the United Nations Financing for Development preparatory process at the NGO Hearings Week, November 2000. As UN NGO representatives, we hoped that the Financing for Development "track" in the UN system would prove to be fertile ground for our tax policy approach.

Each of the five major UN global conferences of the 1990's -- enormous endeavors that had attracted more than 100,000 dedicated participants from around the world -- had brought forth a number of strong and clear action agendas. Creating these documents entails a meticulous -- and impressive -- process of consensus building. Each and every word and phrase is carefully crafted with tremendous care and consideration for meaning and nuance. The process involves substantial time, effort and concentration on details, with UN member state delegates sometimes working long past midnight to meet important deadlines. Sometimes UN NGO representatives have opportunities to present their views as well. The problem was, these good ideas and proposed policies were just not being implemented. There were no significant strides forward for poverty eradication, ending starvation, housing the homeless and provisioning basic services for all.

After reviewing the situation, the UN saw the problem: no funding was coming forth to bring these action agendas into reality. Hence the next UN major global conference, held in 2002 in Monterey, Mexico after three preparatory conferences was to launch a new Financing for Development track within the UN system.

Throughout all three preparatory conferences at the UN building in New York, we stood at the doorways of the UN assembly halls and distributed our policy paper to both NGOs and official UN nation state ambassadors and other delegates. We meticulously combed through the preparatory documents, suggesting changes in wording that would describe the importance of land value taxation and resource rent funds to finance development. We worked with the NGO Financing for Development working group to get statements into the official document. At one point we did succeed in getting a few words into an NGO statement that was presented on the main floor during one preparatory conference.

All to no avail. Our most frustrating moment came during a UN NGO session across the street at the Church Center. I had hoped to have at least five minutes to describe this policy approach to other UN NGO people. About two minutes into my talk, the chairman shut me down. I still do not know why. Perhaps because I was not an insider of the UN NGO core group that met regularly in New York.

By the time the Financing for Development conference in Mexico rolled around, I was feeling hopeless about influencing the process and did not even attend. My colleague Jeffrey Smith was in Mexico at the time and decided to go. He gave a side event workshop and made some contacts. But nothing really went anywhere and as far as I can see, the Financing for Development process is floundering. And we still see no big breakthroughs in ending hunger, homelessness and hopelessness on the planet.

Nonetheless, readers should find this paper of interest. In it, I succinctly described the land value tax policy in a global context. I then describe working models of this approach, and end with a call for a Global Resource Agency that would offer five clear benefits to the world. To my knowledge, Ralph Borsodi first proposed such an agency. He was a profound thinker and visionary who deserves to be far better known.

One more note on this article. It contains the statement that this policy approach is "under serious consideration by the Russian parliament, the Duma." It was, at the time. My colleagues Fred Harrison, Tatiana Roshkoshnaya, and Nic Tideman, among others, worked very hard for many years urging Russia to adopt the land value tax policy approach after the Soviet Union collapsed. They had support at top levels. But in the post-Gorbachev era of chaos and kleptomania, the neoliberal economic paradigm of privatization won out, and Russia experienced one of the largest natural resource grabs in world history. President Vladimir Putin was listening in on their earlier conversations about "the land question." To this day he still advocates capturing the resource rent of Russia's lost natural heritage and to some extant has succeeded in wresting back control of Russia's natural resources to benefit the Russian people as a whole.

13. Local to Global Dimensions of Ecotaxation, Land Value Taxation and Citizen Dividends. James Robertson, a British author of several important books on alternative economics, co-founded The Other Economic Summit (TOES) and the New Economics Foundation. He organized a one-day symposium at the Oxford Centre for the Environment, Ethics and Society on May 14, 1998 at Rhodes House, Oxford University. The conference was called Sharing Our Common Heritage: Resource Taxes and Green Dividends. This is the paper I presented that day.

In the citation for the gold medal awarded to James for his outstanding work, Mikhail Gorbachev called James "An outstanding example of a modern thinker at the service of society." James Robertson was probably the very first scholar to put together the several components of what I now call "holistic, integrated green tax shift." He designed this symposium to bring together experts on three major components of the new economic paradigm: ecotaxation, land value taxation, and citizen dividends.

I was honored to be one of the invited speakers, along with David Marquand, Tatiana Roshkoshnaya, Philippe van Parijs, and Mason Gaffney. Vandana Shiva was also scheduled to speak but could not come. India had just announced its success in building an atomic bomb and she chose to remain there to lead protests. Vandana was appalled that public funds had been directed to develop weapons of mass destruction rather than to meet the basic needs of India's many impoverished people. Lucy Silfa, director of the Henry George School of Social Science in the Dominican Republic, presented in Vandana's place. Lucy spoke brilliantly and movingly about conditions in the Dominican Republic and how they could be substantially improved if a land value tax policy was implemented.

In this talk the section on citizen dividends is a bit too brief but I provide details on the ethical underpinnings and practical policy examples of ecotaxation and land value taxation. I also describe the concept of "subsidiarity" as it relates to local-to-global taxes on specific types of resources.

The paper lays out guidelines for an integrated local-to-global public finance system based on the principle of the common heritage of earth's land and natural resources. It proclaims that the planet and all its resources, including land, water, forests, minerals, the atmosphere, electro-magnetic frequencies, and satellite orbits are the common heritage of all and must no longer be appropriated for the private profit of the few to the exclusion of the many.

All of the papers presented that day, along with books by James Robertson and other important information on alternative economics can be found at www.jamesrobertson.com

14. Alaska Permanent Fund: A Model of Resource Rents for Public Investment and Citizen Dividends. Fred Harrison, author of several important books on the land problem and land value tax policy, asked me to write this paper for the Spring 2002 issue of *Geophilus*, a beautiful journal that he launched and edited as a publication of the Land Research Trust. Six issues of *Geophilus* were published before it unfortunately folded. I was grateful for the opportunity to do some in-depth research on this very important successful model of an oil resource rent fund, probably the best one to date.

In this paper I describe the form and function of the Alaska Permanent Fund as a model governmental institution for collecting and distributing natural resource rents, particularly oil, and I suggest ways to improve the Fund. I also analyze fundamental issues regarding natural resources and territorial claims and show how a Global Resource Agency could collect and distribute transnational resource revenues.

This paper was also one of the five winning essays of the There Are Alternatives Project of the McKeever Institute of Economic Policy Analysis. It was published in an edited version in Fall 2005 in *Dialogues*, a publication of the Canada West Foundation.

15. Citizens Dividends and Oil Resource Rents: A Focus on Alaska, Norway and Nigeria. My colleague Jeffrey J. Smith, a peripatetic Johnny Appleseed-type activist and advocate for the land value tax policy, strongly promotes the idea of distributing resource rents as citizen dividends. Jeff urged several of us to engage with the United States Basic Income Guarantee (BIG) movement. Coordinated by Oxford University economist Karl Widerquist, BIG had leaped across the pond from BIEN - the Basic Income European Network (now the Basic Income Earth Network). And BIG had embedded its annual conference within the annual conference of the Eastern Economics Association.

The stage was set and Jeff helped put me on it. The challenge was to persuade the BIG people that the very best source of revenue for a citizen's dividend was the resource rent from surface land and natural resources. Since the Alaska Permanent Fund was one heckuva good example of distributing resource rent as citizen dividends, I had to include it in the paper I presented in the U.S. Basic Income Guarantee Network (USBIG) track of the Eastern Economic Association 30th Annual Conference held February 20 - 22, 2004 in Washington, DC.

This article contains many facts and figures and concludes with these three recommendations:

1. Use information and communication technologies fully to provide transparency in extractive resource industries.
2. Invest resource rent from non-renewable resources in socially and environmentally responsible ways and primarily in the needed transition to renewable energy based economies.
3. Rent funds based on oil and other non-renewable resources should transition towards capturing substantial resource rents from surface land site values (ground rent) and other permanent and sustainable sources of rent so they could be distributed as citizen dividends.

This paper is now referenced in the bibliography of the 302-page report titled Experiences with Oil Funds: Institutional and Financial Aspects, a June 2006 publication of ESMAP, the Energy Sector Management Assistance Program of the World Bank.

16. Women, Earth and Economic Power. This short essay, printed in my short-lived publication, GEODATA, draws on what we know of land tenure systems before the rise of patriarchy. I describe the difference between land tenure patterns that flow from a consciousness of the interconnectedness of all life, and land tenure systems based on male dominance and control. It has been a long time since a counsel of governance listened to a counsel of women before deciding whether or not to go to war. If we deeply honored and listened to the feminine perspective perhaps we would find a way beyond war to solve our problems.

This is the only piece in this collection that mentions the innovative work and writings of Silvio Gesell. This German economist proposed that ground rent be the source of payments to support women in their role as mothers and homemakers. Thus, ground rent payments would be an equivalent to primitive women using the land and soil to meet basic needs. Yes, we could also extend this to men in the role of primary caretaker of children. So relax Mr. Mom, we have you covered!

17. Harvard Club of New York Speech on the UN Conference. On October 28, 1996 I spoke about my experience as an NGO delegate to the UN Habitat II Conference in Istanbul as part of a panel at the Harvard Club of New York. In this brief talk I describe the challenges surrounding the primary focus of the conference: housing as a human right. I trace this concern to the problem of wealth inequality and from there to the need for equitable land access and secure land tenure. I point to promising sections of the 65-page document which was the outcome of the conference, endorsed by consensus of the official delegates from 183 nation states: the Global Action Agenda for Adequate Shelter and Sustainable Human Settlements.

18. Sharing Our Common Heritage via the Tax Shift Agenda. This was my keynote speech at the annual conference of the Council of Georgist Organizations annual conference in Portland, Oregon in August 1998. I first describe how corporate-led globalization was, and still is, pushing people off their lands, patenting seeds for private profit and control, and enclosing the commons of the genetic code itself. I then point out several global movements and organizations that seemed at the time to hold great potential for securing the human right to common heritage resources via fundamental reforms.

One such movement emerged from the United Nations Conference on Environment and Development (the Earth Summit) held in Rio de Janeiro, June 3-14, 1992. A total of 172 governments participated and 108 sent their heads of state or government. Some 2,400 representatives of non-governmental organizations (NGOs) attended, with 17,000 people at the parallel NGO Forum, who had so-called "consultative status." An important achievement was an agreement on the Climate Change Convention which in turn led to the Kyoto Protocol. The Convention on Biological Diversity was opened for signature at the Earth Summit. It made a start towards redefinition of *money supply* measures that did not inherently encourage destruction of natural ecoregions and so-called uneconomic growth. The Earth Summit outcome document also asked signers not to "carry out any activities on the lands of indigenous peoples that would cause environmental degradation or that would be culturally inappropriate."

Reading this speech nearly a decade later, I think I paid insufficient attention to another fact mentioned in it. The chair of this first major global conference that included so many people from all over the world was also a leader of several corporations with massive land holdings that were acquiring and privatizing major water and other natural resources and displacing indigenous people from their lands in Central America in order to promote tourist development. Is it any wonder that the world has gone backwards instead of forwards on the goals set forth at the Earth Summit? In hindsight it appears to have been one great green wash of a conference. We will never reach our environmental and social goals if the current economic structures and powers continue to rule the world.

Reflecting in 2007 on my optimistic state of 1998, I confess that the "promised land" seems ever more elusive. Having watched the horrors of the Iraq War for several years and experienced chronic anxiety that the United States could attack Iran with its new "earth penetrator" nuclear weapons, I admit to sometimes feeling overwhelmed with despair. It is difficult to keep lighting our candles in the windy cold. We are living through yet another dark night of the collective human soul. Those of us with candles need to shine together if humanity and other forms of life on this planet are to survive and ever again thrive.

People like us can learn something from wild geese. As they fly long distances in V formation, the lead goose takes the brunt of the elements while those behind fly on the uplift of energy generated by those in front of them in the V pattern. When the lead goose tires it falls back in the flock and another goose flies forward into the most energy-consuming and challenging lead position. Sometimes I'm a lead goose, sometimes I fall back. This is natural; we must do it to avoid burn out and total despair.

Despite the lack of real progress toward the goals of the Earth Summit, something on my wish list in this 1998 speech has in fact come to pass. UN Habitat produced a document on which 183 UN member states agreed at the global conference in Istanbul in 1996. It called for land access to eradicate poverty and recommended capturing land value for the people using land-based taxes. The good news, nearly ten years after this speech, is that UN Habitat's recently launched Global Land Tool Network is developing a major program to implement land value capture worldwide as a key policy necessary to achieve the Millennium Development Goal of significantly improving the living conditions of 100,000,000 slum dwellers by 2020.

19. Pennsylvania's Success with Local Property Tax Reform -- The Split Rate Tax. In 1990 I packed up my two kids, their hamsters, some household items and 24 boxes of books and papers and left the San Francisco Bay Area. *Fled* the Bay Area might be more accurate. I had several reasons for moving home place to small-town Pennsylvania. City life was driving me crazy. Crime, congestion and high housing costs were yielding a low quality of life in Oakland. I did not know how to raise children in a city that had no safe open places for them to play. The children would know their grandparents and cousins. Schools were better and safer back where I was born. A big scary earthquake had hit the Bay Area in 1989. And several cities in Pennsylvania were succeeding with local applications of the land value tax policy. On this last point, California was in a hopeless situation, at least for the foreseeable future, with the misguided voter lockdown of the property tax under Proposition 13. So it seemed that I could contribute more to my cause if I just moved back to Franklin County. I was right.

The Jerome Levy Economics Institute of Bard College invited me speak at their conference on Land, Wealth and Poverty held November 2 – 4, 1995. This conference was an excellent opportunity to review the land tax movement in Pennsylvania. In the Pennsylvania's Success paper I give an overview of the policy and some details on its impact in the fifteen cities that had adopted it to varying degrees (more have since done so). The term "split rate" means that the property tax valuation on buildings is kept separate from that on land. Removing the tax on buildings provides an incentive to make improvements; taxing land value curbs land speculation and encourages the use of valuable urban sites. In combination, this policy provides both a carrot and stick to restoring cities and making housing affordable.

Here is a key statement from the paper: "Research based on building permits issued in the three-year period before and after the implementation of the two-rate tax policy in Pennsylvania cities consistently shows significant increases in building permits issued after the policy was put into place."

Now, an increase in building permits might not sound like a very exciting economic indicator. But please consider this point fully. If the building stock is deteriorating and houses are boarded up, then once-thriving neighborhoods are degraded and increasingly depressed – along with the people in them. The research solidly indicates that even modest applications of this tax policy move communities towards renewal and renovation. This is the good news of the Pennsylvania story.

This paper was published in *The American Journal of Economics and Sociology* in April 1997 and is a slightly revised version of my talk at Bard. A later version of this paper briefly elaborates the earth trusteeship concepts of John McConnell, the founder of Equinox Earth Day, and credits him as a co-author. An edited version also appears in *A World That Works: Building Blocks for a Just and Sustainable Society*, a 1997 TOES (The Other Economic Summit) book edited by Trent Schroyer and available from Apex Press.

This paper was also quoted in *An Introduction to Two-Rate Taxation of Land and Buildings* by Jeffrey P. Cohen and Cletus C. Coughlin, published in the Federal Reserve Bank of St. Louis *Review*, May/June 2005. Cohen and Coughlin begin their article with these two quotes:

In my opinion, the least bad tax is the property tax on the unimproved value of land, the Henry George argument of many, many years ago. – Milton Friedman, 1976 Nobel Prize laureate in economics.

The property tax is, economically speaking, a combination of one of the worst taxes – the part that is assessed on real estate improvements...and one of the best taxes – the tax on land or site value. – William Vickrey, 1996 Nobel Prize laureate in economics.

20. How Pennsylvania Boroughs Got the Land Tax Option. This is the sordid saga of the ultimately successful five-year effort to pass enabling legislation so boroughs of Pennsylvania could use the land value tax option. Our campaign was not sordid. That label properly fits the backstabbing and partisan politics we encountered as we worked to pass this benign bill – an option-only or "may bill" that required no funding allocation. This brief amendment to the Borough Code simply granted this tax reform as an option for the state's 1000 boroughs -- an option that the cities already had available to them.

Within this political adventure story readers may find some sections that could help in efforts to pass this type of legislation elsewhere. These are: (1) the initial resolution passed by the Chambersburg Town Council which signaled our local state legislative officials to take on sponsorship of the bill; (2) the piece we used to educate legislators about the land value tax policy; and (3) the entire land value tax option bill.

We nearly lost this one, and then won in the end with a vote of 198 for and 2 abstaining. A nearly unanimous agreement on tax reform. Amazing, huh?

21. Pennsylvania Farmers and the Split Rate Tax. Enabling legislation for the split rate tax option had proceeded gradually over the years. By the time I moved to Pennsylvania all three categories of cities (based roughly on population) could take advantage of this tax reform option. But where I come from, there are no cities, only smaller towns classified as "boroughs." My hometown of Chambersburg was not allowed to implement this policy. I needed to get a bill passed by the state legislature – a daunting challenge if ever there was one. I tell the story of this five-year effort and our ultimate success in the next article. I mention it here because, in the course of the legislative work, I realized that the Pennsylvania State Farm Bureau had major concerns about any bill that included both the words "land" and "tax."

I put this research paper together for the legislative proceedings on how the so-called Borough Bill could impact farmers. The farm lobby did succeed in amending the bill, so that essentially no borough with a farm within its limits could implement this tax reform, but the bill did eventually pass and it might not have without this paper. My research showed clearly that the tax would actually benefit working farmers. In fact, it was so convincing that some legislators were worried about adding the amendment because of their concern that it might actually hurt farmers.

Before I wrote this paper I knew that this tax shift would not hurt working farmers and would actually help them: curbing speculation in farm land, would keep land affordable, while removing taxes on farmers' homes, barns and other buildings would be a tax relief. What I did not know until I did the research was how much it would benefit working farmers (as opposed to both working and idle land speculators). I conclude the paper with ten clear reasons why this policy would benefit farmers and end with this statement:

> Our evidence thus suggests that the split-rate tax policy approach, especially with a heavy reduction of millage (tax) rates on building values, would significantly enhance incentives for the continuation and expansion of a viable, efficient, and sustainable agriculture in Pennsylvania and anywhere else if used.

A few years later, the historian Ken Wenzer, who has practically memorized all of many writings of Henry George, had a contract with M.E. Sharpe to put together an anthology. He called to ask me if I had any unpublished articles that might be appropriate. I gave him this research paper, which he edited in his usual highly meticulous manner. It can now be found in *Land Value Taxation: The Equitable and Efficient Source of Public Finance*, which Sharpe published in 1999.

22. Lunch and Lecture with Ralph Nader. He is still a hero to me. If the majority of Americans could recognize a man of high integrity, unwavering conviction, brilliance and true inner strength, Ralph Nader would be our president today. We would not have innocent blood on our hands from wars of aggression for full-spectrum dominance in the guise of bringing democracy to the world. Ralph's presidential campaigns were wake-up calls. He put his alarm ringer on high volume but to no avail. The snoring continues.

It was my honor to organize a small group for lunch with Ralph at the White Dog Café in Philadelphia on March 25, 2000. We raised a modest amount for his campaign and had the opportunity for some one-on-one time with him.

Ralph clearly knows how to connect the dots from a "military budget twisted into a grotesque excess" to the wealth gap, through the "trivialization of the media" to "initiatory democracy where people are not simply following a movement, but they themselves become leaders who are putting forth and implementing ideas to create a better political and economic system." All these ideas, and more, are included in this piece.

Later that afternoon, at the Wharton School of Law at the University of Pennsylvania, he gave a stirring speech to hundreds of students and members of the Green Party. Ralph said many important things that I summarize or quote in this article. Those of us who had lunch with him that day were especially pleased at this statement:

> We need a big debate on different kinds of taxation, to talk about how corporations are freeloading on public services and getting tax breaks while taxes are falling on workers and smaller businesses. We need to open a debate about land taxation and Henry George, to tax bad things not good things, and not tax people who go to work everyday.

Ralph gave us another choice, beyond the least bad party. How tragic that we did not take it.

23. Diary of an Outreach Activist. One of the wonderful aspects of living a life dedicated to the service of people and planet is the many opportunities to travel all over the world on missions of meaning and purpose. This diary, published in Land and Liberty in 1999, includes brief vignettes of four such intellectually, culturally and spiritually rich experiences in Thailand, the Netherlands, New York City, and Oaxaca, Mexico. I include a photo of the amazing meditation structure built by the Dhammakaya Foundation taken on the day of the awe-inspiring Lights of Peace event.

24. IMF and World Bank Protest. I attended the epic Mobilization for Global Justice protests against the International Monetary Fund (IMF) and the World Bank (WB) held the week of April 8 to 17, 2000, in Washington, D.C. The piece is a phantasmagoric description of the sights, sounds, textures, tones, dialogs and discussions of 50,000 plus individuals of valor who gathered from all corners of the world during that sunny but serious week.

If you have never experienced this type of event yourself, the piece should give you a bittersweet flavor of the global struggle for justice. The bitter is the knowledge of the massive and unnecessary suffering on the planet. The sweet is being in solidarity with high-minded justice-loving sisters and brothers from all around the world. As I again read the story several years after this one-of-many such protests, sometimes I think I see a small shift in the WB's policies. I know that some people inside both the WB and the IMF sincerely want a better world for all. I know that those of us with "good will and special skill" are finding each other and strengthening and expanding our networks.

Recently I was rather surprised to discover that my article on Citizens Dividends (#15 in this volume) was mentioned in a WB publication entitled *Experiences with Oil Funds: Institutional and Financial Aspects*. When I was there among the throngs protesting the WB in 2000, I never imagined that my ideas would be incorporated into a WB paper in 2006. Perhaps some people inside those Washington circles are indeed awakening.

25. D.C. Protest Provides New Insights. This guest essay for the Chambersburg Public Opinion gives a brief overview of my experiences at the Mobilization for Global Justice, detailed in the previous article, and also describes the breakthrough in using peaceful civil disobedience and the non-violent strategy developed by Mohandas Gandhi and Martin Luther King.

26. Professional Super Hero. In 1997, INsider, a magazine distributed on college campuses nationwide, published this interview Adam Monroe conducted with me.

I cannot find either this article or an Internet URL for INsider, so the magazine must have either folded or been transformed into something else. I cannot find Adam either, but I do have a hard copy of the INsider interview somewhere in my archives. Adam's compelling questions led me to reflect on the UN and the roles of UN NGOs, specifically the one I have represented for the past twelve years, the International Union for Land Value Taxation. He also elicited some of my thinking on the global struggle for economic democracy.

It is interesting to read our concerns about the MAI – the Multilateral Agreement on Investment – as its outcome was uncertain at the time of the interview. We now know that due to people power and the Battle of Seattle during the 1999 World Trade Organization Ministerial, the MAI came tumbling down. But it reared its power-hungry head again with the 2003 push for another trade agreement. It was the same quest for corporate rule with a slightly different name. This failed as well, thanks to the united efforts of more than twenty poor countries. I think you'll like the Princess Leia quote from Star Wars near the end of the interview.

27. O! Say Can You See: A Perspective on the Current Crisis. The title is taken from the first line of the "Star Spangled Banner," the official national anthem of the United States. I gave this talk at the Books Not Bombs/Stop Iraq War Forum organized by students at Shippensburg University, Pennsylvania on March 5, 2003.

So many millions of people came out in the streets or organized forums like this in an effort to prevent the war. To me, nothing more clearly indicates a dysfunctional democracy than the fact that a government can launch a war using its citizens' tax dollars of the citizenry and risking or taking our lives and our children's lives with so little respect for the views of all of us.

This speech is a call to stop the momentum towards the Iraq war, a call to use global governance structures to abolish war and solve international conflicts, and a call to pledge allegiance to the earth and its people as an interconnected whole. I briefly analyze resource wars and describe the transition of the United States from republic to empire, using a quote from Dr. Stephen Pelletier, a former professor at the U.S. Army War College in Carlisle, Pennsylvania.

The media was blasting the phrase "shock-and-awe" at us at that time. The world would soon see those words made manifest. In March 2003 I would never have dreamed that in June 2004 I would be spending time with a U.S. Air Force squadron leader who was involved in the shock-and-awe Iraq attack. More on that in article 29.

28. Letter to a Church. This was published as a guest editorial in the *Public Opinion*, a Gannett newspaper in Chambersburg, Pennsylvania. Members of a nearby United Brethren Church frequently left notes on my doorstep inviting me to their services; this letter was my response. My parents had raised me in the fundamentalist, conservative United Brethren faith, a Protestant sect. I went to Sunday School and church every week and Bible School and special evangelical services every summer. I was "born-again" at age 10. By age 13 I was asking many questions and not finding sufficient answers.

My needs for emotional healing, interpersonal conflict resolution, intellectual understanding, and spiritual insight were in no way fulfilled by my affiliation with my parents' church. This letter is an appeal to organized mainstream Christianity to end the hypocrisy and begin to live the teachings of Christ's message of love and peace.

29. A Friend of Mine Bombed a Friend of Mine. This was another guest editorial in the November 1, 2004 *Public Opinion*. The title the editor gave it was "War in Iraq touches many lives near and far." This essay is only six paragraphs long. In that brief space I tell a little story about my friendship with two men and their relationship to the "Shock and Awe" bombing of Baghdad. I end the story with a simple but profound thought from Martin Luther King.

This short personal story points to the great mission before us: abolishing war on Planet Earth. War is a completely unacceptable way to resolve conflicts. We can learn nothing more from it. "Thou shalt not kill." Period. No exceptions.

Each of us needs to decide if our children and our children's children are to live full lives. If political leaders will not abolish war, then we the people must stop paying for it and stop offering up our children and ourselves for slaughter.

30. Economics of War and Peace. The current Iraq war and the potential for a US attack on Iran are affecting everyone in the world on some basic level, whether physical, emotional, mental and/or spiritual. In the 1940s, during another time of war, Ralph Borsodi, Mildred Loomis, and other decentralist, pacificist, "alternative" economists were influenced by the ideas of Henry George; they composed a series of four simple graphs to portray how a simple economy builds into a war economy and how to mold it back into a peace economy. Lindy Davies, director of the Henry George Institute, later graphically redesigned these four rough graphs and they became my framework for this four-part article.

I presented this final article of this anthology in summary form on February 23, 2007 on the Economists for Peace and Security panel at the Eastern Economics Association 33rd Annual Conference in New York. In it, I first describe a simple economy in which people secure their basic needs via fair access to land and natural resources. Then I articulate the root injustice built into our current economic system that lets an elite few privately appropriate the economic surplus. From this dynamic the military-industrial-financial complex emerges, along with an imperialistic U.S. foreign policy.

The fourth graph depicts a new role for democratic governance: Earth Rights Democracy. This system captures the "rent" of nature's gifts to benefit the people as a whole via a type of public finance reform that simultaneously lifts taxes from those actively producing wealth. I provide several practical examples of this policy, to point the way towards a world of peace and plenty.

The Distalfink Bird is part of Pennsylvania Dutch (Deutch = German) culture.
It is supposed to bring "Good Luck" to all. The photo was taken at Aradhana, the author's home and headquarters of Earth Rights Institute's East Coast office.

I am putting the finishing touches on this book while on a weeklong silent retreat with about 200 people led by Gangaji, a wonderful spiritual teacher. We are gathered at Tenaya Lodge in the awesome expanses of Yosemite National Park in California. Here, I experience abundance, joy and deep inner peace. All needs are fully met. My prayer is that we soon put in place an economic system that will enable each and every member of our human family to secure basic material needs with dignity and time to spare. Everyone can then enjoy the adventure of mental, creative and spiritual expansion during this brief sojourn on Planet Earth.

Shalom…Amen…Saalom…Om…………………………………………...………

-1-

Democracy, Earth Rights and the Next Economy

When land became a commodity and lost its status as provider and sustainer of life, Western civilization began its history of subjugation and exploitation of the earth and earth-based cultures.
— John Mohawk

Why precisely do we want to change land ownership? The answer seems to me to be quite clear: to inhibit land speculation, to inhibit the private exploitation of the scarcity-value of land, to inhibit as we might say the 'cornering' of land.
— E. F. Schumacher, "Think About Land"

This was one of the three Twenty-First Annual E. F. Schumacher Lectures given at Amherst College, Amherst, Massachusetts on October 27, 2001. Amory Lovins and John Todd gave the other two lectures that day. Hildegarde Hannum edited the lecture and it was published as a Schumacher Society booklet in 2002.

Beginning with a sweeping overview of the historical period of European land enclosures, it next threads the way through the philosophy of John Locke and the founding of democracy in the United States and then connects the dots from the Civil War period to the rise of an imperialistic foreign policy in the 20th century. The lecture is an appeal for a new form of democracy based on equal rights to the land and resources of the earth. This ethic and practical policy approaches are described as urgent next steps towards establishing "earth rights democracy."

Introduction by Susan Witt, Executive Director, E. F. Schumacher Society

How can the young be expected to defend their homeland when they come home to find they have no stake in the land? The inequitable distribution of land ownership affects our society, our politics, our environment, our communities - and ultimately our sense of well-being as a people. Alanna Hartzok has worked tirelessly for more than twenty-five years to right this injustice. It is not surprising that it was Robert Swann, founder of the Community Land Trust movement in this country, who recommended Alanna as a Schumacher Society speaker.

Alanna Hartzok is vice-president of the Council of Georgist Organizations, which has thirty-five member organizations nationwide, and she is state coordinator of the Pennsylvania Fair Tax Coalition. In 1993 she initiated tax reform legislation and helped work it through the state legislature to nearly unanimous passage of Senate Bill 211, signed by Governor Thomas Ridge in November 1998.

Alanna's published articles on tax reform have been useful to legislators in the states of Pennsylvania, Maryland, New Jersey and New York. She is one of several people featured in *Planet Champions: Adventures in Saving the World: New Paths to Peace, Prosperity, and Human Rights*. Please join me in a big Schumacher Society welcome for Alanna Hartzok.

I am truly honored to have been invited by the E. F. Schumacher Society to be a lecturer today. I admit that "Democracy, Earth Rights and the Next Economy" is a big topic for a lecture series traditionally based on the idea that small is beautiful. Yet to be fully aware of the particulars of the small - whether in terms of a small community or town or in terms of working to build a more locally-based appropriate economy - as the E. F. Schumacher Society and the Institute for Community Economics, both of which were founded by Robert Swann, have done so steadfastly over the years, it may be necessary, or at least useful, to grasp the biggest and most expanded perspective in which that smallness is contained. From that vantage point, combined with the unique particulars of our special place on earth, we can then more clearly know what seeds had best be planted in that smallness of our local towns and communities.

In this lecture I will be addressing the land problem and how to solve it in such a way that we could release billions of dollars of funds to invest in the natural capitalism Amory Lovins described to you earlier today. Amory talked about low-cost bamboo strong enough to build houses. A little bit of land can provide enough bamboo to grow your house out of that land. But what if you have no land? I will also elaborate on the concept of earth rights, pinpoint the fatal flaw in democracy as currently constituted, explore the history of the problem, and, lastly, describe work in progress that would seem to be essential building blocks of the Next Economy.

It is clear to so many of us now that our current form of economy - some call it monopoly or corporate capitalism - does not serve the highest and best interests of either the people or the planet. Permit me to dream for a moment, for sometimes out of our visions flow new realities. Here is my wish list for the Next Economy:

The Next Economy will be deeply unifying. Moving beyond either/or to both/and, it will embrace the diversity of human cultural expressions. The Next Economy will be built upon the highest values of both the Left and the Right. It will be a fair economy and a free economy, using but not abusing the earth and her many resources. It will steadily, and in some places rapidly, grow out of the old economy as more and more humans grasp its principles and implement its policies. The Next Economy will have first and foremost the well-being of all the people on this planet. It will be based on the triple bottom line of social justice, restoration and protection of the environment, and the strength and stability to provide security in basic needs.

The needs of the people and the needs of the planet are one and the same: protection, care, validation, respect, appreciation, and creative expression. Thus, the ethics of the Next Economy will flow out of a profound perception that the rights of human beings and the rights of the planet are one and the same. The Next Economy will be founded on ethics so simple and basic that thoughtful human beings will say, "Yes, this is true." The force of truth is a liberating force, always has been and always will be. Mahatma Gandhi knew and taught this. Gandhi lived according to this *sattyagraha*, the truth force.

Let us explore these truths, starting with a most obvious one: Would you agree that everyone sitting and standing in this room, no matter where on earth they originally came from, is a human being? Does this seem so obvious that it is not worth mentioning? Years ago a friend named Gene Haggerty took upon himself a one-man mission. He traveled around the world asking political and other leaders to sign a statement affirming their belief that, beyond the colors and shades, the faiths and creeds, we are all human beings. Although I could not grasp the Zen of it at the time, I now understand that this was Gene's ingenious way of reminding them of this most basic truth - the "primal holism of the human experience on earth."

Other basic questions: do human beings have a right to exist? Is this an equal right? Does the planet have a right to exist? Are these important questions, or are these absurd questions? Is existence itself a "right" or is it a miracle and a mystery? The great ideals of human rights and equality are based on recognition that you and I have an equal right to exist. The fact that we are all human beings with equal rights to exist is the truth upon which were built important agreements such as the Declaration of Independence, the Bill of Rights and the International Declaration of Human Rights. Alas, these fine declarations, like so many others that have been agreed upon by governments and their citizenry, have not yet brought us a world of peace and plenty for all.

In August, I spent some time one afternoon in Baltimore talking with Councilwoman Bea Gaddy, who passed away a few weeks ago at the age of 78. Dr. Gaddy, an African American, had for many years worked to take care of basic needs for food and shelter in the inner-city neighborhoods. We sat together for a while that sweltering afternoon, talking and sipping ice water at a card table in front of the row house that was her social services home base. Dr. Gaddy said, "I grew up poor in Baltimore, but I never thought I would see things get worse and worse here as they have the past few decades. People call me sometimes in the middle of the night, saying 'Ms. Gaddy, I can't sleep, I'm just hungry.'"

We in the United States freed the slaves, but we have not freed all the people - not even in Washington, New York, Baltimore, and Boston, the cradles of our democracy - from the pain of hunger. As we fully confront the reality of hunger, homelessness and basic needs insufficiencies in this country and in the many other countries that now call themselves democracies, it becomes starkly clear that there is a major flaw at the core of how democracy is constituted. Surely persistent hunger and homelessness in America is not what the founding fathers envisioned for the year 2001!

Human Rights to the Earth

We are all human beings with equal and inalienable rights to life. Yet there is a crack in the Liberty Bell, there is something not sufficiently well crafted, some dimension not understood or perhaps not able to be fully affirmed by European men at the time of the founding, no matter how well intentioned and thoughtful some of them might have been. This imperfection was destined to divide the rich and the poor, to protect the powerful and neglect the needy in our country and throughout the earth. We did not have the industrial technology to form a large durable metal bell at the time, nor did we have the political technology to form a fully and fairly functioning democracy.

Thomas Jefferson, Ben Franklin, and Tom Paine understood that their work was just a beginning step, which the venture of democratic governance would need to proceed with periodic revisions and perhaps even revolutions, hopefully nonviolent. Over the years - step by step, struggle by struggle - the full right to participate in the experiment of democracy yielded the right for all to vote and own land - if they could find a way to buy it. While many are comfortable, the fact remains that there are far too many Americans working too hard for too little. The widening mouth of the wealth gap now threatens to consume many who had made it into the middle class. In the USA today the top 1 percent of the people has more wealth than the bottom 90 percent.

More questions in search of first principles: Who are we human beings? Where did we come from? Where are we going? What we do know for certain is that the human body is composed of earth elements. We are walking, talking bags of rock and salt water, recyclers of plant and animal material, inspiring and expiring the gaseous fires. There is no ultimate separation but rather a unity, as our earthly bodies are bound to the enlivening energy of the sun and, in subtle ways yet to be fully realized, we are galactic beings as well and are mysteriously related to the entire universe. Our existence as creatures of flesh and bone is totally dependent on the land and natural resources of the earth. This earth, which no one of us made, is simply a given.

Eli Siegel, an American poet and philosopher, in his 1946 essay "Ownership: Some Moments," stated, 'How the earth should be owned is the major economic question of this time; as it is the oldest." In another essay, "Self and World," he declared: "The world should be owned by the people living in it. Every person should be seen as living in a world truly his."

Other voices on earth rights:

Thomas Berry: "Humans in their totality are born of the earth. We are earthlings. The earth is our origin, our nourishment, our support, our guide... Thus the whole burden of modern earth studies is to narrate the story of the birth of humans from our Mother Earth."

Chief Seattle: "This we know. The earth does not belong to man; man belongs to the earth. This we know. All things are connected like the blood which unites one family. All things are connected."

Patricia Mische: "The more we grow in awareness of our own sacred source, the more we discover that our own sacred source is the sacred source of each person and all that is in the universe."

Henry George: "Do what we may, we can accomplish nothing real and lasting until we secure to all the first of those equal and inalienable rights with which.... man is endowed by his creator - the equal and inalienable right to the use and benefit of natural opportunities."

The important and vital truth not enunciated or affirmed in our founding democratic covenants is the truth that we, each and every one of us, has an equal right to the earth as our birthright. How did we lose this simple truth, the primal perception that the earth is the birthright of all people?

In his essay "The Problem of the Modern World" John Mohawk states: "When land became a 'commodity' and lost its status as provider and sustainer of life, Western civilization began its history of subjugation and exploitation of the earth and earth based cultures. For nearly five centuries people have been coerced from their landholdings. The problem, in the English-speaking world, has its roots in the sixteenth century."

The Enclosures

To understand how it came to be that this most basic and obvious human right - the right to the earth - was somehow left out of the founding documents of democracy, it will serve our purpose here to go back to the centuries of European history that Mohawk is talking about, to the Enclosure Period. This is the time of violent direct suppression of the indigenous people of Europe. Between the thirteenth and seventeenth centuries, masses of peasants were evicted from their holdings or saw their common lands fenced off for sheep.

The Enclosures were introduced after the signing of the Magna Carta in 1215. This was the great charter that King John was forced by the English barons to grant. Traditionally interpreted as guaranteeing certain civil and political liberties, the right to land for the common people was not among them. The first legal act to enforce enclosures was the Statute of Merton of 1235, which spoke of the need "to approve (meaning improve) the land in order to extract greater rent." From whom do you think they were extracting those rents?

The enclosures redefined land as "private property" and thereby gave it the status of a commodity, tradable within an expanding market system. Since the majority of people were denied access to the land and were forced to become wage laborers, labor also became a tradable commodity. The enclosures were justified by its perpetrators as necessary in order to make "improvements."

The words of Robert Ket, who led the Peasants' Revolt of 1549 against the enclosures, heavy taxes, and other abuses, are quoted in the 1992 Special Issue of *The Ecologist*, "Whose Common Future?":

> The common pastures left by our predecessors for our relief and our children are taken away. The lands, which in the memory of our fathers were common, those are ditched and hedged in and made several; the pastures are enclosed, and we shut out. Whatsoever, the fowls of the air or fishes of the water, and increase of the earth - all these do they devour, consume and swallow up.... We can no longer bear so much, so great, and so cruel injury; neither can we with quiet minds behold so great covetousness, excess and pride of the nobility.... While we have the same form and the same condition of birth together with them, why should they have a life so unlike unto ours, and differ so far from us in calling?

The rebellion of 1549 was one of many peasant revolts in old Europe. Sixteen thousand insurgents formed a camp near Norwich and "scoured the country around, destroyed enclosures, filled in ditches, leveled fences." A poem from the Enclosures period has the line:

> The law hangs the man and flogs the woman
> Who steals a goose from off the commons,
> But turns the greater scoundrel loose
> Who steals the commons from the goose.

Martin Luther

Until the 16th century the Church was the Catholic Church. Its corruptions provoked the rise of Protestant Reformism. In 1524 the peasants of Swabia, a region in what is now Germany, brought Martin Luther a document Twelve Articles, appealing to him for his understanding (see Earle Edwin Cairns, *The Christian in Society*, pp. 8-16). The peasants said it was their intention "to excuse in a Christian way the disobedience and even the rebellion of the peasants" and to describe "the basic and chief articles ... concerning the matters in which they feel they are being denied their rights." The peasants based each one of their Articles on specific chapters and verses of the Old and New Testament. They requested release from serfdom, relief from heavy taxation, fair and just laws, and access to what was once their commons - the forests, fields and water resources - to meet their basic needs. In response Luther wrote his "Admonition to Peace" urging the princes to be kind and the peasants to be peaceful and the appointment of an arbitration commission. Before the "Admonition to Peace" could be published, the land was flooded with insurrection, arson, pillage, and murder.

The disturbances among the peasants were establishing an association between the Reformation and revolution that was alienating many of Luther's supporters while his refusal to identify the Reformation with the program of The Twelve Articles antagonized many of the common people. For Luther the real problem was to defeat the Devil. It was more important to him that law and order be maintained and the gospel be preached than that the pleas of the peasants be addressed. The peasants had gone to Luther for moral and spiritual support and to respectfully communicate their conditions and requests to him. Instead of standing in solidarity with the poor and oppressed as Jesus had done, Luther wrote pamphlets calling for the punishment of "the thieving, murderous gangs of peasants." Regarding the peasants as unruly pagans, Luther believed their rebellions were instigated by Satan.

Beginning with the first act of enclosure and throughout the following period of several hundred years, as the land was enclosed the women and men and the earth-based religion of the peoples of northern Europe were brutally repressed. Women who practiced healing and agriculture, who had their own lands and were leaders of their communities were tortured, hanged, or burned at the stake. The Holy Inquisitions was essentially a women's holocaust; about 85 percent of those killed were women. Some say their murders numbered in the millions. I consider this to be the most significant story of the past two thousand years for women of European descent. Much of what we have learned about history is just that - "his story." The women's holocaust is a terrible "her story" and my sisters are still recovering on deep levels of their collective psyche from that horrific repression, torture and murder. The European indigenous women were strong and clear wild women with equal status to their men. They could stand their ground because they had access to the common lands. The imperial forces called them witches. Martin Luther said, "I would have no compassion on the witches! I would burn them all."

How did the forces of Christianity, based upon the stories of a loving, healing Jesus, come to be aligned with the forces of an imperialist state and a corrupted church? To answer this question let us now fast-forward to the twentieth century and the questions of a man in another part of this world.

Early Christian Teachings

Charles Avila was a Catholic seminarian in the Philippines in the 1960s. One of his professors in the Divine Word Seminary constantly criticized the Church's utter lack of identification with the poor. He persuaded Avila and other students to accompany him on his regular visits to prisoners in various Philippine jails. During his visits Avila heard story after story of how these people had been evicted from lands they had tilled for generations. He came to realize that what was referred to as "the Peasant Question" was literally that – the question the peasants asked. It was a question on the level of "first principles" which are very rarely subjected to review, but which form the threshold of all our thinking. The Peasant Question was this: "What is just with regard to the land?"

Avila learned from the leading lawyer in the peasant movement that the philosophy of ownership which was the basis of property laws and practices in the Philippines, as well as of most modern legal systems, actually went a long way back in history - all the way back to Roman law. Roman law developed the ownership concept that legitimized the accumulation of wealth by a few at the expense of the impoverishment of the many. As Avila was thinking about a topic for his seminary dissertation, he wondered whether there might be early Christian philosophers of the period of the Roman Empire who had anything significant to say about the ownership concept. Most of the faculty warned him that he would be wasting his time pursuing this topic; his social justice professor, however, urged him to dig into the Latin and Greek writings concerning that period.

Avila scoured through 383 volumes and discovered that the early Christian leaders indeed had all dealt with the question of ownership and Roman law. The writings he discovered were of great assistance to the Filipino peasant movement. In 1983 Avila published his research and these patristic writings as a book entitled *Ownership: Early Christian Teachings*. Over and over again, Avila found, early Christians had railed against the Roman law concept of ownership as an "exclusive and unlimited right to dispose of a thing, to the exclusion of all others." The Roman land law of *dominium* meant the legalization of property in land originally obtained by conquest and plunder. The original Judeo-Christian land ethic had been that of *koinonia* - land was God's gift to the community as a whole for the *autarkeia* or self-sufficient livelihood of all.

One of Jesus's tasks was to restore the original intent of the Jubilee, the period every fifty years when lands were to be returned to their original owners or their heirs: "[The Lord] has anointed me to preach good news to the poor...to proclaim release of captives...to set at liberty those who are oppressed, to proclaim the acceptable year of the Lord." (Luke 4:18). As theologian Walter Brueggeman explains in *Land: the Foundation of Humanness* the "acceptable year" is the year of the Jubilee. The "release of captives" is the release of debt slaves who had lost their land because they could not pay their mortgage. A crucial aspect of Jesus's mission was the re-assertion of the land rights of the poor and displaced. The Bible expresses the fundamental recognition that the earth is the Lord's, to be fairly shared and stewarded by all:

> The land must not be sold beyond reclaim, for the land is Mine; you
>   are but strangers resident with me. – Lev. 25:23
> The profit of the earth is for all. – Eccles. 5:9
> Woe unto them that join house to house, that lay field to field, till
>   there be no place. – Isaiah 5:8
> Restore, I pray you, to them even this day, their lands, their vineyards,
>   their olive yards, and their houses. – Nehemiah 5:11

Christianity lost its mission of economic justice when it became the official religion of the Roman Empire and was adapted to or grafted onto, the Roman land law of dominium. From that time forward Christianity went hand-in-hand with the forces of conquest of the land-grabbing imperialist state. As Archbishop Desmond Tutu once said, "Before the Europeans came to Africa, we had the land and they had the Bible. We bowed our heads to pray, and when we opened our eyes, we had the Bible and they had the land."

We are searching for clues to how it came to be that fewer than three hundred multi-billionaires now have as much wealth as three billion people - half the population on earth at this time. We are asking why millions of people die from hunger and disease each year when there is enough to meet basic needs for everyone. Let us journey back now once again to our "old country" before returning to our "new country" in America.

More Enclosures

Thomas More (1478-1535), Chancellor of England, who some say was the most learned justice and scholar in the realm at the time, made passionate pleas against the cruel injustices when whole villages were being pulled down to make way for the more profitable industry of sheep farming and families were turned adrift onto the roads to starve. His plan for a better England was based upon a thorough Common Ownership. More was murdered as a martyr. The root meaning of this word martyr is "one who remembers and cares."

In England in 1648 the Diggers were sounding a lot like land-rights prophets. Gerrard Winstanley, in his "New Law of Righteousness," clearly saw the forces at play when he said, "The rich, in their enclosure saying 'this is mine' and the poor upon the commons saying 'this is ours, the earth and its fruits are common.' ... Leave off dominion and lordship one over another for the whole bulk of mankind are but one living earth!"

Over several hundred years 4,000 Private Acts of Enclosure were passed covering some 7,000,000 acres. Probably the same sized area was enclosed without application to Parliament. About two thirds involved open fields belonging to cottagers while one third involved commons such as woodland and heath. In the census of 1086, more than half the arable land belonged to the villagers. By 1876, only 2,225 people owned half the agricultural land in England and Wales and that 0.6 per cent of the population owned 98.5 per cent of it. As newer agricultural methods and technologies were applied, landowners could raise the rents of their lands by phenomenal amounts. As the cash economy developed, the rent money accumulated into the hands of the landholders and the plight of the people worsened. To survive, they sometimes were forced to borrow money from the landholders at high rates of interest.

Ireland's story at the end of the Enclosures period is that of many in the Third World today. In 1801 Britain made Ireland part of its empire and dissolved the Irish Parliament. By now the Protestants had the upper hand and were given a voice in the British Parliament while the Catholic majority had none. Heavy taxation was placed on Irish goods, and the British controlled almost all of Ireland's farmland. Tenant farmers had to give their entire crops to the landlords as rent. When their subsistence potato crops failed from blight, there was nothing to fall back on. Some three million people died of starvation and disease between 1845 and 1849, while one million fled to the US and Canada. Ireland's population of eight million was cut in half. During the famine Ireland exported to England enough grain, cattle, pigs, butter and eggs "to feed the Irish people twice over" as one Irish historian put it. This information is from an article by Elizabeth Ward called "When Ireland was Europe's Ethiopia" in *Scholastic Update* (Dec. 15, 1986).

Let us go to America now and examine the foundations of liberty and democracy.

John Locke and the Crack in the Liberty Bell

To fully understand the severe limitations in our current form of democracy it is necessary to trace the thread of the democratic ideal back to its fundamental tenets. Pondering the problem of persistent poverty within a democratic system of government, Richard Noyes – a former recent New Hampshire State Representative and editor of the book, *Now the Synthesis: Capitalism, Socialism, and the New Social Contract* – identifies the current land tenure system as "the one great imperfection, the snag on which freedom catches."

Noyes shows us that the "Age of Reason gave us a thesis with flaws." John Locke's *Second Treatise on Civil Government*, the political bible of the founding fathers, held that "the great and chief end of men's uniting into commonwealths, and putting themselves under government is the preservation of their property." The central understanding was that only through the guarantee of property rights could the individual really be free.

In further defining property rights Locke stated that "every man has a 'property' in his own <u>person</u>," so that anything a man has "removed from the common state," anything with which he has "mixed his own labor," is rightfully his own. The securing of this right was to be the main duty of a democratic government. Locke also affirmed "God has given the earth to the children of men" (Psalm 115:16).

But the trouble lies with Locke's Second Proviso regarding property. He maintained that it was correct for the individual in a state of nature "to mix his labor with land and so call [the produced wealth] his own since there was still enough [land] and as good left, and more than the yet unprovided could use." Locke said that people in England who wanted land could go to America to stake a claim from the vacant commons, the *terra nullia* of Roman law. This was justification for the Europeans to take land from the native peoples. Because they didn't have titles to the land, that made it vacant.

In the Second Proviso the reasoning of the primary mentor of the founding father was faulty and limited. In his justification for land enclosures and privatization Locke failed to grasp the consequences for democracy of a time like ours when so few humans would come to control so much of the earth, to the exclusion of the vast majority. Nor could he have known how the forces of an industrial economy would drive land values to such heights, to the benefit of landowners and bank lenders rather than wage earners. The property-in-land problem, insufficiently scrutinized by John Locke and the founding fathers, is the crack in the Liberty Bell. It is the root dilemma of democracy. Having life and liberty without land rights breeds unhappiness, unemployment, wage slavery, suffering, militarization and even death. Democratic government as presently constituted, because it is not grounded and embedded in the principle of equal rights to the earth, cannot build a world of peace and justice.

Thaddeus Stevens and the Civil War

Thaddeus Stevens was a Civil War congressman from south-central Pennsylvania, where I come from. He was Speaker of the House for many years, a radical advocate of the abolition of slavery and the major proponent of land reform during Reconstruction. He wanted the fertile plantation lands of the South to be allocated to the freed slaves and poor whites. In his view this plan would also help to solve the race problem by uniting freed slaves and poor whites on an economic basis.

Stanley Elkins and Eric McKitrick quote Stevens in Thaddeus Stevens: Confiscation and Reconstruction: "No people will ever be republican in spirit and practice where a few own immense manors and the masses are landless. Small independent landholders are the support and guardians of republican liberty."

Stevens wanted the large landholdings seized, with forty acres and a mule to farm them allotted to each former slave. This would do justice to those whose uncompensated labor had cleared and cultivated the southern land, he reasoned. He envisioned a land of productive and independent small farms. After this allocation there would still remain millions of acres -- 90 percent of the land in fact -- which could be sold to help pay the national debt, reduce taxes, and provide pensions for Union soldiers and reimbursement for citizens whose property had been destroyed during the war.

Confiscation was very much a live political issue in 1867, but the forces against Stevens prevailed and his land reform work failed. Even a respected radical journal of the time (*The Nation*) stated that for the government to give land to freedmen would suggest that "there are other ways of securing comfort or riches than honest work...No man in America has any right to anything which he has not honestly earned, or which the lawful owner has not thought proper to give him." As if the slaves had not worked long and hard enough!

Yet William P. Fessenden, one of the most powerful Senate Republicans at the time, commented, "This is more than we do for white men." The *New York Times* expressed most clearly the fears felt by northern men of property:

> If Congress is to take cognizance of the claims of labor against capital...there can be no decent pretense for confining the task to the slaveholder of the South. It is a question, not of human loyalty, but of the fundamental relation of industry to capital; and sooner or later, if begun at the South, it will find its way into the cities of the North... Any attempt to justify the confiscation of Southern land under the pretense of doing justice to the freedmen, strikes at the root of all property rights in both sections. It concerns Massachusetts quite as much as Mississippi.

The final step of the Second American Revolution, the provision of an economic underpinning to the blacks' newly won freedom, was not taken. Later, visionary social justice activists like Bob Swann, inspired by his mentor Ralph Borsodi's thinking on trusteeship, launched the Community Land Trust movement to secure land rights for some. After studying the Jewish National Fund in Israel and the Gandhi-inspired Gramdan movement, which placed donated land in trusteeship for the benefit of the poor, Swann then worked with Slater King, a cousin of Martin Luther King, Jr. They secured 4,800 acres of land in Georgia for African Americans. New Communities and the Featherfield Farm project remain the largest Black-owned single-tract farm in America. Despite isolated examples like this, economic injustice -- the land and land rent problem, combined now with the money and interest problem -- is grounds for the next revolution of the American people.

Martin Luther King on Vietnam and Land Rights

Martin Luther King, Jr., another prophet and martyr, saw that our government's resistance to land reform extended beyond our own borders. In "Beyond Vietnam: A Time to Break Silence," a speech delivered on April 4, 1967, in New York City, he said:

> For nine years following 1945 we denied the people of Vietnam the right of independence. For nine years we vigorously supported the French in their abortive effort to recolonize Vietnam. After the French were defeated it looked as if independence and land reform would come again through the Geneva agreements. But instead there came the United States, determined that Ho [Ho Chi Minh] should not unify the temporarily divided nation, and the peasants watched again as we supported one of the most vicious modern dictators – our chosen man, Premier Diem.
>
> The peasants watched and cringed as Diem ruthlessly routed out all opposition, supported their extortionist landlords and refused even to discuss reunification with the north. The peasants watched as all this was presided over by U.S. influence and then by increasing numbers of U.S. troops who came to help quell the insurgency that Diem's methods had aroused.... [T]he long line of military dictatorships seemed to offer no real change, especially in terms of their need for land and peace.

King wrote in his Letter from Birmingham City Jail:

> I am sure that each of you would want to go beyond the superficial social analyst who looks merely at effects and does not grapple with underlying causes. True compassion is more than flinging a coin to a beggar; it understands that an edifice which produces beggars needs restructuring.
>
> An intelligent approach to the problems of poverty and racism will cause us to see the words of the Psalmist -- "The earth is the Lord's and the fullness thereof" -- are still a judgment upon our use and abuse of the wealth and resources with which we have been endowed.

The Carter Doctrine and U.S. Imperialism

Let us now focus for a moment on Jimmy Carter, an American president who started out with kind intentions and ended up with cruel ones.

The Carter team had pledged itself to non-intervention in the Third World, to a sincere commitment to arms control, and to work for worldwide human rights. Carter accomplished much along these lines in the beginning of his term in office, but in the end he reversed himself and fell victim to Cold War fever. Following the Soviet invasion of Afghanistan in 1980 President Carter issued his famous statement to a joint session of Congress in which he said, "An attempt by any outside force to gain control of the Persian Gulf region will be regarded as an assault on the vital interests of the United States of America (and) will be repelled by any means necessary, including military force."

As Michael T. Klare points out in his important new book, *Resource Wars: The New Landscape of Global Conflict*, the United States began a military build-up in the Persian Gulf area at that time which has continued to this day. The Carter Doctrine was invoked during the Iran-Iraq war of 1980 - 88 and again in August 1990 when Iraqi forces occupied Kuwait.

How is it that Jimmy Carter, our "best-intentioned of presidents" is remembered as the proponent of a doctrine of US national security based on "might makes right"? The remarkable transformation of Carter-the-kind-Christian from peacemaker to warmonger showed his susceptibility to Cold War fever and lack of any firm ground to stand on regarding the relationship of human rights to land rights and democracy. He played into fears that the godless communists were conspiring to take over the world, ignored the true economic principles of the Judeo-Christian tradition, and seemed to be unaware of the imperialist forces at play in the U.S. government.

When the first President Bush sent American troops to Saudi Arabia in 1990, Klare quotes him as telling the nation: "Our country now imports nearly half the oil it consumes and could face a major threat to its economic independence.... [T]he sovereign independence of Saudi Arabia is of vital interest to the United States."

The Carter Doctrine continues to be used to justify elite vested interests wresting control of land, oil and mineral resources in many areas of the earth in the name of the American people and the security interests of our "democratic" state. We the people of the United States, who comprise 5 percent of the world's population, now control 30 percent of the world's resources. All over the world we are claiming vital mineral, oil, and land resources as part of our national security and militarizing those areas. Today we are playing the "great game" for control of the three trillion dollars worth of oil and gas resources in the Central Asian republics. George W. Bush, our new "kind-Christian-president," tells he is "trying to be careful." What or who will stop us if we cannot stop ourselves?

Joseph Stiglitz on Land and the Global Elite

Joseph E. Stiglitz is one of three economists to win the Nobel Prize in economics this year of 2001. In 1999 he was fired from his position as Chief Economist with the World Bank after he began to speak about his concerns. In an interview in 2001 with Greg Palast, a writer for *The Observer* (London), Stiglitz described in detail the four-step plan used by the international banking institutions to extract wealth from around the world. In his view the process leads to financial barbarism, pillage and plunder and has resulted in immense suffering, starvation and destruction. "It has condemned people to death," Stiglitz said bluntly in the interview.

When Palast asked Stiglitz what he would do to help developing nations, Stiglitz proposed radical land reform and an attack at the heart of "landlordism," including excessive rents charged by the propertied oligarchies worldwide. When

Palast asked why the Bank didn't follow his advice, Stiglitz answered, "If you challenged it (property rights in land), that would be a change in the power of the elites. That's not high on their agenda."

Growing numbers of us are appalled and chilled to our bones at what the World Bank (in which the U.S. Treasury has a 51 percent controlling interest), the International Monetary Fund, and other instruments of international finance and control are doing to our world. The anti-globalization protesters of today represent the voices of the world's peasants, past and present, now joined by middle-class people from many countries. Placing our country and our state, county and city or town on the firm and fair foundation of the human right to the earth is one of the most important endeavors of our age.

What Are We Going to Do About It?

In 1979 I was giving a workshop in Pasadena about Henry George and land rights economics when an elder raised her hand and said: "We know this. Now what are we going to do about it?" I did not know at the time that she was Mildred Loomis or who Mildred Loomis was, but she was to become a great friend and mentor of mine. Some called her the grandmother of the counterculture. She was a close friend of Ralph Borsodi and in association with him played an influential part in founding the modern intentional community movement. Mildred also kept in touch with the land-value-tax movement and clearly understood how both of these approaches to land rights drew from the important work of Henry George.

I have thus far presented several dimensions of the great and unsolved land problem from various vantage points. Now I will describe five ways by which the earth can be claimed for the benefit of the people as a whole, detailing ways and means for securing common rights to water, oil and mineral royalties, and the rent of surface land:

- Direct action by exploited and mobilized citizens;
- Enlightened earth rights state institutions;
- Politicians who are true representatives of the people;
- Enlightened vote of the citizenry; and
- Environmental tax reform.

Direct Action by Exploited and Mobilized Citizens

An example of direct action by exploited and mobilized citizens is the story of the Bolivian Water War, as Maude Barlowe told it in her article on water privatization in the summer 2001 Bulletin of the International Forum on Globalization.

International Monetary Fund and World Bank policies have given corporate access to many water systems in developing countries. In the city of Cochabamba the Aguas Del Tunari Company, a local subsidiary of the San Francisco based Bechtel Corporation, was the only bidder for the city's water supply. After privatization, with the water system in the control of this company, rates increased and even tripled for some of the poorest customers. Water was shut off completely for others. No infrastructure improvements were made. Citizens who had built family wells or water irrigation systems decades earlier suddenly had to pay the company for the right to use the water.

An alliance of labor, human rights, environmental, and community leaders organized and fought back with peaceful marches. A public referendum showed that the vast majority wanted the company out, but they were either ignored or met with police violence. Using Gandhian tactics they engaged in strikes and blockades to take back their water. The government declared a state of siege, arrested the protest leaders, shut down radio stations, and sent in a thousand soldiers. A teenager was killed and many others wounded. After weeks of confrontation the government backed down and ended the contract with the corporate raiders. Bechtel then threatened to sue the national government for lost investments and potential lost profits based on a bilateral investment treaty.

No one was providing the city with water while the government and the corporation were in dispute. Then the water company workers began running the water system themselves with the help of the coalition that had been built. The water workers held regular community meetings to determine the need for water; they reduced prices, built new tanks, and laid pipes to bring water service to neighborhoods that had never had it before. The service was fairly and efficiently cooperatized with the full support and inclusion of the workers and the community.

The Cochabamba Declaration, the basis for coalition actions, holds that:

1. Water belongs to the earth and all species and is sacred to life, therefore, the world's water must be conserved, reclaimed and protected for all future generations and its natural patterns respected.
2. Water is a fundamental human right and a public trust to be guarded by all levels of government; therefore, it should not be commodified, privatized or traded for commercial purposes. These rights must be enshrined at all

levels of government. In particular, an international treaty must ensure these principles are noncontrovertable.

3.   Water is best protected by local communities and citizens, who must be respected as equal partners with governments in the protection and regulation of water. Peoples of the earth are the only vehicle to promote democracy and save water.

Enlightened Earth Rights State Institutions

Under the Alaska Constitution all the natural resources of Alaska belong to the state to be used, developed and conserved for the maximum benefit of the people. The Alaska Permanent Fund was established in 1976 as a state institution with the task of responsibly administering and conserving oil royalties and other resource royalties for the citizenry. The principle of the Fund is invested permanently and cannot be spent without a vote of the people, whereas the income can be spent. The legislature and the Governor decide annually how it will be used.

In 1980, after four years of debate, the Alaska Legislature established the Alaska Permanent Fund Corporation to manage the assets of the Fund. That same year the Legislature also created the Permanent Fund Dividend Program to distribute a portion of the income from the Permanent Fund each year to eligible Alaskans as direct personal dividend payments.

Individuals who received the annual dividends each year from 1982 to 2000 have received a total of $18,511. In the year 2000 more than half a million citizens received dividends of $1,963 per person, which amounts to nearly $8,000 for a family of four. Overall, the dividend program has dispersed more than $10 billion into the Alaskan economy.

Beautifully designed literature describes in detail the various components of the Fund. An Annual Report is distributed each year. There is an extensive accountability program and open meetings with opportunity for citizen participation. Citizen interest in the Fund's operation and activities is strong. Earnings undergo special public scrutiny. The Alaska Permanent Fund is a well-managed and transparent earth rights institution. It is a remarkable pioneering model of a fair and effective way to secure common heritage wealth benefits for the people as a whole.

Politicians Who are True Representatives of the People

Public officials who sincerely see their role as servants of the common good can be found in most of our towns and cities. Once they understand practical earth-rights policies, they want to help put them in place. This has been true in Pennsylvania, where local officials are implementing a property-tax reform that is direct lineage of the land-rights ideas of Henry George and, even further back, of Thomas Paine.

Paine came upon the idea of land-value taxation in France in the days preceding the French Revolution when the Physiocrats, the court socio-economic advisors, were whispering into the ear of King Louis XIV, "Poor peasants, poor kingdom; poor kingdom, poor king." Quesnay and Turgot were telling the king he must tax the land and not the common people, but it was too late and events turned bloody.

Paine said: "Men did not make the earth…It is the value of the improvement only, and not the earth itself, that is individual property…Every proprietor owes to the community a ground rent for the land which he holds." (*The Complete Works of Thomas Paine*, edited by Philip Foner, p.611). The International Declaration on Individual and Common Rights to Land says:

> Ground rent is the value that accrues to the land alone apart from any improvements created by labor. This value is created by the existence of and functioning of the whole community. To allow this value to be appropriated by individuals means that land can be used not only for the production of wealth but also as an instrument of oppression of human by human. This leads to severe social consequences that are everywhere evident.

In Pennsylvania civic officials in twenty municipalities are implementing a local tax reform based on this understanding. Pennsylvania's pioneering approach to public finance decreases taxes on buildings, which encourages improvements and renovations, and increases taxes on land values to discourage land speculation and profiteering. Shifting the tax burden from buildings to land values promotes a more efficient use of urban infrastructure and urban land while decreasing the trend towards sprawl. The benefits of development can be broadly shared when housing maintains affordability and public coffers are solvent. Pennsylvania's capitol city of Harrisburg was in shambles in 1980 when it began to shift to land value tax; now the city taxes land values six times more than buildings.

Harrisburg's mayor, Stephen Reed, sent the following letter to Patrick Toomey – businessman, civic activist, and member of the Home Rule Commission of Allentown:

> The City of Harrisburg continues in the view that a land value taxation system, which places a much higher tax rate on land than on improvements, is an important incentive for the highest and best use of land in already developed communities, such as cities.….
>
> With over 90 percent of the property owners in the City of Harrisburg, the two tiered tax rate system actually saves money over what would otherwise be a single tax system that is currently in use in nearly all municipalities in Pennsylvania.
>
> We therefore continue to regard the two-tiered tax rate system as an important ingredient in our overall economic development activities.
>
> I should note that the City of Harrisburg was considered the second most distressed in the United States twelve years ago under the Federal dis-

tress criteria. Since then, over $1.2 billion in new investment has occurred here, reversing nearly three decades of very serious previous decline. None of this happened by accident and a variety of economic development initiatives and policies were created and utilized. The two-rate system has been and continues to be one of the key local policies that has been factored into this initial economic success here.

This city has a resident population of 53,000. Here are a few of the improvements mentioned in the Harrisburg literature:

- Vacant structures, more than 4200 in 1982, today less than 500.
- Today there are 4,700 more city residents employed than in 1982.
- The crime rate has dropped 22.5% since 1981.
- The fire rate has dropped 51% since 1982.

Enlightened Vote of the Citizenry

The city of Allentown, also in Pennsylvania, showed us how this policy can be voted in by an enlightened earth rights citizenry. Joshua Vincent, director of the Center for the Study of Economics, recounted the fierce recall battle that ensued in Allentown after citizens voted in a city Home Rule Charter that included a change in property taxes to a two-tier system that would, gradually over five years, shift the burden to land values.

Vincent saw that the effort to put the land tax back on the ballot and defeat it was being driven largely by used-car dealers with large lots and shareholders of the Allentown Fair Grounds, an immensely valuable 42-acre site in the middle of the city that had always enjoyed a sweetheart property tax deal. With the help of money from statewide car dealer associations, the opponents bought television and radio time and used billboards and airplane trailer banners to paint Henry George's ideas as "socialist." They warned (falsely) that churches would have to pay the land tax. But the pro-land-tax forces, lead by a former city councilman who had been pushing for it for twenty years, mounted an intense grassroots education effort -- and the tax passed again by a comfortable margin.

Since the move towards land-value taxation, Allentown has been experiencing steady gradual improvements, as have all the Pennsylvania cities that have been implementing earth rights policy.

Environmental Tax Reform

The state of the earth now requires that the costs of industrial production and human commercial activity no longer be externalized onto the global commons. The environmental movement has been discovering how to harness tax policy in order to protect the earth.

Sufficiently high user fees and pollution permits encourage business and industry to find more efficient and cost-effective controls. Pollution taxes function as pay-for-use fees for common heritage resources of land, water and air and make the tax system work for the people and the planet. Green taxers also aim to eliminate numerous subsidies deemed no longer necessary, environmentally or socially harmful, or inequitable. Green tax policy is poised to radically redirect the incentive signals of the world's taxation systems that now promote waste, not work. Enviro think tanks like Worldwatch Institute, Center for Sustainable Economy, Northwest Environment Watch, and the Institute for Ecological Economics are building the conceptual framework.

A look at the current approximate composition of the world's $7.5 trillion tax pie reveals that 93 percent of taxes fall on work and investment while only 3 percent is collected from environmentally damaging activities. A mere 4 percent of global tax revenues is captured from natural resource use and access fees. The challenge before us is to bring about change in tax policy all around the world so that people will pay for what they take, not what they make.

Work in Progress

This past decade the Russian parliament, the Duma, has been grappling with the question of land privatization as it relates to the transition to a market economy. As Joseph Stiglitz observed when he was with the World Bank, Russia's natural resources have been pillaged for the profits of a few. Earth rights colleagues in Britain and the US -- Fred Harrison, Nic Tideman and others -- have been working quite closely with certain Russian leaders as they search for a different kind of economy, one beyond both Left and Right. Many Russian officials in positions of power are pushing the policy of land rent for the people. This effort is an uphill struggle against the neocolonizers and the international banking institutions. Battle lines are drawn between those who would privatize rent, meaning concentrate land wealth into the hands of a few, and those who would socialize rent, which means basing the Russian state on the common right of the people to the land of mother Russia as financed by land rent for the people as a whole.

In the Dominican Republic my friend Lucy Silfa is hard at work as she has been for the past fifty years. As director of the Henry George School of Social Sci-

ence there, she has educated tens of thousands of people about earth rights principles and policies. Journalists, government representatives, economists, military top
brass, and prisoners have graduated from her classes. The President of the Dominican Republic was one of her students. Recently he gave her a letter to take to
others in the government. The essence of the letter is, "Open your door to Lucy,
listen to her and do what she says."

She is now trying to pry land ownership and valuation information out of a
bureaucracy so that a feasibility study can be done before recommending a tax shift
plan for this small island state. As in Russia and almost everywhere else, we are up
against the international banking establishment's plan for this country.

Philadelphia, where Henry George was born in 1839, is one of the most exciting points of play in the land value tax movement at this time. The city's first tax
law was a land tax voted into place on January 30, 1693. Over the ensuing centuries
Philadelphia lost its land tax and fell prey to one of the highest wage taxes in the
country. There has been sporadic interest in land value taxation over the years, but
the movement is coming into its own. In 1998 we organized a Public Finance Alternatives Forum attended by around sixty people, among them an Assistant City
Controller. After reviewing the evidence for the benefits of the switch to land value
tax in other Pennsylvania cities, the Controller's Office hired one of our land value
tax colleagues to help research the possibilities for Philadelphia.

Support for the idea is rapidly growing. A number of informative and favorable stories have appeared in the *Philadelphia Inquirer*, *The Public Record* and *Philadelphia
City Paper*. Leaders in the anti-globalization movement and Green Party like Mike
Morrill and Anne Goeke are supporters along with the leadership of the Greater
Philadelphia Association of Realtors and the Chamber of Commerce. Strange bed-
fellows, eh? Well, land-value tax is a pro-active, practical and sensible approach to
the revitalization of the city. It is highly unifying because nearly everyone benefits.
Those most likely to be against it are land speculators and people who profit from
high land and housing costs. There is a possibility that certain banking interests
could also try to stand in the way, the reason being that when land becomes more
affordable and purchasing capacity rises as the result of shifting taxes from labor to
the land, banks will then be unable to capture as much interest from mortgages.
These vested interests will be outvoted and voted out as the people learn once
again how to make democracy work for the good of the whole.

Earth Rights and Information Technology

The powerful tools of information technology can well serve our work in securing
the earth as our birthright. Cities and towns are putting property values and tax
information into computer databases and onto the web, where this information is
transparent and easily accessible. Geographic information systems (GIS) are com-

puter maps containing detailed data. City assessor Ted Gwartney and political scientist Bill Batt are pioneering the use of GIS for land value tax research.

Information technology will be of great assistance to us in finding answers to these important questions: Who owns the earth? How much do they profit? How much land rent do they pay into the common fund?" LANDSAT satellite technology can help us determine if land, water and air resources are being polluted or destroyed. Those indicators can serve as red flags indicating the need to levy pollution taxes or fines. All of these concerns can be monitored by the masses via computer technology. Safeguarding the planet and the people will become the "best game on earth" – a wonderful phrase coined by Norie Huddle.

Conclusion

The Next Economy will deeply respect and value all life on earth. It will recognize that we as human beings are trustees and caretakers of the many life forms that dwell here with us. The Next Economy will extend the democratic mandate to solve the land problem by affirming the equal right of all people to the earth. It will have a balanced and just relationship of citizenry to government with enlightened public finance policy based on land and land rent for the people. Money will be issued and circulated as a service for the people as a whole rather than used as a mechanism for the exploitation of the many by the few. As land and natural-resource rent is socialized and wages are fully privatized (meaning untaxed), capital will cooperatize in ways similar to the Mondragon cooperatives of the Basque region and the models described by E. F. Schumacher, Louis Kelso and others.

The Next Economy will be global, as people are freed to move beyond borders and boundaries and claim the whole earth as their birthplace. It will be highly decentralized as well, with people living and producing for their basic human needs within the constraints and parameters of local ecological systems. The Next Economy will build a world that works for everyone, with plenty of time to expand our minds and elevate our spirits. Will we live to experience the Next Economy? Will we see it come of age? We each have a role to play to bring it forth. Let's get to it!

References:

Avila, Charles. *Ownership: Early Christian Teachings*. Maryknoll, NY. Orbis Books/Maryknoll, NY: 1983.

Barlow, Maude. "Water Privatization and the Threat to the World's Most Precious Resource: Is Water a Commodity or a Human Right?" *International Forum on Globalization Bulletin*, Summer 2001.

Berry, Thomas. "The Spirituality of the Earth" in *Toward a Global Spirituality: The Whole Earth Papers #16*. East Orange, NJ: Global Education Associates, 1982.

Cairns, Earle Edwin. *The Christian in Society*. Chicago: Moody Press, 1973.

Elkins, Stanley and Eric McKitrick. "Thaddeus Stevens: Confiscation and Reconstruction." *The Hofstadter Aegis: A Memorial*. New York: Alfred A. Knopf, 1974.

Ferrell, John. "This Land Was Made for You and Me." *Rain Magazine*, June 1982.

Foner, Philip, ed. *The Complete Works of Thomas Paine*. New York: Citadel Press, 1945.

George, Henry. *Social Problems*. New York: Robert Schalkenbach Foundation, 1996. First published 1883.

_____. *The Science of Political Economy*. New York: Robert Schalkenbach Foundation, 1992. First published 1898.

Hamilton, Leonard, ed. *Gerrard Winstanley: Selections from His Works*. London: The Cresset Press, 1994.

Hartzok, Alanna. "The Alaska Permanent Fund: A Model of Resource Rents for Public Investment and Citizen Dividends." *Geophilos* (London). Spring 2002.

_____. "Financing Local to Global Public Goods: An Integrated Green Tax Shift Perspective." *Taxation Alternatives for the 21st Century. Proceedings of the 1999 Global Institute for Taxation Conference on Fundamental Tax Reform*. New York, September 30, 1999.

_____. *Financing Planet Management: Sovereignty, World Order and the Earth Rights Imperative*. 2nd ed. New York: Robert Schalkenbach Foundation, 1995.

_____. "Pennsylvania's Success with Local Property Tax Reform: The Split Rate Tax." *American Journal of Economics and Sociology*, April 1997.

Huddle, Norie. "The Best Game on Earth." www.bestgame.org.

King, Martin Luther, Jr. "Beyond Vietnam: A Time to Break Silence." A speech delivered on April 4, 1967, at a meeting of Clergy and Laity Concerned at Riverside Church in New York City.

Klare, Michael T. *Resource Wars: The New Landscape of Global Conflict*. New York: Henry Holt, 2001.

Mische, Patricia. "Spirituality and World Order" in *Toward a Global Spirituality*. The Whole Earth Papers #16. East Orange, NJ: Global Education Associates, 1982.

Mora, Barbara and Monic Sjoo. *The Great Cosmic Mother: Rediscovering the Religion of the Earth*. San Francisco: Harper, 1991.

Newcomb, Steven T. *Pagans in the Promised Land*. Eugene, OR: Indigenous Law Institute, 1992.

Noyes, Richard. *Now the Synthesis: Capitalism, Socialism and the New Social Contract*. London: Shepheard-Walwyn, 1991.

Paul, Leslie Allen. *Sir Thomas More*. New York: Roy Publishers, 1959.

Roodman, David Malin. *The Natural Wealth of Nations*. Worldwatch Institute. New York: Norton, 1988.

Siegel, Eli. "Ownership: Some Moments." *The Right of Aesthetic Realism to Be Known* (Periodical of the Aesthetic Realism Foundation), May 5, 1999.

_____. "Self and World." *The Right of Aesthetic Realism to Be Known*, Dec. 22, 1999.

Smith, Gaddis. *Morality, Reason, and Power: American Diplomacy in the Carter Years*. New York: Hill and Wang, 1986.

"Whose Common Future?" A Special Issue of *The Ecologist*, July/August, 1992.

Wolff, Edward N. *Recent Trends in Wealth Ownership*, 1983—98. Calculations based on 1998 Survey of Consumer Finances conducted by the Federal Reserve Bank.

Image from E. F. Schumacher Society.

-2-

Who Owns the Earth?

Published in *Perspectives*, a publication of Basic Economic
Education Foundation, San Diego, 1987

The task of conservation, restoration, and rational use of the earth is vitally linked to the question of "Who should own the Earth?" The ever widening gap between rich and poor, both within and among nations is a primary source of conflict and violence, a trigger mechanism for warfare. The root cause of this local to global mal-distribution of wealth problem is the inequitable ownership and control of the planet's land and natural resources.

The ownership of land resources and valuable land-sites ultimately determines the social, the political and consequently the mental and physical condition of a people. Attaining an ethic of wise and careful stewardship of the Earth is likewise inseparable from the task of securing the well-being of individuals. The health of the human being and the health of the Earth are interrelated. It is unlikely that environmental degradation will cease until the exploitation of the human being is alleviated. The pressures upon those who are themselves exploited to exploit in turn each other and the environment is great.

Wholistic Perspective

These issues are not separate. They cannot be ordered in a linear progression of steps one, two, three - disarm, restore the environment, then work on economic justice issues. Human survival must be secured on all fronts simultaneously if it is to be secured at all. The causes and conditions of warfare, environmental exploitation, and human degradation cannot be considered apart from each other but are woven into the institutionalized fabric of the current state of the world. The whole cloth must be woven anew.

Peace is not only the ability to resolve conflicts non-violently but to ascertain conditions of basic justice and fairness in human interactions. Force has most often predominated over fairness in the long history of human affairs. Territorial conflict has for millennium been a root cause of war. The price of peace has too often been the cost of continued injustice and conditions of economic servitude. Veterans of war, little more than mercenaries to begin with in many cases, come home to want and poverty.

Fifty percent of the homeless in America today are estimated to be veterans, and fifty percent of those served in the Vietnam War. Military induction has been the only way to "be all you can be" for millions of America's lower class people. Many risked their life for "their homeland" yet had no inherent right to any part of that land when they returned home.

Basis for Justice

Can a safe and secure planet be inhabited by a few masters and many slaves? The various states and cities comprising the USA may be "safe" from invasion from each other because of the initial agreements of confederation that created the nation state two hundred years ago. Yet there is ever mounting death and violence among the underclass that find survival increasingly more difficult while the middle class is being steadily taxed into oblivion. An enduring peace must secure justice, yet the actual basis for justice lies in affirming and restoring economic rights, a subject about which there is not yet enough consensus for the kind of unity or purpose and action essential to the task.

For instance, peace advocates recommend that a department of peace be established in order to teach strategies of non-violent conflict resolution. But from what established ethic can a conflict be resolved between a landowner with 1000 acres of land and 1000 landless peasants? Do we divide the land in half and give each of the landless a small parcel so that the large landowner now holds 50%? Do we equally distribute all the land so that each peasant has one acre? But some acres will surely be better located or have richer soil than others. And what about the children?

Maldistribution of Wealth

The cry of "Land and Liberty" of the Russian revolutionaries led to a Marxist-Leninist, state-bureaucratic socialist remedy, but with curtailment of individual freedoms and with an economic elite emerging nonetheless a few decades down the road. The American Revolution proclaimed "life, liberty and the pursuit of happiness" but adopted Europe's Roman-based land law system. In the USA today, three percent of the population owns 95 percent of the private land, land values rise faster than wages, and the resulting mal-distribution of wealth is securing the very conditions that our forefathers and mothers had hoped to escape.

The paucity of real non-violent solutions to the problem of the concentration of land and resource ownership has led by default to violent upheavals and poorly conceived arrangements that are often short-lived. The landlord is killed but the peasants fight and compete against each other only to have once again the powerful and ruthless few emerge to control the many.

Equal Rights to Earth

No, these are crude attempts at solving the problem. Just as every human being strong and weak is considered of inherent equal value as a person with the right to self-expression, so every human must have a fair and equal right to the Earth itself. The right to the Earth cannot be vulnerable to the whim of partisan politics. The right to the Earth must be vested in the people themselves, in a way that can be understood and monitored by the average individual.

Need for a New Synthesis

Those of good will who would improve the conditions of the poor and the people as a whole are polarized into the right/left, Democrat/Republican traditional camps. While their good intentions may be similar, their means are in direct opposition, leading not to balanced progress but to barren compromise, resulting in increasing human and environmental degradation.

No matter how grand the goal, without a consensus of means and method well-intentioned and progressive people on both sides of the political seesaw will just keep bouncing up and down, ultimately going nowhere except deeper into the hole in the ground at the middle. Meanwhile, the institutionalized Roman land tenure system continues to make rot out of our political democracy and a mockery of ideals of human freedom as the under-classes are the first to be strangled by the unidentified and invisible hand of creeping land rent.

Capitalist-Socialist Dilemma

Socialist type solutions to the problem have resulted in unwieldy and inefficient bureaucracies that, while more evenly distributing produced wealth, depress productive powers by inhibiting individual freedom and incentives. Capitalist arrangements, while maximizing efficiency in production through competition and reward for individual incentive, cannot resolve the mal-distribution of wealth problem because of the basic flaw in putting the land base in the same market category as labor-produced wealth.

The real power in any new political grouping such as the "Peace and Environmental Coalition" and other "Green" efforts will emerge firmly when the right/left, Republican/Democrat tension is resolved not through compromise but through the articulation and actualization of a solid and dynamic synthesis. Such a higher middle ground must arise from an appreciation and unification of the highest values of both sides. Namely, concern for fairness in the distribution of wealth and collective societal needs as emphasized by the left and individual freedom and incentive with efficiency in production valued by the right.

The Keystone of Synthesis

There is a way to attain both fairness in distribution and maximum efficiency in wealth production, of securing collective needs and furthering individual freedom. The approach is based on the equal right of all to the land and natural resources and the right of the individual to the products of labor. The method based on this ethic is to collect for the people as a whole the "ground rent" which means the value of land and natural resources, and to remove taxes on labor.

A condition of "ownership" of any particular landsite or natural resource is payment of the ground rent back to the community as a whole. Ground rent is the proper source of public finance for the collective needs of the community. The "commonwealth" is thus supported by the "common wealth." Alternatively, ground rent can be redistributed by direct payment back to all individuals, much as a company returns dividends to its stockholders.

It is not necessary for each person to own land outright in order to secure his or her fair share of the Earth. Persons "owning" land or resource rights would profit through their labor, which is untaxed, not through the privilege of exclusive ownership. If they have a better located land site or richer mineral lands, they pay higher ground rents back to the community, thus equalizing results of labor applied to greater or lesser valuable natural resources.

There is no need to forcefully confiscate land titles in order to secure the equal right of all to the Earth. With ground rent as the source of public finance the people as a whole become the ^{3}owner^2 and a title deed functions as a "lease" agreement. The community "allows" individual private use of sites on the condition that its fair rental value is paid to the community. If a particular land site is misused or abused, then the community must charge a higher rate to pay for damages and cost of restoration. Thus there is individual incentive for proper care of the Earth.

The Necessity of Ground Rent as Finance Source

Public finance on all levels - local to global - must be collected from that which is the "commonwealth"- the ground rents of the land and resource base. Taxes from any other source raised for whatever worthy goal or peace or environmental needs, food, jobs or medicine, ultimately depress wages and capital formation necessary to secure basic human needs while the inevitable increase in land values is pocketed by the few who own the land. We must always ask the bottom line question when proposing ideas for a safe and restored planet: "Who benefits and who pays?"

Thus we see that the source of public finance is every bit as important as the purpose to which public funds are directed. Just as the health of the roots of a tree is crucial to the production of abundant fruit, so must public funding come from the proper base in order to procure a healthy wholesome society. Advocating the redirection of tax dollars away from armaments and toward peace education and conflict resolution, away from environmentally damaging activities and toward restoration and stewardship will not automatically better conditions of life for the majority of people. Ending the arms race will not in itself free resources, which will then feed the hungry and house the homeless.

Whatever immediate advantage might be wrought from a redirection alone of tax dollars will in due time be annulled by increase in land values to the benefit of those few holding title. Financing redirected from the military budget and into food stamps or subsidized housing or rent supplements will again be to the ultimate advantage of landholders who can charge just that much more for agricultural and residential lands, and we are back again at square one or worse.

Greens are on the Right Track

Fortunately, "Green" efforts in several countries have included platform planks that do advocate ground rent as the basis of public finance even though other parts of their agendas are sometimes contradictory in terms of means and methods.

On the global level the Law of the Seas Covenant is an example of a ground rent basis for public needs as it has affirmed that ocean resources are the common heritage of all and a proper source of funding for global institutions.

-3-

Land for People, Not for Profit

This article was published in *Green Revolution*, Vol.56/No. 4, 1999 and also published on the Bulletin Board website of United Nations Center for Human Settlements' Global Campaign for Secure Tenure.

Summary: This essay makes a clear distinction between the benefits derived from secure title to land and the market distortions caused when land is used as a commodity for investment and speculation. It briefly explores historical antecedents to capitalist arrangements of land tenure and title, taxation and banking systems. Finally, it articulates the rational for land value taxation policy, as recommended by the United Nations Center for Human Settlements Habitat II Action Agenda, and suggests that a Community Land Trust leasehold system may be the most beneficial way to secure land tenure for squatters and landless people.

On the United Nations Center for Human Settlements (UNCHS or Habitat) Global Campaign for Secure Tenure website, under the categorization of Land Ownership, Freehold Tenure is identified with free market proponents and with the use of land as an investment and speculation commodity. In the Bulletin section of the website UNCHS intern Anna-Karin Jatfors of the Land & Tenure Unit Shelter Branch states the following:

> .... when dwellers have access to secure tenure, their land and property become a source of wealth and investment in their own right, with increasing value over time. Experience has shown that the granting of secure tenure actually increases the value of the land and property, while the insecure tenure of informal settlements keeps the land economically undervalued and prevents dwellers from reaping the economic benefits from the land on which they live.

Land held for investment and speculation, however, inflates land value, making land access more difficult for some, impossible for many. This is the policy area - the question of what happens to land values when there is secure tenure - where there is the least understanding and thus the greatest challenge. Yes, freehold tenure as usually contracted allows land to become a source of investment. But is this good? How can land speculation, an inevitable concomitant of the commodification of land, be anything other than a hindrance to secure tenure for all?

It is important to separate the security of use rights that a land title grants from the land value enhancement that also results from secure land tenure. Freehold tenure is not the only form of tenure that can provide security of use rights. Other forms of legal contracts for land, such as Community Land Trust (CLT) lease agreements, also provide security of use. It is not actually the type of ownership; it is the secure title that stipulates who may use the land and sometimes also how the land may be used.

When the title is secure, thus firming up the agreement as to which individual or group is to thereby have exclusive use rights to a clearly demarcated land parcel, then the land can be productively used. This guarantees that what is sown can also be reaped, so to speak. Simultaneous with the legal agreement as to title, there may be an enhancement of land value because the use right has been clarified, from perhaps a formerly untitled or disputed status to secure tenure status.

In squatters' areas around urban centers, the land potentially has relatively high value. The potential value becomes actual value as soon as the title is secured, even before any improvements are made to the land. Thus we have seen cases where squatters go from being poor landless people to relatively wealthy people with the stroke of the land title pen.

While a clear title to land gives the security of use rights, under current private property regimes it also permits owners to speculate and profit from land as a market commodity. Thus we have also noted cases where landless people who have been given secure title sometimes quickly sell their land for immediate cash benefits. When they are unable to obtain employment to pay rent for housing, the cycle of poverty and landlessness begins anew.

Jatfors states that with secure tenure "land and property become a source of wealth and investment in their own right." She assumes that this is a solution when in fact, from a macroeconomic perspective, the commodification of land is a major problem.

Holding land as investment property and a way to accumulate wealth is actually maladaptive to a market economy. This tenure approach has been identified as a primary cause of the maldistribution of wealth problem that is rampant in capitalist systems. Land cannot respond to supply and demand dynamics. There can be increasing demand for land but there is never a corresponding increase of supply as the supply of land was determined aeons ago by whatever unfathomable forces of the universe created it.

The commodification of land and land speculation inflates land values to the point where those who have only labor to contribute to the productive process must pay ever-higher amounts for access to land for shelter. Taxation placed upon wage labor further decreases purchasing capacity. Those with the most valuable land, and there is always the situation that some land is more valuable than others, have an advantage over those with less valuable land. Having a more advantageous position, the holders of the better lands see their wealth increase above and beyond the wealth of those with the poorer land and those who have no land at all. They then frequently use their greater wealth and power to acquire additional land.

Soon land values rise more rapidly than wages. Workers must borrow to pay for land. They borrow from those who already have acquired surplus wealth and have deposited their funds in banks. Now the landless must pay interest in order to buy land. The people with surplus wealth become even richer. If the workers lose their jobs and cannot pay the mortgage, they must surrender their land to the banks.

The commodified land tenure and land-backed mortgage banking system is the problem, not the solution. We see this problem throughout the world now, for instance in the unbridled power of big financial interests to force people off of lands for so-called development projects, such as big dams which displace millions of people and supply water and electricity primarily to a few wealthy landholders and businesses rather than to all on an equitable basis.

Most of the people who are landless squatters around the urban centers in the developing world have been pushed off of their lands in rural areas, displaced from self-sufficient lives where they had direct access to land and resources to provide for their basic needs. This is the extensive dimension of the land problem - the fact that so few now control so much of the land and resources of the world.

One of the major functions of governance is to grant clear titles to land and other property. Democratic governance as presently constituted has unfortunately not been greatly concerned about how the land was obtained in the first place. We need only reflect for a moment on the fact that in the USA, for example, land was acquired by the colonizers from the native peoples under the old Roman Empire land laws of "dominium" - the legalization of land acquired by conquest and plunder. George Washington and other Founding Fathers were heavily involved in extensive land acquisition and speculation. Only white males were allowed to own property. The power of the state was used to enforce the land rights of the most aggressive and greedy.

When other groups were legally enabled to obtain land titles, practically the only way land could be acquired was through purchase. If we take this further back historically, we note that many of those who wanted to buy land had either come to America as indentured servants who had been in debtors' prisons in old Europe or Africans who had been captured into slavery. A much earlier condition of many in Europe had been that of indigenous peoples who were then subjected to the forces of colonization and empire under Rome, had later become serfs and peasants for large landed estates, and then had been forced off of the land under the Enclosure Acts.

During the Enclosure Acts period, from approximately 1350 up through the 1700s, landless people crowded into squalid cities where they were hungry and impoverished and frequently put into prison for petty crimes or the failure to repay their debts. Many were forced or tricked into indentured servitude in the New World. Some went there in desperation, with hope of a better life. But the best land had already been claimed before their arrival. After their seven years of servitude in America, their only way to access land was through purchase, never by right. Land tenure in the West, as far back as the Roman Empire, has been rooted in the legalization of title to land originally acquired by conquest and force. Democratic political rights have not given us democratic economic rights. We can exercise our right to free speech all day long but it in no way guarantees that we can have a secure place to sleep at night.

Democratic systems of governance have not given us equitable land tenure systems. In no instance historically did democratic governments procure the right to land as a human right. In no instance today do democratic governments affirm the equal rights for all to the land and resource base that sustains all life. This reality is important to keep in mind when considering how to implement truly equitable systems of land tenure today.

The intensive dimension of the land problem is what we confront as an economy "develops" under the current capitalist system. The intent to make money from land as a commodity and an investment is called "rent seeking." As development proceeds land values rise. Some few people are in positions to collect the increased land values, while other people have to borrow money from banks. Banks then collect ever-increasing ground rent - the profit from increased land value - as private profit. Investments are made, production increases, land speculation continues, and land values increase more rapidly than wages. Governments then increase taxes on middle class wages in order to pay for welfare programs for the poor. But soon workers are pressed down again to subsistence levels and below and the middle class gets angry or perhaps just depressed - if there is still a middle class remaining. The shining hope of progress has been dashed to pieces upon the hard rocks of wealth concentration.

Note that the world's richest 20% now pocket 86% of the world's gross domestic product; the middle 60% has just 13%; and the poorest 20% have but 1%. The income gap between the top fifth and the bottom fifth is now 74 to 1, compared to just 30 to 1 in 1960. These figures and the ones in the following paragraph are from the UN Human Development Report, 1999.

We see now how it has come to pass that the assets of the world's 200 richest people more than doubled between 1994 and 1998, to over $1 trillion, how the world's three richest people have come to have assets greater than the combined economic output of the 48 poorest countries, and the root cause of why 55 nations have seen real per capita incomes decrease over the last decade. The human relationship to the earth is a most fundamental and basic relationship. In the capitalist system, this most important relationship is established on the basis of conquest and commodification. This criminal maldistribution of wealth must be stopped. We need to make some fundamental changes. We need political and economic systems based upon the human right to land and resources. We need governance and land titles that can secure tenure and a genuinely free AND fair market system for all. Land values must be delinked from the privatization category, the debt and private banking system delinked from its backing in land, and labor must be freed from taxation.

The way forward has been endorsed by the consensus of 165 nation states as stated in the UN Habitat II Action Agenda from the 1996 conference in Istanbul. The Ensuring Access to Land section (B.3.c.) states both the principle and the policy approach:

> Every government must show a commitment to promoting the provision of an adequate supply of land in the context of sustainable land-use policies. While recognizing the existence of different national laws and/or systems of land tenure, governments at the appropriate levels, including local authorities, should nevertheless strive to remove all possible obstacles that may hamper equitable access to land and ensure that equal rights of women and men related to land and property are protected under the law.

The recommended policy approaches delineated in the Habitat II Action Agenda include land value assessments, land based forms of taxation, land value recapture, and technology and education programmes to support land administration systems.

Land value taxation policies shift taxes off of labor and productive capital and onto land and resources, thus collecting ground rent for the benefit of all rather than the profit of a few. Freeing labor from taxation assures maximum purchasing capacity. Collecting ground rent through land value recapture and land value taxation provides an equitable and sufficient source of public funds to finance infrastructure for water and sewage systems, transportation, education and other community services. Land also maintains affordability when it is freed from speculation and private profiteering.

While we are preparing to implement city and country wide land value taxation, we can model this approach through Community Land Trust leases which secure title and tenure to the poor and landless while eliminating the problem of the commodification of land.

A Community Land Trust (CLT) is a legal not-for-profit landholding entity with a democratically elected board and transparent accounting procedures. A CLT issued land lease clearly demarcates land boundaries and which individuals or groups are granted secure tenure and use rights to a particular parcel of land.

Under a CLT lease, land maintains affordability because there is no capacity for land speculation or profiteering. The Trust land cannot be sold so it does not have a purchase value for land users but does have a fair rental value, which in remote rural areas would be extremely low. With no selling price, only a fair lease fee, there is no need to borrow mortgage money for land purchase. This significantly lowers the cost of land for housing and other useful activities.

A CLT lease clearly states the use for which the land is being leased, including environmental covenants, the amount of land rent to be paid into the Trust, and the method of calculation for determining land rent. It also includes sublease and termination agreements and defines a process of arbitration should there be any conflicts.

The money collected from land rents can be allocated for (1) capitalization and maintenance of needed community infrastructure - water, sewage, transport, public safety, and education, and/or for (2) interest free revolving loan funds made available for housing construction and the development of small or cooperative business activities.

This approach provides needed services without taxing labor or productive capital and takes private profiteering out of banking and loan arrangements. Freed from taxation, production can proceed efficiently. Freed from usury the money system can now begin to function like a public trust.

Land tenure, taxation policy, and banking systems are all intricately interrelated. As we address all three in a just and equitable manner we will surely see wonderful progress in securing quality affordable housing and useful employment for all.

-4-

Green Economics:
A Decentralist, Bioregionalist, Globalist Agenda

Published in *Land and Liberty*, August 1985.

Our nation state systems are in transition toward a new world order that is a synthesis of both the political and the economic rights that have been advanced throughout the world during the past two centuries. On one hand the nation state is too large and on the other too small for the undertakings necessary to lead us into the 21st century. We must both and at the same time decentralize certain political and economic functions to more local levels and appropriately centralize certain functions to the global level.

Additionally, if the Green movement is to be consistent with its earth-centered values, it must as a whole endorse bioregionalism. If bioregionalism is to be internally and externally consistent with itself, it must in turn adopt an appropriate system of political and economic governance. The bioregion would then serve as an intermediary level between the local and the global.

A Green economic agenda in a decentralist, bioregionalist, and globalist framework would be a synthesis of the highest values of right and left. As such, it would be capable of uniting caring and thoughtful people from both sides of the body politic. The concern is for both efficiency and individual freedom in economic production and exchange as well as fairness in the overall distribution of wealth and just rewards for labor of all kinds.

The production and exchange of wealth in any society takes place within the constructs and constraints of two major systems: land tenure and money. In the United States, 3% of the population owns 95% of the private land, the top 10% owns 86% of all net financial assets, and 5% owns virtually all the capital wealth. To solve this maldistribution of wealth problem, the foundational underpinnings of the economy must be set on the moral and ethical ground of basic fairness.

A financial elite should not control the money system. Non-profit banks should issue and retire currency and should loan to the kinds of business enterprises which will broadly distribute ownership of wealth. The government's role would simply be to establish and enforce a standard monetary unit applicable to the issuance of currency.

We need a fundamental reorientation in our system of land tenure to provide a framework for the ecological use of land and to give effective recognition to the fact that land is a common heritage to which everyone is equally entitled.

Green taxation policy should be rooted in an ethic of fair rights to the earth for all. The dual problems of territorial conflict and the maldistribution of wealth can thus be addressed at their source. An overall policy of full ground rent collection, in lieu of most other forms of taxation, should be implemented whereby the socially created value of surface landsites and the unearned value of the oil and mineral deposits of the earth are shared by all. Ground rent is thus the appropriate revenue source for funding ecological restoration efforts and peacekeeping through world law. Dividends can also be refunded directly back to the people.

Within the framework of sound and ethical systems of land tenure and money, we envision a three-tier economy. Natural monopolies such as transportation, communications, and certain utilities and large scale key industries such as steel and other forms of heavy manufacturing should have a high degree of social input and control on the most local, decentralized level feasible.

The second tier consists of cooperatives and worker-owned industries and businesses formed through freedom of association and choice rather than through coercive mandates. The third tier is that of individual and family owned small businesses - shops, restaurants, services, and such.

Environmental costs should be factored into the total costs of production and polluters should be heavily penalized. While our economic goal is the production of high quality goods and services that satisfy genuine human needs, economic production is not an end in itself. Ultimately, economic production must further the evolution and development of the human being on the emotional, mental and spiritual planes.

Nobel Prize
Winner
Wangari
Maathai
planting a
tree in Kenya.

-5-

Restructuring Economic Relationships

Published in the Analysis and Commentary section of
Geodata, Issue Number 2, Winter 1988.

Chief Sitting Bull said to Annie Oakley:
"The white man knows how to make everything,
but he does not know how to distribute it."

The problem of the severe maldistribution of wealth in the United States clearly has not been solved by the predominant 20th century economic theories and policies. Keynesian economic policies of transfer payments through various New Deal and Great Society programs now stand revealed as short-term, stopgap reforms by which the middle classes were taxed more heavily so that the poor could have merely a subsistence existence. Reaganomics peeled off some of the band-aids but the wounds did not heal -- they only bled more profusely.

We must also dispel the fantasy that technological invention can solve our economic crisis. There is no machine that can save us. Our advanced technology has become labor enslaving and displacing rather than labor saving and enhancing because of the extreme concentration of capital ownership.

The primary task is to restructure the economic relationships of our society. We can rely on the traditional economic policies of neither the right nor the left. An ethic of fair play must inform the inputs of economic production: land and resource ownership, capital ownership and finance policy.

We need to rethink the whole area of work, jobs, and wages. In addition to fair wages and equal pay for equal work we must add another factor – all workers have a right to own a fair share of the capital they produce.

This right stems form the obvious fact that labor, whether blue collar, white collar, pink or polka dot, makes the capital. Our challenge is to correct this fundamental injustice. The labor power of employees on nearly all levels of the economic ladder has been steadily usurped through mechanisms of wealth concentration.

That labor may reap its due rewards, a wide variety of employee stock ownership plans as developed by Louis Kelso and others should be implemented, as well as industrial cooperative models such as the highly successful ones utilized by the Basque people of Mondragon, Spain.

The extreme concentration of capital ownership grew largely out of an earlier concentration of land and natural resources ownership. Land speculation continues to be a major concentrator of wealth.

Most of our cities and neighborhoods currently function like mini-third world countries. The goods and services we produce ultimately trickle up into the banking accounts of the very wealthy through various wealth concentration mechanisms such as real estate speculation, usurious money lending, concentration of capital ownership and diverse currency manipulation practices.

Studying and analyzing the economic structures of our communities will help us to realize what must be done to move toward a thorough democratization of economic arrangements.

We need to know the answers to questions such as:

- Who owns the land and natural resources of our city / region?
- What are and who owns the major industries?
- What is imported and what is exported?
- Who pays what taxes and what for?
- Who is hungry, homeless, and hopeless and why?

Answers to the above questions will give us a high degree of awareness from which to direct our efforts toward securing a broad base of ownership of capital and fair share rights to land and natural resources.

The author rides with Apache and Navajo friends down cliffs into the sacred and ancient lands of Canyon De Chelly.

- 6-

Earth Rights Democracy: Land Ethics and Public Finance Policy as if People and Planet Mattered

Presented at the Richard Alsina Fulton Conference on Sustainability and the Environment, Wilson College, Chambersburg, Pennsylvania, March 26 – 27, 2004.

Evaggelos Vallianatos, in his reflections on Why Small Farmers are Essential to Democracy, said: "When democracy thrived in Greece, so did farming. The two were inseparable." He noted that those who worked very small plots of land, not philosophers, laid the foundations for ancient Greek democracy. "Democracy was the Greek smallholders' answer to tyranny and the genius of Greek civilization," says Vallianotos, who well remembers the joys and pleasures of childhood on the small Greek farm where he grew up. "My father's farming was wrecked when the Americans converted Greece to agribusiness," he tells us.[1]

Somehow our world has become complex. Stress related emotional and physical illness continues to rise. Most of us are born landless, without any real place to be. Our parents were probably paying rent or a mortgage while we were growing up. They did the best they could, and then we launched into the world of labor. While some never made it to the first rung of the ladder, others found employment as highly skilled laborers. An educator is a type of highly skilled laborer. Usually, the more highly skilled a laborer is, the further removed he or she is from the land. Yet that which all of the laborers need to survive comes ultimately from the earth itself.

Who owns the earth?

- A United Nations study of 83 countries showed that less than 5% of rural landowners control three-quarters of the land.
- Just 342 farm properties in Brazil cover 183,397 square miles - an area larger than California. [2]
- 86% of South Africa is still owned by the white minority population.
- 60% of El Salvador is owned by the richest 2% of the population.

- 80% of Pakistan is owned by the richest 3% of the population.
- 74% of Great Britain is owned by the richest 2% of the population.
- 84% of Scotland is owned by the richest 7% of the population.
- At best, a generous interpretation would suggest that about 3% of the population owns 95% of the privately held land in the United States.[3]
- 568 companies control 22% of our private land, a land mass the size of Spain. Those same companies land interests worldwide comprise a total area larger than that of Europe - almost 2 billion acres.
- Urban Land Institute calculations show that more than half of all corporate earnings are generated by real estate and real estate-related activities.[4]
- In Florida, 1% owns 77% of the land. Other states where the top 1% own over two-thirds of the land are Maine, Arizona, California, Nevada, New Mexico, and Oregon.[a]

Eli Siegel once said: "How the earth should be owned is the major economic question of this time.... The world should be owned by the people living in it.'[5]

By some estimates, one percent of the population owns at least 60% of the land value in western countries. The value of all land in the United States in 1990 was $3.7 trillion.[6] By now that number is likely to be more than $6 trillion. The federal government no longer tracks land ownership and values. Apparently such numbers are too politically sensitive.

Let us take an example of how the average American family experiences the land problem. In smaller cities a typical $120,000 house will be on a $30,000 lot. In major population centers a house costs double, triple or even 10-times that price. In parts of California a comparable home would be $400,000; in parts of Washington, DC it would be $800,000. Labor and material prices for these homes are relatively equal. The price difference is the cost of land functioning under the "law of rent" as described by classical economist David Ricardo.[7]

Under our current economic system, the price of land is paid by the producers of wealth - labor - to those who amass wealth from unearned income for which they do not labor. Those who receive this unearned income from land price escalation are primarily (1) those who already own large amounts of land or land of high value; (2) those who are earning interest from real estate speculation; and (3) financial institutions via mortgage payments.

We must grasp the injustice at the core of our economic system. We need to understand how far we have strayed from reality and how we have been led into

---

[a] United States Senator Jesse Helms read these facts and figures into the Congressional Record in 1981 as his way of "proving" that there was no need for land reform in the US as land is more concentrated in ownership in the US than in Central America where the US was waging wars against those seeking land reform.

illusionary games of finance. Patricia Mische said, "The more we grow in awareness of our own sacred source, the more we discover that our own sacred source is the sacred source of each person and all that is in the universe."[8]

Near a large metro area, a farmer can sell land at a price of $20,000 to $60,000/acre and in some cases even more. The farmer takes this cash and looks for another farm to buy farther from the city. Using a 1031 (tax-free) exchange he rolls the profits into another farm. Another group of agricultural land buyers are investors who conclude that land is a good investment after watching farmland prices go up. Farmers sitting on significant equity in land they already own also add to their current land base at higher prices when they perceive that land values are on the rise.[9] Farmland thus loses its utility value for agriculture and becomes a "good investment" - a cash cow to be milked for all its worth.

For most farmers, the value of farmland comprises the majority of net worth. The recent land price boom has been driven primarily by low interest rates. Because of these low interest rates, a young couple living in a metropolitan area can now buy a $150,000-200,000 home. As a result of these new buyers, real estate developers are able to buy farmland at extremely high prices and develop entry-level to middle-income homes.

John Mohawk fully grasped the problem of our land tenure system. He said, "When land became a 'commodity' and lost its status as provider and sustainer of life, Western civilization began its history of subjugation and exploitation of the earth and earth based cultures."[10]

Today, this subjugation and exploitation is eroding middle class America as well. While the larger land parcels are bought with cash or very little debt, working people take on substantial amounts of debt to buy their small house plots. This further widens the wealth gap.

Americans are working longer and harder just to buy someplace, somewhere, to rest their weary bones at night. The United States is a super rich nation that spends a huge amount on health care and has multitudes of sick people. The Health Olympics tracks the correlation between illness, longevity and economic injustice as indicated by the wealth gap. This indicator shows that the greatest health hazard in the United States is the economic gap between the rich and the poor. With greater economic inequality comes worse health - lower life expectancy and higher mortality rates. The U.S. spends the most money on health care but ranks 26th in life expectancy on the Health Olympics 2003 chart. All of the countries that rank higher in the Health Olympics have a smaller gap in income distribution between their richest and poorest citizens.

Worldwide less than 300 multi-billionaires now have as much wealth as three billion people, which is half the six billion population of the planet. Just three people have as much wealth as the people of 48 countries. In the United States, the wealth gap has been steadily growing since the 1970s. Currently, the top one percent of our population has accumulated more household wealth than the bottom 95 percent. The bottom 90% has only 29% of household wealth. The wealthiest 1% owns 49% of all stocks and mutual funds; the next 9% own 36% and the bottom 90% own 15%.[11]

Robert Reich said, "We now have more national income and national wealth concentrated in fewer hands then we've had since the gilded age of the late nineteenth century. This poses a fundamental threat to democracy."

One of the most disturbing aspects of life in this very wealthy country is the persistence of hunger. The U.S. Department of Agriculture (USDA) reports, based on a national U.S. Census Bureau survey of households representative of the U.S. population, that in 2002 11.1 percent of all U.S. households were "food insecure" because of lack of resources. Of the 12.1 million households that were food insecure, 3.8 million suffered from food insecurity that was so severe that USDA's measure classified them as "hungry." The report showed that food insecurity and hunger increased in the United States for the third consecutive year. Since 1999, food insecurity has increased by 3.9 million individuals: 2.8 million adults and more than one million children. In 2002, 34.9 million people lived in households that were unable to purchase adequate food and thus experienced food insecurity, compared to 33.6 million in 2001 and 31 million in 1999.[12]

The U.S. Conference of Mayors in their Sodexho Survey 2003 also reported that hunger and homelessness continued to rise in major American cities over the last year.[13] Twenty participating cities reported that unemployment and various employment-related problems were the leading causes of hunger. Other causes most likely contributing to hunger include low-paying jobs (13 cities) and high housing costs (11 cities). Participating cities were most likely to attribute homelessness to a lack of affordable housing (21 cities), mental illness and the lack of needed services (20 cities), substance abuse and the lack of needed services (19 cities), and low-paying jobs (17 cities). The survey documents significant unmet need for shelter in the cities surveyed. Eighty-four percent of the cities reported that emergency shelters have turned away homeless families due to lack of resources.

To remedy this injustice we must understand the land problem. Thomas Berry said, "Humans in their totality are born of the earth. We are earthlings. The earth is our origin, our nourishment, our support, our guide... Thus the whole burden of modern earth studies is to narrate the story of the birth of humans from our Mother Earth."[14]

The millions who are hungry and homeless in America are unlikely to ever have sufficiently well paying jobs or any jobs at all. Two million manufacturing jobs have evaporated since 2000. Manufacturers are either off-shoring jobs to China or automating as fast as they can. Information jobs are fast moving to India. Today there are roughly 15 million Americans working in manufacturing jobs. Every year for the next 15 years, a million or so Americans will lose their manufacturing jobs.

In 15 or 20 years, there will be zero people in America working in manufacturing jobs.

Those who still have jobs are less secure than they have ever been before. More than 40 million Americans have no health insurance and 140 million are facing soaring health costs. Retirement savings are at an historic low.

The richest 10% of capital owners own 71% of America. If current trends continue they will own it all. They are now financing the robotic revolution. Robots are going to create completely automated factories in the very near future. Automated retail systems like ATMs, kiosks and self-service checkout lines are just the beginning. These systems will proliferate and evolve until nearly every retail transaction will be handled in an automated way. By 2022 computers run at one trillion operations per second. Computers with the capacity of the human brain could cost as little as $500.[15]

What will become of democracy? What will become of "we the people?" What kind of life awaits our children and grandchildren if they have no jobs and no income to buy food or shelter?

Henry George had this insight more than a century ago:

> Our primary social adjustment is a denial of justice. In allowing one man to own the land on which and from which other men must live, we have made him a bondsmen in a degree which increases as material progress goes son. It is this that turns the blessings of material progress into a curse.[16]

Either we will be in bondage, or we will build an economic democracy and be free to celebrate life on this amazing planet. We must find the way and quickly. The forces of concentration of wealth and power have nearly overpowered us. A poem in The Lord of the Rings mirrors the mythic times we are living: "One ring to rule them all, one ring to find them, one ring to bring them all, and in the darkness bind them." We are bound and the cord is tightening. "Full spectrum dominance" is the phrase the elite have coined to describe their intention to rule the world.

We are on the threshold of the second American revolution. We need to proceed with the non-violent approach taught by Thoreau, Gandhi and King. We need to build an economic democracy based firmly on this most basic principle - the earth belongs equally to everyone as a birthright.

Thomas Jefferson gave us a first principle ethic when he said, "The earth is given as a common stock for men to labor and live on."

Abraham Lincoln told us:

> The land, the earth God gave to man for his home, sustenance, and support, should never be the possession of any man, corporation, society, or unfriendly government, any more than the air or water, if as much. An individual, company, or enterprise should hold no more than is required for their home and sustenance.

All that is not used should be held for the free use of every family to make homesteads, and to hold them as long as they are so occupied.

Tom Paine gave us a policy approach to the problem of escalating land values
when he said:

Men did not make the earth...It is the value of the improvement only, and not the
earth itself, that is individual property...Every proprietor owes to the community a
ground rent for the land which he holds.

Several early political economists had begun to grasp the problem and the solution.
John Stuart Mill was aware that:

Landlords grow richer in their sleep without working, risking, or economizing.
The increase in the value of land, arising as it does from the efforts of an entire
community, should belong to the community and not to the individual who
might hold title.

Henry George said:

Do what we may, we can accomplish nothing real and lasting until we
secure to all the first of those equal and inalienable rights with which....
man is endowed by his creator - the equal and inalienable right to the
use and benefit of natural opportunities.[17]

Thus far we have looked at how the land problem is the root cause of the wealth
gap. Sustainability people are well aware of the costs to the planet when wealth and
power spiral into the hands of so few. Loss of species and topsoil, deteriorated air
and water quality, global warming - the list of catastrophes and potential catastrophes grows each day. Those with clear vision frequently feel frustrated by lack of
power and financing to remedy these problems.

War is the last topic to touch upon before describing how we can adjust - add
justice to - the economy so that profits can serve people and planet. Most every war
throughout all the ages has been fought over land and natural resources. During
the past one hundred years, governments have been destabilized and wars have
been fought over land and natural resources in Indonesia, Vietnam, Iran, Iraq, Nigeria, Chile, El Salvador, Nicaragua, Guatemala and many other small countries.

We have seen oil conflicts in the Persian Gulf, the Caspian Sea Basin, Nigeria
and the South China Sea and water conflicts in the Nile Basin, the Jordan, Tigris-
Euphrates and Indus River Basins. Internal wars have been or are being fought
over minerals and timber in Angola, Sierra Leone, Liberia, the Congo, Bougain-
ville/Papua New Guinea, Borneo, Brazil and Indonesia. Hostilities over valuable
gems, minerals and timber are under way in Angola, Brazil, Burma, Cambodia,
Columbia, Congo, Indonesia, Liberia and the Philippines.

Michael Klare astutely observes in his book *Resource Wars*:

> What we are seeing is the emergence of a new geography of conflict - a global landscape in which competition over vital resources is becoming the governing principle behind the disposition and use of military power.... the result is a new strategic geography in which resource concentrations rather than political boundaries are the major defining features.[18]

A few days ago I saw a large earthworm wriggling around frantically in a puddle of water contained in plastic sheeting, so there was no way it could escape. I picked up the worm, and then carelessly threw it in the bushes. The worm snagged on a rose thorn. I was angry at myself, having saved the worm and then murdered it. Again I carefully picked up the helpless creature and laid it gently on the ground. A few moments later, much to my relief, the worm began to wriggle and find its way underground.

I am certain that most of you at this sustainability conference are like me in this way. You respect life and living things. Some of you take spiders outside instead of smashing them, set out food or water for birds and use have-a-heart traps for mice and groundhogs. And yet, you and I are murderers. We murder other living things. We murder children, women and men. Part of our time each day pays for the killing of human beings just like us. We do this because our lives are embedded in an unjust economic system that breeds war and destruction. We do this because we pay for this with our hard-earned tax dollars. Each day we hand over fistfuls of money to build weapons of mass destruction, fuel dangerous, dirty and polluting technologies, and subsidize huge conglomerates that concentrate the wealth of the world for the power of an elite few.

What if we, instead, were to find a way to share the earth? What if we, instead, were to find a way to end tax tyranny and align our visions and values with how we finance government? The way forward is coming into sight.

Ecological economists are attempting to cost the earth - to put a dollar amount on the services that the planet provides. The cost of earth services is, as we might suspect, multi-trillions of dollars. Geonomic economists are calculating resource rents - the market value of surface land and natural resources - and are finding that for the US the amount could be as much as half of GDP. Visionary philosophers say these sums represent our common heritage and should profit the many, not the few. A prophet once said, as recorded in Ecclesiastes (5:9), "the profit of the earth is for all."

In 1996, the UNCHS - United Nations Center for Human Settlements - issued a global agenda for ensuring access to land that weaves together person/planet concerns and states in part:

Access to land and legal security of tenure are strategic prerequisites for the provision of adequate shelter for all and for the development of sustainable human settlements affecting both urban and rural areas... The failure to adopt, at all levels, appropriate rural and urban land policies...remains a primary cause of inequity and poverty. It is also the cause of increased living costs, the occupation of hazard-prone land, environmental degradation and the increased vulnerability of urban and rural habitats, affecting all people....

Within the UNCHS document, adopted by consensus of all UN member states, are the crucial recommendations d, h, and k:

(d) Apply transparent, comprehensive and equitable fiscal incentive mechanisms, as appropriate, to stimulate the efficient, accessible and environmentally sound use of land;

(h) Consider the adoption of innovative instruments that capture gains in land value and recover public investments; and

(k) Develop land codes and legal framework that define the nature of land and real property and the rights that are formally recognized. [19]

Decades earlier, another international conference produced a document which provided such a land code and framework that defined land rights. The International Declaration on Individual and Common Rights to Land declared that the earth is the common heritage of all and that all people have natural and equal rights to the land of the planet. By the term "land" is meant all natural resources. The Declaration says:

Subject always to these natural and equal rights in land and to this common ownership, individuals can and should enjoy certain subsidiary rights in land.

These rights properly enjoyed by individuals are:
- The right to secure exclusive occupation of land
- The right to exclusive use of land occupied.
- The right to the free transfer of land according to the laws of the country.
- The right to transmit land by inheritance.

These individual rights do not include:

- The right to use land in a manner contrary to the common good of all, e.g., in such a manner as to destroy or impair the common heritage.
- The right to appropriate what economists call the Economic Rent of land.

The Economic Rent is the annual value attaching to the land alone apart from any improvements thereon created by labor. This value is created by the existence of and the functioning of the whole community wherein the individual lives and is in justice the property of the community. To allow this value to be appropriated by individuals enables land to be used not only for the production of wealth but as an instrument of oppression of human by human leading to severe social consequences which are everywhere evident.

All humans have natural and equal rights in land that may be exercised in two ways:

- By holding land as individuals and/or
- Sharing in the common use of the Economic Rent of land.

The Economic Rent of land can be collected for the use of the community by methods similar to those by which real estate taxes are now collected. That is what is meant by the policy of Land Value Taxation. Were this community created land value collected, the many taxes that impede the production of wealth and limit purchasing power could be abolished.

The exercise of both common and individual rights in land is essential to a society based on justice. But the rights of individuals in natural resources are limited by the just rights of the community. Denying the existence of common rights in land creates a condition of society wherein the exercise of individual rights becomes impossible for the great mass of the people.[20]

These two important international documents lay out how we can build economic democracy based on the equal right of all to the land and resources of the planet. They give us both the ethics and the policies whereby the earth can be secured as the birthright of all people. They carry forward the previously quoted earth rights democracy ideas of Thomas Paine, John Stuart Mill, Thomas Jefferson, Abraham Lincoln, and Henry George. Several progressive think tanks[21] are developing public finance frameworks - sometimes called "green taxation policy" - that are fundamentally based on the ethic and policies of these two important international documents. The goal of green tax policy is to create a system of public finance that strengthens and maximize incentives for:

- Fair distribution of wealth
- Environmental protection
- Basic needs production
- Provision of adequate government services
- Peaceful resolution of territorial conflicts

Green tax reform makes a clear distinction between private property and common property. Private property is that which is created by labor. Common property is that which is provided by nature. Green tax policy removes taxes from wages and other private property and increases taxes and user fees on common property. Reducing taxes on labor increases purchasing capacity, reducing taxes on capital encourages efficiency. Shifting taxes to land and resources curbs speculation and private profiteering in our common property and is a practical way to conserve and fairly share the earth.

Captured in brief sound bites, tax waste, not work; tax bads, not goods; pay for what you take, not what you make; and polluter pays become tax shift principles readily translated into voter friendly policy recommendations with broadbased political support.

Green tax policy seeks to ELIMINATE SUBSIDIES that are environmentally or socially harmful, unnecessary, or inequitable. Slated for drastic reduction or complete removal by Green Scissors and other tax cut campaigns are subsidies for:

- Energy production
- Resource extraction
- Commerce and industry
- Agriculture and forestry
- Weapons of mass destruction
- Green tax policy aims to ELIMINATE taxes on:
- Wages and earned income
- Productive and sustainable capital
- Sales, especially for basic necessities
- Homes and other buildings

Green tax policy INCREASES taxes and fees, thus capturing resource rents on:

- Emissions into air, water, or soil
- Land sites according to land value
- Lands used for timber, grazing, mining
- Ocean and freshwater resources
- Electromagnetic spectrum
- Satellite orbital zones
- Oil and minerals

These tax policies[22] both enhance the power of the people as a whole and trigger environmental improvements. One of the first examples of environmental tax reform as a two-pronged incentive strategy - raising taxes on the use of resources while decreasing taxes on income - was in 1991 when Sweden began levying a carbon dioxide tax and, in conjunction with it, cut the income tax. Other countries followed Sweden's lead, as Denmark, Spain, the Netherlands, United Kingdom, and Finland cut taxes on personal income and wages and raised taxes on motor fuel, coal, electricity, water, waste, carbon emissions, pesticide, natural gas, and other energy sales. These were small shifts, to be sure, the largest being Denmark which eco-shifted 2.5 percent of total tax revenues.

In the US, J. Andrew Hoerner, a senior research scholar with the Center for a Sustainable Economy, a nonprofit public interest research organization based in Washington, DC, has compiled a Survey of State Initiatives detailing 462 environmental tax provisions currently in place at the state level. "We are still learning how to design environmental taxes and tax incentives, and many current approaches to environmental taxation will surely be found wanting," says Hoerner. "But there is a danger in a rush to judgment, in trying to impose a single theoretical paradigm on the immense diversity of emerging instruments."

Movements are underway in several countries, some detailed in the appendix of this paper, to collect increasing amounts of resource rents for public benefits. The Alaska Permanent Fund is one such excellent example of a transparent, public institution that collects and distributes resource rents for the people as a whole. Under the Alaska Constitution all the natural resources of Alaska belong to the state to be used, developed and conserved for the maximum benefit of the people. The Alaska Permanent Fund was established in 1976 as a state institution with the task of responsibly administering and conserving oil royalties and other resource royalties for the citizenry. The principle of the Fund is invested permanently and cannot be spent without a vote of the people.

In 1980, the Alaskan Legislature created the Permanent Fund Dividend Program to distribute a portion of the income from the Permanent Fund each year to eligible Alaskans as direct personal dividend payments. Individuals who received the annual dividends each year from 1982 to 2003 have received a total of more than $20,000. Alaska is the only state where the wealth gap decreased during the past decade. There is strong citizen interest in the Fund's operation and activities. The Alaska Permanent Fund website (apfc.org) keeps current all investment and distribution activities of the Fund. Also posted on the website are stories, puzzles and games for teachers to use in their classes to educate their students about the Fund.

The Alaska Permanent Fund is a well-managed and transparent earth rights institution. It is a remarkable pioneering model of a fair and effective way to secure common heritage wealth benefits for the people as a whole. However, the challenges of global warming and non-renewable resource depletion dictate that oil and other non-renewable resource rents should be invested in socially and environmentally responsible ways and primarily in the needed transition to renewable energy technologies.

The handful of non-renewable resource rent funds in the world should be citizen empowered to both increase their resource rents and royalties and should transition towards capturing substantial resource rents from surface land site values (ground rent) and other permanent and sustainable sources of rent, such as hydropower points, electromagnetic spectrum and satellite orbital zones. Resource rent funds should be established worldwide from the local to the global level.

Cities in Pennsylvania have been pioneering the ways and means to capture the value of land for public benefits. Civic officials in twenty municipalities of this state are decreasing taxes on buildings, which encourages improvements and renovations, and increasing taxes on land values to discourage land speculation, encourage good site use, and furthers access to more affordable land. Shifting the tax burden from buildings to land values promotes a more efficient use of urban infrastructure and recaptures the values that society creates. The benefits of development can be broadly shared when housing maintains affordability and public coffers are solvent.

Pennsylvania's capitol city of Harrisburg was in shambles in 1980 when it began to shift to land value tax; now this city of about 55,000 people taxes land values six times more than buildings. Harrisburg's mayor, Stephen Reed, writes:

> The City of Harrisburg continues in the view that a land value taxation system, which places a much higher tax rate on land than on improvements, is an important incentive for the highest and best use of land.... With over 90 percent of the property owners in the City of Harrisburg, (this) tax system actually saves money over what would otherwise be a single tax system that is currently in use in nearly all municipalities in Pennsylvania. .... the City of Harrisburg was considered the second most distressed in the United States twelve years ago under the Federal distress criteria.
>
> Since then, over $1.2 billion in new investment has occurred here, reversing nearly three decades of very serious previous decline. None of this happened by accident and a variety of economic development initiatives and policies were created and utilized. The (land value tax) system has been and continues to be one of the key local policies that have been factored into this initial economic success here.

Here are a few of the improvements mentioned in the Harrisburg literature:

- The number of vacant structures, over 4200 in 1982, is today less than 200.
- With a population of 53,000, today there are 4,700 more city residents employed than in 1982.
- The crime rate has dropped 22.5% since 1981.
- The fire rate has dropped 51% since 1982.

There are many more examples of the successful implementation of resource rent and green tax policy approaches than can be mentioned in this paper. Movements for land value taxation and resource rent for revenue are now underway in other states and in England, Scotland, South Korea, Russia, Nigeria, Namibia, Australia and Venezuela. Historically, versions of this public finance approach have resulted in substantial land reforms in Taiwan, Japan and the central valley of California.

Green tax reform is a comprehensive, holistic framework and could become a universally accepted approach to public finance policy. The policies and principles of green tax reform can provide the underpinnings for worldwide economic democracy. Freedom to live or work in any part of the globe would also further equality of entitlement to the planet.

Green tax policy provides a basis for the resolution of resource wars and territorial conflicts. There would be no more private profit as unearned income from earth resources. Instead, transparent and accountable resource agencies would collect resource rents and distribute those funds in public services or as direct citizen dividends. With fundamental democracy in rights to the earth firmly established through legal means and mandates, basic needs would be secured for all and the militarized national security state and its bloated budgets could wither away.

Full resource rents from surface land would eliminate the need for land mortgages as land could be secured on the basis of a simple annual fee according to land value. No other charges would fall on the backs of labor and thus wages and purchasing capacity would increase. Secure private home ownership would be the rule. Labor with access to affordable land would produce quality affordable housing for all.

It has been calculated that nearly half of corporate profits comes from real estate related activities. A tax on land would thus fall heavily on corporate held lands that cannot escape from taxation via offshore accounts and other tax shelters. With the power of the people focused with laser clarity on the task of taxing monopolistic land holdings, corporate rule would erode. Labor would gain affordable access to land resources and capital. The products of labor on land would increasingly be owned and controlled by voluntary cooperative organizations. The removal of federal subsidies for agribusiness combined with affordable land access will give a great impetus to organic, sustainable agriculture.

Green tax policy is a mechanism for full cost recovery of environmental damages. A condition of the permission to extract resources or to use water or air would be the advanced payment of environmental security deposits. While heavy pollution taxes would drastically increase incentives for clean technologies, the environmental security deposits would only be returned if the land resource was left in an acceptably healthy condition.

There is a huge task ahead of us. The incentive signals of the world's taxation systems currently promote waste, war, environmental damage, and the concentration of wealth. Approximating the composition of the world's $7.5 trillion tax pie reveals that 93% of taxes fall on work while only 3% is collected from environmentally damaging activities. A mere 4% of global tax revenues is captured from natural resource use and access fees. A modest global tax shift scenario proposed by David Roodman at Worldwatch Institute would collect 15% from environmental damage, 12% from land use and resource royalties (to total $900 billion each year) and cut environmentally harmful subsidies by 90%. This would free up an additional 8% of current revenues ($600 billion) and permit a nearly one-third reduction on wages and capital to 65% of total global taxes.[23]

Public finance legislation is underway in several states based on green tax shift calculations done by Northwest Environment Watch for the Pacific Northwest. This bolder and more detailed green tax shift scenario is detailed in these "before" and "after" pie diagrams next page.[24]

The planet and all its resources of land, water, forests, minerals, the atmosphere, electro-magnetic frequencies, and even satellite orbits are the common heritage of all and must no longer be appropriated for the private profit of a few to the exclusion of the many. As we place this fundamentally just earth rights ethic within a fully established green tax agenda, the profits of the earth will benefit the people and the planet and secure an age of peace and plenty for all.

No child should live and play in squalor like this. Earth Rights Democracy would secure an equal right to earth as a birthright for everyone through fair land tenure and tax policy.

Current Revenue Source

**Projected Revenue Source
Stage One Reform**

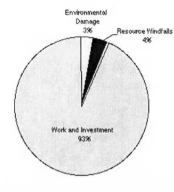

Environmental
Damage
3%

Resource Windfalls
4%

Work and Investment
93%

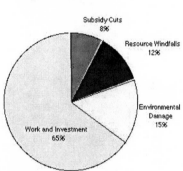

Subsidy Cuts
8%

Resource Windfalls
12%

Environmental
Damage
15%

Work and Investment
65%

Source: David Malin Roodman, *The Natural Wealth of Nations: Harnessing the Market for the Environment* (New York: W.W. Norton & Company/World Watch, 1988)

Tax Shift Scenario for the Pacific Northwest

Diagram on left shows current, below is projected under tax shift.

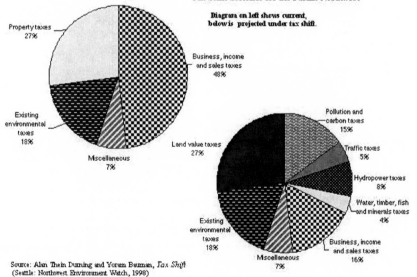

Property taxes
27%

Business, income
and sales taxes
48%

Existing
environmental
taxes
18%

Miscellaneous
7%

Land value taxes
27%

Pollution and
carbon taxes
15%

Traffic taxes
5%

Hydropower taxes
8%

Water, timber, fish
and minerals taxes
4%

Existing
environmental
taxes
18%

Business, income
and sales taxes
16%

Miscellaneous
7%

Source: Alan Thein Durning and Yoram Bauman, *Tax Shift* (Seattle: Northwest Environment Watch, 1998)

1 E.G. Vallianatos, *Why Small Farmers are Essential to Democracy*, The Progressive Populist, August 1-15, 2002, p. 6.

2 Worldwatch, Oct. 1988.

3 Peter Meyer, *Land Rush - A Survey of America's Land - Who Owns It, Who Controls It, How Much is Left*, Harpers Magazine, Jan. 1979.

4 Urban Land Institute, *America's Real Estate*, 1997, p. 14.

5 Eli Siegel, essay on *Ownership: Some Moments* in The Right of Aesthetic Realism to be Known, a periodical of the Aesthetic Realism Foundation, 5/5/99.

6 J. W. Smith, *Economic Democracy: The Political Struggle of the Twenty-First Century*, 3rd edition, p. 309.

7 Smith, *ibid.*, pp. 306 & 309.

8 Patricia Mische, *Spirituality and World Order*, published in Toward a Global Spirituality: The Whole Earth Papers #16, Global Education Associates, 1982, p. 7.

9 Richard Brock, *Farmland Prices EXPLODE*, The Corn and Soybean Digest, Mar 1, 2004.

10 John Mohawk, *The Problem of the Modern World*, CREATION, May/June, p. 18.

11 Edward N. Wolff, *Recent Trends in Wealth Ownership*, 1983-98.

12 Edward N. Wolff, *Recent Trends in Wealth Ownership*, 1983-98.

13 Economic Research Services, USDA, http://www.ers.usda.gov/publications/fanrr35/

14 For Berry and other Earth Ethics quotes see: http://www.earthethics.com/archive_of_quotes.htm

15 See Robotic Nation articles at: http://www.roboticnation.blogspot.com/ or http://www. marshallbrain.com

16 Henry George quote from *Progress and Poverty*, Chapter 26: The Call of Liberty.

17 Henry George, *Social Problems*, Robert Schalkenbach Foundation, p.202.

18 Michael T. Klare, *Resource Wars: The New Landscape of Global Conflict*, New York: Henry Holt, 2001, p 214.

19 For the UNCHS document go to United Nations website www.uno.org or to www.earthrights .net publications section.

20 Originally composed and declared at a conference of the International Union for Land Value Taxation held in 1949.

21 For instance, books, papers and studies published by Worldwatch Institute, Northwest Environment Watch, Robert Schalkenbach Foundation, Center for Economic Studies, Institute for Land Policy, Land and Labor Campaign, Land Reform Scotland, Earth Rights Institute, New Economics Foundation. For others see Council of Georgist Organizations and International Union for Land Value Taxation websites.

22 For these and additional examples, references and details on green tax policies see several articles by Alanna Hartzok posted on Earth Rights Institute: www.earthrights.net.

23 David Malin Roodman, *The Natural Wealth of Nations: Harnessing the Market for the Environment*, New York: W. W. Norton & Company/World Watch, 1998.

24 Alan Thein Durning and Yoram Bauman, *Tax Shift*, Seattle: Northwest Environment Watch, 1998.

-7-

Forget the Old Tax Fights:
All Should Enjoy the Profits from Nature's Gifts

Published in The Charleston Gazette *Viewpoints*, April 16, 2007.

Although I live in Pennsylvania, I have had a special affection for West Virginia, having lived and worked there some years ago. Recently, a West Virginia friend sent me a series of interesting viewpoints from The Charleston Gazette. There is a thread of important perspectives running through them all.

John David wrote on Nov. 27, 2006, about his concerns regarding the growing wealth gap between the super rich and the rest of us. He is disappointed with recent "Band-Aid" actions of the state's Legislature, which brought only "a little of something for everyone" rather than a deeply rooted solution "to help eliminate poverty." He then describes the Alaska Permanent Fund, which captures the "resource rent" from oil and other natural resources for the benefit of all residents of the state. "Resource rent" is a term that describes the profit that accrues to the gifts of nature above and beyond the necessary returns to labor and capital.

David is on to something we really need to learn more about. Each October, this innovative institution distributes checks of equal amounts to everyone, ranging from several hundred dollars to nearly $2,000 each year. These "citizen dividend" payments have made Alaska the only state in the country where the wealth gap has decreased rather than increased during the past several years. Think about it. A significant proportion of profits are due to the gifts of nature, and Alaska's state constitution vests ownership of natural resources in the people of the state. Is this not an elegant policy approach?

Which brings us to the heart of the matter — the question concerning just and fair ownership of the gifts of nature. In West Virginia, much of the coal mining lands are "owned" by large companies that are not headquartered in the state. These are often companies that are not the "working" companies that organize labor and capital to do the hard job of mining the coal. Yet these outsider, non-working companies collect enormous amounts as lease fees from the productive coal companies, simply because they hold paper titles. The money that the paper title-holding companies demand and receive from the working companies is entirely "resource rent" and rightly belongs to the people of West Virginia.

Resource rent is being drained out of West Virginia by paper title-holding companies while most taxes fall on workers and productive capitalists. This is the problem that continues to relegate most West Virginians to a socioeconomic power status like that of many Third World countries. These countries are said to have *a resource curse*. Though richly endowed with the gifts of nature, they are plagued with poverty and environmental devastation just like West Virginia. John David is right. His state greatly needs an institution similar to the Alaska Permanent Fund.

In his Dec. 8, 2006, commentary, Russell Sobel says, "by increasing the cost of doing business and reducing profitability, this plan would reduce and even destroy the incentive for future capital investment and new business development in our state." Sobel is locked in the old labor vs. capital paradigm and does not understand the concept of "resource rent." He has yet to consider the idea that unearned income accruing to the gifts of nature rightly belongs to the people as a whole. He does not yet grasp that there is a contemporary way to secure everyone's birthright to God's gifts of land and natural resources, thus freeing the energies of both labor and productive capital. Neither labor nor capital made the earth. Certainly we can all agree to this basic and most obvious truth.

If West Virginians were to capture resource rent, the unearned income now going to outsider paper title-holding non-working companies, then taxes on both workers' wages and on the rightful profits of working business owners could and should be substantially reduced. The essence of the conflict is not that of labor versus capital, but that of all those who contribute mental and physical energy to the productive process vs. those individuals and companies that are monopolizing the gifts of nature.

From this perspective and policy approach, private ownership or enclosure of land and natural resources is made conditional upon paying a fair fee for that privilege to the people as a whole. This is another way of saying that it is important to collect property taxes based on natural resource and surface land values, while reducing taxes on wages, productive capital and other privately created wealth such as our houses and all other buildings. This ethic and policy approach can be viewed as an emerging new understanding of the role of governance. I sometimes call it "earth rights democracy."

John David responded to Russell Sobel on Dec. 18, 2006, with an even stronger focus on the wealth divide and the question of "who owns the earth?" by reminding us that all current titles can be traced back to land that was "taken from the Native American people." In a democracy, we are supposed to have equal rights as human beings. Is it not time that we constitute democracy on equal rights to our planet's land and natural resources, and institute practical policies based on this ethic?

David also stated "West Virginia's wealth is tied to land and energy resources". Is not all tangible wealth everywhere tied to the gifts of nature? Look around from where you now sit reading this. Is there anything, other than human beings and nature itself, which you see that has not come from mental and physical exertion upon the gifts of nature?

By January 31, Arthur Rybeck had taken a particular interest in the John David-Russell Sobel dialogue. In his commentary, Rybeck describes the so-called "two-rate property tax" that numerous cities in Pennsylvania have been putting into place. The policy has indeed been proving successful here. It is based on the reasoning that taxes should be shifted off our houses as well as productive labor and capital and that government should collect resource rent. Homeowners love it. Most pay less than with the old form of property taxes. They can fix up their houses without fear of a tax increase for their efforts.

Mayor Stephen reed, recently voted Number One mayor in the country and Number Three in the world, says that this form of property tax is a key policy that brought Harrisburg from the status of second most distressed city in the United States in 1980 to a high quality of life now.

Perry Man, in his February 9 commentary, puts forth some important economic truths and correctly credits Henry George as one of the great forerunners of the newly emerging "beyond the old right and the old left" land tenure and tax policy paradigm. It seems to me from his tone of writing, however, that Mann has observed so much corruption and self-serving in the Legislature that he has little hope that West Virginia can ever emerge from its current status as an internal Third World country.

"The villains are those who make the laws," Mann wrote. But in a democracy, the ordinary people are supposed to have something to say about the making of the laws. I note that Mann is a lawyer. And I sense he has a good heart underneath his bleak despair.

So I ask you now, Perry Mann, might you be willing to lend a hand to the people of West Virginia to assist them in establishing the new laws and taxation policies that can enable everyone in West Virginia to have a life worth living?

Author's note - The day after this was published in the *Charleston Gazette* I received this message by email: I enjoyed your article in the *Gazette* and agree with all my mind and heart with your views and goals. I would be happy to work toward the end you are working toward: more equity and justice in the world. Give me a pragmatic assignment or a suggested way to go to help and I will do my best to advance your goals. Aside from working to save the earth, I have no ambition but to help bring political and economic right to the peoples of the world who have long been denied it. -- Perry Mann

Citizens Alliance for a Responsible Environment protests
the degradation of their mountains and pollution of the land
and water of West Virginia.

-8-

Public Finance Based on
Judeo-Christian Teachings

Presented at the Christianity and Human Rights Conference at
Sanford University, Birmingham, Alabama, November 2004.

Summary: This paper makes a case for a new form of democracy based on human rights to the earth as a birthright, linking this to the Judeo-Christian Jubilee Justice tradition and Old and New Testament teachings. The paper concludes by describing a tax fairness practical policy approach based on these ethics.

The United Nations Millennium Declaration was adopted by the world's leaders at the Millennium Summit of the United Nations in 2000. Secretary General Kofi Annan has said that the Declaration "captured the aspirations of the international community for the new century and spoke of a world united by common values and striving with renewed determination to achieve peace and decent standards of living for every man, woman and child."[1]

All UN Member States pledged to achieve several Millennium Development Goals by the year 2015, including (1) reduce by half the proportion of people living on less than a dollar a day; (2) reduce by half the proportion of people who suffer from hunger; and by 2020, (3) achieve significant improvement in lives of at least 100 million slum dwellers.

The basic framework for these goals was set forth in the Universal Declaration of Human Rights, adopted by the UN General Assembly on December 10, 1948. Article I states "All human beings are born free and equal in dignity and rights." Article 25 says that:

> Everyone has the right to a standard of living adequate for the health and well-being of himself and of his family, including food, clothing, housing and medical care and necessary social services, and the right to security in the event of unemployment, sickness, disability, widowhood, old age or other lack of livelihood in circumstances beyond his control.

The International Covenant on Economic, Social and Cultural Rights was adopted and opened for signature, ratification and accession by the General Assembly on December 16, 1966 and entered into force on January 3, 1976. The Covenant proclaims these economic human rights, among others: "the right to wages sufficient to support a minimum standard of living, to equal pay for equal work, and equal opportunity for advancement." In addition, the Covenant forbids exploitation of children, and requires all nations to cooperate to end world hunger.

Nearly every UN member state has signed and ratified this important Covenant. The United States, Cambodia and Liberia have signed but not ratified it. Our government, founded upon clearly articulated political human rights, is floundering in the field of economic human rights.

The US Census Bureau reports that the number of Americans living below the poverty line jumped by 1.3 million to 35.9 million or 12.5 percent of the population last year. The latest U.S. Conference of Mayors Sodexho Hunger and Homelessness Survey reports that hunger and homelessness continue to rise in major American cities.[2] More than 3.5 million people, or 1.25 percent of the US population, are living in city streets or homeless shelters. The number of homeless grew by around 19 percent in 2003 and 13 percent in 2002. Twenty-three of the 25 surveyed cities reported that lack of affordable housing was the leading cause of homelessness. Twenty participating cities reported that unemployment and various employment related problems were the leading causes of hunger.

There is a significant lack of decent affordable housing in the United States. The growing gap between wage earnings and the cost of housing leaves millions of families and individuals unable to make ends meet. According to the National Low Income Housing Coalition, families across the country would need to earn a "housing wage" of $15.21 an hour, nearly three times the current minimum wage, to afford a two-bedroom apartment at the average fair market rent.[3] In states with median housing costs, a minimum wage worker would have to work 89 hours each week to afford a two-bedroom apartment at 30% of his or her income, which is the federal definition of affordable housing.[4] Currently, five million rental households have "worst case housing needs," which means that they pay more than half their incomes for rent, live in severely substandard housing, or both.[5]

Economic Research Service of the United States Department of Agriculture released its annual report on household food security for 2002. It was no surprise given the recent increases in poverty that hunger and food insecurity rose for the third year in a row. A food insecure household is defined as a household that faces limited or uncertain availability of food. In 2002, 34.9 million people lived in households that were food insecure, 1.26 million more people than in 2001. This number includes 13.1 million children. The number of people living in households where someone was hungry also increased by 300,000 to 9.3 million. About 567,000 kids lived in homes where children were hungry, 100,000 more than the year before. The prevalence of food insecurity rose from 10.7 percent in 2001 to 11.1 percent in 2002, and the prevalence of food insecurity with hunger rose from 3.3 percent to 3.5 percent.[6]

The wealth gap is increasing in the US. According to the latest Federal Reserve data, the top 1% of the population has $2 trillion more wealth than the bottom 90 percent.

Perceptions of the causal factors of these statistics and the suffering of so many who lack basic necessities in this wealthy country are most often simplistic explanations - these people lack money and they lack money because they lack jobs or their wages are too low, or housing costs are too high. For those concerned about the growing wealth gap in America and worldwide, and the resultant poverty, homelessness, hunger and food insecurity, the dilemma usually bogs down into supply or demand side efforts to find solutions. But the root cause is a deeper injustice.

The primary cause of the enormous and growing wealth gap is that the land and natural resources of the earth are treated as if they are mere market commodities from which a few are allowed to reap massive private profits or hold land and resources out of use in anticipation of future profits. Henry George, the great 19th century American political economist and social philosopher, proposed a solution to a problem that too few understood at the time and too few understand today. Early Christian teachings drew upon deep wisdom teachings of the Jubilee justice tradition when they addressed this problem. The problem is the Land Problem.

The Land Problem takes two primary forms: land price escalation and concentrated land ownership. As our system of economic development proceeds, land values rise faster than wages increase, until inevitably the price paid for access to land consumes increasing amounts of a worker's wages. In classical economics, this dilemma is called the "law of rent" and has been mostly ignored by mainstream economists. The predictability of the law of rent - that land values will continually rise - fuels frenzies of land speculation and the inevitable bust that follows the boom. A recent Fortune cover story informs us that there are big gains and huge risks in housing speculation in about 30 predominantly coastal markets that encompass 100 million people. Since 2000, home prices in New York, Washington, and Boston have surged 56% to 61%. Prices jumped 58% in Miami and Los Angeles and 76% in San Diego where the median home price countywide is $582,000. The gap between home prices and fundamentals like job growth and incomes is greater than ever.[7]

The second form of the Land Problem is the fact that in most countries, including the United States, a small minority of people own and control a disproportionately large amount of land and natural resources. Data suggests that about 3% of the population owns 95% of the privately held land in the US. Less than 600 companies control 22% of our private land, a land mass the size of Spain. Those same companies land interests worldwide comprise a total area larger than that of Europe - almost 2 billion acres.[8]

In order to show that there was NO NEED for land reform in Central America because our land in the US is even more concentrated in ownership than Central America, Senator Jesse Helms read these facts into the Congressional Record in 1981: In Florida, 1% owns 77% of the land. Other states where the top 1% own over two-thirds of the land are Maine, Arizona, California, Nevada, New Mexico, and Oregon.

A United Nations study of 83 countries showed that less than 5% of rural landowners control three-quarters of the land. Other studies on land ownership report these facts: In Brazil, 2% of landowners hold 60% of the arable land while close to 70% of rural households have little or none. Just 342 farm properties in Brazil cover 183,397 square miles - an area larger than California. In Venezuela, 77% of the farmland is owned by 3% of the people. In Spain, 70 per cent of the land is owned by 0.2 per cent of the people. In Britain, 69 per cent of the land is owned by 0.6 per cent of the population. Just 158,000 families own 41 million acres of land while 24 million families live on four million acres.[9]

The basic human need for food and shelter requires access of labor to land. With access to land people can produce the basic requirements of life. Access to land provides an enabling environment for life itself and thus meets the minimum requirement of love, meaning fairness in human relations based on the fundamental equal right to exist. The Land Problem in its two forms - the inequitable ownership and control of land and natural resources and the treatment of land as a market commodity - is the root cause of the great amount of human deprivation and suffering from lack of the basic necessities of life. And yet the human right to the earth is missing from the Bill of Rights, the Universal Declaration of Human Rights, and the Covenant on Economic, Social and Cultural Human Rights.

Democratic governance has not yet concerned itself with a "first principle" question. This question concerns property rights in land - property rights in the earth itself. The question is, "Who Should Own the Earth?" The question of "Who Should Own the Earth?" is a fundamental question. In venues when this question is asked, the answer is always the same. The answer is, "everyone should own the earth and on an equal basis as a birthright."

The right to the earth has yet to be pronounced in human rights covenants. Democracy is unclear, ethically weak, and on shaky ground when it comes to the question of the right to the land and resources of the earth. Democracy as presently constituted lacks this most fundamental and basic human right - the equal right to earth. The right to the earth is the great undiscovered revolution in both American and global politics.

Early Christian teachings on the Land Problem, however, were clear and precise. The question of "Who Should Own the Earth?" was unequivocally answered. The land ethic of the early Christian communities was that of *koinonia* meaning essentially that God was the sole owner of the earth which was given as a gift to all for the *autarkeia*, the self-reliant livelihood, of all. In the words of John Chrysostom, Bishop of Constantinople at the close of the fourth century, "The very air, earth, matter, are the Creator's; and so are you yourself... and all other things also."

When Christianity became the state religion of the Roman Empire, the early Christian teachings on land were overtaken by the Roman land laws of *dominium* - a legalization of property in land originally obtained by conquest and plunder. A largely corrupted Christianity, uprooted from its early teachings on land ownership, too often went hand in hand with the exploitation and degradation of centuries of colonial conquests. A statement by the great South African Archbishop Desmond Tutu addressed this point in a succinct and profound manner. He said, "When the missionaries came to Africa they had the Bible and we had the land. They said 'Let us pray.' We closed our eyes. When we opened them we had the Bible and they had the land."[10]

Charles Avila, in his profoundly important book entitled *Ownership: Early Christian Teachings*, explored the early church fathers' view of property rights in land. He contrasted these teachings to Roman property rights law. In his chapter on "The Concept of Ownership" Avila states:

> The concentration of property in private hands began very early in Rome and was indeed based on the foundational and legitimizing idea of absolute and exclusive individual ownership in land. This was the same idea that would come to form the basis of the slave owning, the feudal, and the capitalist (including the pseudo-socialist, or state-capitalist) economic systems successively. Modern civilization has not yet discarded this antiquated ownership concept, which was originally derived from ancient Rome. In fact, it seems to us, this is one of the main roots of the present global crisis, in which the rich become richer because the poor become poorer.[11]

Avila further noted that "the distinction in legal terminology between "real" and "personal" property is the survival in words of an ancient real distinction between property held in both theory and practice as common by its very nature and property which was the fruit of one's labor." [12] Avila said that modern social thinkers:

> advocate the promotion of social justice without stopping to think that individual ownership of nature's bounty might be socially unjust in itself. And yet patristic thought insisted long ago that there could be no real justice, or abolition of poverty, if the koina, the common natural elements of production, are appropriated in ownership by individuals.[13]

Here are a few Patristic period quotes on land ownership that Avila compiled in his book:

Ambrose: How far, O ye rich, do you push your mad desires? Shall ye alone dwell upon the earth? Why do you cast out all the fellow sharers of nature and claim it all for yourselves? The earth was made in common for all. Why do you arrogate to yourselves, exclusive right to the soil?

St. George the Great (Pope 590 - 604) rebuked the Romans when he said: They wrongfully think they are innocent who claim for themselves the common gift of God.

Clement of Alexandria: (The functions of property) -"to be shared," "to minister to" and serve "the welfare of all"; "not for personal advantage as being entirely one's own" but "for those in need"; "to achieve autarkeia" and "to foster koinonia" - constitute the very essence of Clement's view of property.

St. John Chrystostom: God in the beginning did not make one man rich and another poor; nor did he afterwards take and show to anyone treasures of gold, and deny to the others the right of searching for it; rather he left the earth free to all alike. Why then, if it is common, have you so many acres of land, while your neighbor has not a portion of it?

Augustine: He (according to Avila's research) saw that the poor are poor because they have been deprived by the propertied few of the wealth that should belong to all. He laid the blame for this unjust situation squarely on the doorstep of an absolutist and exclusivist legal right of private ownership. He reminded his audience that they were all "made from one mud" and sustained "on one earth" under the same natural conditions, having the same essence and called to the same destiny. He rejected the legalized status quo as inappropriate for human living. Holding that legal arrangements of property rights were of human origin, he asserted that they should be changed, in theory and in practice, in function of a faith-informed ethic based on the true meaning of ownership.

Basil the Great: He saw that a privileged few were exceedingly rich, ostentatious, and powerful, inasmuch as wealth, particularly the wealth-producing resource, land, was concentrated in the hands of the few. He taught a philosophy of ownership based on the view that God was Father and giver and Provider for all, and that therefore a few must cease stealing the food-producing resources that God had destined for the use of all.

Basil admits a certain right of laborers to the product of their labor but asks the landlords by what right they exercise ownership over their vast estates:

> Which things, tell me, are yours? Whence have you brought them into being? Whatever you have produced, or brought into being, may justly be yours. However, it is land that has made the landlords rich, and land is not something they have brought into being.

Speaking to the rich Basil said:

You are like one occupying a place in a theatre, who should prohibit others from entering, treating that as one's own which was designed for the common use of all.... If each one would take that which is sufficient for one's needs, leaving what is in excess to those in distress, no one would be rich, no one poor. Did you not come naked from the womb? Will you not return naked into the earth?[14]

Jesus pointed to Old Testament teachings regarding land ethics. According to some contemporary theologians, one of the tasks of the mission of Jesus was to restore the original intent of Jubilee. In Luke 4:18, by way of Isaiah 61:1-3): "He has anointed me to preach good news to the poor, to proclaim release of captives. To set at liberty those who are oppressed, to proclaim the acceptable year of the Lord."

As theologian Walter Brueggeman explains in "Land: The Foundation of Humanness"[15] the "acceptable year" is the year of the Jubilee when the land was to be returned to the original holders. The "release of captives" is the release of debt slaves who had lost their land because they could not pay the mortgage. A crucial aspect of Jesus' mission was the reassertion of the land rights of the poor and displaced.

The early Christian land ethic echoed Old Testament teachings concerning land rights. Hear these voices anew:

The land must not be sold beyond reclaim, for the land is Mine; you are but strangers resident with me. - Lev. 25:23

The profit of the earth is for all. - Eccles. 5:9

Woe unto them that join house to house, that lay field to field, till there be no place. - Isaiah 5:8

Restore, I pray you, to them even this day, their lands, their vineyards, their olive yards, and their houses. - Nehemiah 5:11

During the 15th century and several centuries thereafter, the "commons" (land that had always been available for free use by the community) were enclosed by the wealthy or powerful for private use only. This accelerated the rise of the market economy, for without land, peasants had to survive by their wits and their abilities to manufacture. The emerging economy that used money as a primary medium of exchange opened up an opportunity for the landless to acquire land - they could now buy it. But working to accumulate enough wealth to buy land, instead of asserting an inherent human birthright to the earth, is akin to a slave's saving enough money, by cleverness, skill and extra hard effort, to buy him or herself into freedom.

We must not forget that mainstream institutionalized Christianity once promulgated the doctrine that the right of some humans to hold other humans as slaves was encoded in the Bible. After much struggle and centuries of suffering, it gradually dawned on the majority of people that slavery was unjust and it was abolished. A similar awakening regarding the land problem lies in our future, hopefully the near future. Several great sages of our own recent history held the vision for a just land ethic. Their statements could be useful to us today:

Thomas Jefferson - The earth is given as a common stock for men to labor and live on.

Abraham Lincoln - The land, the earth God gave to man for his home, sustenance, and support, should never be the possession of any man, corporation, society, or unfriendly government, any more than the air or water, if as much. An individual, company, or enterprise should hold no more than is required for their home and sustenance. All that is not used should be held for the free use of every family to make homesteads, and to hold them as long as they are so occupied.

Henry George - Our primary social adjustment is a denial of justice. In allowing one man to own the land on which and from which other men must live, we have made them his bondsmen in a degree which increases as material progress goes on. This is the subtle alchemy that in ways they do not realize is extracting from the masses in every civilized country the fruits of their weary toil; that is instituting a harder and more hopeless slavery in place of that which has been destroyed; that is bringing political despotism out of political freedom, and must soon transmute democratic institutions into anarchy.

Charles Avila, again in *Ownership: Early Christian Teachings*, wrote:

> On first reading Henry George (*Progress and Poverty*) almost twenty years ago when doing research for this volume, I was particularly struck by the similarity of his arguments, and even analogies, to those of the fourth century Christian philosophers on the topic of land ownership. [16]

Henry George, the great American political economist and land rights philosopher (1839-1897), eloquently confronted the enigma of the wealth gap in his masterwork *Progress and Poverty* and set forth both an ethical and practical method for holding and sharing the land as a sacred trust for all. He made a clear distinction between property in land and property in wealth produced by labor on land. He said that private property in human made wealth belonged to the producer and that the state should not tax wealth produced by human labor. George said:

> To abolish these taxes would be to lift the whole enormous weight of taxation from productive industry. The needle of the seamstress and the great manufactory;

the carthorse and the locomotive; the fishing boat and the steamship; the farmer's plow and the merchant's stock, would be alike untaxed. All would be free to make or to save, to buy or to sell, unfined by taxes, un-annoyed by the tax-gatherer. Instead of saying to the producer, as it does now, "The more you add to the general wealth the more shall you be taxed!" the state would say to the producer, "Be as industrious, as thrifty, as enterprising as you choose, you shall have your full reward! You shall not be fined for making two blades of grass grow where one grew before; you shall not be taxed for adding to the aggregate wealth.[17]

In an economic system such as ours that uses money as a medium of exchange, land and resources come to have monetary value. In asserting that the gifts of nature are common property and should be equitably shared by all, George saw that in a just society the ownership of land and natural resources would be conditional upon the cash payment to all of a fairly assessed tax, or land rent, for the exclusive right to God's gifts. Thus the collection of land rent for the community as a whole would replace the taxation of productive endeavors. Those with more and/or better-located land would pay more into the common fund, while those with little or no land would pay much less or nothing at all.

As George explained it:

> ...the value of land is at the beginning of society nothing, but as society develops by the increase of population and the advance of the arts, it becomes greater and greater. In every civilized country, even the newest, the value of the land taken as a whole is sufficient to bear the entire expenses of government. In the better-developed countries it is much more than sufficient. Hence it will not be enough merely to place all taxes upon the value of land. It will be necessary, where rent exceeds the present governmental revenues, commensurately to increase the amount demanded in taxation, and to continue this increase as society progresses and rent advances.[18]

The author of Common Sense, Tom Paine, was onto the same idea when he said:

> Men did not make the earth...It is the value of the improvement only, and not the earth itself, that is individual property...Every proprietor owes to the community a ground rent for the land which he holds.

Enormous sums are currently accruing as unearned income to a relatively few individuals, families and corporations who are holding large amounts of land, very valuable and well-located land, and natural resources as their own exclusive private property. These enormous land values and resource rents are also accruing as unearned income to banks holding mortgages based on exploitative compound interest rates. It may be of interest to note that the word "mortgage" means "dead hand." Truly, when one must work so many years of ones life to pay off a mortgage, one productive hand is as if dead in terms of producing for oneself, as the labor of that hand pays the mortgage. For the 33% of citizens (40 million people) in the United States who are renters, there is not even equity ownership to look forward to after a life of labor. For the more than three million homeless people in American and the multi-millions who are homeless around the world, what Henry George said in 1879 holds true today and is worth repeating:

> Our primary social adjustment is a denial of justice. In allowing one man to own the land on which and from which other men must live, we have made them his bondsmen in a degree which increases as material progress goes on.[19]

Not only is the land ethic of Old and New Testament prophets and Henry George virtually the same, the policy approach of "resource rent for revenue" also known as "land or site value taxation" has its corollary in the approach called for by the ancient rabbis in their discussions about the finer and little known details of Jubilee.

Talmudic rabbinical discussions considered how fairly to partition the land of Canaan among the tribes under Joshua. Those with poorer land were to be given more acreage and those with more fertile land would be given less. As for land disadvantageously situated, the adjustment was to be made by money; that is to say, those holding land nearer the city (Jerusalem) should pay into the common treasury the estimated excess of value pertaining to it by reason of its superior situation, while those holding land of less value, by reason of its distance from the city, would receive from the treasury a money compensation. Upon the more valuable holdings was to be imposed a tax, or lease fee, the measure of which was the excess of their respective values over a given standard, and the fund thus created was to be paid out in due proportions to those whose holdings were in less favorable locations. In this, then we see affirmed the doctrine that natural advantages are common property, and may not be diverted to private gain.[20]

Roman law undermined the Christian land justice teachings and the early Christians were attacked and persecuted. Similarly, there was a great movement to discredit the teachings of Henry George. Pope Leo XIII issued the Rerum Novarum Encyclical in 1891 that propounded an exclusivist right to private property in land, exhorting those without land to work harder, longer and smarter to save money from which to buy land.[21]

Money from vested interests poured into the University of Chicago, Columbia University and other emerging schools of economics to thwart and obscure the understanding and the solution to the land problem and the wealth divide. Academics were paid to undermine Georgist economics that had followed in the classical tradition, and to instead develop an approach to economics that minimized the contribution of nature's gifts to the production process. Land, the term in classical economics that denotes all gifts of nature, was made a secondary factor, a mere subset of capital. The two major factors became Labor and Capital. The intellectual crime of the century - the neoliberal economics paradigm - has predominated in the field of economics ever since.[22]

Yet the truth of George's *koinonia* based economics endured through the work of several schools, publishers and research organizations established during the first half of the 20th century, both in the US and worldwide. In 1949 this movement issued An International Declaration on Individual and Common Rights to Land.[23] The policy approach urged by Henry George and Thomas Paine as a way to assure human rights to the earth's resources was successfully implemented in part and to varying degrees in several places throughout the world.

As a result of decades of steady education and promulgation, there are now 18 municipalities in Pennsylvania that have adopted a so-called split-rate property tax which shifts taxes away from buildings and onto land according to site value. This approach is based on the understanding that the property tax is actually two types of taxes - one upon building values, and the other upon land values. This distinction is an important one, as these two types of taxes have significantly different impacts on incentive motives and development results. Decreasing the tax on buildings gives property owners the incentive to build and to maintain and improve their properties. As the levy on land values is increased, land speculation and poor land utilization, an example being slum buildings and boarded up buildings, are discouraged. The signal thus sent to property holders is to either improve their properties or sell them to someone who can do so. Either way, labor and capital gain access to land to improve and augment the building stock. The tax incentives are harnessed correctly to encourage effort directed to the provisioning of housing and other basic human needs.[24]

Shifting the tax burden in this way discourages land hoarding and encourages good land utilization. It promotes a more efficient use of urban infrastructure (such as roads and sewers), decreases the pressure towards urban sprawl (as there is significant infill development), and assures a broader spread of the benefits of development to the community as a whole.

Researchers have carefully recorded the number of building permits issued in the three-year period before and after the split-rate was put in place. In every instance, the number of building permits increased significantly after the implementation of this reform. As the city improves, without the need for subsidies, the land values gradually increase, thus providing the city with an increasing source of revenue for public services. With this system, land values maintain a natural correlation to the overall health of the city. Land values do not peak and spike as they do under conditions which promote land speculation and profiteering. As development stabilizes, land values also stabilize. Thus it is possible to have a self-financing city with citizens reaping the full rewards of their labor and creativity.

The experience with this form of taxation in the 18 municipalities of Pennsylvania points towards the possibilities of a self-renewing city. But until we greatly reduce or eliminate the burden of federal income and payroll taxes and the billions of dollars of wasteful and inequitable corporate subsidies, we will only have a partial realization of the promise. Nonetheless, there is much we can learn from the split-rate tax cities in Pennsylvania, upon several of which we shall now focus.

Harrisburg, the capital of Pennsylvania, provides one of the best examples of the benefits of shifting taxes away from labor and productive capital and onto land according to site values. In 1981 Harrisburg was listed as the second-most distressed city in the nation under criteria used by the federal government. A review of the gains made in effective economic development activities since then has produced significant results, and the sharp reversal of nearly three decades of previous serious decline. Beginning with the implementation of the split-rate property tax and gradually increasing the tax on land while decreasing the tax on buildings, Harrisburg has sustained an economic resurgence that has garnered national acclaim. It twice won the top United States community honor as All-American City, along with the top state recognition from the state Chamber of Business and Industry as Outstanding Community in Pennsylvania, all because of Harrisburg's development initiatives and progress.

As of 2001, the value of taxable real estate was over $2.2 Billion, versus $212 Million in 1982. Over 26,000 building permits were issued from 1982 representing over $2.65 Billion in new investment. Even adjusted for inflation, this is more than for any period since Harrisburg became a municipality in the year 1791, with most of this investment undertaken since 1990. There are over 5,500 businesses on the city tax rolls in 2001 compared to 1,908 in 1981. The numbers of vacant structures, over 5,500 in 1982, have been reduced by 85% to less than 400. The crime rate has dropped 53% and fire rate has been cut by 72%.[25]

Harrisburg Mayor Stephen Reed has written several letters to officials of other cities telling them that the split-rate tax has been a key to the remarkable renewal of his city.

The citizens of Allentown, the third largest city in Pennsylvania with a population of 105,000, voted for the land value tax system in 1994 and it was instituted in 1996. The difference between the land and building rates was expanded in each of the following four years. Michael Rosenfeld, the executive director of that city's Redevelopment Authority, says that the benefits of this tax approach are evident. The value of both new commercial construction and of new residential construction increased substantially after the shift to land value taxation. Nearly three out of every four properties in Allentown saw some sort of tax cut. Today, many of those properties have new or better buildings on them, stabilizing the tax base to the point where there has been no need for a tax increase in five years. The number of building permits in Allentown has increased by 32% compared to the three-year period before the land value tax reform.

Allentown and Bethlehem are both in eastern Pennsylvania and are roughly comparable as to size and economy. In that Allentown adopted this tax approach and Bethlehem did not, there was an opportunity to compare the two. Allentown's new construction and renovation grew by 82% in dollar value in the three years after it adopted two-rate LVT as compared to the prior three years. Its new construction and renovation grew 54% faster than Bethlehem's new construction and renovation despite the infusion of much federal grant money into Bethlehem (but not into Allentown) during 1997-99.[26]

The small cities of Washington and Monessen, both in southwestern Pennsylvania, are roughly comparable as to size and economy. Monessen has the common form of property tax which taxes building value significantly more than land value. After Washington adopted the split-rate tax in 1985, it saw its new construction and renovation increase by 33% in dollar value following this tax reform as compared to the prior three years. During the same time period, Monessen's new construction and renovation decreased by 26%.[27]

Studies comparing Oil City, Pennsylvania, which shifted its tax base starting in January 1989, with Franklin, a comparable neighbor municipality, found that Oil City experienced a 58.2% increase in new construction and renovation in the three years after it adopted a two-rate property tax as compared to the three years before, whereas Franklin experienced a 12.2% decline during the same time periods.[28]

In 1995, Professor Nicholas Tideman, the Chairman of the Economics Dept. at Virginia Tech University and his then-graduate student, Florenz Plassman, now a professor at the University of Binghamton, N.Y. completed a highly technical, peer reviewed study of land value taxation in Pennsylvania. To quote from the conclusion of their study: "The results say that for all four categories of construction, an increase in the effective tax differential is associated with an increase in the average value per permit. In the case of residential housing, a 1% increase in the effective tax differential is associated with a 12% increase in the average value per unit. From the perspective of economic theory, it is not at all surprising that when taxes are taken off of buildings, people build more valuable buildings. But it is nice to see the numbers."[29]

Dr. Steven B. Cord has done an exhaustive review of 237 studies of land value taxation from all over the world. In every instance there was an increase in construction and renovation after the policy was enacted, indicating that there were previously unmet needs for housing and other living and working space. [30]

A meticulous study conducted by Dr. Mason Gaffney entitled "Rising Inequality and Falling Property Tax Rates"[31] refutes the common belief that property tax relief would be good for farmers. His research showed that property tax relief for agricultural land increases the likelihood that it will attract those looking primarily for tax shelters and speculative investments. Such nonproductive incentives ultimately inflate land values overall, making it increasingly difficult for working farmers to access and maintain acreage for viable agricultural enterprise.

The high price of land means that the modern food and agriculture system provides no options for those who cannot find a paying job other than subsistence on charity or government supports. Those with minimum wage incomes are finding it increasingly difficult to afford decent housing. These social problems and pressures are bound to increase with the cut-off of welfare and other government subsidies to the poor.

Intensively managed small farms and well-designed ecological villages could produce a diverse range of food, fiber, livestock, and energy products for local markets. Bio-intensive farming methods depending on renewable energy sources can yield both social and environmental stability. The establishment of labor and bio-intensive small farming operations can be greatly furthered by land value tax policies that remove taxes on labor and productive capital while promoting affordable land access. A shift to land value taxation will likely have the following benefits in the rural area:

- Discourage speculation in land
- Reduce the price of land to equate with its value for production
- Enable new entrants to more easily obtain land
- Limit farm sizes to those of the most productive units
- Enable the reduction of taxation on earnings and capital
- Reduce interest rates as land became more affordable
- Prevent rural depopulation
- Encourage owner-occupation rather than absentee ownership
- Promote more responsible use of land
- Promote a rural renaissance.[32]

The success of the Wright Act is an example of how properly implemented land based taxes can promote a rural renaissance. This legislation, passed by California in 1887, allowed communities to vote to create irrigation districts for building dams and canals and to pay for them by taxing the increase in land value. Once irrigated, land was too valuable for grazing and too costly for hoarding. So cattlemen sold fields to farmers at prices the farmers could afford. In ten years the Central Valley was transformed into over 7,000 independent farms. Over the next few decades, vast tracts of treeless, semi-arid plains became the "bread basket of America" and one of the most productive areas on earth. It is a prime example of how land value taxation can promote and enhance the viability of both an efficient and equitable agricultural base - without government subsidy.

Private banking institutions eventually undermined this equitable and successful public finance approach. Now taxpayers nationwide subsidize the irrigation needs of agribusiness. Self-financing development projects reduce the necessity for debt finance; so do not contribute to the profits of rent-seeking institutions. These exploitative institutions, which concentrate wealth in the hands of the few, will continue to sabotage this policy approach until sufficient numbers of people have a better understanding of the land ethic of *koinonia* and this fundamental approach to securing the human right to the earth.

One of the best examples of the beneficial results of an ethic of koinonia in natural resources is to be found in the state of Alaska where an "earth rights" constitution gives ownership of the oil and other natural resources of the state to the citizens of Alaska on an equal basis. The Alaska Permanent Fund invests the state's oil resource rents, the interest from which funds cash dividend payments directly to all adults and children resident in the state at least one year.

The Fund ended fiscal year 2004 on June 30 with a 14.1 percent return and a total value of more than $27.4 billion, according to currently available Alaska Permanent Fund Corporation figures. More than $24,000 per person has been distributed to citizens of Alaska since 1982. Note that Alaska is the only state in the US wherein the wealth gap has decreased during recent decades.[33]

The Alaska Permanent Fund is an innovative and important model of resource rents for citizen dividends, but with worldwide oil production nearing peak, it is the opinion of this writer that oil resource rents had best be directed to the development of renewable energy technologies. The electromagnetic spectrum, geo-orbital zones, and surface land values would be a more appropriate source of rent distribution as citizen dividend payments.

Had the land problem been addressed in the south after the Civil War, a more equitable distribution of wealth and overall prosperity would have been the likely result. It can be instructive to review this earlier effort to secure land rights in America.

On March 3, 1865, just weeks before the end of the Civil War and almost a year prior to the ratification of the 13th Amendment, the Freedmen's Bureau was created by Congress. According to Section 4 of the First Freedmen's Bureau Act, this agency shall have authority to set apart for use of loyal refugees and freedmen such tracts of land within the insurrectionary states as shall have been abandoned or to which the United States shall have acquired title by confiscation or sale, or otherwise; and to every male citizen, whether refugee or freedman, as aforesaid there shall be assigned not more than forty acres of such land.

Introduced into Congress by Thaddeus Stevens this portion of the Freedmen's Bureau Act was defeated by Congress on February 5, 1866 by a vote of 126 to 36.[34] Lands that had been distributed to freedmen were reclaimed and returned to the previous owners. There was to be no land reform for the South. Northern industrialists feared that giving land to freedmen and poor whites in the South could have led to similar demands for land by the people in the North, which, if implemented, would assuredly have greatly limited the supply of cheap labor available for factory work in the industrial North.

Abraham Lincoln sounded a warning when he said in 1865:

> Corporations have been enthroned.... An era of corruption in high places will follow and the money power will endeavor to prolong its reign by working on the prejudices of the people...until wealth is aggregated in a few hands...and the Republic is destroyed.

We live in yet another age of rapid privatization of the remaining commons. The airwaves, also known as the electromagnetic or radio-frequency spectrum, the most valuable resource of the information economy, are being given away to huge media corporations. Economists estimate that in the United States alone the commercial value of access to it could be more than $750 billion. There is a rush to patent plant material around the world. The attempt to patent sections of the DNA code itself is but a modern expression of previous centuries of enclosures.

The band-aid safety nets of the 1940s and 50s are unraveling and a new Gilded Age is upon us. The wealth gap is growing. Wages for nearly everyone have stagnated or are declining. Ever escalating land values push housing prices beyond the capacity of millions to secure adequate shelter. Worldwide, a billion people live in degrading destitution lacking basic needs. Local conflicts and global wars are waged for control of land and natural resources. Tax funds that could build a world that works for everyone instead are being directed to biochemical weapons research, building space laser weaponry, and neo-colonial warfare.

It has been said that the only two certainties in life are death and taxes and that the power to tax is the power to create or destroy. The story of the birth of Jesus is on one level the story of a family on a long and onerous journey to pay taxes imposed by the Romans upon the people of the land.

We urgently need to establish land tenure and tax policies based on the deepest wisdom of the Judeo-Christian tradition - a truth based on the perception of the unity of life, that God creates all, and on the realization of the brotherhood and sisterhood of the one humanity. The privilege of holding large amounts of land or highly valuable land as individual private property needs to be a conditional, not an absolute right. For justice to prevail, the right to exclusive access to land must be granted only upon payment of full and fairly assessed land value taxes and resource rents.

We have at hand a powerful solution and a way to secure a world of peace and plenty. We need to constitute democratic governance on the firm foundation of equal rights to the land and resources of the earth, an "earth rights democracy" which removes the burden of taxes from the backs of those who labor and instead directs government to collect the value of our common wealth for the benefit of all. A morally correct form of taxation may not lead to everlasting life, but it WILL promote and sustain the conditions for lives worth living on planet earth.

ADDENDUM

Episcopalian: People without land or without any control over the value of land lack security in a major dimension of their lives. - National Bishops General Convention, Action Proposal for Economic Justice, 2/22/88

A great deal of what is amiss alike in rural and in urban areas could be remedied by the taxation of the value of sites as distinct from the buildings erected upon them. - William Temple, a former Archbishop of Canterbury, in *Christianity and Social Order*

Equity insists that we cease levying taxes on the fruits of human toil, and make the monopoly value of land be the exclusive basis of taxation. - Episcopal Bishop C.D. Williams

Methodist: All creation is the Lord's and we are responsible for the ways in which we use and abuse it. We believe that Christian faith denies to any person or group of persons exclusive and arbitrary control of any other part of the created universe.

Catholic: The land is a gift of the Creator to all men and therefore its richness cannot be distributed among a limited number of people while others are excluded from its benefits. - Pope John Paul II, "Bahia Blanca", Brazil, 1986

God intended the earth and all things in it for the use of all peoples, in such a way that the goods of creation should abound equitably in the hands of all, according to the dictate of justice, which is inseparable from charity. - *Pastoral Constitution on the Church in the Modern World*, Vatican II

The rights of land ownership and of free bargaining in land are subordinated to the fundamental right of man to obtain the necessities of life. In the force of the fundamental claim of the Commonwealth there is no unconditional right of land ownership. - Pope Paul VI, "Populorum Progressio", 1967

Every man, as a living being gifted with reason, has in fact from nature the fundamental right to make use of the material goods of the earth. - Pope Pius XII

Relevant Quotes:

The problems that exist in the world today cannot be solved by the level of thinking that created them. - Albert Einstein

The minority, the ruling class at present, has the schools and press, usually the Church as well, under its thumb. This enables it to organize and sway the emotions of the masses, and make its tool of them. - Albert Einstein

What the public wants is called 'politically unrealistic.' Translated into English, that means power and privilege are opposed to it. - Noam Chomsky

The greatest triumphs of propaganda have been accomplished, not by doing something, but by refraining from doing. Great is truth, but still greater, from a practical point of view, is silence about truth. - Aldous Huxley

True compassion is more than flinging a coin to a beggar; it understands that an edifice which produces beggars needs restructuring. A true revolution of values will soon look uneasily on the glaring contrast of poverty and wealth. - Martin Luther King

An intelligent approach to the problems of poverty and racism will cause us to see the words of the Psalmist - "The earth is the Lord's and the fullness thereof" - are still a judgment upon our use and abuse of the wealth and resources with which we have been endowed. - Martin Luther King

---

[1] Implementation of the United Nations Millennium Declaration, Report of the Secretary General, August 27, 2004.

[2] U.S. Conference of Mayors - Sodexho Hunger and Homelessness Survey 2003 *Hunger, Homelessness Still On the Rise in Major U.S. Cities; 25-City Survey Finds Unemployment, Lack of Affordable Housing Account for Increased Needs,* December 18, 2003

[3] National Student Campaign Against Hunger and Homelessness http://www.nscahh.org/hunger.asp?id2=8802

[4] National Low Income Housing Coalition, 2001

[5] Why Are People Homeless? NCH Fact Sheet #1 Published by the National Coalition for the Homeless, September 2002, http://www.nationalhomeless.org/causes.html

[6] Household Food Security in the United States, 2002 Economic Research Service, USDA http://www.ers.usda.gov/publications/fanrr35/

[7] Shawn Tully, "Is the Housing Boom Over?" *Fortune,* September 27, 2004

[8] Peter Meyer, "Land Rush - A Survey of America's Land - Who Owns It, Who Controls It, How much is Left" *Harpers,* January 1979

[9] For references and further details on land ownership statistics: http://www.earthrights.net/geodata.html

[10] The Quotes Center at http://teachers.sduhsd.k12.ca.us/gstimson/quotes.htm

[11] Charles Avila, Ownership: Early Christian Teachings, Orbis Books, Maryknoll, 1983, p.8

[12] Ibid.

[13] Ibid. p. 9

[14] Ibid., pp. 134-135.

[15] Walter Brueggeman, "Land: The Foundation of Humanness" *Whole Earth Papers* #17, Global Education Associates

[16] Charles Avila, op.cit., p. 156

[17] Henry George, Progress and Poverty, Book IX, Chapter 1 in paragraph IX.I.5 (Available from Robert Schalkenbach Foundation, http://www.schalkenbach.org/)

[18] Ibid, Book VIII, Chapter 2 in paragraph VIII.II.18

[19] Henry George, "Ode to Liberty" Delivered in San Francisco by Henry George as orator of the day July 4, 1877

[20] The Gemara, Baba Bathra, (122, A) http://www.come-and-hear.com/bababathra/bababathra_122.html See also an essay by Solomon Solis Cohen, "The Land Question in the Talmud"

[21] Mason Gaffney, "Henry George, Edward McGlynn & Pope Leo XIII," NY: Robert Schalkenbach Fdn.., 2000

[22] Mason Gaffney and Fred Harrison, The Corruption of Economics, Shepheard-Walwyn Ltd, London, 1994

[23] Go to: http://www.earthrights.net/docs/declaration.html

[24] Alanna Hartzok, "Pennsylvania's Success with Local Property Tax Reform: :The Split Rate Tax" *The American Journal of Economics and Sociology,* April 1997 http://www.earthrights.net/docs/success.html

[25] "Harrisburg, PA: An Economic Profile 2001" , originally produced and published by Economic Opportunity, Inc.

[26] These figures are based on a study of building-permit data on file in the Allentown city hall done by Benjamin Howells (a science researcher and former Allentown councilman), William Kells (a science-oriented businessman), and Steven Cord (professor-emeritus) in 1999. The study was summarized in *Incentive Taxation* July 2000, p 1

[27] A report of this study, based on building-permit data on file in the Washington and Monessen city halls, can be found in *Incentive Taxation,* October 1988

[28] Building-permit study of these cities reported in Incentive Taxation, Nov. 1994

[29] Tideman & Plassman, A Markov Chain Monte Carlo Analysis of the Effect of Two-Rate Property Taxes on Construction. See the peer-reviewed *Journal of Urban Economics,* pp. 216-47, for the full study.

[30] For details, go to http://www.economicboom.info/

[31] Mason Gaffney, "Rising Inequality and Falling Property Tax Rates," published in Land Ownership and Taxation in American Agriculture, edited by Gene Wunderlich, San Francisco: Westview Press, 1992, p 119

[32] Alanna Hartzok, "Pennsylvania Farmers and the Split Rate Tax " published in *Land Value Taxation: The Equitable and Efficient Source of Public Finance,* an anthology edited by Kenneth C. Wenzer, published by M.E. Sharpe, Inc., New York, 1999 http://www.earthrights.net/docs/pa-farmers.html

[33] URL of the Alaska Permanent Fund: http://www.apfc.org/

[34] Gerene L. Freeman, "What About My 40 Acres & A Mule?" from *Emerging Minds Archives* http://www.emergingminds.org/nov03/diduknow.html

A lily in the water garden at Aradhana,
the East Coast, USA base of Earth Rights Institute.

Odi, a village on the Nun River in Bayelsa State in the Niger Delta area of Nigeria, had a pre-1999 population of 60,000 people. It had the largest number of most educated people in the region. Unfortunately, in late 1999, a massive brigade of the Nigerian army invaded this historic town with a mandate to arrest local bandits for a national crime. Tragically, Odi was completely wiped out in less than a day save three buildings. Today, Odi remains underdeveloped, impoverished, highly and grossly unplanned. Earth Rights Institute, with partners Gordon Abiama and Francis Udisi, has several projects underway in this area.

Marshall Kunoun, a citizen of Odi, and Francis Udisi, Earth Rights Institute's Humanitarian Aid Program Coordinator, travel by boat down the creeks of the Niger Delta for peace talks in June of 2007. This area of coastal southern Nigeria frequently experiences resource conflicts due to the related issues of oil extraction, environmental degradation, and impoverishment of the local population.

-9-

Financing Local to Global Public Goods: An Integrated Green Tax Perspective

Presented at the Global Institute for Taxation Conference on Fundamental Tax Reform sponsored by Price Waterhouse Coopers and St. John's University, New York, September 30, 1999 and published in *Taxation Alternatives for the 21st Century: Proceedings of the 1999 Conference.*

Summary: This paper details a number of successful practices and work-in-progress on green tax shift policies that harness incentives for efficient, equitable, and sustainable wealth production and distribution. Research is cited which shows the impressive potential of green tax reform to help solve major social, economic and environmental problems facing our global civilization. Additionally, presented is an integrated local-to-global public finance framework based on green taxation principles and policies.

World stability and human security require that we re-think the logic of globalization, including the best ways to finance public goods such as health, education, infrastructure, environmental sustainability and efforts for peace and conflict resolution. The challenge is to evolve a coherent, integrated and ethically based local-to-global tax system out of the current public finance hodge-podge of the world's more than 180 nation states.

Green tax shift policy is a rapidly emerging new perspective on tax reform that emphasizes the incentive capacity inherent in public finance policy. From this vantage point, taxation not only raises money necessary to fund governmental services it also reflects the overall value system of a given society, rewarding some activities while punishing others.

The goal of green tax shift policy is the creation of a system of public finance that will strengthen and maximize incentives for:

- Fair distribution of wealth
- Environmental protection
- Wealth production
- Provision of adequate government services
- Peaceful resolution of territorial conflicts

Green tax reform makes a clear distinction between private wealth and common wealth. Private wealth is that which is created by individual and collective labor. Common wealth is that which is provided by nature.

This public finance approach removes taxes from privately created wealth and increases taxes and user fees on common wealth domains used for human economic production. Captured in brief soundbites, "tax waste, not work," "tax bads, not goods," "pay for what you take, not what you make," and "polluter pays" become tax shift principles readily translated into voter friendly policy recommendations with broad based political support.

Reducing or eliminating taxes on private wealth means slashing taxes on:

- Income, especially from wages, payroll
- Capital, especially of sustainable quality
- Sales, especially for basic necessities
- Homes and other buildings

With careful calculations usually geared to overall revenue neutrality, green tax shifting balances cuts to the above by increasing taxes and fees on common heritage resource use such as:

- Emissions into air, water, or soil
- Surface land sites according to land value
- Public lands for timber, grazing, mining
- Electromagnetic spectrum
- Geo-orbital zones
- Oil and minerals
- Fish in the ocean
- Water resources

Green tax shifters also aim to eliminate numerous subsidies deemed no longer necessary, environmentally or socially harmful, or inequitable and unfair. Slated for drastic reduction or complete removal are subsidies for:[1]

- Energy production
- Resource extraction
- Waste disposal
- Agriculture and forestry
- Private transport and the infrastructure it requires
- Investments designed to exclude labor from production.

So far these reforms have been proceeding in a patchwork manner, but what matters is that the process has begun and the principles are being clearly articulated. Combining the efficiency and fairness taxation criteria of both Adam Smith and Henry George, green taxes largely conform to what a "good" tax should be:[2]

- Cheap to collect
- Fall as clearly and directly as possible on the ultimate payer
- Embody no favoritism or special exceptions
- Correspond to the payer's ability to pay
- NOT bring about undesirable economic distortions.

Distilled to the essence, taxes should be cheap, direct, equal and benign. It is imperative that the fiscal policy for good democratic governance be guided by these fundamental principles. Unfortunately, most taxes are not based on what a good tax should be, but instead current public finance mechanisms largely exploit both people and the planet.

World Revenue Review

The incentive signals of the world's taxation systems promote waste, not work. Approximating the composition of the world's $7.5 trillion tax pie reveals that 93% of taxes fall on work and investment while only 3% is collected from environmentally damaging activities. A mere 4% of global tax revenues is captured from natural resource use and access fees.[3]

A global tax shift scenario proposed by David Roodman at Worldwatch would collect 15% from environmental damage, 12% from land use and resource royalties (to total $900 billion each year) and cut environmentally harmful subsidies by 90%. This would free up an additional 8% of current revenues ($600 billion) and permit a nearly one-third reduction on wages and capital to 65% of total global taxes.[4]

Other researchers have calculated the potential for a total shift onto the full collection of resource rents, as will be detailed later in this paper. While being more ambitious in scope, this would also provide increased benefits through even stronger incentives for environmental protection and efficient, equitable wealth creation.

Billions of dollars have been loaned by the World Bank or channeled through the United Nations Development Program (UNDP) since 1965 to strengthen the capabilities of developing countries and to promote higher standards of living, faster and more equitable economic growth and environmentally sound development. While these explicitly stated UNDP goals are laudable, they have fallen far short of the mark.

Between 1994 and 1997 UNDP spent almost $6.5 billion. Of that amount, 26 percent went to eradicating poverty and livelihoods for the poor; 25 percent went for good governance; 24 percent for environmental resources and food security; 23 percent for public resources management for sustainable human development; and 2 percent for "other" which includes gender programs.[5]

But parts of our global economy are becoming weaker, with some 2 billion living below the poverty line (which is to say they earn less than the equivalent of $300 annually.) In the past 15 years, per capita income has declined in more than 100 countries and individual consumption has dropped by about one percent annually in more than 60 countries.[6] Clearly, larger detrimental influences have more than offset programs established by national and international aid agencies.

In 1960, the poorest countries, accounting for 20 percent of the world's population, had 5 percent of the world's income; the richest 20 percent had a 63 percent share. By 1990, the corresponding share of the poorest had declined to a mere 1.3 percent.[7]

The gap between the world's rich and poor has continued to widen with the richest one fifth now having 85 percent of the world's income. The 20% of the world's population that lives in the richest countries have generated almost three-quarters of the cumulative carbon dioxide emissions that are a primary cause of global warming. A fifth of the world's population is consuming four-fifths of all resources consumed annually, many of which are non-renewable.[8]

The world enjoys a $25 trillion economy. According to the United Nations, it would take just $80 billion to finance an anti-poverty program that could provide access to basic social services for all who are empoverished. "It is an ethical scandal that we do not provide the basics of education and health for everyone in a world with a $25 trillion economy," says Richard Jolly, author of the UN's Human Development Report (1997).[9]

UNDP now defines its major roles as eradicating poverty and providing an "enabling environment for social development."[10] To further these goals UNDP intends to contribute to the sustainable management of environment and resources and establish basic social services for everyone. It is hoped that those working through this and other agencies responsible for global well-being will grasp the potential of green tax reform. If they do, they will have to fully confront the challenges of the world's present inequitable and inefficient tax systems.

UN officials point out that the cost of eradicating poverty is just one percent of the world's income. But since governments fund UNDP and other UN programs, and governments rely primarily on the taxation of wages, efforts to stimulate economic development are paid for by the income of workers throughout the world. And because the increase in land values which accompanies development is not recaptured for the common good, these efforts frequently have the unfortunate side effect of enriching the few who own and control land and resource wealth and pay low or no fees, taxes, or royalties for their privileges. The way the current market system is structured, as development proceeds, the rich/poor gap grows. A new philosophy and development approach is needed for the 21st century.[11]

Green tax principles are an explicit and well-reasoned set of values and goals that can be succinctly stated - tax more heavily the behaviors that use and harm the earth's land and natural resources and untax activities we want to support and promote.

To reach the goals of equitable, sustainable development, closer attention must be given to the question of "Who benefits and who pays the taxes?"

Recommendations contained in UN documents, which advocate taxes on land and resources to ensure equitable access and to recapture land values enhanced from development activities, must be heeded.[12] Activities that damage common heritage resources of air, fresh water, land and sea must be penalized.

The footprint of industrial man is now pressed into every bit of the planet. High levels of poisonous industrial chemicals have been found in the Arctic peoples. If the entire world were to have the same patterns of consumption as the industrialized countries, total global industrial output would need to rise by four to tenfold depending on future population levels. Pollution levels would be unimaginable. But because of the poverty of the poorest one fifth of the world's population, there is a need for a new model of sustainable 'eco-industrialism' that is less energy and resource-intensive.

Market Efficiency and Ecological Equity

The state of the earth now requires that the costs of industrial production and human commercial activity no longer be externalized onto the global commons. But bureaucratic regulations to prevent pollution are often complex, unwieldy and expensive. Sufficiently high user fees and pollution permits which encourage business and industry to find more efficient and cost-effective controls are examples of green tax incentives that limit harmful outputs.

The "Economists' Statement on Climate Change," signed by over 2500 economists including eight Nobel laureates, is the strongest formal recommendation for green tax shifting that has emerged to date. Noting that the Intergovernmental Panel on Climate Change had determined that there was indeed a discernible human influence on global climate, the statement urges market-based policies as the most efficient approach to slowing climate change. "The United States and other nations can most efficiently implement their climate policies through market mechanisms, such as carbon taxes or the auction of emissions permits. The revenues generated from such policies can effectively be used to reduce the deficit or to lower existing taxes."[13]

The exact structuring of the proposed taxes or auction permits is crucial in terms of global equity considerations. In 1990 the World Resources Institute (WRI) recommended apportionment of the responsibility for the carbon dioxide and methane emissions that contributed to global warming. However, it was found that the countries that produced the larger quantities of these gases had been given larger shares. In other words, those who had polluted the most would continue to have the right to pollute the most. The Centre for Science and Environment (CSE) launched a critique of the model, claiming that global environmental space should be equitably shared amongst all human beings on earth.

CSE's "Statement on Global Environmental Democracy"[14] points out that the South needs ecological space to grow but that this space has already been colonized by the North. Recognizing the complexity of existing local-to-global property rights, two different economic approaches are recommended. For pollution from products originating within nations, market-pricing mechanisms should be modified through public policy so that ecological costs of production and consumption are internalized. For global resources, "the sustainable use of global common property should be encouraged through equitable entitlements."

CSE sets forth a precise policy approach for the equitable apportionment of global common property. "Within a globalized economy, those who consume more than their fair share of the world's environmental space must be asked to buy the extra space from those who do not consume their share. And those who consume beyond their own share should pay economic penalties to a global fund which would compensate those affected by the resulting environmental damage, and underwrite a prevention programme."[15]

Equity is a moral, ecological, and political requirement for a sustainable future. Green tax shifting is based upon the principle of equity of access to resources for all nations and peoples. Calculations determine the amount of resources that can be consumed relative to population size and the allowable amount of pollution that can be discharged into the environment. "The equity principle is fundamental to a modern, humane capitalism, and its proponents should support free and fair access to resources as the crux to providing quality of life for all" is how Michael Carley and Philippe Spapens express it in their book *Sharing the World*.[16]

Viewed from the ethic of equal rights to the creation, the undertaxation of land and natural resources is a form of theft from the common heritage. Governments charge much less than they could and should for the extraction and use of resources. Unfortunately, it is the case that much collusion between government and vested interests factor into this unequal equation. Fortunately, an organized and focused citizenry can remedy the situation. All can join in on one of the most revealing games on earth - who owns the planet and what is it worth?

Here are a few examples of common wealth rip-offs:[17]

- In the 1970's and 80's President Marcos granted cheap timber concessions to his allies, which then generated $42 billion in profits for an elite 480 families while impoverishing millions of rural people by ruining their land.
- In Indonesia, loggers paid only $500 million in 1990 for rainforest logging concessions, worth some $3.1 billion (in 1997 dollars). For every dollar that flowed into the country as aid, another dollar flowed out to timber magnates with ties to President Suharto.
- In California's Imperial Valley large-scale farm owners hold rights to a quarter of the flow of the Colorado River, water from which is delivered for free via a federally funded 80-mile canal. In the Central Valley, the government charges many farmers only $2.84 for a thousand cubic meters of water, but other farmers pay 28 - 50 times as much for water from a state irrigation project.
- Hardrock mining is nearly free on public lands in Canada and the USA. In 1994 a Canadian firm bought 1,950 acres of federal land in Nevada for $5,190; once mined the tract contained gold worth $10 billion - 2 million times as much as the transaction price.
- In Alaska's Tongass National Forest, one of the world's largest temperate rainforests, 500-year old trees are turned into cellulose for disposable nylon stocking. Between 1982 and 1988 the government spent $389 million on roads and other services for private clearcutting operations yet earned only $32 million.
- The US has just given away to private corporations the right to digital portions of the electromagnetic spectrum valued at $70 - $110 billion.

Here are examples of public collection of common wealth revenues:

- In 1992 Honduras began public auctioning of timber concessions and succeeded in raising sale prices from $5 to $33 per cubic meter of timber.
- The Philippines also began reforming timber-pricing policies in the 1990s, and now captures about 25 percent of the value of its timber, up from 11 percent.
- In contrast to the timber private windfalls, Indonesia now captures 85 percent of the in situ value of its petroleum deposits, enough to generate a quarter of its tax revenues.
- Norway is also collecting substantial royalties from its oil reserves and is putting much of it into a pension fund whose value is expected to climb to $25,000 per Norwegian by 2000.

- Developing countries charges to industrial-county governments for fishery access now total $500 million to $1 billion a year.
- Costa Rica, home to 1 in 20 of the world's terrestrial species, is charging for access to the genetic secrets of their biological wealth. The Merck drug company has agreed to pay to the country's Instituto Nacional de Biodiversidad $1 million for providing 10,000 biological samples.
- A 1996 auction of airwave frequencies brought $10 billion into the US government, more than any other auction in history.

Resource Trusts for Public Revenue

Let us be clear that the strategy of shifting taxes off of work and onto the use of land and other natural resources is contained within a system that gives monetary value to the contributions of both labor and land. The shift depends on institutions of market value land assessments and mineral valuation. Nature is thus ascribed value in its commodified forms.

Privatization of formerly common lands subordinated both people and social institutions to the market economy. But these same market forces, harnessed differently, can be used to provision an environmentally sustainable and socially stable base for the expansion of human potential into limitless realms of mental and spiritual expression.

Levying user charges on natural resources may require fine-tuning which takes into account various other values, such as cultural, historical, and generational. Even so, such efforts may arouse the suspicion of those seeing the limitations of market systems. Writers such as Michael Goldman are concerned about new forms of social control that can lead to intensified exploitation of all forms of nature. Goldman states:

> If we are to learn anything from the 1992 Earth Summit in Rio - the Greatest Commons Show on Earth - it is that the objective of the Summit's major power brokers was not to constrain or restructure capitalist economies and practices to help save the rapidly deteriorating ecological commons, but rather to restructure the commons (e.g., 'privatize,' 'develop,' 'make more efficient,' 'valorize,' 'get the price right') to accommodate crisis-ridden capitalism.[18]

Al Andersen at the Tom Paine Institute[19] acknowledges this concern and recommends that a large part of common heritage wealth be excluded from the monetized economy to be held as trust lands for parks, paths, roads and nature reserves providing habitats for all species.

Land and resources in what is now both the public and private sectors can be used as market commodities yet still be treated as common heritage wealth. This does not require as great a stretch as one might imagine. Zoning practices allow a degree of community control in land use decisions on private land, and current forms of property tax do collect a portion of land revenues to fund local government. User fees for grazing and timber and mineral extraction on public lands are usually much too low, but they are being collected.

These kinds of current land use rules can be viewed as covenants which condition land access. Local-to-global trusts, administered by democratically elected and carefully monitored trustees, could be responsible for enforcing land use and user fee covenants and for wisely and equitably allocating the funds collected. The Internal Revenue Service could be transformed into a multi-tiered Internal Resource Revenue Service.

The Alaska Permanent Fund functions as a good example of a resource trust. When Alaskans found themselves with billions of dollars of state oil revenues which began flooding state coffers in 1974 they chose three uses for these monies: (1) let state government use part of it for schools, highways, and other infrastructure; (2) return a large portion to citizens directly through annual cash dividends (the 1998 amount was $1,540 per-capita); and (3) invest the remainder in a portfolio of stocks and bonds, so that dividends would continue after the oil runs out.[20]

Peter Barnes envisions a similar type of trust for the sky. The sky can be viewed as a container for the carbon wastes of the fossil fuel industry. The sky's waste absorption capacity has become a scarce and finite resource that has been given away on a first come first served basis. But viewed in this way, the sky is clearly a common heritage resource and for industrial society it is literally worth trillions of dollars.

Barnes plan is to establish a Sky Trust whose underlying asset is America's share of the atmosphere's carbon absorption capacity. The trust structure is a market-based entity that can own and manage assets, charge for use of its assets, and periodically distribute its income to shareholders ("beneficiaries" in trust terminology). It has a board of trustees who are legally responsible for its actions and it declares a mission, which its trustees are legally bound to fulfill. Barnes' calculations show that revenue from atmospheric rent could exceed $1 trillion over the next 15 years.

"In essence, the Sky Trust would be a scarcity rent recycling system whose underlying formula is: from each according to his use of scarce sky, to each according to his equal ownership," says Barnes.[21]

Others also project massive potential for common heritage resource revenues. California resource economist Mason Gaffney has compiled a detailed list of rent yielding natural resources that are part of the proposed green tax base. Major sources of rent include energy, specifically hydrocarbons, uranium and hydro; hardrock minerals; fresh water and adjunct resources for recreation, fishing, navigation, reservoir sites, watersheds, waste disposal; timberlands; electromagnetic spectrum; geosynchronous orbital bands and LEO (Low Elevation Orbits); geothermal, wind and solar sites; the gene pool, which includes seed patents; natural herbs, medications, and breeding stock.

Gaffney concludes, "Aggregate resource rents, in a tax-free economy, would be adequate to replace all present taxes. That conclusion is subject to a comprehensive definition of rent."[22]

Addressing Deadweight Loss

Taxes on labor and production, wages and capital, have destructive consequences that result in economies that are much smaller than they could be. The same application of labor and capital could produce much more if they were untaxed. Public finance economists refer to the destructive effects of taxation as the *excess burden* or *deadweight loss* meaning that people have to work harder to achieve the desired output.

Careful calculations of numbers from all the G7 countries show that there could be a significant gain in output and per capita income with a shift to public collection of rent for resources. Overall it is estimated that the G7 economies had levels of output in 1993 (last year figures were available) that were only 52 percent to 77 percent of what they could be with a full green tax reform program. The US had the lowest taxes and the highest level of output at 77 percent of total possible estimated capacity, followed by Canada at 64 percent. Trailing were the higher tax nations of Japan at 58 percent and UK at 55 percent.[23]

It was estimated that for the US economy in 1993, the reduction in excess burden of taxation that would have been possible by relying primarily on rent for public revenue was $784 billion or 14 percent of net domestic product. In terms of the 1998 economy in 1998 dollars, this means that a better public finance system could yield an increase of about $1 trillion in the well-being of citizens. The reductions in excess burden as percentages of net domestic product are even greater for the other G7 economies, because of their higher current taxes.[24]

Taxes on wages and capital depress the net income that could otherwise be claimed by the owners of land and natural resources. With removal of these taxes, land and resource rents would increase considerably and could then be recaptured and distributed as government services or direct citizen dividends for the benefit of all. Those that own or use the gifts of nature would be charged for the privilege so that nature's wealth could not be hoarded or monopolized by the few. "Pay for what you take, not what you make" is the soundbite.

During 1995, collective profits of the world's top 500 companies rose by 15 percent to US$323 billion, while the size of their workforces remained approximately constant.[25] Separating productive capital from resource rents, it can be understood that a substantial portion of the "profit" of these corporations is drawn from their private claim to land and natural resources.

Land ownership statistics are hard to come by, but a 1979 study found that in the US 568 companies controlled 301.7 million acres of US land - more than 11 percent of total land area and 22 percent of all the private land. Those same companies' land interests worldwide comprised a total area larger than that of Europe - almost two billion acres.[26] A mere 2.5 percent of landowners with more than 100 hectares controlled nearly three-quarters of all the land in the world, with the top 0.23 percent controlling over half.[27] The concentration in land ownership has continued, but such statistics are the well-kept political secrets of the neo-liberal economic legacy that made land and natural resources a mere subset of capital.[28]

Tax Waste Not Work

Tax changes that enhance the position of workers AND trigger environmental improvements are the order of the day. One of the first examples of environmental tax reform as a two-pronged incentive strategy - raising taxes on the use of resources while decreasing taxes on income - was in 1991 when Sweden began levying a carbon dioxide tax and, in conjunction with it, cut the income tax.[29]

Other countries followed Sweden's lead, as Denmark, Spain, the Netherlands, United Kingdom, and Finland cut taxes on personal income and wages and raised taxes on motor fuel, coal, electricity, water, waste, carbon emissions, pesticide, natural gas, and other energy sales. These were small shifts, to be sure, the largest being Denmark which eco-shifted 2.5 percent of total tax revenues.[30]

In the UK, a study proposing an increased escalatory tax on road fuel of 17.6 percent per annum and the revenue generated used to decrease employers' national insurance contributions could increase employment by 1.275 million in about ten years. More conservative modeling suggests a gain to the UK economy of 400,000 to 700,000 jobs that could reduce unemployment by a quarter. A CO2-reduction energy scenario in Belgium forecasts a growth in employment of 27 percent in 2000 with a reduction in energy consumption and CO2 emissions of 8.5 percent. Reducing value-added taxes on products that are not energy-intensive would encourage their use.[31]

In the US, Andrew Hoerner, a senior research scholar with the Center for a Sustainable Economy, a nonprofit public interest research organization based in Washington, DC, has compiled a "Survey of State Initiatives" detailing 462 environmental tax provisions currently in place at the state level. "We are still learning how to design environmental taxes and tax incentives, and many current approaches to environmental taxation will surely be found wanting," says Hoerner. "But there is a danger in a rush to judgment, in trying to impose a single theoretical paradigm on the immense diversity of emerging instruments."[32]

Tax shift scenarios are being detailed for state and regional levels. A Northwest Environment Watch (NEW) proposal for the Pacific Northwest - British Columbia, Idaho, Oregon, and Washington - encompasses 84 percent of provincial, state and local revenue. The model reduces taxes on business, income and sales from 47 percent to 16 percent, with the loss being made up for by pollution and carbon taxes and taxes on traffic, hydropower, water, timber, fish and minerals. The 27 percent property tax, falling as it does more on buildings then on land values, is shifted to a pure land tax.[33]

This NEW scenario was the first to thoroughly integrate land value, or site value, taxation with environmental tax reform, and thus addresses a potential problem with some forms of ecotaxation. The very success of ecotax policies based on the polluter pay principle means that this tax base could shrink as incentives for energy conservation expand. Similarly, total tax take on non-renewable resources could eventually plummet as we begin to rely more on renewable energy such as wind or solar.

The advantage of including land value taxation as an ecotax is that surface land values either increase or decrease depending on the intensity of economic development. It is a tax base that automatically adjusts to a community's need for public finance. The more people and economic activity is focused on a particular area of land, the higher the land values and the greater the potential tax base. A tax or user fee based on land value is thus a stable and consistent source of public funds. Additionally, land value taxation provides a key to both political and economic decentralization.

Exploding Inequality

The addiction to the pounds of flesh that the nations have been extracting from their citizens will have to be cured. Many of us, at least in the US, now believe that there is excessive power and control wielded at the federal level. We feel disenfranchised by those who have concentrated economic wealth and now have disproportionate influence on the political process. Our hard-earned dollars are extracted from us without our consent and spent in ways that we do not approve. We are being subjected to taxation without representation.

The United States income tax is not the progressive tax that it used to be and that it was meant to be. The income tax enacted in 1913 was fair and simple and only twenty pages long. Only the richest 5% of households paid income taxes, which were actually more on capital gains than on wages.[34] Most of the "progress" in the income tax since then has been in progressively pushing the tax burden onto middle and lower income wage earners and in increasing the size of the loopholes and shelters for the wealthy.

With the addition of Social Security taxes, the income tax steadily devolved into a stiff payroll tax whose surpluses cover budget deficits. But the payroll tax is a highly inequitable flat tax. Everyone pays 7.65 percent (the self-employed pay 15.3 percent) UNTIL wages reach $68,400, after which they are not taxed at all!

Ted Halstead, founder and former president of Redefining Progress proposes a $10,000 payroll tax "personal exemption" similar to the one that already applies to income tax, with the resulting $140 billion gap filled by pollution permit fees. Such a tax shift would "strengthen our economy, boost wages and job creation, fix our troubled tax system, and protect the environment, all without raising the deficit," says Halsted.[35]

Meanwhile the growth in the federal government brought a growth in federal benefits, the bulk of which go to the well to do. Peter Peterson estimated an annual flow of $570.7 billion to the non-poor versus $109.8 billion to the poor. The average benefit to households with income over $100,000 exceeds that to households with under $10,000.[36]

This trend is clearly mirrored in rising income inequality and stagnating middle and lower class wages. Though annual growth rates for household income were positive for all income groups in the previous three decades, from 1973 to 1994 average incomes declined for 60 percent of the US population. In comparison, average real income increased 27.2 percent for the top fifth and 44 percent for the top 5 percent.[37] Currently the richest 20 percent reaps 55 percent of income and owns 80 percent of the wealth.[38] The richest 1 percent of US citizens possesses greater wealth than the bottom 90 percent.[39]

The combined wealth of the Forbes 400 richest Americans increased $114 billion during the 12-month period from September 1, 1997 to September 1, 1998 - an average addition of $285 million for each of those who were already wealthy. Put in terms of wages based on a 40-hour week and a 50-week year, which comes to $97,603 an hour, which is an hourly increase in their wealth at 18,416 times the federal minimum wage.

Between 1989 and 1997, 86 percent of stock market gains accrued to the top 10 percent of households while 42 percent went to the wealthiest one percent.

From 1983 to 1995 (the latest Fed figures), only the top five percent of households saw an increase in their net worth and only the top 20 percent experienced any increase in their income. Average wealth fell for everyone else. Median financial wealth (net worth less home equity) was $11,700 in 1997, lower than in 1989. In 1996, the Census Bureau reported record-level inequality; with the top fifth of households claiming 48.2 percent of national income while the bottom fifth has just 3.6 percent. Average middle class savings are enough to maintain the current standard of living for only 1.2 months, down from 3.6 months in 1989.[40]

The willingness and ability to work no longer guarantees an adequate standard of living. The share of US households with at least one child that were living below the poverty line despite having a full-time worker rose from 8.3 percent in 1975 to 11 percent in 1996, for a total of 3.65 million families.[41]

Cut the Pork

Clearly, there needs to be some major reshuffling of the ground rules of the economic game. Green tax reform can greatly reduce or eliminate the unhealthy predatory practice of taxing wage incomes and other forms of labor. Removing taxes from working people would significantly increase purchasing capacity while shifting taxes onto land and resources, the source of all tangible wealth, would prevent monopoly and speculation in the fundamental basis of life. Weaned off of the sweat and blood of working people and put on the proper diet of natural resource revenues and pollution fees, the nations should be able to efficiently meet the basic minimum governing requirements of all their citizens.

On the way there, we have a major weight reduction program looming. The wealthfare state has created substantial transfer payment programs in the form of subsidies for the already wealthy. Much unsustainable and inefficient economic activity is actually paid for by government. There are numerous subsidy programs that may have been helpful in the past but have outgrown their intended purposes and now represent a privileged largesse from the public trough. Eliminating tax drains by removing these subsidies is another key green tax shift strategy.

Tax shifters are pushing for and succeeding in the elimination of billions of dollars of subsidies that are deemed no longer essential. Subsidy elimination campaigns are underway in Europe and North America. In the US, the Green Scissors Coalition, an alliance of environmental groups and conservative tax cutters led by activists from Friends of the Earth, Taxpayers for Common Sense, and the U.S. Public Interest Research Group (PIRG), is lobbying Congress to save taxpayers nearly $51 billion by cutting federal programs that harm the environment and waste money.

Green Scissors has succeeded in getting Congress to cut more than $24 billion in wasteful and environmentally harmful spending programs since 1995.

Subsidies targeted by the Green Scissors '99 campaign include:

- **Money-Losing Timber Sales** Requiring the Forest Service to stop subsidizing timber industry clearcuts on National Forests would save $555 million and stop promoting the destruction of our Forest Heritage.
- **Coal and Oil Research and Development** Eliminating the coal, petroleum, and diesel research programs that benefit large, profitable fossil fuel and auto companies would save $1.6 billion and reduce subsidies that encourage global warming.
- **Wasteful Water Subsidies** Eliminating federal subsidies for water projects would protect the quality of our drinking water and wildlife habitat and protect taxpayers. For example, cutting the environmen-

tally damaging Animas-La Plata dam and irrigation project would save taxpayers $503 million. Reducing the budget for the Army Corps of Engineers' ineffective and harmful flood control construction program would save $1.25 billion.

- **Wildlife Services Livestock Protection Program** Slashing funding for ineffective attempts to control wolves, coyotes and other predators for western ranchers would save taxpayers $50 million.

- **Diesel Engine Research for Cars and Light Trucks** Eliminating research funding for diesel engines, which emit harmful levels of air pollution, would save taxpayers $220 million.

- **Radioactive Recycling Subsidies** Canceling the Department of Energy's noncompetitive contract to "recycle" radioactive metals and other atomic weapons and nuclear power wastes into consumer products would save $251.6 million.

"These outrageous programs flatten our forests and our pocketbooks, drain our rivers and the Treasury, contaminate the environment and the democratic process," says U.S. PIRG Staff Attorney Lexi Shultz.

Pay For What You Take, Not What You Make

Behind the front lines of the subsidy-cutting revolution, Redefining Progress think-tankers are devising several scenarios for federal green tax shifting for the United States. Taxes or fees would be increased or new taxes levied on carbon, air pollutants, gasoline, virgin materials, public resources, water pollutants, electricity, natural gas, coal for industrial combustion, and residential fuel oil. Increased revenue from these sources would permit major tax reductions on income and payroll taxes and also significant decreases on business taxes and some forms of capital gains, such as on new tax investments and home sales.[42]

Many green tax theorists avoid issues of how collected taxes should be dispersed and distributed. To state opinions on how public funds are spent could raise additional controversies and divert the debate from the important tax shift focus on tax sources. Most tax shift scenarios are therefore carefully crafted so as to be revenue neutral, projecting the same amount of tax revenues as is currently collected.

While the revenue neutrality approach may work well for tax shifters intending to gain political leverage on federal levels, this writer is at liberty to make one further nation state dietary recommendation. The world would be safer, saner, and more secure with a major weight loss program for bloated, bulging military budgets. Additionally, since green taxation presents an equitable approach to sharing the world, territorial conflicts could much more readily be resolved by peaceful means.

Several tax shift models indicate that some nations could fully substitute income taxes with resource rents. Calculations show that 17.5 percent of national income is the rental value of land and natural resources for the UK. For 1996, national income in that country was 675 billion pounds, (using the United Nations numbers) which gives a land rent of 118 billion pounds. Further, factoring in 108 billion pounds as the estimated value of government services provided by the state as the entity in sovereign control of the land, which can be considered as also coming out of land rent, then the total land rent for UK comes to 226 billion pounds. This is 33 percent of the National Income of 675 billion pounds, which is thus sufficient to wipe out all UK taxes on income.[43]

For the purposes of local-to-global tax harmonization and integration, the argument for shifting some resource rents and pollution fees upwards to the global and a substantial portion downwards to strengthen the local base means a significant decrease in overall federal taxation for most nations.

Responsible Decentralization – Stronger Local Economies

While top-heavy federal tax policy has enriched the rich, burdened the poor, and flattened the middle class, cities have declined along with the people in them. The poverty rate in central cities increased from 14 percent in 1970 to nearly 21 percent in 1993, according to the 1995 US Bureau of the Census. In Atlanta, which ranks second among America's big cities in its rate of violent crime, 43 percent of the children in its central city live in poverty.[44] Detroit has lost 50 percent of its population and 40 percent of its job base in four decades. Philadelphia and Washington have lost respectively one quarter and one fifth of their populations in the last 25 years and contain tens of thousands of homeless.

Despite rising GDP, many indicators of American quality of life are falling. The Index of Social Health, published each year by Fordham University in New York, combines 16 measures of well-being into a single numerical index. Since 1970, America's social health has fallen more than 45%. In 1993, the most recent year for which data is available, six of the indicators - children in poverty; child abuse; health insurance coverage; average weekly earnings; out-of-pocket health costs for those over 65; the gap between rich and poor - reached their worst recorded levels.[45]

While cities die, billionaires thrive. The pay of top earners is now 212 times higher than that of average employees, up from a multiple of 4 in 1965. During 1995, salaries and bonuses of chief executives in the US rose by 10.4 percent compared to a 2.9 increase in average earnings.[46]

In 1975 there were 350,000 millionaire households (0.5 percent of all households). In 1996 there were 3.5 million millionaire households (3.5 percent of all households).[47] In 1929 there were two billionaires. In 1944, after Roosevelt's Great

Society programs were put in place, there were no billionaires. In 1978 there was one billionaire, but by 1994 there were 120.[48]

Downshifting the tax base can provide a strong and sustainable source of public finance for our ailing cities while making sure that everyone pays their fair share for the land sites they hold. A type of tax shifting that is particularly suited to the local level can largely remedy the sick social conditions in the urban cores. The place to look is the frequently maligned property tax. A fundamental green tax shift reform of the property tax has the potential to transform the world's cities into places of safety, functionality, beauty and prosperity for all. But the incentive capacity of the property tax has to be realigned.

Currently the major portion of the property tax falls on buildings, thus discouraging renovations and improvements to the built environment. A lessor portion of the property tax falls on land values, which part can be rightly viewed as a resource rental fee. Urban sites are valuable as places of production and exchange. Undertaxed, urban site rental incomes accrue to the few who own these valuable sites without any compensatory labor on their part. The private appropriation of site rental values can be viewed similarly to the private profits that accumulate from the extraction of oil, minerals, and other natural resources.

Taxing surface land falls in line with other forms of green tax shifting and contains a special boon for decentralizing economic and political power to the local level. Shifting taxes off of buildings and onto sites will decrease land speculation and encourage higher and better use of urban lands, which often now have large swaths of boarded up commercial and residential buildings or are entirely vacant. Additionally, more intensive use and reuse of already serviced urban land sites will reduce sprawl and increase efficiencies of scale for infrastructure and public transportation, all desirable environmental objectives.

The late Nobel Prize winning economist William Vickrey of Columbia University was a strong proponent of a land value only form of property tax. "Site value taxation in the long run tends to diminish urban sprawl, increasing densities and site values at the center and usually diminishing them at the periphery."[49]

Currently the property tax is a relatively small proportion of all taxes and weighs more heavily on buildings than on land values. In Western Europe, real estate taxation generates about 5 percent of tax revenue. Property is more heavily taxed in the US, Canada, and Japan, yielding about 12 percent of revenue, but again land values are underassessed relative to buildings. David Roodman of Worldwatch Institute says that "If property taxes in North America and Japan were replaced with pure land value taxes and if land value taxes reached the same level in the rest of the world, they could generate 12 percent of global tax revenue, or $900 billion a year.[50]

While this is an impressive number, since global tax revenue is estimated to be about $7.5 trillion, this is a relatively small percentage of the overall tax yield. Other calculations show that a full land value tax could generate a significantly greater proportion of taxes.

A study by the New Economics Foundation in London calculated that half the tax revenue in the UK - some $140 billion a year - could be raised through a land value tax set at 75 percent of annual rental value. Ninety-eight percent of this would come from land used for housing, offices, factories, or mining, not for farming. Combined with a sizable energy tax, this could fund the abolition of all taxes on income, payroll, sales, profits, and buildings and also pay for a "Citizen's Income" in the form of stipend checks for several hundred or thousand pounds for each resident each year.[51]

Land value taxation (also called "site rental public revenue") appears to be a potent green tax shift tool, based on some real-world experience in its application. For example, fifteen cities in Pennsylvania are reforming their tax base via a property tax reform that shifts taxes off of buildings, to encourage construction and improvements, and onto land value, to discourage land speculation and poor site use.[52] An added advantage is that sites maintain affordability of access.

Harrisburg's Mayor Steven Reed, in describing his city's remarkable recovery from "second most distressed city in the USA" by official federal criteria, has stated that the shift to land value taxation "has been and continues to be one of the key local policies that has been factored into this initial economic success here." A substantial decrease in vacant structures (over 4200 in 1982, less than 500 currently), significant increase in well-employed city residents, and lowered crime and fire rates are among the several quality of life indicators which affirm the positive benefits of this tax reform.[53]

Interestingly, this basic approach to local public finance underlies the success of a number of countries ranking high on the Index of Economic Freedom. Compiled by the Wall Street Journal and the Heritage Foundation, this index assigns scores for ten areas including taxation and property rights. Hong Kong is on top of the 1998 list. Hong Kong's land has been in the public domain since it's founding in 1983. It is leased to users via auctions and this revenue funds government services. Singapore ranked second in the Index and that state also holds most of the land in the public domain. New Zealand placed fourth after oil-revenue rich Bahrain, and it, too, has relied heavily on the rent of land as public revenue. In seventh place was Taiwan, a country that also draws a significant proportion of public revenue from the rent of land.[54]

As has been seen, the income tax is no longer a genuinely progressive tax. A land value tax IS a progressive tax because the share of wealth that is land tends to increase with total wealth. As described by land economist Mason Gaffney, the land tax is progressive for two reasons:[55]

- It is not shifted, so only an owner and not a tenant bears it.
- The ownership of land is highly concentrated. As a consumer good, land is a superior good and a status symbol. And as investment, land promises capital gains type income with minimal management problems, traits that attract the wealthy buyer.

The richest 10 percent of Americans own 60 - 65 percent of private land by value, calculates economist Clifford Cobb of Redefining Progress.[56] This figure includes land indirectly owned through corporations. By area, it is estimated that 3 percent of the population owns 95 percent of the privately held land in the US.[57] In Brazil, the wealthiest 1 percent hold title to half the countryside.[58] Those who profit from control of land resources are wealthy as a group all over the world.

As the world's economies have become more intertwined, large asset holders have been able to shuttle their wealth to low tax or tax free zones in other countries. The elimination of taxes on labor and productive capital would eliminate the problem of offshore tax evasion. No tax to evade equals no tax evasion. An advantage to taxing in-place tangibles of land and natural resources is that they cannot be easily hidden.

"Since a plot of earth can never sidle across a national border to avoid taxation, (taxing) natural resources give governments a sort of protective barrier against the corrosive forces of international tax competition," says David Roodman.[59]

Global Resource Agency

But there is another level of competition and exploitation fast underway. The 20th century has opened vast new frontiers that promise great wealth and power to those with the technology to stake a claim. These new territories lie beyond the jurisdiction of national governments. If issues concerning their use and ownership are not addressed at the global level, they may overwhelm all our efforts to strengthen local economies.

The thinking of academicians and policy makers concerning the so- called "new global commons" strives to direct supranational decision making on the grey areas of global real estate: the earth's ozone, deep seas, 'biodiverse' reserves, the North and South poles, the air waves.[60]

These are not "grey areas" for tax shifters like Land and Liberty editor Fred Harrison, who gives dire warning regarding future territorial expansion, seen not as horizontal but vertical territory. "...shifting into gear is the quest for the rents of outer space and the rents of natural minerals below the surface of the ocean beds. And there are also the rents from our genes..."[61] These are global common heritage domains whose resource rents should be captured for the benefit of all, not pillaged for private profit.

There is an urgent necessity for the creation of a Global Resource Agency responsible for monitoring the global commons (e.g., the ozone shield, global forest reserves, fish, biodiversity) determining rules for access, issuing permits and collecting resource revenues. Such a body could also assume substantial authority for equitably distributing fees collected and levying fines and penalties for the abuse of common heritage resources.

There are numerous domains for raising global revenue.[62] One of the main categories are fees for the use of the global commons, which would include parking charges for satellites placed in geostationary orbits, royalties on minerals mined or fish caught in international waters, charges for exploration in or exploitation of Antarctica, and use of the electromagnetic spectrum.

Other significant global revenue sources include taxes or fees based on the polluter-pay principle, such as international flights or aviation kerosene, international shipping, or dumping at sea. Some would place a tax on the international arms trade. While not a user fee or pollution charge per se, taxes on weapons of destruction certainly would fall on the "bads" side of the "tax bads not goods" green tax ethic. Considering the damages due to war and violence, funds raised from arms trading charges might well be placed into contingency funds both for conflict resolution to prevent open warfare and for post-war reparations, although some advocate the abolition of the arms trade altogether.

Revenue raised from access fees for the use of the global commons could be used to fund necessary sustainable development programs, environmental restoration, peacekeeping activities, or as backing for low-interest loans to help eradicate poverty. Funds are also needed on the global level to finance justice institutions such as the World Court and the International Criminal Court and to facilitate policy convergence in areas such as trade, currency exchange, and human rights.[63] A portion of these funds could also be distributed as direct "world citizen dividends" similar to the Alaska Permanent Fund.

Are there signs of an emerging Global Resource Agency with the necessary legal authority suited to the tasks outlined above? Alas, the nation state system has not yet agreed to arrangements that would permit the United Nations or any other transnational body to operate with independent funding and thus be in a position of sovereignty over nations. But the emergence of such an agency is an imperative if we are to create a world that works for everyone.

Places to watch for how major players are now financing the planet are the International Monetary Fund (IMF), the World Bank, the newly established UN related Global Environmental Facility and the Global Sustainable Development Facility.[64] Places to look for components of a Global Resource Agency include the UN Commission on the Limits of the Continental Shelf and the Committee on Energy and Natural Resources for Development.

David Korten, former expert development specialist turned critic, suggests that the IMF be replaced by a United Nations International Finance Organization, empowered to write-off international debts, regulate international financial markets and currencies, balance trade accounts, and collect and administer a tax on foreign exchange transactions. Additionally, he advocates that the World Bank be closed, as its main role has been that of creating indebtedness of poor countries.[65]

While some national governments, backed by vested interests that are profiting from the current system, might balk at the idea of a Global Resource Agency, many others would find it a welcome institution if it were truly capable of promoting stability and economic equity for their peoples. The push for its creation may have to come from a unity of these countries plus a powerful network of non-governmental organizations (NGOs), similar to the kind of organizing it took to establish the International Criminal Court in 1998.

Some people might object to the idea of a Global Resource Agency out of fears that it would add another top-heavy level of bureaucracy to an already governmentally burdened world. But those at Global Education Associates, a UN-affiliated NGO focused on building better world institutions, and others who favor strengthened global governance ask us to imagine the shape of the emerging world as a pyramid with three basic levels: a small tier at the top for global institutions, a greatly slimmed down second band of national governments, and a vast sturdy base of local governance.[66]

Local to Global Public Finance Tiers

Green tax reform has the potential for becoming a comprehensive and universally accepted approach to public finance policy that can readily be integrated into such a three-tier system of local-to-global governance. Suitable tax bases for the funding of cities, regions, and states and at the global level can be clearly delineated through identifying appropriate tiers of common heritage domains. The following descriptions of these public finance tiers will serve to summarize the main points that have been expounded in this paper:

Surface land values, such as sites for homes, business and industrial activities, are well suited to finance towns, cities, counties and townships. Progressively shifting taxes OFF OF productive efforts such as building homes, working and organizing businesses, and ON TO land values prevents land speculation and monopoly, thus keeping land affordable while workers keep what they have earned in the process. This type of full-on green tax shift also would be recommended for rural areas where it has potential for non-coercive land reform which could underpin the transition to organic farming and a revitalized rural "eco-village" culture.[67]

State, regional, or national bodies are best constituted to collect user fees for forestry, mineral, and oil resources. For nations with significant amounts of public lands, user fees for grazing, timber, or mineral extraction would be significantly increased. The electromagnetic spectrum would be leased via auction rather than being given outright to the private sector. Precise configurations for the allocation of resource rentals between the state, regional and federal levels would vary according to the situation of particular nations.

Globally, as aforementioned, there is the need to establish some sort of Global Resource Agency to collect user fees for transnational commons. The Global Resource Agency could also be responsible for distributing resource revenues equitably throughout the world as calculated by formulas based on population, development criteria and currency purchasing capacity. Revenues collected would also provide the funding for global agencies responsible for justice, peacekeeping, and fair trade.

Percentages of total resource revenues collected could be disbursed up or down these several tiers based on criteria of equity, as some nations and regions of the earth are better endowed with natural resources than others. Freedom to live or work in any part of the globe would also further equality of entitlement to the planet.

The Earth is the Birthright of All People

It is overly simplistic to view the world as being divided between the rich North and the poor South. In the North there are significant numbers living in poverty and despair while in the South there are those with the riches of royalty. The structural systemic problem of the misdistribution of wealth is a global phenomenon. The 358 billionaires with a combined net worth of $760 billion - equal to the poorest 2.5 billion people of the world - have profited from the virtual enslavement of everyone else.[68]

Taxes structured along these lines would do much to level the economic playing field worldwide, both within and among nations. A coherent and integrated local-to-global green finance system would fundamentally alter the status quo and would give every person a stake in the planet as a birthright. With basic needs securely met for all, humankind would be free to advance to a higher dimension of expression and realization.

We can do no better than to end this paper with a quote from a great tax shift pioneer, visionary, and planet champion, Fred Harrison:

"Privatized rent is the last great injustice inherited from the earliest civilizations. The anti-social prejudices that protected it through four millennia ought not to be tolerated by any society with a claim to being democratic and governed by principles of justice. The Challenge of the Millennium is to empower people to convert a legacy of trillion dollar losses into the riches that would finance the social and environmental needs of all nations in the 21st century."[69]

[1] From "Factor 10 Club Carnoules Declaration," (Wuppertal Institute :1995), in Michael Carley & Philippe Spapens, Sharing the World:Sustainable Living & Global Equity in the 21st Century (London: Earthscan Publications Ltd., 1998) 180.

[2] Hanno Beck, Brian Dunkiel. and Gawain Kripke, "A Citizens Guide to Environmental Tax Shifting" (Friends of the Earth : 1999) www.foe.org

[3] David Malin Roodman, The Natural Wealth of Nations: Harnessing theMarket for the Environment (New York: W.W. Norton & Company/Worldwatch,1998)166.

[4] Ibid.166.

[5] C. Gerald Fraser, "United Nations Development Programme at Crossroads" (Earth Times, May 16 - 31, 1999) 15. www.earthtimes.org

[6] Ibid. 14.

[7] Ibid.

[8] Carley & Spapens, op.cit. 3.

[9] Fred Harrison, The Losses of Nations (London: Othila Press Ltd.,1998) , xvii.

[10] C. Gerald Fraser, op.cit.14.

[11] For a detailed exposition of a new development approach in line with green tax policy, see David Smiley, Third World Intervention: A New Analysis, (Redfern, Australia: New South Wales Henry George Foundation,1998).

[12] See for example the UN Habitat II Action Agenda , Section B, 55 &56, "Ensuring Access to Land," endorsed by consensus of 183 nation state representatives in Istanbul on June 15, 1996.

[13] For complete text, see the Redefining Progess website

[14] Anil Agarwal & Sunita Narain, "The Sharing of Environmental Space on a Global Basis" in Sharing the World, op.cit. 177.

[15] Ibid.

[16] Ibid. 68.

[17] David Roodman, op.cit. 114-129.

[18] Michael Goldman, Privatizing Nature: Political Struggles for the Global Commons (London: Pluto Press, 1998) 23

[19] Al Andersen, Tom Paine Institute , "An Educational Challenge Designed to Achieve Economic Justice Worldwide" at www.csf.colorado.edu/sustainable-justice

[20] Peter Barnes, "The Pollution Dividend" (The American Prospect, May-June 1999 , Number 44) 61.

[21] Ibid. 64-65.

[22] Mason Gaffney, "An Inventory of Rent-Yielding Resources" in appendix of Harrison, ibid. 221-231.

[23] Nicolaus Tideman & Florenz Plassman, "Taxed Out of Work and Wealth: The Costs of Taxing Labor and Capital" from Harrison, op.cit. 147.

[24] Ibid.148.

[25] Carley & Spapens, op.cit. 160.

[26] Peter Meyer, "Land Rush: A Survey of America's Land - Who owns it, who controls it, how much is left," Harper's Magazine, January 1979.

[27] Susan George, How the Other Half Dies (Penquin Books, 1976) 24.

[28] For a thorough exposition, see Mason Gaffney & Fred Harrison, The Corruption of Economics, Shepheard-Walwyn, 1994, which can be ordered from the Robert Schalkenbach Foundation, www.progress.org/books

[29] Hanno T. Beck, "Ecological Tax Reform," in Land Value Taxation, Kenneth C. Wenzer, ed. (New York: M.E. Sharpe, 1999) 222.

[30] Roodman, op.cit. 161.

[31] Ibid. 162.

[32] J. Andrew Hoerner, "Harnessing the Tax Code for Environmental Protection: A Survey of State Initiatives" in State Tax Notes, Special Supplement, Tax Analysts, April 20, 1998.

[33] Alan Thein Durning & Yoram Bauman, Tax Shift (Seattle: Northwest Environment Watch, 1998) 76.

[34] Chuck Collins & John Miller, "Tax Reform Follies," Dollars and Sense (March/April 1999) 14.

[35] David Brauer, "The Eagle Dies on Friday," Utne Reader, September-October, 1998.

[36] Peter Peterson, 1994, as stated in research paper of Mary M.Cleveland, November 1, 1995.

[37] M. Jeff Hamond, Tax Waste, Not Work (San Francisco: Redefining Progress, 1997) 21.

[38] Roodman, op.cit.188.

[39] David Kotz, "How Many Billionaires Are Enough?" New York Times, October 19, 1986.

[40] Statistics from the above two paragraphs compiled by Jeff Gates, a former counsel to the US Senate Committee on Finance and author of The Ownership Solution (Addison Wesley, 1998) as reported in Yes! A Journal of Positive Futures, Fall 1999, 53.

[41] Roodman, op. cit. 203.

[42] Hamond, op.cit. 71-81.

[43] Harrison, op. cit. 125 - 126.

[44] Hamond, op.cit. 23.

[45] Carley and Spapens, op.cit. 33.

[46] Ibid. 160.

[47] Source: Affluent Market Institute, T. Rowe Price Associates.

[48] As stated from sources noted in David C. Korten, When Corporations Rule the World, (Copublished by Kumarian Press, Inc. , West Hartford and Berrett-Koehler Publishers, Inc., San Francisco, 1995), 62 & 65.

[49] Harrison, op.cit.144.

[50] Roodman, op.cit. 127.

[51] James Robertson, Benefits and Taxes (London: New Economics Foundation, 1994) as found in Roodman, op.cit. 126.

[52] Alanna Hartzok, "Pennsylvania's Success with Local Property Tax Reform: The Split Rate Tax" American Journal of Economics and Sociology 56, no. 2 (April 1997) 205.

[53] Ibid. 210.

[54] Fred Harrison, op.cit. 119.

[55] Ibid. 205.

[56] Clifford Cobb et. al, "Fiscal Policy for a Sustainable California"(San Francisco, CA: Redefining Progress,1995) as reported in Roodman, op.cit. 190.

[57] Meyer, op.cit.

[58] Fabio L.S. Petrarolpha, "Brazil: The Meek Want the Earth Now," Bulletin of the Atomic Scientists, November/December 1996, as reported in Roodman, op.cit. 190

[59] Roodman, op.cit. 190.

[60] Barnes, op.cit. 21.

[61] Harrison, op.cit. 93.

[62] List source is Overseas Development Institute as found in Carley & Spapens, op.cit.179.

[63] Along these lines, see Global Public Goods: International Cooperation i n the 21st Century, edited by Inge Kaul, Isabelle Grunberg and Marc A. Stern (New York: Oxford University Press, 1999).

[64] For details on these two, see www.corporatewatch.org.

[65] Korten, op.cit. 323.

⁶⁶ Jack Yost, *Planet Champions, Adventures in Saving the World* (Portland: Bridge City Books, 1999) 26, describes the vision of GEA founders Gerald and Patricia Mische.

⁶⁷ For a detailed exploration of research regarding land value taxation and its affect on agriculture, see Alanna Hartzok, Pennsylvania Farmers and the Split-Rate Tax, as found in Wenzer, op.cit., 239-267.

⁶⁸ Statistics cited by Richard J. Barnet, "Stateless Corporations: Lords of the Global Economy," The Nation (December 19, 1994) 754.

⁶⁹ Harrison, op.cit. 120 and back cover.

Dave Wetzel, Annie Goeke, Heather Wetzel and Alanna Hartzok at the UN Habitat World Urban Forum in Vancouver, 2006. Dave, Vice-Chair of Transport for London, UK, is holding a copy of J.W. Smith's book, *Money: A Mirror Image of the Economy.*

10

Financing Planet Management: Sovereignty, World Order and the Earth Rights Imperative

First published January 1994, the 2ⁿᵈ edition printing was January 1995, both by the Robert Schalkenbach Foundation.

We have reached the deplorable circumstance where in large measure a very powerful few are in possession of the earth's resources, the land and all its riches, and all the franchises and other privileges that yield a return. These monopolistic positions are kept by a handful of men who are maintained virtually without taxation . . .we are yielding up sovereignty.

– Agnes de Mille (1905-1993)

Heaven has its reasons, Earth has its resources, and Man has his political order, thus forming with the first two a triad. But he would err if he failed to respect the ground rules of this triad and infringed on the other two.

– Xun Quang Xunzi, 3rd century.

D efining the parameters of sovereignty is a key component of the world order dialogue as it struggles to reach consensus regarding the boundaries and prerogatives of power.

Sovereignty is the status of a person or group of persons having supreme and independent political authority. In dealing with the concept of sovereignty, we are dealing with the reality of power. It is a power over territory, over land and water, oil and minerals, as well as those life forms that have miraculously emerged out of the mud of the earth.

The kings and queens of Europe, Africa, and Asia were sovereigns. They reigned supreme and were thought to be divine. They descended from those having the strongest might and force to prevail over territory. The larger and richer the territory they could hold under their power and authority, the higher their status. They were both feared and courted by other humans.

These were the dominators who ruled the land and made the rules. Their rules became law. Their territorial law was that of *dominium* – the legalization of control over lands originally obtained by conquest and plunder. All real estate was the royal estate. Might made right, as the rules of power became the laws of the land.

Peter Hansen, executive director of the Independent Commission on Global Governance, has stated:

> The United Nations cannot by the nature of things, have the formal attributes of sovereignty, which has been defined around a territory, around a (specific) population, because centralized control of a sovereign body with a given territory and population, is not the same thing as a sovereign U.N. To assume that it would be is not a very meaningful way, in my opinion, to define the subject. (World Peace News, November 1993)

But it seems to me that the U.N. has in fact been defined around a given territory, that territory being the planet as a whole, as well as a specific population, which is all the planet's people. The issue here is not that of populations and boundary lines, but of the demarcation of power and control over the earth that is the foremost "formal attribute of sovereignty" to be debated.

To speak of enforceable world law is to speak of world power. A world legislature would have the power to make the laws of the land and to make the rules for the territory of the earth. And this is what concerns me, because we have not yet discussed the rules of territorial control and ownership in sufficient detail.

Consider these realities:

Fact: A U.N. study of 83 countries showed that less than 5% of rural landowners control three-quarters of the land.

Fact: The most pressing cause of the abject poverty which millions of people in the world endure is that a mere 2.5% of landowners with more than 100 hectares control nearly three-quarters of all the land in the world, with the top 0.23% controlling over half. [1]

Fact: At best, a generous interpretation would suggest that about 3% of the population owns 95% of the privately held land in the U.S. [2]

Fact: According to a 1985 government report, 2% of landowners hold 60% of the arable land in Brazil while close to 70% of rural households have little or none. Just 342 farm properties in Brazil cover 183,397 square miles—an area larger than California. [3]

Before a global authority, be it a reformed United Nations or a federal world government, can be trusted to wield power benignly, the problem of the current undemocratic control of the earth must be addressed. Innumerable battles and wars have been fought, and many are currently in progress, over territorial control. The fair and peaceful resolution of such conflicts requires a deep consideration of ethical principles regarding land tenure.

Dr. I.G. Patel, Independent Commission on Global Governance member, governor of the Reserve Bank of India, and former director of the London School of Economics stated:

> We cannot talk (sensibly) about what kind of global government we want until
>   (1) Agreement is reached on how to deal with the causes of international problems and
>   (2) If we are going to have governance or government we will have to do something about poverty.[4]

Dr. Patel is correct in his perception that the world order movement has not dealt sufficiently with these issues. While there is a fair amount of unanimity regarding the basic outline of a democratic global political structure, i.e., the need for a democratically elected legislature, a world judiciary to interpret and apply world laws, and an executive to administer and enforce the laws, there has not yet been sufficient thought applied to the consideration of root causes of poverty and international conflict.

The problem is that democracy has not "grounded" itself. We have not yet extended democratic principles down to the ownership and control of the earth. Democratic government as presently constituted, and democratic world government as currently proposed, ungrounded and unembedded in equal rights to the earth, cannot create the world of peace and justice that we seek.

The Crack in the Liberty Bell

To fully grasp the nature of the severe limitations in the current ideology of the world government movement, it is necessary to follow the thread of the democratic ideal back to its fundamental tenets. Pondering the problem of persistent poverty within a democratic system of government, Richard Noyes, New Hampshire State Representative and editor of *Now the Synthesis: Capitalism, Socialism, and the New Social Contract*, identifies the current land tenure system as "the one great imperfection, the snag on which freedom catches."

Noyes shows us that the "Age of Reason gave us a thesis with flaws." John Locke's Second Treatise on Civil Government, the political bible of the founding fathers, held that "The great and chief end of men's uniting into commonwealths, and putting themselves under government is the preservation of their property." The central understanding was that only through the guarantee of property rights, one's own body included, could the individual really be free.

In further defining property rights, Locke stated that "every man has a `property' in his own `person'", so that anything a man has "removed from the common state," anything with which he has "mixed his own labor," is rightfully his own. The securing of this right was to be the main duty of a democratic government.

Locke also affirmed "God hath given the world to men in common." But the trouble lies with Locke's Second Proviso regarding property. Locke maintained that it was correct for the individual in a state of nature to mix his labor with land and so call it (produced wealth) his own "since there was still enough (land) and as good left, and more than the yet unprovided could use."

In the Second Proviso the reasoning of the primary mentor of the founding fathers was faulty and limited. Locke failed to perceive the consequences for democracy of a time when so few humans would come to control so much of the earth, to the exclusion of the vast majority. Nor could he have known how the forces of an industrial economy could drive land values to such highs, to the benefit of landowners rather than wage earners.

The property-in-land problem, insufficiently scrutinized by John Locke and the founding fathers, is the crack in the Liberty Bell. It is the root dilemma of democracy. Life and liberty without land rights breeds unhappiness, unemployment, and wage slavery.

Adam Smith was of no more help than John Locke when it came to solving the land problem. Although initially he made clear distinctions among land, labor, and capital, he soon began using the terms capital and land as synonymous factors. Consequently, mainstream economists have treated land as essentially no more than a subset of capital in their own two-factor (capital and labor) macroeconomics. This is why they have failed to understand the grave problem of the maldistribution of wealth that has grown out of the fact that a minuscule percentage of the world's people have come to control and consume the vast majority of the earth's land and natural resources.

The Common Heritage Principle and Public Finance

The resolution of the dilemma of democracy can be found in a three-factor (land, labor, capital) macroeconomic approach. The products resulting from the interaction of land and labor are rightfully held as individual private property, while land (which term includes all natural resources) is recognized as the common heritage.

Once the human right to the earth is firmly established in the minds and policies of a democratic majority, land will no longer be taken by the few from the many either by the force of military might or by the mechanisms of the market. The market's ability to place value, combined with the efficiency of money as an exchange medium, results in a range of prices for land sites and natural resources. Those who simply "own" earth resources, contribute nothing as such to the productive process. Yet under the current private property ethic, they are in an advantageous position of power and can extract the ransom of what economists call "ground rent" from both labor and productive capital.

But if we now apply the common heritage principle to land, then it follows that ground rent, which is a measure of natural resource value, must be treated as "common property." The next step which three-factor economists take is to link this insight with the public finance system. Voila! The policy imperative becomes clear. A way to affirm the equal right of all to the common heritage is to collect the ground rent for the benefit of the community as a whole, a policy frequently referred to as "land value taxation."

Confiscatory taxes on labor and productive capital should gradually be removed, as the value of earth resources becomes the proper source of funding for the community as a whole. The "common wealth" finances the commonwealth.

Three-factor economists thus advocate a practical policy that will solve the problem of Locke's Second Proviso, which falsely assumed no limitation to natural resources. Democracy can now be established on the firm foundation of equal rights to the earth, our common heritage.

While this perspective is newly emerging, it is not new. No less a figure than Tom Paine stated, "Men did not make the earth... It is the value of the improvement only, and not the earth itself, that is individual property... Every proprietor owes to the community a ground rent for the land which he holds." Where does that leave us in our consideration of the world order movement, the concept of "sovereignty," and the need for financing the activities of the U.N. or any other global body?

The New Democratic Covenant

Clearly, the mandate of a benevolent yet powerful sovereign global governmental body must be to protect the property rights of the bodies of individuals as well as the products of their labor (private property), as well as to protect and to fairly share our common body Mother Earth. This is the new territorial imperative, the new democratic covenant, and the higher synthesis resolving what has been the difficult and too-often-destructive dialectic of left versus right.

A properly constituted global authority will seek to further these principles both within and among the current nations. Once the world order movement grasps the importance of the new territorial imperative of equal rights to earth, then it follows that ground rent (land value) should be advocated as the appropriate source of public finance from local to global levels.

Examples of Ground Rent Policy

This taxation approach is not merely theoretical but is being implemented, at least in part, in a number of places. In the United States, enabling legislation in Pennsylvania gives cities the option of shifting their property taxes off of buildings (productive capital) and onto land values only (common heritage). The fifteen cities taxing land values at the higher rate have been experiencing statistically significant economic benefits.

Alaska retained its oil lands as public land, subject to fair leasehold arrangements for use plus a tax on each barrel pumped for market. Assets in the Alaska Permanent Fund are about $13 billion. There are no state income or sales taxes, and every citizen of Alaska receives an annual dividend of about $1000 each with an additional $250 per month to every citizen 65 years or older.[5]

Movements in this direction are underway through- out the world. In the spring of 1993, representatives of eighty Russian cities signed a resolution to reform their public revenue system in this manner.

On the global level, the Law of the Seas, the Moon Treaty, and the treaty now governing Antarctica are all based on the common heritage principle, a principle that now must be extended worldwide to include surface lands, as well as oil and mineral resources.

Hatching Many Birds out of One Egg

As the taxation of land values, essentially a "user fee" system, becomes an integral component of the agenda of planet management, several birds will begin to hatch out of one egg. Simultaneously,

* Land tenure will be based on fairness, not force, thus ameliorating territorial conflict, a root cause of war;
* Land resources can be equitably allocated;
* The economic playing field is leveled;
* A genuinely free market is encouraged;
* The gap between the rich and poor narrows; and
* The necessary collective activities of humanity are properly funded, which include peacekeeping and the restoration and protection of the environment.

Common Heritage Funding: Local to Global

It has been suggested that such a system of finance would be based on principles of subsidiarity in terms of implementation. Clearly delineated governing bodies can collect the ground rent of certain specific types of land resources from the local to the global level.

Thus, cities and counties would draw their funding from the ground rent of surface lands; regional authorities would collect the ground rent of oil and minerals, and global governing agencies would be funded by a percentage from these two levels as well as that of deep sea resources, the electromagnetic spectrum, satellite orbital zones, and other transnational resources.

Democratic rights to the planet can be vested in the people as a whole in a way that can be understood easily and administered practically. The advent of the information revolution combined with the personal computer enables such a system to be monitored by the masses. Who owns what, where, and how much ground rent they pay into the common fund could become the most enlightening computer game on earth.

A Warning and an Appeal

If we fail to tax land values for the common fund, the concentrated control of earth in the hands of the few will continue unmitigated, thus advancing the conditions of social turmoil which too often burst into flames of hatred, murder, and war.

Marx is in the morgue, and in the West there is a dawning realization that the huge bureaucracies of the welfare state, which confiscate the wages of the middle classes through the income tax in the attempt to provide a safety net (rather than a safe nest!) for the poor, are not only unwieldy but unworkable as well.

I am appealing to my brothers and sisters in the world order/planetary peace and justice movements to deeply consider the fundamental assumptions of the planet/people relationship as it concerns the entire question of land tenure. I trust that this consideration will discard both the power politics of *dominium* as well as the market construct of buying and selling our Mother Earth for private profit.

Currently, certain monetary and debt repayment policies and practices of the World Bank and the International Monetary Fund are strangling the economies and harming the people of many developing nations. This reality relates to the theme of this exposition in a major way.

A significant proportion of the "profit" that has poured into the global banking system in the past several decades was not a product of honest labor, but was in fact a pool of funds generated from the ground rent of oil resources. These funds were loaned to numerous developing countries where they were frequently of benefit to the ruling elite rather than the people as a whole. However, the debt repayments have now fallen upon the middle class and poor citizens who neither voted for nor gained from the borrowed money.

Morally and ethically, a vast amount of the funds of the International Monetary Fund and the World Bank represent a theft from the global commons. Under the common heritage principle, these funds would have been used to benefit the people of the world either by direct dividends or as interest free loans through a revolving loan fund type of system.

These "oil theft loans" made by the world financial institutions should therefore be declared illegal and invalid. In the future, any other money loaned to governments by global financial institutions should be repaid from the ground rent of the indebted nations. Such repayments would therefore fall primarily upon those who are unjustly reaping the benefits of valuable land holdings rather than further burdening the struggling wage earners, small business owners, and the oppressed poor.

Unless a reformed or empowered United Nations or other world government is built firmly upon the principle of equal rights for all to our planet, then both the government and the planet will be controlled by a handful of vested interests. It is up to the intellectual leadership of the world order movement to grapple with this issue NOW - to stop hedging and waiting for the messiah of world government to descend.

Before we purport to know the global governmental recipe for success, let us consider how to make one city succeed. What would it take for the wealth gap between rich and poor to begin to narrow each year instead of widening, for the murder rate to plummet rather than skyrocket, for the schools to become safer rather than scarier?

If the present political structure of democracy were sufficient for the task, then Washington, D.C. would be the New Jerusalem, Philadelphia would truly be a city of brotherly love, and every slice of the Big Apple would taste sweet.

To have peace on earth, we must work to create the conditions for peace in our own towns and cities. If we would revitalize our urban habitats by improving schools and libraries, creating livelihoods and affordable housing, and maintaining safe and beautiful parks and playgrounds, then we must urge our city council members to collect the ground rent of land to finance public services and greatly reduce or eliminate most other forms of taxation.

If the politics of the planet are to be based on fairness rather than on force, then equal rights to earth must become the guiding principle, the sovereign, supreme rule. The fundamental human right that now needs to be affirmed is this:

The Earth is the Birthright of All People

About the author: Alanna Hartzok co-chaired the Alternative Economic Commission at Conference on Global Governance sponsored by the Association of World Citizens and the Campaign for A More Democratic United Nations (CAMDUN).

Comments on "Financing Planet Management" included in the printed pamphlets follow:

World citizens must be concerned with the growing gap between rich and poor in the world and within democracies. Conventional economics has failed miserably. Alanna Hartzok's application of the common heritage principle to land and 'land value taxation' offers a refreshing new approach.
   - Ross Smyth, President, World Government Organization Coalition

Alanna Hartzok has recognized that the earth is the birthright of all peoples and that prevailing notions of state sovereignty must yield to the new thinking that the only real sovereigns are the people If we are all to live together in peace and dignity, it must become a reality that the land, the sea, and the air we breathe are a common heritage to serve the basic rights of human kind.

- Dr. Benjamin B. Ferencz, Prosecutor, Nuremburg War Crimes Trial, Adjunct Professor of International Law, Pace University

Alanna Hartzok has given us a fascinating account of the economic necessity of building democracy in human terms from the ground upwards. World governmentalists should start their re-think from here.

- Dr. Jeffrey J. Segal, Co-Founder, Campaign for a More Democratic United Nations

I enjoyed reading "Financing Planet Management" and found it to be a valuable contribution to the quest for world government on a democratic basis. We do need to have a politics based on fairness and with the earth as our birthright.

- Leland P. Stewart, Founder, Unity-In-Diversity Council

I'm very much in favor of the ideas proposed in your paper. I agree very much with you that world federalists and world governmentalists need to think through the fundamentals of economic justice.

- Jack Yost, United Nations NGO Representative, World Federalist Movement

Your paper is a cogent and convincing reply to the appeal for an economic engine to propel the 'democratic world order', 'global peace and justice', and 'environmentally sustainable development' movements. It is an evocative introduction to a crucial worldwide discussion by citizens locally and opinion-makers internationally and confirms your qualifications to serve as a coordinator for the Campaign for a More Democratic United Nations (CAMDUN).

- Dr. Harry H. Lerner, Co-Founder, CAMDUN

One thing that has troubled me about the world government concept is the fact that our continuing failure to be able to use power wisely at any local level, with which I am familiar, casts doubt on the possibility that we homosapiens would be able to do any better at the highest level.

Your essay correctly isolates land title as the modern day weapon-- the one which has so recently replaced the Auchelian 'almond-shaped hand axes' Louis S. B. Leakey found at Olduvia, and the even earlier thigh bones which seem to have bashed in so many skulls. Your essay is calculated to focus the attention of the world peace movement at a critical place.

- Representative Richard Noyes, New Hampshire State House of Representatives

Many organizations that advocate peace, human rights, or alleviation of poverty suggest temporary charitable measures or a future ideal solution to world problems, at once inadequate on one hand and frustrating on the other. Alanna Hartzok in *Financing Planet Management* makes a vital connection for creating world peace and order. In this concise but insightful narrative, the author has us realize the importance of providing a sound base from which democracy, justice, and equitable opportunity can proceed.

- Hal Sager, Media Producer, Trustee, Common Ground-USA

We are fond of citing history yet refuse to act in accordance with the lessons that are apparent. Past civilizations have collapsed and perished by their own making and by stubborn adherence to their profit and power paradigms. The unchecked depletion and destruction of natural resources and eco-systems, is an old story repeating again and again. In every case where there was the holding of land by the few out of the hands of most, the result was the horror of war or economic collapse.

The nation-state country clubs have not been able to rise from the muck of myopic views and economic illusions. Hartzok drops the veils through which we see economics and courageously calls for a gentle revolution in our relationship to the planet-one that is not only necessary, but also vital to our very survival.

- Mary Rose Kaczorowski, Action Coalition for Global Change, Ten Mile River Association

Hartzok has a firm, intuitive grasp of basic economic and political principles.

- Dr. Mason Gaffney, Professor of Economics, University of California, Riverside

Dr. Harry Lerner, President, Communications Coordination Committee for the United Nations and co-founder of CAMDUN – Campaign for a More Democratic United Nations.

Many Great Lawgivers and Economists Have Said Landed Property IS DIFFERENT!

Adam Smith – Ground rents are a species of revenue which the owner, in many cases, enjoys without care or attention of his own. Ground rents are, therefore, perhaps a species of revenue which can best bear to have a peculiar tax imposed upon them.

Thomas Jefferson – The earth is given as a common stock for men to labor and live on.

Tom Paine – Men did not make the earth... It is the value of the improvement only, and not the earth itself, that is individual property... Every proprietor owes to the community a ground rent for the land which he holds.

John Stuart Mill – Landlords grow richer in their sleep without working, risking, or economizing. The increase in the value of land, arising as it does from the efforts of an entire community, should belong to the community and not to the individual who might hold title.

Abraham Lincoln – The land, the earth God gave to man for his home, sustenance, and support, should never be the possession of any man, corporation, society, or unfriendly government, any more than the air or water, if as much. An individual, company, or enterprise should hold no more than is required for their home and sustenance. All that is not used should be held for the free use of every family to make homesteads, and to hold them as long as they are so occupied.

Leo Tolstoy – Solving the land question means the solving of all social questions. Possession of land by people who do not use it is immoral-just like the possession of slaves.

Henry George – Our primary social adjustment is a denial of justice. In allowing one man to own the land on which and from which other men must live, we have made them his bondsmen in a degree which increases as material progress goes on. It is this that turns the blessings of material progress into a curse.

Dr. Sun Yat-Sen - The [land tax] as the only means of supporting the government is an infinitely just, reasonable, and equitably distributed tax, and on it we will found a new system. The centuries of heavy and irregular taxation for the benefit of the Manchus have shown China the injustice of any other system of taxation.

The author signing the Earth Charter.

[1] Susan George, *How the Other Half Dies*, Penguin Books, 1976, p. 24
[2] Peter Meyer, "Land Rush-A Survey of America's Land - Who Owns It, Who Controls It, How Much Is Left", *Harpers*, January 1979
[3] Worldwatch Institute, October 1988
[4] World Peace News, November, 1993
[5] For more on the Alaska Permanent Fund go to www.apfc.org

11

Acting As If the Second Assembly Already Exists
Building the Second Assembly on the Firm Foundation of Fairly Sharing the Earth

First presented at a conference organized by Harry Lerner and Jeffrey Segall, co-founders of CAMDUN – Campaign for a More Democratic United Nations – this paper was included in the anthology *Building a More Democratic United Nations: Proceedings of the First International Conference on a More Democratic UN*, edited by Frank Barnaby, published by Frank Cass, 1991. The proposed Second Assembly would be an organ of the UN established to represent the world's citizens as members of civil society, linked with the UN General Assembly in which the governments represent citizens as subjects of the member states.

I am concerned about increasing the speed and effectiveness of our efforts to create a UN Second Assembly. The clearer an idea becomes, the sooner it can be realized. The sooner we arrive at a general agreement as to the form and structure of this new organization, the more quickly it can be assembled.

The suggestion has been made that the Second Assembly is to be a representative body of 500 people elected or in some way selected according to the population base of various regions of the world. Assuming general agreement to this plan, we have the keystone for a clear course of action.

I propose that we proceed along the following lines:

1. The 500 population regions need to be identified from which the 500 representatives will be drawn. The regional boundaries need to be delineated, at least approximately in the beginning.

2. Regional coordinators need to be identified, at least one per region, as quickly as possible. If there are several people wishing to play coordinating roles, no one should be discouraged. Everyone interested in the task should be encouraged to work together, cooperatively in this effort.

3. The leadership can be drawn from regional NGO bodies, from various service groups, or even local elected officials who have demonstrated a sincere concern for the betterment of world affairs. There is no need for a rigid or pre-determined method of selection at this time.

4. The task is not simply that of forming the Second Assembly, great as that is. In order to have enlightened leadership in the Second Assembly the job of regional coordinators and their work with local groups is proposed as follows:

    - Identify the points of person/planet pain in the region. In other words, where in the region are the places of greatest human suffering and environmental degradation?
    - Identify the reason(s) for the person/planet pain in the region.
    - Develop proposals for the solution of these problems.

In developing such plans, coordinators should adhere to the principle of subsidiary. The problem should be redressed at the lowest level of governance possible, starting with the local neighborhood or community, working up through town or township, city or county levels to the state or nation state. Second Assembly coordinators should, of course, give particular attention to those problems that can be solved primarily through global action.

This last point presents an interesting dilemma. At what moment in time can the reality of the Second Assembly be expected to have assumed sufficient power to be a force for healing on the planetary level? Must we wait for some sort of consensus agreement as to all the details concerning this new body? Until the General Assembly accepts the idea of the Second Assembly and makes it 'official'? Until it has its own system of finance?

Let us assume a much more existential approach to the process. Let us simply proceed with the above objectives, acting 'as if' the Second Assembly is already an official body.

I propose that in forthcoming international meetings on the subject of UN reform there be an enactment of the Second Assembly. Each region that can be represented will have a delegate and an alternate chosen from among the region's coordinators, if there is more than one coordinator in a region. An agenda will need to be compiled and the rules of order established. This enactment will proceed with discussion of items of significant concern and will make its decisions accordingly.

Methods of implementation of the proposals and resolutions arrived at by this Second Assembly enactment must be taken seriously. They should be sent as a press release to the media and announced as widely as possible throughout the globe.

Likewise acting seriously 'as if', coordinators/regional representatives will need to assume actual personal responsibility for the resolutions as far as they are able. I see no other way for the average person of good will to be prepared to assume greater leadership in global affairs than by actually practicing leadership in this way.

Other than the power to influence public opinion, as significant as that can be, the Second Assembly will have no greater reality until it can command material resources. In order to command material resources the Second Assembly must do exactly what all governing bodies must do to some extent – establish a system of finance. Revenue generation for the implementation of Second Assembly programs will be the single most important consideration in birthing the reality of the Second Assembly. The source of funds for such revenue generation is a matter of not small consequence.

Rather than further burden the labor of individuals through income taxes, tariffs, or taxes on productive capital, the Second Assembly should look to the 'common heritage fund' for its revenue. The principle behind the common heritage fund is that the land and natural resources of the earth and indeed the natural resources of the universe should be fairly shared by all. Territorial and natural resource disputes are most often at the root of war and conflict. Thus, the common heritage fund as a source of finance for Second Assembly programs will in itself be peace promoting. Other sources of financing will, conversely, impede the Second Assembly's efforts at global conflict resolution.

The common heritage fund as a source of finance for global governance has already been established to some extent by the United Nations. The Law of the Seas Conference determined that the UN should collect a considerable percentage of the value of minerals mined from the deep seas. The Moon Treaty has also been under consideration and is based on similar principles.

Agreement that the common heritage fund is the appropriate source of financing for global governance will become increasingly important as we advance through the next decades. The principle that natural resources should be fairly shared can be of enormous assistance in settling current conflicts as well as potential disputes over the use of outer space. For instance, how can there be fair access to the L5 zones? These are the points equidistant between the earth and the moon in which a satellite or space station can hang suspended and supported equally by the gravitational fields of both bodies. The common-heritage-fund principle would enable the establishment of lease fees for the use of these and other natural resources including the electromagnetic spectrum.

Common agreement as to this principle would be of enormous assistance in resolving the current crisis in the Middle East - a conflict primarily over oil and land. The common heritage fund can be applied to the generation of public revenue on regional and local levels as well, thus creating a kind of resonance among the levels from local to global. It has been suggested that the surface land rents or leases are the most equitable source of revenue for local governance and that subsurface mineral leases are appropriately left to regional levels.

The importance of connecting public finance policy with the problem of the inequitable control of our earth's resources cannot be overemphasized.

Susan George in *How the Other Half Dies* says that "The most pressing cause of the abject poverty which millions of people in this world endure is that a mere 2.5% of landowners with more than 100 hectares control nearly three quarters of all the land in the world - with the top 0.23% controlling over half."

How we hold the earth is how we hold each other. The needs of the person and the needs of the planet are one and the same. If this is true, as increasing numbers of us believe it to be, then building Second Assembly on the firm foundation of fairly sharing the earth will result in a great healing of both planet and people.

Members of the ecovillage development team in the town of Odi in the Niger Delta of Nigeria are taking initiatives for a sustainable green future of peace and plenty.

12

Land Value Taxation and Resource Rent Approach to Financing for Development

This policy paper was co-authored by Alanna Hartzok and Pat Aller and submitted by the International Union for Land Value Taxation to the United Nations Financing for Development Preparatory Process at the NGO Hearings, November 2000.

Public finance policy can be structured to enhance both private sector economic activity and public sector services. A fundamental reform in tax policy can optimize incentives for a productive market economy while also providing money for education, health care and other social services, as well as infrastructure. Such reform promotes a different kind of market system whereby wealth is fairly distributed and basic needs for all are met. Does this sound too good to be true?

We are accustomed to compromise and trade-offs, to sacrifice one goal for another. That a systemic reform can simultaneously promote economies that are both free AND fair may seem to be an impossible ideal. But a public finance perspective, variously known as land value taxation, green tax shifting, or resource rental offers such a reform. It is estimated that approximately 93% of taxes collected worldwide fall on labor and economic production. Removing the tax burden on all forms of labor and productive activity can greatly enhance private sector enterprise, especially small business.

Freed from taxation, workers get increased purchasing capacity and investors more funds to invest. Shifting taxation ONTO the economic base of land and natural resources has other positive consequences. Taxes would function as user fees for what are essentially common heritage resources. Investments in land speculation would be curbed, thus freeing funds for productive activities.

Taxing land sites according to land value promotes urban and rural land reform, providing affordable access to land for homes, businesses and farming. Sufficiently high resource rental fees, captured for public sector benefits, promote more careful and efficient use of natural resources by the private sector. Conversely, the undertaxation of natural resources leads to their over-exploitation. A high access cost for nonrenewable resources can also stimulate investment in renewable energy and other sustainable technologies, as less profit can be made on extracting irreplaceable resources.

Several UN bodies have recommended this approach or urged its consideration. The United Nations Centre for Human Settlements (Habitat) included it in
the 1996, as well as the 1976, declarations. The 1996 Habitat agenda states:

> The failure to adopt, at all levels, appropriate rural and urban land policies and land
> management practices remains a primary cause of inequity and poverty. It is also the
> cause of increased living costs, the occupation of hazard-prone land, environmental
> degradation and the increased vulnerability of urban and rural habitats, affecting all
> people, especially disadvantaged and vulnerable groups, people living in poverty and
> low-income people. [B.75]
>
> Apply transparent, comprehensive and equitable fiscal incentive mechanisms, as ap-
> propriate, to stimulate the efficient, accessible and environmentally sound use of land,
> and utilize land based and other forms of taxation in mobilizing financial resources for
> service provision by local authorities; [76(d)]
>
> Consider the adoption of innovative instruments that capture gains in land value
> and recover public investments. [76(h)]

The Food and Agriculture Organization's International Fund for Agricultural Development has a global consortium of intergovernmental and civil society organizations, The Popular Coalition, which urges governments to "establish land-tax systems, especially for underutilized land and land held for speculative purposes."

A paper distributed by the UN at the April 2000 prepcom of the Commission
for Social Development also urged a land value tax as the most immediately feasible way of coping with global poverty. The author of Department of Economic
and Social Affairs Discussion Paper 11, Professor Anthony Clunies-Ross, recommends "full exploitation of the possibilities of taxes precisely targeted on the site
value of land and the rents of other natural resources."

The International Union for Land Value Taxation and its 60 member organizations are working to implement these recommendations. The policy is to shift
taxes OFF labor and productive capital (thus increasing everyone's purchasing capacity and wealth creation incentives) and ONTO land and natural resources (thus
curbing speculation and private profiteering in the world's common heritage). Such
a tax shift makes land prices affordable for housing, other basic needs production
and infrastructure.

When we fail to tax land values adequately, as they rise during development,
and tax wages instead, workers soon cannot afford housing and other basic necessities unless they work longer or go deeper into mortgage debt. What should be the
true purpose of a market economy and development - to efficiently provide for the
needs of all - is undermined. Under the current model, which commodifies land
and resources, land prices become a greater proportion of the costs of production
as development proceeds. This primary cause of the widening rich/poor gap demonstrates the law of rent, a concept little understood even within the field of eco-

nomics. As private profits accumulate from resource rents and interest payments, the gap between rich and poor keeps growing year by year.

Most "poor" countries are not poor. Rather, their people are poor, because the countries' valuable land and other natural resources are controlled by only a few. Land value taxation promotes both urban and rural land reform. Land values rise because of population growth or concentration and because of infrastructure and other services provided by the public sector.

Reducing taxes on wages and productive capital while recapturing the increase in land values (resource rents) BACK to the public sector assures both a fair and functional market economy and a continuing source of tax funds for the public sector. The public fund can also be a source of low-interest loan financing to community members. Under this arrangement, the people themselves become beneficiaries of both resource rents and interest payments. The recapture of rises in land value and the revolving of loan monies all within the public sector enables countries to develop with less need for outside funds.

Examples of land value tax and resource rent approach to financing for development:

- Harrisburg, the capital of Pennsylvania, was in 1980 on the Federal list as the second most distressed city in the United States. The city gradually reformed its municipal tax policy by shifting taxes OFF of buildings and ONTO land site values. Now taxes on buildings have dropped and land is taxed five times more heavily. With land sites freed from speculation and underuse and buildings less burdened by taxes, labor and capital went to work restoring the city, now considered to be one of the highest quality of life cities in the US.

- Seventeen other municipalities in Pennsylvania have put this policy in place, all with proven benefits of economic regeneration as indicated by increased building permits and other criteria. This approach generates steady urban renewal in Sydney, Australia. Hong Kong and Singapore capture land rent primarily by nationalizing land and renting it out.

- There has been some experience with land value taxation in urban areas of nations of Eastern Africa. Some cities in the Republic of South Africa have had benefits from collecting a portion of land rent as revenue. The Land Resettlement Minister of Namibia is currently working to implement this approach. It is also under serious consideration by the Russian parliament, the Duma.

- The Alaska Permanent Fund is an excellent example of the use of resource rents to not only finance government but to provide an ongoing fund for both public investments and cash payments to citizens.

Under the Alaska Constitution, the natural resources of Alaska belong to the residents of Alaska and are to be used, developed and conserved for the maximum benefit of the people. In 1969 the state auctioned off the drilling rights on tracts of land at Prudhoe Bay. The original $900 million was spent to provide for basic community needs like water and sewer systems, schools, health, education and other social services. In 1976 the voters approved a constitutional amendment to establish the Alaska Permanent Fund, which required that a set percentage of wealth from state-owned mineral resources be preserved to benefit future generations of Alaskans. While the principle cannot be spent without a vote of the people, it must be invested to generate earnings.

By 1999 the Fund had a balance of $26.4 billion and investment earnings of $2.5 billion, more than double state oil revenue.

In the United States, the Fund is larger than any single endowment fund, private foundation or union pension trust. It would rank among the top 3 percent of the Fortune 500 companies in terms of net income. It is one of the largest lenders to the U.S. government. A large portion of these well-managed funds are paid out as citizen dividends to each man, woman and child who has resided in Alaska for at least one year. From 1982 through 1998 the dividend program paid out almost $7 billion to Alaskans through the annual distribution of per-capita dividend checks. Dividend payments this year 2000 are the highest ever - $2000 for each individual.

These public finance principles apply at the global level, too. The Commission on Global Governance recognized that global taxation is needed "to service the needs of the global neighborhood." Global taxes, based on the use each nation makes of global commons, could include: (1) taxes and charges on use of international resources such as ocean fishing, sea-bed mining, sea lanes, flight lanes, outer space, and the electro-magnetic spectrum; and (2) taxes and charges on activities that pollute and damage the global environment, or that cause hazards across or outside national boundaries, such as emissions of CO_2, oil spills, dumping wastes at sea, and other forms of marine and air pollution.

A Global Resource Agency, similar to the Alaska Permanent Fund, could collect global resource rents for distribution and investment. This would provide a stable source of finance for UN expenditures for peacekeeping, environmental preservation and restoration, and to finance justice institutions such as the World Court and the International Criminal Court. Some of the revenue might be distributed to all nations according to their populations, reflecting the right of every person in the world to a "global citizen's income" based on an equal share of the value of global resources.

A Global Resource Agency with this mandate would:

- Encourage sustainable development worldwide;
- Provide substantial financial transfers to developing countries by right and without strings, as payments by the rich countries for their disproportionate use of world resources;
- Help to liberate developing countries from their present dependence on aid, foreign loans and financial institutions which are dominated by the rich countries;
- Reduce the risk of another Third World debt crisis; and
- Recognize the shared status of all human beings as citizens of the world.

This land ethic and policy has potential to benefit all and has deep roots in the history of economic justice. A full Jubilee 2000 and beyond plan would not only reduce or eliminate debt, but would also promote systemic reforms in land tenure and taxation. This is the kind of "structural adjustment" the people of the world really need.

The Financing for Development process could further this tax shift approach by:

1. Worldwide education and information,
2. Encouragement of implementation on the local and national level, and
3. The creation of a body of experts to assist with the transition to this policy.

The International Union for Land Value Taxation and its 60 member organizations are ready to work in partnership with the Financing for Development process, UN agencies, member states and other development NGOs for the implementation of this fundamental tax shift.

Children from the village of Odi on the Nun River, Bayelsa State, Nigeria.

13

Local to Global Dimensions of Ecotaxation, Land Value Taxation and Citizen Dividends

This paper was presented at Sharing Our Common Heritage: Resource Taxes and Green Dividends, a symposium organized by James Robertson and the Oxford Centre for the Environment, Ethics and Society on May 14, 1998 at Rhodes House, Oxford University.

Private interests by and large pilfer common property. - Winona LaDuke

Concerned world citizens are wringing their hands because Rio Earth Summit objectives for sustainable development have fallen far short of the goals established in 1992. Frequently the United States and other industrialized countries are blamed for insufficient political will in committing finance resources to developing countries and to environmental repair programs. But with taxpayers in the 'developed' world on the verge of revolt, where is the money to come from?

We have arrived at a time of great struggle and opportunity to reconstitute democratic governance on the basis of a new vision and mandate concerning individual and common property rights to earth. Private property rights advocates and common property rights advocates will appear to be in numerous arenas of confrontation and conflict until the proper balance can be struck.

Ward Morehouse, a director of the program on Corporations, Law and Democracy, has put forth a call for broad based public debates on the theme of democracy and property rights. Morehouse has found interesting parallels[1] between the International Declaration on Individual and Common Rights to Earth propounded by the International Union for Land Value Taxation and Free Trade in 1949, and Native American environmental activist Winona LaDuke's call for a Common Property Constitutional Amendment. The amendment would affirm that there are resources that are common property and no individual interest has the right to destroy those common properties whether it is air, water, ocean, fish, or forest.

In a fall 1996 speech in Boulder, Colorado, LaDuke noted that while the Fifth Amendment protects private property by asserting the right not to have it taken or confiscated by the government, there is no corresponding preservation for common property under the Constitution. "The absence of that protection means that common property is by and large pilfered by private interests," she concludes.

The Economists' Statement on Climate Change with its attached monumental compilation of signatories (2,509 as of March 1, 1997) concludes that "The United States and other nations can most efficiently implement their climate policies through market mechanisms, such as carbon taxes or the auction of emissions permits. The revenues generated from such policies can effectively be used to reduce the deficit or to lower existing taxes."

This policy recommendation has relevance beyond the particulars of global climate change. It provides the beginning point for a broad based consensual framework for a set of principles and policies that can integrate common heritage protection goals with market economy incentives. The growing use of so-called 'ecological taxation' policies shows promise of a similar alignment of vision and values.

J. Andrew Hoerner of the Washington has compiled the most comprehensive listing of ecotaxation policies in the United States, D.C. based Center for a Sustainable Economy.[2] "Harnessing the Tax Code for Environmental Protection: A Survey of State Initiatives" identifies and categorizes 462 such provisions and provides a short description, the tax rate, base and a legal citation for each.

"Environmental tax measures in the states have been adopted in a haphazard and uncoordinated fashion," says Hoerner. "States have only scratched the fiscal, environmental, economic, and social goals. Given the chaotic status of environmental taxation, states have an opportunity to reap considerable benefits by simply adopting the best practices from other states."[3]

Making the polluter pay for the abuse of natural resources is just a short step away from making the user pay for what is taken from common heritage resources. Resource taxes work somewhat like a rental or interest payment for the use of assets that are owned by all of us, ranging from the broadcast spectrum to the air we breathe.

In the United States, the federal government owns and manages over 650 million acres of public land. These areas contain huge amounts of valuable natural resources that should not simply be given away or sold at low costs to private interests. In their 1997 book[4] *Tax Waste, Not Work*, associates of Redefining Progress delineated proposals for revenues from user fees for the following:

- Increase recreation fees to pay for park maintenance.
- Raise grazing fees on public lands.
- Rent or auction the broadcast spectrum.

- Impose higher user fees on the inland water system.
- Charging market rates for electricity sold by federal Power Marketing Administrations;
- Establishing charges for airport takeoff and landing slots to ensure that the scarce resource of public airspace is put to best use; and
- Charging more substantial royalties and holding fees for hardrock mining on federal lands.

Arising from ecotaxation approaches to environmental concerns is an emergent new perspective on public finance policy that has the potential for a clear synthesis of objectives that formerly appeared to be polarized. With big government approaches, conflicts over public funds from competing interests were exacerbated. Environmentalists often appeared to be anti-business and anti-labor, as these constituents experienced environmental regulations as added costs and burdens.

With ecotaxation based on the "polluter pays" principle, industry and individuals have an open range of choices to modify and adapt their behaviors to minimize the amount of tax paid. Human creativity can be brought to bear in any number of ways to solve environmental problems. With the payment of increased user fees for limited natural resources, resource users may very well discover ways to do more with less of these resources. With decreased private profits from natural resources, private finance could flow more readily into recycling operations and renewable resource technology development, yielding a win for both needed new environmentally sound private enterprises and the public at large.

Perhaps the greatest potential that ecotaxation has for synergizing various private sectors, social and environmental objectives is that rather than draining the public purse, this approach fills it. With the increase in public funds coming from ecotax dollars, corresponding cuts can be made in the taxation of both business and labor. Tax shifters ask, why not develop a socially useful tax system that would tax those things we need less of and untax those things of which society wants more?

One of the items that this brand of tax shifters agrees we need more of is purchasing capacity and economic equity for wage earners. In the U.S., tax shifters are now pointing their fingers at the payroll tax, which has been increased seven times since 1980 and is the greatest tax burden for most families. Although reform options now in the public dialog fail to account for these high taxes on labor, tax shifters say that if tax reformers are serious about helping working Americans and small business while enabling people to move from welfare to work, then the payroll tax must be addressed.[5]

Undoubtedly, the tax shift vision gives a powerful, coherent, rational underpinning and therefore a restored legitimacy to the field of public finance. Individuals should be able to keep more of the fruit of their efforts, but should pay for the costs that they impose on others. Since tax shifters also advocate drawing increased public revenue from resources already owned in common, all citizens could come to receive direct dividend payments similar to the Alaska Fund oil dividends (of $1000 and more) distributed each year to residents of that state.

Tax Pollution, Not Paychecks could be the next reform slogan for America's Northwest. The Seattle based Northwest Environment Watch (NEW) has put forth one of the most brilliant tax-shift proposals in a recently released book entitled *Tax Shift* by Alan Thein Durning and Yoram Bauman. Replacing most of the existing tax codes in the Northwest with taxes on pollution and other environmental ills would prevent hundreds of premature deaths, safeguard the environment and raise economic output by at least $5 billion, say the NEW researchers who have analyzed how a revenue-neutral environmental tax shift would affect the Northwest states and British Columbia.[6] The proposal would untax 'goods' such as paychecks and profits and tax 'bads' such as pollution, resource depletion, sprawl, and traffic jams.

NEW is frontrunner among the tax shift think tanks in the promotion of yet another form of tax shifting - a shift within the property tax itself. An important distinction not yet grasped by other tax shift proponents is that the traditional property tax is actually two conflicting taxes rolled into one; it is a tax on the value of buildings and a tax on the value of the land under the buildings. The NEW scenario shifts taxes off buildings to encourage upkeep, maintenance and quality housing stock and replaces this with a stronger tax on land values that encourages compact development and contains sprawl. The entire 27% of the property tax would be shifted onto land values only.

The NEW report concludes that their proposed tax shift for 1996 for the Pacific Northwest - British Columbia, Idaho, Oregon, and Washington - would have encompassed 84% of provincial, state and local revenue. It says:

> The tax shift would have eliminated almost two-thirds of existing taxes on retail sales and corporate and personal income. Pollution, hydropower, and land value taxes would have yielded the most revenue.

Perhaps the Northwest tax shifters will be looking to Pennsylvania for some guidelines on their proposed major property tax shift towards land value taxation. Sixteen cities in 'Penn's Woods' have opted for the so-called "split-rate" tax which enables localities to reduce taxes on buildings, thereby giving property owners the incentive to build and to maintain and improve their properties, while increasing taxes on land values, thus discouraging land speculation and encouraging infill development. This revenue neutral shifting of the tax burden promotes a more efficient use of urban infrastructure (such as roads and sewers), decreases the pressure towards urban sprawl, and assumes a broader spread of the benefits of development to the community as a whole.[7]

A recent study by University of Maryland economists, Wallace Oates and Robert Schwab,[8] compared average annual building permit values in Pittsburgh and 14 other eastern cities during the decade before and the decade after Pittsburgh greatly expanded its two-rate tax. Pittsburgh had a 70.4% increase in building permits while the 15 city average decreased by 14.4% of building permits issued.

The City of Harrisburg, considered the second most distressed in the U.S. fifteen years ago, has reversed nearly three decades of very serious previous decline. The number of vacant structures, over 4200 in 1982, is today less than 300. With a resident population of 53,000 nearly 5,000 more city residents are now employed. The crime rate has dropped 22.5% and the fire rate has dropped 51%.

Harrisburg Mayor Stephen Reed has stated that the shift towards the land value tax system is 'an important ingredient in our overall economic development activities...(and) continues to be one of the key local policies that has been factored into this initial economic success here.[9]

Mayor Anthony Spossey of the small city of Washington, Pennsylvania, population 15,000, likewise relates the many benefits of this form of tax shifting. He says, "The budget has really shown vast improvements.... We now have a capital improvements budget and have been able to do things we had not been able to do before."[10]

Recently in the Republic of South Africa municipal authorities in the newly formed Greater Cape Metropolitan Area made a major decision to move directly to land value taxation.[11] (Editor's note: There has been an unfortunate policy reversal since this article was written.) The Property Valuation Ordinance is being revised to allow for rating of land values only and to remove technical obstacles to revaluation of all metropolitan properties. Land value taxation currently plays an important role in the local tax base of other RSA cities as well. It is hoped that President Mandela may come to understand the importance of this policy approach so that it can be more broadly applied throughout South Africa and on the federal level as well. Although Mandela has stated his distrust of borrowing from international lenders, he has yet to fully comprehend the public finance and revenue generating potential of the land and resource base of his own country.

Land tenure and resource management systems, which had been established during the colonial era, were retained after countries in Latin America, Africa and Asia established democratic forms of government in mid-century.[12] They claimed vast amounts of formerly indigenous and native controlled forests, agricultural lands, minerals and water within their borders or permitted these resources to remain largely under the control of foreign powers. Under the guise of economic development, many began cashing in these natural resources at bargain basement prices, filling their own private coffers while the majority of their fellow citizens remained in conditions of abject poverty.

Meanwhile in the so-called developed world, the purchasing capacity of the family head of household gradually eroded to the point that two adults must now work full-time in the cash economy to provide for a family's basic living expenses. High land values have driven up housing costs.

Without access to raw materials and with declining purchasing capacity, individual workers, small business entrepreneurs, and entire governments have turned to pools of money available at high interest rates from local, national and international banking systems. But sound, secure, sustainable economies have not grown from such arrangements and the degradation of human and natural resources continues.

We are herein enunciating the guidelines for an integrated local-to-global public finance system based on the principle of the common heritage of earth's land and natural resources. It is through affirming the peoples rights to the value of earth's land and raw materials now controlled by the few that the many will be able to secure access to debt-free private property for homesites and sustainable, independent and fulfilling livelihoods.

The clarity of thought and integrity of values set forth in the tax shifting policy approach provides a compelling base for action for major tax reform on all levels. The goal is nothing short of a non-violent revolution required to free wage slaves and those now living in dire conditions of poverty and homelessness throughout the world. In order that the many may make a living, the few must stop making a killing.

Nearly all regions of the planet have sufficient land and natural resources and the human skills required to supply the basic necessities of all. As was clearly stated in the United Nations Habitat II Action Agenda endorsed by 183 nation state representatives in Istanbul in June of 1996:

> The failure to adopt, at all levels, appropriate rural and urban land policies and land management practices remains a primary cause of inequity and poverty. It is also the cause of increased living costs, the occupation of hazard-prone land, environmental degradation and the increased vulnerability of urban and rural habitats, affecting all people, especially disadvantaged and vulnerable groups, people living in poverty and low income people.

Reducing taxation on labor will increase purchasing capacity, lowering taxes on physical capital will lower the costs of life necessities, while charging for resource use via ecotaxation and land value taxation will yield the funding for investments in infrastructure, education, health and other public goods without the need to borrow from the elite controlled banking systems such as the International Monetary Fund and the World Bank.

The planet and all its resources, including land, water, forests, minerals, the atmosphere, electro-magnetic frequencies and satellite orbits are the common heritage of all and must no longer be appropriated for the private profit of the few to the exclusion of the many. As we place this fundamentally fair ethic within a fully established tax shift agenda, any person or group making use of more than their fair share of the earth's resources should pay full user fees for those resources to Common Heritage Funds, administered as a trust for all people, or to be distributed as direct citizen dividend payments from the local to the global level.

Worldwide ecotaxation can be based on principles of subsidiarity in terms of implementation. Clearly delineated collection authorities from the local to the global level can tax specific types of land resources. Towns and cities could draw their funding primarily from user fees for residential, commercial and industrial landsites; counties could focus on agricultural, pasture and forest land; regions and states might draw their funds primarily from water, mineral, and oil resources; global governing agencies established for purposes of peacekeeping and environmental restoration, protection, and monitoring could target fund collection from the electromagnetic spectrum, the sea, ocean mineral deposits, and geosynchronous orbital zones. Percentages of these resource rents could be channeled up and down the local-to-global range for flexibility and maximum fairness and efficiency. Citizen dividend payments from earth resource fees could be distributed at all levels.

The key to enacting such a fundamental and wide-ranging tax reform agenda is a critical mass mobilization of popular support. It would seem that the tax shift policy approach has the potential to unite the constituent necessary for significant political action. No doubt, this agenda will be carried forth in incremental stages as is in fact occurring now, with momentum building as positive, life-affirming benefits are realized from place to place.

Although the obstacles to creating a beneficent world order may at times appear insurmountable, energy and attention must be brought to focus on the required changes necessary to create a world that works for everyone. Proactive "Campaigns for the Earth"[13] in various forms and guises have already begun linking and enlisting citizens of the world in a great global effort for peace, justice and care of the earth.

I think it can be readily perceived that the call for common property rights by Winona LaDuke, for biodiversity covenants by Vandana Shiva and the goals of land rights and other social justice movements worldwide can be affirmed and furthered by the principles and policies of tax-shifting. Common property rights can be properly aligned with private property rights. Affirming the existence of common rights in land and natural resources creates a condition in society wherein individual economic interests can be advanced for all. The enigma of the misdistribution of wealth, which has for so long plagued market economies, thus can be redressed through the resultant broad-based sharing of the benefits of free market and private incentive systems.

Essentially, democratic governance can now be firmly established on the human right to the planet itself.

[1] From a March 9, 1998 email from Ward Morehouse to Alanna Hartzok.

[2] Andrew Hoerner, "Harnessing the Tax Code for Environmental Protection: A Survey of State Initiatives," available from Center for a Sustainable Economy, 1731 Connecticut Ave., NW, Suite 500, Washington, DC 20009.

[3] Ibid. p. 4.

[4] M. Jeff Hamond, *Tax Waste, Not Work: How Changing What We Tax Can Lead to a Stronger Economy and a Cleaner Environment*, includes writing by Stephen J. DeCanio, Peggy Duxbury, Alan H. Sanstad, Christopher H. Stinson with an introduction by Paul Krugman. April 1997, available from Redefining Progress, One Kearny St., 4th Fl., San Francisco, CA 94108 or email: <info@rprogress.org>.

[5] Ibid., p14.

[6] From "Tax Pollution, Not Paychecks, Would Help Economy, Environment, and Health," the Executive Summary from the book Tax Shift by Alan Durning and Yoram Bauman.

[7] Alanna Hartzok, "Pennsylvania's Success with Local Property Tax Reform: The Split Rate Tax," American Journal of Economics and Sociology, Vol. 56 No. 2, April, 1997.

[8] "Urban Land Taxation for the Economic Rejuvenation of Center Cities: The Pittsburgh Experience," by professors Wallace Oates and Robert Schwab of the Univ. of Maryland, 1992.

[9] From a letter from Mayor Stephen Reed of Harrisburg to Patrick Toomey, October 5, 1994.

[10] This statement is edited from a transcript of Mayor Anthony Spossey's presentation at the Tax Reform Forum held on May 2, 1997 at Shippensburg University, Shippensburg,, PA.

[11] Godfrey Dunkley, "Good news as Cape Town Chooses SVR," *Land & Liberty*, Winter 1997, p.11.

[12] David Malin Roodman, "Paying The Piper: Subsidies, Politics, and the Environment", Worldwatch Paper No133, December 1996, p.20 (from Worldwatch Institute, 1776 Massachusetts Ave., NW, Washington, DC20036, USA).

[13] For example, Foundation for the Earth, 2120 13th St., Boulder, CO 80302, USA or Global Awareness In Action, Inc., 14 Les Plateaux, Anse St-Jean, Quebec, Canada G0V 1J0 or Action Coalition for Global Change, 55 New Montgomery St., Suite 219, San Francisco, CA 94105 USA, email: <acgc@apc.org>.

14

The Alaska Permanent Fund: A Model of Resource Rents for Public Investment and Citizen Dividends

Published in the Spring 2002 issue of Geophilos, a publication of the Land Research Trust, this paper was also one of the five winning essays from "There Are Alternatives Project" of the McKeever Institute of Economic Policy Analysis. A shorter version was also published in Dialogues, a publication of the Canada West Foundation, fall 2005.

Summary: Wars are often fought over the ownership and control of land and natural resources. Inequitable ownership and wasteful, unsustainable use of the earth's resources are root causes of both the unjust wealth gap between the rich and the poor and the depletion and collapse of our natural resource base. This paper describes the form and function of the Alaska Permanent Fund as a model governmental institution for collection and distribution of natural resource rents, particularly oil, and makes suggestions for improvement of the Fund. It also presents an analysis of fundamental issues regarding natural resource and territorial claims and urges the establishment of a Global Resource Agency to collect and distribute transnational resource revenues.

If you were a third grade student in the state of Alaska, one day in school you would play a game called Jennifer's Dilemma. The game tells the story of a little girl who has discovered a box of valuable coins. Her dilemma is deciding what to do with an unexpectedly large amount of money. It is a way for young children to learn about their own yearly windfall fortunes from the Alaska Permanent Fund. In the year 2000, each one received a dividend check for nearly $2000. The Alaska Permanent Fund is a case study in a new concept of the role of government - that of agent to equitably distribute resource rents to the people, thereby securing democratic common heritage rights to land and natural resources.

Purchased from Russia in 1867, Alaska became the 49th state in 1959. Under the Alaska Constitution (Article VIII. Section 2. General Authority) all the natural resources of Alaska belong to the state to be used, developed and conserved for the maximum benefit of the people. Ten years after statehood the first Prudhoe Bay oil lease sale yielded $900 million from oil companies for the right to drill oil on 164 tracts of state-owned land. Compared to the 1968 total state budget of $112 million, this was a huge windfall. By legislative consensus, the original $900 million was spent to provide for basic community needs such as water and sewer systems, schools, airports, health and other social services.

Although the oil fields were proving to be the largest in North America, Alaskans came to agree that a portion of this wealth should be saved for the future when the oil runs out. In 1976 voters approved a constitutional amendment, proposed by Governor Jay Hammond and modified by the legislature, which stated that at least 25% of all mineral lease rentals, royalties, royalty sale proceeds, federal mineral revenue-sharing payments, and bonuses received by the State shall be placed in a permanent fund, the principal of which shall be used only for those income-producing investments specifically designated by law as eligible for permanent fund investments.

The Alaska Permanent Fund was thus established as a state institution with the task of responsibly administering and conserving oil and other resource royalties for the citizenry.

There are two parts to the Fund: principal and income. The principal is invested permanently and cannot be spent without a vote of the people. Fund income can be spent, decisions as to its use being made each year by the legislature and the Governor.

The Fund was established as an inviolate trust, meaning that the principal of the Fund is to be invested in perpetuity. The Fund thereby transforms non-renewable oil wealth into a renewable source of wealth for future generations of Alaskans.

Oil started flowing through the Trans-Alaska Pipeline in 1977, at the time the world's largest privately financed construction project. In February of that year, the Fund received its first deposit of dedicated oil revenue of $734,000. All income from the Permanent Fund was to be deposited in the state general fund unless otherwise provided by law. What to do with the earnings generated and how they would best benefit the present generation of Alaskans engaged Alaskans in debate for the two decades following the establishment of the Fund.

Like Jennifer with her box of coins, the dilemma was what to do with the growing income from the Fund. Would it best be saved for the future or managed as a development bank for Alaska's economy? After a four-year debate the Alaska State Legislature decided in 1980 in favor of a savings trust for the future. The Alaska Permanent Fund Corporation was created to manage the assets of the Fund.

The same year the Legislature also created the Permanent Fund Dividend Program, retroactive to January 1, 1979, to distribute a portion of the income of the Permanent Fund each year to eligible Alaskans as a dividend payment. By the end of 1982, after a couple years of wrangling with the U.S. Supreme Court over constitutional details, all residents of Alaska - every woman, man and child - who applied for and who were found eligible (must be at least one-year resident) received their first dividend which was $1000. This was the historic beginning of an annual program paying to Alaskan citizens a fair and equal share of the wealth from publicly owned resources.

In 1987 the Permanent Fund Dividend Division was created within the Department of Revenue to consolidate responsibilities for the administration and operation of the dividend program. Through the dividend distribution program, the Fund puts more new money into the state's economy than the total payroll of any industry in Alaska except the U.S. military, petroleum and the civilian federal government. Compared to the wages paid to Alaskans by basic industry, dividends make a greater contribution than the seafood industry, construction, tourism, timber, mining and agriculture. For a considerable percentage of Alaskans, the dividend adds more than 10 percent to the income of their family. This is particularly true in rural Alaska.

Those who received dividends each year from 1982 - 2000 have received a total of $18, 511. There were 582,105 citizens who received a total of $1,143,172,725 in dividends in the year 2000, which amounted to an individual dividend of $1963 per person. Overall, the dividend program has dispersed more than $10 billion into the Alaskan economy. The principle of the Fund was nearly $26 billion as of June 19, 2001.

There is strong citizen interest in the Fund's operation and investment activities. Earnings of the Fund undergo special public scrutiny since any expenditure of such earnings must be subject to the legislative appropriation process. Beautifully designed and printed literature is available which describes in detail the various components of the Fund. An Annual Report is distributed each year. Under the policy guidance of the Fund's six trustees and the executive director and staff selected to execute it, there has developed an extensive accountability program and open meetings with opportunity for citizen participation.

The Alaska Permanent Fund Corporation website (www.apfc.org) keeps current all investment and distribution activities of the Fund. The history of the development of the Fund, its incorporation, details concerning its management, along with up-to-date information on the Fund portfolio and dividend pay-out amounts can all be found on the website.

Also posted therein are lesson plans that can be downloaded for teachers to use in their classes such as Jennifer's Dilemma, other teaching stories, and puzzles and games to further education and interest in the Fund. From the website one can email any questions and receive a direct reply from a knowledgeable Fund trustee or employee.

The Alaska Permanent Fund is a well-managed, transparent and democratic institution. It is a remarkable pioneering model of a fair and effective way to secure common heritage wealth benefits for the people as a whole. While undoubtedly an institution worthy of replication worldwide, there are, however, aspects of the Fund that upon close examination reveal the beginnings of another dilemma.

Charlie's Challenge and the Prudent Investor Rule

Let's call this dilemma "Charlie's Challenge." Imagine now that Jennifer has given Uncle Charlie some of her valuable coins to invest in the best and safest way possible. Jennifer trusts Uncle Charlie to do a good job because he is an expert investor. Charlie invests in a diversified portfolio of stocks, bonds and other securities, including real estate. Having carefully explored potentially good deals for real estate investments in "the lower 48", Charlie selects several properties, including one in the City of Philadelphia. Philadelphia has low property taxes, state and federal monies pouring into the city and "free enterprise zones" so land values will surely be rising. Real estate in this city looks like a good investment for Jennifer.

However, unbeknownst to Charlie, there is a growing citizen's movement in Philadelphia that is set on capturing for the people of that city the equivalent of Alaska's oil wealth - the value accruing to a different type of valuable natural resource - the surface land sites of Philadelphia. Charlie's Challenge is this: when he becomes aware that the citizen's movement for land value taxation in Philadelphia will cut into profits for Jennifer's dividend investment fund, what will he do? Will he try to keep the resource rents of Philadelphia flowing into Jennifer's portfolio or might he decide to help the citizens of Philadelphia establish their claim to the resource rents of their own territory? Or will he simply withdraw funds from real estate investments that may not be so profitable once land values are recaptured by the city for the benefit of its citizenry?

Charlie's Challenge is quite literally the situation that is emerging for the Alaska Permanent Fund Corporation and its Board of Trustees. The Fund now owns investment property in the city of Philadelphia. There is indeed a growing citizen movement in that city to shift taxes onto the value of land sites, thereby recapturing resource rents as a common heritage right for the citizens of the territory of this municipality.

Keep in mind that the Fund is now so enormous ($26 billion) that it has the power to grab significant amounts of resource rents from anywhere on earth. Within established foundation guidelines of the "prudent investor rule" the Trustees' goal is to earn slightly better than average rates of return with slightly below-average levels of risk. In other words, the Fund is managed under normal investment procedures and criteria. And under normal investment rules, there are no established ethical criteria for socially responsible investing. In fact, the Fund makes a special point that it minimizes risk and within that constraint maximizes investment yield and does NOT engage in "social" or "political" investing.

In other words, mandated by law to secure the continued prosperity of the citizens of Alaska now and into the future, the Fund is in the position to make substantial profits from land and natural resources from people all over the world via Fund investments in real estate[1] and stocks, as profits from the latter also include substantial amounts of land and resource rent.

Thus the Fund faces this ethical challenge of global dimensions. Established to secure common heritage rights to rents and royalties from the oil and natural resources of Alaska for the citizens of Alaska, it is now beginning to extract resource rents from other territories. Unbeknownst to people elsewhere who have not secured their own rights to common heritage resources is the fact that Alaskan people are "stealing" their resource rents through perfectly legal, "responsible" and yes "prudent" investment mechanisms.

From this perspective, Charlie's Challenge is a dilemma of monumental proportions. As people all over the world begin to awaken to and indeed demand their rights to the rents of common heritage resources, investment portfolios will never again be the same. The Alaska Permanent Fund and all other public and private investment funds will have to look elsewhere to generate profits - maybe to investments in renewable energy technologies that could help ALL of us when the oil runs dry.

Viewed holistically, and as a fundamental paradigm shift in property rights ethics, the Alaska Permanent Fund opens yet other important dimensions of inquiry.

The state of Alaska receives federal money for substantial federal military installations. The military is established to protect the territory of the United States and this protection secures the rights to US land and resources for the people of the US as well as non-nationals who have legal title to American lands. The military, paid for by US citizens out of federal income taxes, is protecting Alaskan citizens' rights to the resource royalties they are now collecting through the Fund. Through providing protective services, all US citizens are contributing to the value of Alaska oil resources and thus to the dividends paid to Alaskans, but getting no value in return, as the federal government is not taxing Alaskan oil wealth.

Additionally, the Fund is now so large that it is a major source of loans to the US government via US savings bonds. So not only are US citizens from the other 49 states contributing through their tax dollars to the value of Alaska oil resources via military expenditures, they now have to pay interest on the federal debt to the Fund out of their own hard-earned income taxes. And where, one might ask, are the Alaska Permanent Fund equivalents for the other oil producing and mineral mining states? Many large corporations owning these oil and mineral lands sometimes pay no taxes whatsoever. They engage in other ventures such as agribusiness at a loss, write the loss off against their oil profits, and end up with no "profits" on the books to be taxed.

Resource Rights and Territorial Claims

Let us deepen our inquiry concerning property rights in land and natural resources as it relates to the Fund, checking in again with Jennifer and Uncle Charlie. What would Jennifer do if she met up with another claimant to her valuable coins? What if someone informed Jennifer that the box of coins was originally theirs, because they had found the box first, and had simply put it on the shelf where she had found it? Now they had returned and wanted it back.

Here we confront issues of the establishment of rights to territory by discovery and prior claim. Jennifer "discovered" the coins but someone else claims them as originally theirs. If Jennifer refuses to surrender her coins to the prior claimant, the situation could deteriorate to violence and bloodshed, mayhem and murder, or even a lawsuit. Uncle Charlie better supply Jennifer with some really big guns or funds for an extensive court battle. Claim could then be determined by force in the former or cunning in the latter.

There is a miasma of problems with trying to establish territorial rights by any of these methods, either discovery or prior claim, by military force or by current legal mechanisms. The persistent conflict in the Middle East comes readily to mind, as do indigenous land issues and the wounds of historic land grabs still festering throughout Latin America. Less well-known are the raw realities of the concentration in the ownership and control of land and resources in the United Kingdom, Scotland, and the United States, all first world countries where a few individuals or corporations own massive amounts of natural wealth.

And now back to Alaska with the really big question. Upon what basis is the exclusive claim of the people of Alaska to the oil resources of Alaska? Let us consider the history of this claim.

The state takes its name from the Eskimo word "Alakshak." The "prior claim" by original occupancy would appear to be exclusively that of the indigenous people. Russia claimed Alaska by right of discovery after it was sighted by Vitus Bering in 1741. Purchase was negotiated by the US government's Secretary of State William H. Seward who bought Alaska from Russia in 1867 for $7.2 million, about two cents an acre. Was the purchase by the United States and thus the transfer of rights to exclusive claim legitimate on the basis of Russia's prior claim by discovery?

World War II had a substantial impact on Alaska as the United States sent thousands of workers there to build defense installments and the Alaska Highway. In 1942 the Japanese occupied several Aleutian Islands, the only part of North America that was invaded during the war. "Might makes right" enables an exclusive claim to be secured and maintained and frequently is the origin of the claim itself. But does the ability to maintain a territorial boundary through military protection stand up as an appropriate basis for exclusive claim?

Is the exclusive claim of the people of Alaska to the oil resources of Alaska theirs by right of that state's constitutional law? Legally, yes, a legality that was put in place well after United States Federal and State Constitutional law was established for the "lower 48" states, and much later than the land of North America was grabbed by force of conquest from indigenous peoples. That a state constitution and a democratic vote of the people established a basis and a mechanism for equal rights to natural resources is a phenomenal and profoundly important human rights achievement and should be acknowledged as such.

Nonetheless we must question whether democratic process itself is a sufficient basis for an exclusive claim to natural resources by people residing in a particular territory. If that territory contains resources essential for the well-being of everyone else on earth, then the absolute control of that resource by the people of that territory, no matter how democratic the internal politics may be, would give those people undue and unjust power and control over the people of the rest of the world.

Thus we see that the basis upon which the citizens of Alaska stake their exclusive claim to the oil and natural resources of Alaska is a complex historical weaving of territorial claims by discovery, purchase, military might and democratic law. Interestingly, the land right due to occupancy or "prior claim," negated as a way to secure an exclusive claim of indigenous peoples to the territory by the several ensuing methods of claim by newcomers, finds its mirror in the Alaska Permanent Fund requirement that an individual must reside in Alaska for at least twelve months in order to qualify for the Fund dividend payments. Time-determined occupancy is certainly one way to stake a claim to the benefits of natural resources in a territory, reminiscent of earlier US homesteading approaches to land rights. But here again, we must ask if this is a sufficient ethical basis for an "exclusive" claim?

The essential question then is this: Is it fair and just to exclude people from everywhere else in the world from benefiting from the extremely valuable, nature created oil deposits of Alaska because of any of these territorial rights rules and negotiations? Are any of these methods of claiming territory more moral and ethical, more in alignment with truth and justice, than others? In other words, is there a moral and ethical hierarchy, if you will, of territorial claims, some being more "right" than others?

We must conclude that while some of these means to claim may be more just or fair than others, the exclusive claim of the people of Alaska to the oil royalties of Alaska cannot be made on the basis of either prior claim, discovery, purchase, ability to maintain and secure possession, constitutional law, or length of residency.

Ultimately, the only rational, supportable, moral, just and ethical basis upon which the citizens of Alaska can assert a claim to the oil resources of Alaska is by birthright to the gifts of nature. And that cannot be an exclusive claim. The claim by birthright can only be legitimate if it is acknowledged that all other human beings have an equal claim to land and natural resources. The deepest ethical dimension of territorial rights recognizes that humanity is one and indivisible in its fundamental claim to the earth as a birthright of all.

People from the rest of the world, with no oil in their territories, can only establish the right to oil by purchase or force. If they are dependent on oil to develop and advance their economies, but only are able to purchase and not profit from oil, then these people will remain in a subservient and mendicant relationship to the controllers and claimers of oil rich territories until the oil runs dry. By then the Alaska Permanent Fund will have an even larger investment portfolio by which to extract land and resource rents from people elsewhere. This is the fundamental moral and ethical contradiction of the Alaska Permanent Fund and its modus operandi as a "prudently" managed investment trust.

If the Fund trustees and the citizens of Alaska were to deeply consider this common heritage rights basis for their claim of oil royalties and the profit on Fund investments they would certainly come to realize the need for a broader, global, humanitarian role for the Fund - that of assisting people in other parts of the world to secure their own fair share rights to resource rents.

For instance, Africa now accounts for 14 percent of U.S. oil imports, a number that could grow to 25 percent by 2015.[2] Many African countries with oil wealth do not publish their oil revenue in the national budgets. These nations are rife with strife, civil war, corruption and poverty. Humanitarian organizations and many African citizens are calling for transparency and accountability in the management of oil funds and for the use of oil wealth for overall economic development. The Alaska Permanent Fund could play an important role by helping to establish similar funds in these nations.

Additionally, the Fund could develop a screen for its investments that would go beyond even currently established criteria for socially responsible investing. It could decide NOT to invest in land and resource securities and instead TO invest primarily in (1) the development of renewable energy technology; (2) strictly goods and services businesses and industries; and (3) in places and in ways that would support the emergence of forms of governance holding principles aligned with the primary task of the Fund, i.e., the collection of resource rents as a common heritage right for all people on an equal and democratic basis.

It would be a big step in the right direction if people all over the world awakened to their claim to the land and resources of the earth as a birthright and demanded that this right be written into their constitutions, as did the Alaskans. But based on nation state boundaries, this would be insufficient to secure justice in land rights worldwide. Nation states were formed in a number of ways, but primarily through force of conquest. Consequently, some nation states are large and well endowed with land and resources, while others are small or lack natural resources.

Furthermore, former colonial states now independent did not thereby automatically gain control of their resources for their own people.

Global Resource Agency

There is an urgent rational, ethical and democratic imperative for the creation of a Global Resource Agency that would function in some ways similar to, but much more extensively than, the Alaska Fund. The Global Resource Agency would be responsible for (1) monitoring the global commons (e.g., the ozone shield, global forest reserves, fish); (2) determining rules for access to transnational resources (like the oceans, electromagnetic spectrum and satellite orbital zones); (3) issuing use permits; and (4) collecting resource royalties and revenues.

The Global Resource Agency could also assume substantial authority for equitably distributing fees collected from common heritage resources worldwide as calculated by formulas based on population, development criteria and currency purchasing capacity. For example, a percentage of the oil rents from the Alaska Permanent Fund would be collected by the Global Resource Agency and either distributed directly to citizens in regions with no oil resources in a kind of dividend sharing program or made available as interest free loan funds for sustainable development projects in those areas.

The Global Resource Agency could fund institutions and activities needed for global environmental protection, justice, and peacekeeping, such as the World Court and the International Criminal Court. This would in turn contribute to a better and more secure quality of life for the citizens of Alaska and elsewhere who would pay a portion of their resource rents into the GRA. The principle that the earth is the birthright of all on an equal basis would also guide legal decisions made by the courts in determining just solutions to territorial disputes.

The emergence of such an institution is essential if we are to create a world that works for everyone. However it would take years for it to be accepted and created. In the meantime diverse existing United Nations agencies and other intergovernmental institutions and mechanisms could assume the responsibilities listed above. While some nation states which are strongly controlled by vested interests who profit from the current system might balk at the idea of a Global Resource Agency, others would offer their endorsement if it were truly capable of promoting stability and economic fair play for their people. Seed funding and technical assistance from the Alaska Permanent Fund could be provided to work together with these nations and worldwide networks of humanitarian nongovernmental organizations to establish and coordinate the various components, which would then be brought together to form the Global Resource Agency.

Some people might object to the idea of a Global Resource Agency out of fears that it would add another top-heavy level of bureaucracy to an already governmentally burdened world. But those advocating strengthened global governance ask us to imagine the shape of the emerging world as a pyramid with three basic levels: a small tier at the top for global institutions, a greatly slimmed down second band of national governments, and a vast sturdy base of local government, with a primary role of governance on each tier to collect and redistribute land and resource rents and royalties as common heritage funds for the benefit of all. Thus much of the resources raised, decisions made and benefits provided would be at the local level.

Conclusion

The object of the 4000-year-old oriental game of GO is to gain control of territory by capturing enemy stones on a board. You win by forming walls with your stones that surround more territory than do your opponent's stone walls. One of the oldest games known, GO is based on the concept that if you possess land or territory, you have an area to base life on. You then have liberty and freedom. Without land or territory, you do not have anything to base life on and are considered without life, or dead.

Chess, probably invented in India in ancient times, was widespread in Europe in the 16th century when the rules were definitively stabilized. A more directly confrontational and combative game than GO, chess exhibits the same theme of territorial conquest and control as a life or death affair. Both are games of metaphor that mirror real life militarized territorial goals.

Consider for a moment that for thousands of years and millions of hours trillions of brain cells have been trying to take, expand or hold territory in the face of the "enemy." We now live in an age when defining the "other" as "enemy" can lead to the annihilation of both. "Winning" by taking away the territory of the "other" now has a boomerang effect, as numerous intractable civil wars attest. Time, attention, energy and money devoted to securing or maintaining exclusive claim to particular territory now needs to be redirected to save the earth, all of humanity and other life forms from the current threat of overall ecosystem collapse.

The spirit of our age, with the image of the earth as seen from space emblazoned in our mindscape, insists that the circle now be drawn to include all, each and every one of us, as equal claimants to the whole earth itself. This quantum leap worldview can and surely will be the basis for profound changes in institutions of governance, economics and law. The right to the earth itself as a right by birth is the most fundamental human right of all. The Alaska Permanent Fund, based on the democratic constitutional equal right to natural resources, though not a perfect model, is nonetheless one of the most enlightened governmental "works in progress" at this time on earth.

[1] The Fund's real estate portfolio consisted of 63 separate investments with a market value of $2.5 billion as of June 30, 2000.

[2] "Oil for us; hope for them: U.S. trade with Africa should stress value of human rights" by Ian Gary, Philadelphia Inquirer, July 9, 2001

Note: Material for this paper taken from "An Alaskan's Guide to the Permanent Fund, 9th edition, annual reports of the Alaska Permanent Fund Corporation and Alaska Permanent Fund Dividend, and the Fund website, www.apfc.org.

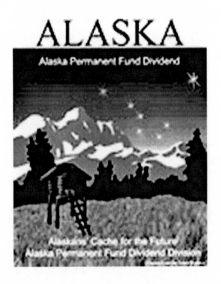

This image is from the website of the
Alaska Permanent Fund Dividend Division.

15

Citizen Dividends and Oil Resource Rents:
A Focus on Alaska, Norway and Nigeria

This paper was presented in the U.S. Basic Income Guarantee Network (USBIG) track of
the Eastern Economic Association 30th Annual Conference held
in Washington, D.C., February 20 – 22, 2004.

Summary: Citizens of Alaska have been receiving individual dividend checks from an oil rent trust fund since 1982. Norway's citizens receive substantial social services and invest oil rents in a permanent fund for the future. Nigeria has yet to establish a similar fund for its oil revenue stream. This paper explores the oil rent institutions of Alaska, Norway and Nigeria with a focus on these questions: Are citizen dividends from oil rent funds currently or potentially a source of substantial basic income? Are oil rent funds the best source for citizen dividends or should CDs be based on other types of resource rents?

The paper recommends full use of information and communication technologies for transparency in extractive resource industries, that resource rent from non-renewable resources should be invested in socially and environmentally responsible ways and primarily in the needed transition to renewable energy based economies, and that oil and other non-renewable resource rent funds should transition towards capturing substantial resource rents from surface land site values (ground rent) and other permanent and sustainable sources of rent for possible distribution of citizen dividends.

Alaska

The Alaska state constitution claims common heritage rights of ownership of oil and other minerals for the people of the state as a whole. Citizen dividend checks are distributed every year in Alaska out of the interest payments to an oil royalties deposit account called the Alaska Permanent Fund (APF) created in 1976 after oil was discovered on the North Slope. The APF is a public trust fund - a diversified stock, bond and real estate portfolio - into which are deposited the oil royalties received from the corporations which extract the oil from the lands of Alaska. The first citizen dividend check from the interest of the APF was issued in 1982 and was for $1000 per every person for everyone in Alaska who had resided in the state for at least one year. Annual citizen dividends have been issued every year since then, for a total of more than $23,000 per person.

In 2003, each of the nearly 600,000 Alaska US citizens (residents of Alaska for at least one year) received a check for $1,107 from the APF. The total amount dispersed was $663.2 million. The $25 billion investment fund's core experienced stock market losses that led to the dividend's decline this past year compared to the several previous years. The amount was $433 less, a 28 percent drop from the 2002 pay out of $1,540, and a 44 percent decrease from the all-time high of $1,964 in year 2000. The amount changes based on a five-year average of APF investment income derived from the bonds, stock dividends, real estate and other investments.

Alaska relies on oil for about 80 percent of its revenue and has no sales or income tax. Alaska state government is mandated to invest 25% of its oil revenue into the APF while the other 75% of oil royalty revenue is dispersed to other government funds to finance education, infrastructure and social services. If 100% of Alaska's oil royalties had been deposited into the APF, it is conceivable that the CD this year could have been about $4,400 or $17,600 for a family of four. But then there would have been no funds for roads, education and other public services and no funds available to run the state legislature - a libertarian dream fulfillment or a social and economic disaster, which one we will never know. If state services were to have been maintained while 100% of oil royalties were deposited in the APF, there would of course have been the need for income, sales and other taxes on wages and production.

At the end of the 2002 fiscal year, the state of Alaska had a deficit of nearly $400 million. State lawmakers frequently debate whether the APF should be used to help run state government, but the Fund is protected by law from being used for government expenditures. Rather than cutting into the Fund and citizen dividends, others are proposing an increase in oil rents and royalties from oil corporations.

On February 5th of this year of 2004, several Democratic Representatives filed legislation to help Alaskans recover a fairer share for their oil. That same week former Alaska Governors Jay Hammond and Wally Hickel stated that it is time to review the fairness of oil tax exemptions contained in a 1989 law known as "the ELF," or Economic Limit Factor. Their viewpoint is that ELF gives unjustified tax exemptions. The Alaska Fair Share bill would redress the Economic Limit Factor and meet the constitutional obligation to make sure Alaska's oil provides "the maximum benefit to the people" as mandated by the state constitution.

Because of the ELF statute tax breaks, Alaska's oil production tax rate has plummeted from 13.5% in 1993 to 7.5% today, and by 2013, it will be down to 4% if the law is not changed. Also because of ELF, 11 of the last 14 fields developed since 1989 pay none or almost none of Alaska's 15% Production Tax. While the state's share for Alaska oil has fallen, corporate oil profits have soared. BP and Conoco Phillips reported net earnings of $9 billion and $7 billion respectively last year. According to the Department of Revenue, at recent oil prices of $30 per barrel the annual share corporations receive for Alaska oil would exceed total state oil revenue by $1.2 billion.

The Alaska Fair Share bill establishes a modest minimum production tax of 5% and would raise an additional $400 million in revenue this year. That approximates the current state budget gap. The bill raises more at higher prices per barrel, and an additional $100 million at average prices, according to the Department. The bill also lets the state share in profits above $20 per barrel by slowly increasing the severance tax above that price. To encourage development, the Alaska Fair Share bill reduces the severance tax rate at low prices, when companies face the prospect of reduced profits, and possible investment losses.

Passage of the bill would alleviate state government expense shortfalls, and would possibly result in higher citizen dividend payments, as more funds would be deposited into the APF. We cannot predict this for certain, however, as the CD's come from the investment portfolio interest, are averaged over a five-year investment period, and determined by the portfolio performance.

We do know that due in large part to the citizen dividend payments combined with the happy consequences of no state income or sales taxes, Alaska is the only state in the United States where the wealth gap has decreased in the past decade. The citizen dividends from the APF are an important and significant source of income, especially for rural families maintaining more land based subsistence lifestyles.

Norway

Norway, one of the world's richest economies, is a model of prudent economic management of resource wealth. So states the IMF 2000 Article IV consultation with Norway. Norway is the top non-OPEC oil exporter, the world's third-largest exporter of oil, and pumps about 3.2 million barrels per day. Norway's oil and gas industry underpins the economy, providing up to 25% of the country's gross domestic product. This country of nearly four and one half million people has a steady growth rate, almost no poverty, and negligible unemployment. Norway has a diverse economy based on agriculture, forestry, fishing and manufacturing, among other things, and its oil industry has developed amid much planning, bargaining, and public debate.

The most recent U.N. Human Development Report ranks Norway the number one place in the world to live, based on a cocktail of indicators about health, wealth and social outlook. Nearly 1% of GDP is spent each year to fight global poverty and enhance peace. Oslo often plays a mediating role in foreign conflicts, from efforts to reconcile North and South Korea to the now foundering Middle East peace process. Norway has created an economy that retained its progressive tax structure, re-invested its oil profits throughout the economy, and saved money to cushion future market shocks.

Norway struck oil in the North Sea in the 1960s. Norwegians' best defense against the decline of the industry that has made it the world's fourth-wealthiest country is the State Petroleum Fund, which is managed by the national Norges Bank. Parliament created the oil fund in 1990, but the state had its first budget surplus only in 1995. Until then, oil income was used to pay down Norway's staggering foreign debt from the tough years before North Sea riches could be exploited. A substantial amount of the profits from the exploitation of a resource that is viewed as belonging to all Norwegians, not just the current generation, is invested in foreign stocks and bonds. The state-owned fund guards against spending too freely on public sector services in boom years so as not to lay off droves of state workers when the economy goes bust.

The Petroleum Fund is an instrument designed to prevent Norway's substantial oil profits from being taken too rapidly into the economy. State bank officials and government leaders believe that dispersing oil revenues directly would overheat the Norwegian economy and suppress private sector growth. Their view is that the resource rent collected from the sale of their natural wealth of oil should be conserved.

Norway has extracted only about 30% of its known oil resources in the three decades and reserves are expected to last 40 more years. But the oil that's left is mostly in depths, distances and quantities that make its extraction less likely to produce profits of the magnitude to which the country has become accustomed.

From the perspective of some, Norway focuses more on how to administer and distribute the assets already acquired than on how new value is to be created. There are generous benefits for both men and women of eight weeks' vacation, liberal sick leave and day care that is reliable and inexpensive. Three-year maternity leaves, broad part-time opportunities and creative application of telecommuting help keep women in the work force. State assistance to single mothers is so generous that there is no need for a father's income.

Norway's State Petroleum Fund is now worth about $60 billion. Many of Norway's citizens fail to see why they should pay some of Europe's highest tax rates when Norway's crude output is worth about $7,000 a year for each citizen, about one fourth of per capita GDP of $28,433. If the $60 billion is invested for a rate of return of 10%, then each Norwegian citizen could receive $1333 as an annual CD. The state's priority instead is to conserve and build the Fund and funnel fund revenue into social benefits.

Nigeria

Two thousand years ago, Pliny the Elder wrote that the two greatest curses of civilization were the discovery of silver and gold. Perhaps oil and gas should be added to the list of natural wealth that ends up damaging more then helping people in many parts of the world that are rich in subsoil resources. This has certainly been the case in Nigeria.

There have been 28 wars waged in Africa in the past three years over the control of mineral resources, many of them in West Africa. Conflicts in Nigeria have been ongoing since oil was first discovered four decades ago. Nigeria is Africa's most populous nation home to more than 130 million people, or one-sixth of the population of the African continent. The giant of West Africa, Nigeria has half the area's population and one of its most highly educated workforces. Nigeria is the fifth-largest supplier of oil to the United States. The Bush administration has recognized African oil as a key US strategic interest as the country seeks more stable sources of petroleum outside the turbulent Middle East.

Nigeria is potentially Africa's richest country. As the world's sixth largest producer of crude oil, with huge reserves of mineral and agricultural riches and manpower, it should be enjoying some of the highest global living standards. But it has some of the lowest living standards in Africa. Surveys conducted by Nigeria's Federal Office of Statistics show that in a 16-year period between 1980 and 1996, Nigeria's poverty level rose from 28 to 66 percent. GDP per person in 1982 was $860, in 1996 it as $280, and now reported to be $290. Numerically, while 17.7 million people lived in poverty in 1980, the population living on less than US $1.40 a day rose to 67.1 million by 1996.

Northern and southern Nigeria are essentially two different countries. Some view the oil-producing region of the Niger Delta in the south as a sort of internal colony of Nigeria. Home to 15 million impoverished people, the Niger Delta region produces 90 percent of Nigeria's wealth. Under the swamps and mangroves of one of the world's richest ecosystems lie vast reserves - an estimated 40 more years of crude and a century of natural gas. The first oil was produced here in 1956. After 40 years of production, there are rutted roads, decrepit schools, few health clinics, and no conduits for running water, and polluted creeks and farmlands. There have been dozens of oil spills and gas flares spew carbon dioxide 24 hours a day. The Niger Delta is one of this country's poorest regions, despite its oil wealth. Most people are struggling to survive on less than $1 a day. Away from the main towns there is no real development, no roads, no electricity, no running water and no telephones.

Most of the oil that has earned Nigeria close to US$340 billion since production began over four decades ago has come from the Niger Delta onshore sites. Some put the number at $300 billion with about $50 billion 'disappeared overseas' meaning stolen by corrupt officials. Shell and other western oil companies extract oil worth an estimated $150 billion a year in recent years from the area. A rough estimate is that Nigeria earns some $10 billion every year from oil.

Based on Nigeria's 1988 population of 100 million, if Nigeria had distributed the entire $340 billion it has received in oil exploration up until year 2000, over a forty-year period, the citizen dividend per person per year would have been about $85. Based on the figure of $10 billion that Nigeria earns every year from oil and a current population of 130 million, distributing the full amount as citizen dividends would yield about $77 per year per person. Based on oil extraction worth of $150 billion a year from the area, and a resource rent of 10% (or $15 billion) charged by the Nigerian government, the annual citizen dividend would be about $115 per person per year.

As noted earlier, GDP per person in 1982 was $860; in 1996 it had fallen to $280. Based on the current GDP of $290, adding the $115 dividend would bring the income per person per year to $405. For a family of four, that would be $1620 per year with the dividend ($1160 without the dividend). Based on the GDP per person in 1982, a family of four would have earned $3440. That same family in 1982 with the dividend of $85 added would have had $3780. While a citizen's dividend in Nigeria would mean a significant increase in annual income, one must note the vastly more substantial decrease in GDP from 1982 up until this time.

After the discovery of oil and with the high exchange rate of US petrodollars compared to Nigerian nairas, palm oil, groundnuts and other previous export products of Nigeria were for the most part eliminated. Nigeria's economy had been mostly subsistence agriculture and fishing, and with the collapse of their few export commodities, the economy took a nosedive for most Nigerians.

What has become of Nigeria's oil wealth? Transparency International's Corruption Perception Index rated Nigeria as the world's most corrupt country (out of 52). Much has been made of the fact that money generated from Africa's oil reserves has been lost in corruption, mismanagement and violent conflict. In Nigeria, an estimated $4 billion in government funds was stolen by the dictatorship of General Sani Abacha in the 1990s. Some estimate that as much as $50 billion in oil revenue has been stolen since Nigeria first began production.

Faced with severe balance of payments problems in the mid 1980s, the then military ruler, General Ibrahim Babangida, adopted International Monetary Fund and World Bank advised structural adjustment programs. The key objective was to ensure that Nigeria serviced its external debt of US $28 billion and maintained macro-economic stability, while cutting back on social spending. Starved of funds, social service institutions began to decay and service delivery in schools and hospitals sharply declined. The World Bank estimates that public spending per capita on health is less than $5 and as low as $2 in some parts of Nigeria, contrary to $34 recommended for low-income countries by the World Health Organization. Infrastructure and utilities began to collapse.

Comparing the $4 billion stolen by Abacha to the $28 billion in external debt that Nigeria was forced to pay by the IMF/WB advised structural adjustment programs, it seems that a case could be made that the greater crime can be found in the neoliberal economic system. As has happened to many other third world resource rich countries, government leaders were urged to use the oil and mineral wealth royalty payments to secure loans for their countries and to buy military equipment and other foreign made commodities. Then the accumulated debt was called in on the backs of the people as a whole.

The IMF and WB could have insisted that a transparent oil rent fund similar to the Alaska Permanent Fund be established as a condition for loans. The fact that the international banking institutions did not act in a responsible manner by promoting transparent public finance institutions and socially just structural adjustments programs but instead put countries into odious debt lends credence to the position that these institutions were established to maintain the predominance of the US dollar as the major global currency over and above any humanitarian or even good governance objectives.

What might happen to the people of Nigeria in the years ahead? President Obasanjo and his administration intend to increase Nigeria's oil reserves to 50 billion barrels by 2010 and to raise its production capacity to five million barrels per day by 2010. Confirmed offshore oil deposits have increased from about 30 percent of the country's total reserves in 1997 to about 50 percent today. As Nigeria moves closer to the reserves and production targets set by Obasanjo, this percentage is likely to increase to more than 70 percent. Since oil production for Nigeria is set to move increasingly offshore of the Niger Delta, people in the region are concerned that they will be left behind once again with no share of the federally controlled oil wealth. Nigerians would be wise to revamp and diversify their economy sooner rather than later.

Given the extent of the corruption, violence, destruction and environmental devastation, perhaps the people of the Niger Delta should make a hard push for the federal government and the oil companies to repair and restore their land and water and then look forward to a new day of sustainable development based on renewable sources of energy and their own capacity for self-directed development. Any oil resource rents that they can draw down from the federal government or finagle directly from the oil companies might better be directed towards capping and tapping the dozens of natural gas flares to provide an energy source for the region that will help it transition to renewable energy of wind, solar, and microhydropower.

Additionally, transparent, interest free (perhaps a 2% management fee only) revolving loan funds for ecovillage and sustainable development projects could be established with the oil revenue, either managed on the federal level or via separately mandated funds on the state level. Thus the oil revenue would be used for internal development projects, not invested externally as is the case with the Alaska and Norwegian permanent funds. As these projects proceed, and the economy gently expands, land values will rise and these funds could then transition towards a surface land rent and distribution fund. A portion of these funds could then be distributed as citizen dividends.

Let us note here that land based taxes and land value recapture policies are recommended in the 1996 Action Agenda of the UN Center for Human Settlements, a document agreed to by all UN member states. The approach was also strongly promoted by ecological economist Herman Daly of the University of Maryland in a very important speech that he gave to the World Bank on April 30, 2002. Although Professor Sala-i-Martin at Columbia University recently wrote a paper advising the World Bank to help establish a fund in Nigeria similar to the Alaska Permanent Fund, those of us who have been advocating for a Niger Delta Fund are now thinking that a sustainable development focus would be better than using the oil revenue for citizen dividends in terms of overall wealth creation for the region.

Nigeria newspapers earlier this week gave us some positive and hopeful stories. President Olusegun Obasanjo has fully endorsed the Extractive Industries Transparency Initiative (EITI) and has inaugurated the National Stakeholders Working Group, a 28-person team that will work to publish all payments made by and to its multi-billion dollar oil industry. Obsanjo wants to hold to account the Nigerian National Petroleum Corporation and its international partners, including Chevron Texaco and ExxonMobil, the Anglo-Dutch major Shell and France's Total.

President Obasanjo also said that whatever resources the country gets from extractive industries should be invested in 'renewable and non-depleting aspects of our national economy. What we should, of course, not do is, advertently or inadvertently, waste these resources because...they are not renewable.' He further stated that 'apart from being non-renewable, I have said on a number of occasions that what God has put in the soil for Nigerians are put in the soil for past, present and future Nigerians... therefore, those of us who are managing it must manage it for all Nigerians - past, present and future. And we cannot do that unless we are transparent...''

Other good news out of Nigeria this past week is that Obasanjo signed into law the Allocation of Revenue Act 2004 which abolishes the dichotomy between onshore and offshore oil production in respect of the principle of derivation for the purposes of allocation of oil revenue accruing to the Federation. This announcement was received with jubilation in the Niger Delta states where state officials described it as a victory for the 'down-trodden people of the Niger Delta.'

All of this is also very good news for those of us working to secure resource rents for the people worldwide and to underpin our political democracies with earth rights democracy ethics and policies.

As the world turns, in a case being investigated by the US Justice Department and the FBI, it is alleged that Halliburton paid over $100 million to bribe Nigerian oil ministry officials and $200 million to bribe government officials surrounding the award of the Nigeria Liquefied Natural Gas project between 1995 - 2002. A Halliburton spokesperson said the company has handed over documents to the Justice Department but insisted that the company did no wrong. She said that Halliburton always maintains the highest ethical business standards.

Climate Change and Other Environmental Considerations

Some environmentalists raise the concern that citizen dividends and social services based on petroleum and other nonrenewable resources rents makes it that much more difficult to shift to renewable sources of energy. Alaskan representatives frequently have voted to open up the Alaska National Wildlife Refuge and other areas for more oil drilling. This writer's first response to this concern is that if citizens do not get a rightful share of these resource rents, then corporations will capture even greater amounts of surplus profits. While this is true, we need to look at the issue in a holistic way.

From the vantage point of a planetary civilization, we clearly need to shift to renewable energy sources. There is clear and compelling scientific evidence of global warming. Climate change is one of the most pressing environmental problems of our time. Carbon dioxide and other gases released by fossil fuel consumption and deforestation is trapping heat in our atmosphere for 100 years or longer, with devastating environmental consequence. It is time to go full throttle in addressing this enormous challenge.

We need to use oil resource rents to shift to renewable energy and sustainable economies. Both the Alaskan and Norwegian petroleum funds invest in stocks, bonds and real estate. Interest from these investments is distributed as citizen dividends in Alaska and for social services Norway. The priorities of the fund portfolios need to be scrutinized and revamped. Currently the investment portfolios are mandated to follow the 'prudent investor rule' meaning that managers must find the balance point between highest profits and lowest risks. Fund investments are not based on or screened for socially and/or environmentally responsible criteria.

Furthermore, those of us working for a full range of resource rents as the basis for earth rights democracy view oil rent fund investment in real estate worldwide as an expropriation of surface land resource rents from other nations and thus are not a just source of interest income for the citizens of oil rent fund countries like Alaska and Norway.

The Alaskan and Norwegian funds, and the Nigerian fund if it is established, need to have socially and environmentally responsible criteria. Investments should be made in renewable energy - wind, solar, green hydrogen, and microhydropower - and in reforestation and other environmental restoration activities. A portion of the funds should be made available as interest free (suggested 2% - 3% management fee) revolving loan funds to people in developing nations to help finance their efforts for sustainable development.

A criterion of the loans should be that the communities receiving the loans begin implementing surface land value (ground rent) recapture in their towns, regions and nations. Land value based resource rent funds, if full ground rent is collected for the people as a whole, promotes land reform and affordable land access for current and future generations in addition to generating funds for public benefits and citizen dividends.

In the US about one half of corporate profits comes from real estate related activities so we know that resource rents from surface lands could be a substantial source of funds for basic income and citizen dividends. In addition to land sites, rents from the electromagnetic spectrum, water power points and satellite orbital zones should be sourced for citizen dividends in the future.

Key Recommendations

In concluding this consideration of oil resource rents as a basis for citizen dividends and basic income payments, here are three key recommendations:

(1) Full use should be made of information and communication technologies for total transparency in revenue raising and expenditure on the part of both government and extractive resource industries, as modeled by the Alaska Permanent Fund and promoted by the Extractive Industries Transparency Initiative.
(2) Resource rent from non-renewable resources should be invested in socially and environmentally responsible ways and primarily in the needed transition to renewable energy based economies.
(3) Oil and other non-renewable resource rent funds should themselves transition towards capturing substantial resource rents from surface land site values (ground rent) and other permanent and sustainable sources of rent, such as hydropower points, electromagnetic spectrum and satellite orbital zones.

REFERENCES

ALASKA:

Alaska Permanent Fund Corporation: http://www.apfc.org/
"Alaska economy taps into oil wealth" by Mary Pemberton, AP, 10/8/2003.
www.boston.com/news/nation/articles/2003/10/08/alaska_economy_taps_into_oil_wealth?mode=PF
"The Alaska Permanent Fund: A Model of Resource Rents for Public Investment and Citizen Dividends" by Alanna Hartzok, published in *Geophilos*, Spring 2002.
"Permanent Fund Dividend No Government Handout" by Representative Harry Crawford www.crawford.akdemocrats.org
"Democrats, Former State Revenue Official, Call for End To Unjustified Oil Tax Breaks" 2/5/04.
www.akdemocrats.org/Documents/020504_End_Oil_Tax_Breaks.pdf

NORWAY:

"Norway looking beyond the oil boom," Department of Energy at Newspage 26-02-00.
www.gasandoil.com/goc/news/nte01744.htm
"Further Regulatory Reforms Would Safeguard Norway's Prosperity"
Directorate for Public Governance and Territorial Development, 02/06/02M
www.oecd.org/document/59/0,2340,en_2649_33735_2514299_1_1_1_1,00.html
"Norway's Labor party aims stay on" by Alister Doyle posted 9/11/01.
www.japantoday.com/gidx/news75407.html
"IMF Concludes Article IV Consultation with Norway"
www.imf.org/external/np/sec/pn/2001/pn0110.htm
"So, This Is Heaven: Norway" by Carol J. Williams, TIMES Staff Writer 11/08/01.
www.oecdwash.org/PUBS/BOOKS/RP034/rp034cp.htm

NIGERIA:

"Oil just clogs the works" by David McWilliams, 3/30/03.
archives.tcm.ie/businesspost/2003/03/30/story651105249.asp
"Nigeria's oil wealth shuns the needy" by the BBC's James Whittington, 12/28/01.
www.news.bbc.co.uk/1/hi/business/1732196.stm
"Obasanjo fiddles while Nigeria's oil wealth burns"
www.afrol.com/News2002/ca001_oil_bishops.htm
"Nigeria And Her Oil Wealth" by Reno Omokri LLB, BL, LLM
www.gamji.com/amviews207.htm
"NIGERIA: IRIN Focus on shift towards offshore oil production"
UN Office for the Coordination of Humanitarian Affairs (OCHA)
Integrated Regional Information Network (IRIN) LAGOS, 4 July 2002.
"NIGERIA: Focus on the scourge of poverty," LAGOS, 11 June 2002.
"NIGERIA: Focus on dispute over offshore oil resources," LAGOS, 9 May 2002.
www.irinnews.org/report.asp?ReportID=28258
"Nigeria's Delta Problem" by C. Payne Luca, October 1999.
www.africare.org/news/editorials/nigeria-delta.html

"Africa: U.S. Interest in Oil Wealth," uploaded 01 June 2003.
www.usafricaonline.com/nigeriaoil.chevrontexaco.html
"Haliburton says 'we're not alone'" by Akanimo Sampson, Bureau Chief, Port Harcourt,
Daily Independent Online, February 17, 2004.
"In Nigeria's Oil Patch, an Unsung Ethnic Voice" by Lara Santoro, August 13, 1998.
www.csmonitor.com/durable/1998/08/13/fp5s1-csm.htm
"Alienation and Militancy in the Niger Delta: A Response to CSIS on Petroleum, Politics,
and Democracy in Nigeria" by Oronto Douglas, Von Kemedi, Ike Okonta, and Michael
Watts, *Foreign Policy In Focus*, July 2003, www.fpif.org/papers/nigeria2003.html
"Obasanjo Wants Transparency Acted, Inaugurates Group" by Josephine Lohor in Abuja.
This Day News, February 17, 2004.
"Obasanjo signs onshore-offshore bill" by Sam Akpe in Abuja, *The Punch*, February 18, 2004.

VARIOUS:

"Managing Oil Wealth" by Benn Eifert, Alan Gelb, and Nils Borje Tallroth, a quarterly
magazine of the IMF, March 2003, Volume 40, Number 1.
www.imf.org/external/pubs/ft/fandd/2003/03/eife.htm
"Norway, Alaska considered as models for Iraqi oil industry" by Marego Athans, KRT
Business News webposted June 10, 2003.
www.oilandgasreporter.com/stories/061003/ind_20030610005.shtml

Gordon Abiama, standing in the above photo, promotes the establishment of a Bayelsa State Oil
Fund that would collect oil resource rent for the benefit of the people of the second largest oil producing state in Nigeria. They are now mired in poverty and pollution of their land and water.

16

Women, Earth and Economic Power

Published in Geodata, Winter 1982.

I do not locate the process of women acquiring land rights in each
woman's isolated struggle within the family, but in a collective struggle
that seeks to build support across multiple tiers of society.
- Bina Agarwal, author, *A Field of One's Own*

Women once enjoyed a special relationship to the land when nomadic tribes shifted to an agricultural way of life. Plants and children were gifts from the gods and woman was the medium for both. Women seemed to have the ability to summon ancestral spirits into her body, and cause fruits and grain to spring from planted fields. In a mystical sense, the earth belonged to the women and they had a religious and legal hold on the land and its fruits.

The human worldview has since moved from an awareness of the interconnectedness of all through the female to the individuality and separateness of individual beings, which is the emphasis of the male principle. The male qualities of force, strength, drive, and individual self-determination led us out of the state of unity with nature that had come to have its own limiting delusions and superstitions.

Land no longer was held in common under the care of the women, but could be acquired by male conquest. Individual landholdings were justified under the Roman law concept of dominium, which gave absolute power to the title-holder to control, use, and abuse.

As women's role in procreation was demystified, so were our ties to the earth cut. Under Roman law women were not generally allowed to own land; currently women own less than 1% of the world's resources.

Ending this age of militarism and environmental rape requires that the male and female forces find a new balance and harmony. Neither nature as the "omnipotent" nor the superiority of individual human beings dominating nature can be a legitimate worldview. We need to affirm the human species as partner with nature.

The biological nature of the mother/infant bond places the responsibilities of childrearing primarily upon women. People now attain less than their full potential because as children they are not given the right kind of stimuli and guidance at the proper moments in their neurological development. The first five years of a child's life require great amounts of love, attention, and skill.

The majority of mothers are now wage earners as well. They are caught, along with men, in a web of economic injustice in which their wage earnings buy less of the basic needs each year.

This injustice stems from the Western land tenure system that has led to the ownership and control of the earth by a small number of people. This in turn is rooted in a deeply ingrained metaphysical error in Western civilization, which sees human beings and the earth as distinctly separate systems.

The various equal rights movements have yet to affirm the most essential right of all -- the equal right of all people to the earth. This is the "equal right" that furthers human unity and acknowledges our interconnectedness not only with each other but also with the earth from which we come and to which we return.

Equal rights to the earth can be practically attained through a ground rent system whereby the community created value of land and resources is collected in lieu of other taxes.

The German economist Sylvio Gisell proposed that ground rent be the source of payments for the support of women in the role of mothers and homemakers. Thus, ground rent payments would be an equivalent to the use of the soil by primitive women. As he put it:

> Every woman could bring up her children without being forced to depend on the financial support of a man. Economic considerations would no longer be able to crush the spirit out of women. A woman would be free to consider the mental, physical, and race-improving qualities and not merely the moneybags of her mate.

Current calculations indicate that such a system would yield $3500 per year per person, children included, or $14,000 for a family of four -- well above the poverty line. Ground rent, when not collected for the community as a whole, adds to the concentration of wealth and builds fortunes for a few individuals.

By placing the economic infrastructure on a base of essential fairness, people as wage earners would reap the full rewards of their labor to the advantage of both women and men of all races. This fundamental reform will facilitate the procuring of other rights and advances needed for human and planetary progress and evolution.

The earth is the birthright of all people.

17

Harvard Club, New York Speech on Habitat II Istanbul Conference

Published in GroundSwell, November-December, 1996.

This paper was presented on a panel at the Harvard Club in New York City on February 28, 1996, that was held to report on the UN Habitat II Conference. Other speakers included: John McConnell, founder of Equinox Earth Day and co-founder of the Earth Society Foundation; Elaine Wolfson, founding president of the Global Alliance for Women's Health; and Carol Smolensky, U.N. NGO representative for the Defense of Children International.

The U.N. is a very important institution but under attack and underfunded. It costs only $2 per person on earth. Compare this to $134 per person for military expenditures. The total operating expenses for the entire U.N. system (including World Bank, IMF, and all the U.N. funds, programs and specialized agencies) comes to $18.2 billion a year. This is less than the annual revenue of a major corporation like Dow Chemical, which took in more than $20 billion in 1994. The budget for the U.N.'s core functions in New York, Geneva, Nairobi, Vienna and five Regional Commissions is only $1.3 billion a year. This is about 4% of NYC's annual budget.

The Turkish hospitality to foreign guests contrasted with the repression of freedoms of speech and expression in Istanbul. Contrapuntal to the Official U.N. Habitat meetings, an Alternative Habitat Conference had been organized by individuals and human rights organizations who perceived a profound hypocrisy in having a major global conference on adequate human shelter and sustainable settlements in a nation state waging a war within its own territory, a conflict, which thus far had destroyed more than 2,000 Kurdish villages and created thousands of refugees, many of whom, now landless and uprooted, were living in extremely substandard and insecure conditions in Istanbul.

The official U.N. conference, with delegates from 183 nation states, had convened at three previous preparatory conferences. The task before them was to finalize a 65-page document that would be the Global Action Agenda for Adequate

Shelter and Sustainable Human Settlements. It was inspiring to watch this assembly working laboriously word by word to a consensus.

The issue of Housing as a Human Right was a major, perhaps the primary, point of contention at Habitat II. The official position of the U.S.A. delegation opposed issuing a clear statement of housing as a human right. The concern was that homeless people might use this as a basis for lawsuits against the government for not providing shelter. That, in my perspective, is perhaps understandable in a time when the proper role of government is currently being rethought and redefined.

But it brings us up against a perplexing reality. If people do not have the purchasing capacity to procure safe, secure shelter for their families, what choices do they have? When the mechanisms of the market economy disallow supply to meet demand to secure basic human needs, then a compassionate society has turned towards government to play a role in the provision of these basic necessities, either through various forms of transfer payments or through centralized control and planning.

Elsewhere there is the realization that the huge bureaucracies of the welfare state, which confiscate the wages of the middle classes through the income tax in the attempt to provide housing and other necessities for the poor, are unwieldy, unworkable and a bandaid at best.

Above and beyond any particular ideology or world view is the raw reality of the horrendous and maldistribution of wealth on planet earth:

- The richest fifth receives 82.7% of total income, while the poorest fifth received 1.4% of world income.
- The incomes of the richest 20% of the world's people are approximately 140 times those of the poorest 20%.
- The world now has more than 350 billionaires whose combined net worth equals the annual income of the poorest 45% of the world's population (The Nation, July 15-22, 1996, "The Limits of the Earth")
- The richest 1% of Americans possesses greater wealth than the bottom 90% (New York Times, 10-19-86, "How Many Billionaires are Enough.")

There is a grave problem with the way the democratic governance is currently constituted. This year at universities throughout our country students have been organizing Forums on The Crisis of Democracy, asking how can democratic institutions remain intact while there is an ongoing concentration of economic and subsequently political power in the hands of so few.

I've come to see the world increasingly as a hologram, as if all of the world is somehow reflected and can be seen in each part of the world. I see similar forces at work in my own small town in rural southcentral Pennsylvania, both for good and for bad, as I saw in the city of Istanbul and see in New York City.

There were 2,000 Kurdish villages destroyed in Turkey, and similar crises elsewhere, but here in our land, witness the decaying and rotting conditions of homes, schools, and infrastructure. Many of us are appalled by the ongoing expropriation of land and mineral resources and the poisoning of the water, earth, and thus the peoples on what remains of the land bases allocated to Native Americans. Perhaps the forces militating against the renewal of human habitat in our own country bear some resemblance to the forces that lead to the blatant destruction of villages and communities throughout the world.

The one reality that is quite obviously contributing to intense human suffering and conflict, that threatens the survival of people and their democratic institutions, is the maldistribution of wealth problem. With a fair distribution of wealth throughout the world, there would be no need for a global conference concerned about securing adequate shelter for all.

My perception is that this problem is clearly acknowledged with the U.N. system and has been acknowledged in all the documents to come out of the five great global conferences of this decade. The question remains, what are we going to do about it?

It is not government's role to provide decent shelter for all, then how can we establish a market economy that functions not only freely and efficiently but also fairly?

The NGO that I represent, the International Union for Land Value Taxation, is part of a world-wide movement that is working to implement a market system that fairly distributes wealth, one that would result in sufficient purchasing capacity for all in order to procure life's basic necessities and even something to spare to make life worth living. Our movement stems from a perspective that has been struggling to emerge for the past 100 years, some would even say for the past 2000 years.

Of primary concern to our movement is how to establish a market system that functions both freely and fairly. The body of knowledge that this movement has spawned has clearly identified the root of the maldistribution of wealth problem and the fundamental flaw in current market economies.

We have not founded our democratic system of governance on what should be a fundamental human right -- the human right to the planet itself.

Here are some land ownership facts:

- A U.N. study of 83 countries showed that less than 5% of rural landowners control three-quarters of the land.

- According to a government report, 2% of landowners hold 60% of the arable land in Brazil while close to 70% of rural households have little or none.

- Just 342 farm properties in Brazil cover 183,397 square miles -- an area larger than California. (Worldwatch, October, 1988)

In order to show there was NO NEED for land reform in Central America because our land in the U.S.A. is even more concentrated in ownership than Central America, Senator Jesse Helms read these facts into the Congressional Record in 1981:

- In Florida, 1% of the population owns 77% of the private land. Other states where the top 1% owns over two-thirds of the land are Maine, Arizona, California, Nevada, New Mexico, and Oregon.

Throughout the world, we see these numbers (compiled by U.K. Quaker Land Research Committee):

- 86% of South Africa is still owned by the white minority population.
- 60% of El Salvador is owned by 2% of the population.
- 80% of Pakistan is owned by 3% of the population.
- 74% of Great Britain is owned by 2% of the population.
- 84% of Scotland is owned by 7% of the population.

Many of our modern nation states were founded on territorial conquest and domination, on the old Roman stance of "dominium" -- the legalization of land acquired by conquest and plunder. And we continue to be ruled by might rather than by what is right. "Neocolonialism" and the globalization of the economy have become code phrases for the challenges arising from earth's control by so few.

Another aspect of this land tenure is that current market mechanisms distort free trade. Buying, selling, and thus profiteering and speculating in land and resources prevents market supply from meeting demand in order to procure shelter and other life necessities for all.

All that we need for life's securities is created by labor applied to land and natural resources. I believe that it is important that the ethics and institutions of democracy are firmly grounded upon the human right to the earth and this ethic be realized in a practical matter through fundamental reforms in our systems of public finance.

In Istanbul our NGO sponsored six forums entitled "The Earth is the Birthright of All People. We described how to implement this right in a practical manner through local to global public finance systems based on the collection of the ground rent of land and resources for the benefit of all. These policies shift the public revenue base away from taxes on labor and productive capital and onto fees for the use of land and natural resources, an approach recommended now by eight Nobel Prize winners and also by equinox Earth Day Founder John McConnell.

Refugees in transit after being forced off their common lands.

Sharing Our Common Heritage via the Tax Shift Agenda

Council of Georgist Organizations speech, August 1, 1998,
as published in *GroundSwell*, Nov.-Dec. 1998.

Groundswell Editor's note: Alanna Hartzok is one of two (Pat Aller serves as alternate) United Nations Non-Governmental Organization representatives for the International Union for Land Value Taxation. She dedicated her speech at the August 1, 1998 banquet at the Council of Georgist Organizations conference in Portland to the memory of the late Betsy Dana, a former Portland resident. Betsy Dana started the Georgist Registry and also the Registry for the World Federalists, with whom she was also active.

Our theme is sharing the common heritage via the tax shift agenda. And basically I am just going to do some sketches of what we are up against in terms of globalization, and the massive privatization of land and resources of the planet, and the kind of havoc that is causing. But also in the crisis of that we have the opportunity to really affirm the whole context, which I see as important to the Georgist movement, of common heritage resources.

There are several movements in that direction that I think are going to really help us in our linkage with a full scale tax shift agenda. And after covering those common heritage activities I want to look at how the tax shift agenda could be a really strong component in a mass local to global movement building.

Corporate Planet, subtitled Ecology and Politics in the Age of Globalization, is a quite impressive work that has just been put out by the Sierra Club. It looks at how the current form of development world-wide, through the World Bank, is using massive amounts of ground rent, privatized through oil resources, to fund development policies that exclude people from the heritage of the land and resource base. For instance, one is a World Bank funded project for corporations (this always seems to get directed to corporations, not to the people themselves to build a dam in Japan that displaced 30,000 rice farmers.

Another one was building roads for hacienda owners in Central America for cotton export, which displaced massive amounts of peasants. They are pushed into the rain forest, and they chop down the rain forest, and then that land is used for export for beef products. And again they are left basically homeless. Logging projects in Africa displaced 200,000 people who were dependent on forests for their livelihood.

This form of development policy has been pervasive. We can look back to 1948 in North Dakota. At that time there was probably the only Indian Tribe who were sustainably farming along the Missouri River bottom. The Army Corps of Engineers and the Bureau of Reclamation decided to put a number of dams on the Missouri River. One they placed right outside of the reservation. Reservations are not national parks for native peoples; they are sovereign territory arranged by treaty. The dam was built, and the dam flooded that whole river bottom and displaced those 1500 Native Americans who then went into poverty and welfare conditions.

The sequel to this 1948 story was in 1991. One of the children born in a tarpaper shack to the displaced Indians, after the flooding of their ancestral territory, went from poverty to graduating from Stanford to law school at Yale. His name is Raymond Cross and in 1991 he found himself leading the case for a settlement for the people who were displaced in 1948. In 1991 he won the case and a $149.5 million settlement for their lands.

Maurice Strong is a board member of corporations that hold massive amounts of land holdings in New Mexico. He was in charge of major development and privatization of hydro-power and other natural resources in Canada and went on to become a major mover and shaker for the past twenty years within the United Nations system. He was chair of the Earth Summit in Rio de Janeiro in 1992. His vested interest in land is quite pervasive. His companies displaced indigenous people in Central America to create lands for tourist development.

One of Strong's most recent acquisitions was that of a major North American aquifer in Colorado, and his intention then was to sell water resources to Denver. The local communities who formerly were in charge of that aquifer had to raise taxes in order to raise legal funds to fight this corporate grab of their water, which previously was a common heritage resource, used for those communities.

So is it any wonder that in the "Rio Plus Five" 1997 conference at the U.N. the results came in that there has been really no progress in sustainable development efforts in the past five years. We have gone backwards. We have an opportunity here to look very clearly at land tenure, taxation and overall financing for development policy, local to global, to set us on a new track.

I want to tell you about the Seed Satyagraha movement in India. Imagine that you were growing heirloom tomatoes in the backyard of your homestead, that the seeds had been passed on for generations, and those seeds were really well matched to the conditions in your particular land. Imagine then that somebody from a thousand miles away came and took the tomato and took that seed and analyzed the genetic DNA patterns of the seed, and then claimed it as the property rights for a particular corporation. And they said that you were no longer allowed to grow your tomatoes. And they then tried to sell you other seeds that would not reproduce and you would no longer have seeds, generation after generation, to keep growing with.

That is essentially what has been happening throughout the Third World with the privatization of intellectual property rights to the genetic code of life itself. While this was happening there were also massive public relations campaigns throughout India by the Cargill Corporation to show the farmers how advantageous it was to buy their seeds, that they could have greater crops with the new seeds, though of course it came with a certain chemical and pesticide base. Because of the glitz of the public relations, of the videotapes and the glossy literature, many of the Indian farmers went along with this and started buying these seeds from Cargill, and started neglecting their traditional seeds that they had used for eons of time.

But when the farmers realized after a very short period of time that these seeds could not produce any more seeds, and they would forever have to buy more seeds, they began to organize and rise in protest. The ten million plus united farmers in India went to the head office and the production center for Cargill Seeds with their crowbars and brick by brick took apart the building. That form of protest idea started with comments from Carla Hills, who was our Trade Representative to the South, saying that our corporations would pry open the Southern Hemisphere markets with crowbars.

There seems to be no end to the efforts to privatize common heritage resources and to find ways to control genetic structure. For instance, the "Terminator" technology can splice a gene into any particular seed so that that seed cannot reproduce. You have to keep buying and buying the seed. This is just one more example of the global reach of the vested interest of the very few. At this point the statistic is that 348 multi-billionaires have now accumulated more wealth than 2.5 billion people. It is hard to grasp.

We are hopefully nearing the end of this monopoly game. And this is what it looks like when you play monopoly. You see all the pieces get into the hands of one person. We are in the greedy grasp of the few right now, and it is just further igniting the people's movements local to global all over the planet to get very clear about the peoples' agenda that is going to create a massive shift in terms of ownership and control of the earth's resources.

I see this shift coming from a number of places. The Indian farmers now have a movement to establish collective intellectual property rights, to affirm property rights that have been vested in the community for eons of time and the experience that the community has had in developing their own sustainably based technology and seed resources. There is the Biodiversity Convention, which affirms the human right to the rich variety of genetic resources of the planet that our United States government has been vetoing for many years. Indian scientist Vandana Shiva is a strong voice for the Biodiversity Convention, portions of that are being adopted as legal guidelines, despite the lack of full ratification.

Then we have The Seventh Generation Act. That is a full cost accounting bill being introduced by a Canadian Member of Parliament from Ontario, Joe Jordan. In this we are seeing some common heritage perspectives working their way into legal formatting. We have the call by Ward Morehouse for a widespread debate on the theme of democracy and property rights, which I think is going to get us into the issue of what are the democratic rights to land; we need to base democracy on the right to the earth itself.

I think the best manifesto for common heritage, combining the private individual and the common rights to earth, was put out by the International Union for Land Value Taxation and Free Trade in 1948. It is printed on the inside of the back cover of my little booklet, "Financing Planet Management," which is available from Schalkenbach Foundation. This is the 50th year of that wonderfully profound and extremely relevant International Declaration on Individual and Common Rights to Earth. We should really be using it and getting it broadly published and distributed. It is just as relevant now as it was in 1948, and is a strong backbone for a lot of the work that our movement is doing.

This year is also the 50th year of the anniversary of the Universal Declaration of Human Rights, so we could also use this year to affirm human rights to the earth. You might want to set aside December 10, which is the exact date for the Universal Declaration of Human Rights, and have some sort of event on that day where we can say that the next step in universal human rights is declaring the right to the planet itself.

I am grateful that Hanno Beck urged me to attend the Tax Shift conference in Washington, D.C. this past April. To me, it was the most optimistic sign of the potential for our movement developing a massive strength that I have seen at any time probably in the last several years. The tax shifters conference was two days long, sponsored by Redefining Progress and the Center for a Sustainable Economy.

The context is developing where environmentalists have come to understand that to have the strong support of the middle classes, they have to have a concern about wages, and to have a base in low income communities there also must be a concern for environmental justice, and a way of building support by business as well. So they saw a way to build a broad range of support by shifting from a bureaucratic command control approach to environmental restoration to a market approach through tax incentives.

This is a really major shift for environmentalists to be making, and it moves them from being a net drain on government resources to increasing the tax base for government. Because there is a strong movement to decrease rather than increase the size of government, environmentalists then realized that they had to have a revenue neutral tax shift, and so they combined the objectives of economic justice with that of supporting legitimate business enterprise by advocating reductions in income, payroll and business taxes. This is certainly a Georgist concept, and though there was not a strong speaker for land value or site value taxation at the Tax Shift conference, Alan Durning's book was given to all conference participants.

Andrew Hoerner of the Center for a Sustainable Economy (CSE) has done an exhaustive survey of over 400 ecotax policies already in place throughout the fifty states. Now they are gleaning the best practices from those 400 policies. CSE has sent to me the work they have done for Pennsylvania, asking me to review that. They are very interested in Pennsylvania's work with the land value tax because some are coming to see that the land value tax is a very important tax shift policy that they need to get well versed in and up to speed on.

CSE is considering focusing on and targeting Pennsylvania for some of their tax shift efforts because of our two-rate land value tax efforts in the 16 cities there. So I think organizing-wise, all of you should get hold of the ecotax research and find out what ecotaxes are already in place in your state, and network with these policy institutes that are talking about the tax shift. There were about 70 people at Tax Shift and they represented about 50 different organizations. Worldwatch Institute and many other major DC think tanks had sent representatives.

Another field that is related that I only recently found out about is the financing for development dialogue. The background to this is that the G-77 (the Group of 77 developing countries, as juxtaposed to the developed countries, G-8, the 8th being Russia) has called for a wide dialogue within the UN system and within the UN members on the theme of "Financing for Development" which they perceive is a real weak point coming out of Agenda 21 from the Rio Earth Summit. They are realizing that there are lots of holes in current development theory and that the development approach of the World Bank and the Bretton Woods institutions is not working to eradicate poverty but is in fact exacerbating the problem.

The invitation has gone out on many levels to join in and link with this dialogue on the best practices for innovative funding sources, and how can we mobilize domestic resources for development. The United States is coming strongly in on this. I first heard about it at a briefing at the UN Mission in New York by David Hale, who is President of U.S. AID. We have also our Treasury Department and other agencies of the U.S. government who are invited. There will be input that you can read on their web site, and they will have meetings on the theme of financing for development for the next two years.

Another place for us to plug in on that dialogue is the United Citizens Network for Sustainable Development, which is probably one of the strongest networks connecting the Non-Governmental Organizations movement of the UN down to the grassroots level in terms of implementing Agenda 21.

The Millennium Peoples Assembly Network (MPAN) is yet another opportunity, and I think a very great one, for our movement to really grow exponentially. This effort is very visionary yet it has mass mobilization potential.

Last fall UN General Secretary Kofi Annan, in looking ahead to the year 2000, announced that the UN is planning for the General Assembly to have its Millennium Assembly and also a Millennium Summit of heads of state. At that time Annan also put forth the call for Millennium Peoples Assemblies worldwide, local to global, regional, national, and continental. This call for Millennium People's Assembly, also being called a Millennium NGO Forum, has mobilized a movement that has been building for 20 years to establish a permanent Global People's Assembly.

During this decade there have been several UN sponsored global conferences such as the Cairo Summit on Population, the Copenhagen Summit on Social Development (where our NGO first began to participate), the Istanbul Habitat II Summit, and others. At these global conferences, the nation states have their meetings and they develop their agendas by consensus, word-by-word, phrase-by-phrase. At the Istanbul one, which I participated in, 183 nation states hammered out by consensus an impressive 165-page document.

Most inspiring to us, and I had talked about this at previous conferences, is the Land Access section of the Habitat II agenda, which calls for land value recapture, and is a pretty thorough going 18-point Georgist policy approach that we need to really keep working with, and get that pushed for implementation.

Also, at these global conferences, the people all come together and they form their own people's agendas. There were 35,000 people at Rio, 50,000 at the Beijing Women's conference and at Istanbul about 18,000 were assembled. Now we are going to take all these agendas, get them very clear, and then work to build a massive local to global peoples movement to break through the monopoly control of the corporations that are bent on ruling the planet. (To get an excellent perspective on this take a look through David Korten's book, When Corporations Rule the World.)

I see the Georgist agenda is already coming to the forefront in the agenda that is being developed. I invite you to become a part of the leadership of this movement for worldwide local to global peoples assemblies so that we will be able to build an agenda process that is going to produce a true global people's document and blueprint for the future. So please consider joining with us in New York for the Millennium NGO Forum and Peoples Assembly in the year 2000.

I hope I have given you some ideas about ways to keep our movement on the move.

Pennsylvania's Success with Local Property Tax Reform: The Split Rate Tax

This paper was presented at the Jerome Levy Economics Institute of Bard College conference on "Land, Wealth and Poverty" held November 2-4, 1995. A slightly revised version was published in the *American Journal of Economics and Sociology*, April 1997. An edited version appears in *A World That Works: Building Blocks for a Just and Sustainable Society*, a 1997 TOES (The Other Economic Summit) book edited by Trent Schroyer and available from Apex Press. This paper was also quoted and referenced in "An Introduction to Two-Rate Taxation of Land and Buildings" by Jeffrey P. Cohen and Cletus C. Coughlin published in the Federal Reserve Bank of St. Louis Review, May/June 2005 edition.

Summary: Fifteen cities in Pennsylvania are pioneering an innovative approach to local tax reform that harnesses market incentives for urban renewal. Opting for the so-called 'two-rate' or 'split-rate' property tax, these cities are lowering taxes on buildings, thereby encouraging improvements and renovations, while raising the tax on land values, thus discouraging land speculation. The resulting infill development as indicated by increased building permits means downtown jobs, efficient use of urban infrastructure, an improved housing stock, and less urban sprawl. Cities in other states are poised to follow Pennsylvania's example.

Pennsylvania's Initiative

Pennsylvania has been experimenting with a new approach to property tax reform which has already begun to attract attention in New York, Maryland, and other states. This policy offers an entirely different angle to the current mainstream dialogue on property tax "reform" which consists mainly of efforts to reduce and curtail the use of property taxes while increasing sales or income taxes.

The property tax is actually two types of taxes - one upon building values, and the other upon land values. This distinction is an important one, as these two types of taxes have significantly different impacts on incentive motives and development results. Pennsylvania's pioneering approach to property tax reform recognizes this important distinction between land and building values through what is now known as the split-rate or two-tier property tax. The tax is decreased on buildings, thereby giving property owners the incentive to build and to maintain and improve their properties, and the levy on land values is increased, thus discouraging land speculation and encouraging infill development. This shifting of the tax burden promotes a more efficient use of urban infrastructure (such as roads and sewers), decreases the pressure towards urban sprawl, and assures a broader spread of the benefits of development to the community as a whole.

Taxing land values, while decreasing taxes on buildings, is sometimes proclaimed as a way to increase development. However, in today's world the word "development" is likely to be a red flag to many ears.

It is important to keep in mind that the purpose of this policy is not first and foremost to encourage development, but rather to assure that the benefits of development be broadly shared while impacting as lightly as possible on existing ecosystems.

Land value taxation was a key policy recommendation made by the Committee on Banking, Finance and Urban Affairs of the House of Representatives, 96th Congress whose groundbreaking report was entitled "Compact Cities: Energy Saving Strategies for the Eighties."

Current mainstream development models and methods in most cases contribute to the maldistribution of wealth. Statistics show that the richest 1% of Americans possesses greater wealth than the bottom 90%.[1] The land value tax, in essence a type of user fee for access to limited natural resources, is a policy that both harnesses market incentives and individual initiative and furthers social cohesion and well-being by narrowing the rich/poor gap. There is even greater need to make this point now, when the direction is towards cutbacks in many social services, the removal of the bandages placed to hold back the hemorrhage of the body politic.

Better tax policy could reduce the need for social services provided via government spending. Land value based public finance policies encourage home improvements and affordable housing. In Pennsylvania 85% of homeowners pay less with this policy than they do with the traditional flat-rate approach. For those who do pay more it is not significantly more and they tend to be wealthier homeowners who can better afford to pay a little more.

Some, indeed, whose business efforts are encouraged by this policy, come out ahead.

The Current Situation in Pennsylvania

There are now 15 Pennsylvania cities (Table 1) using the two-rate approach. Pittsburgh and Scranton implemented this policy as far back as 1913. Since then enabling legislation was passed which gave this option to third class cities as well. Land value tax policy in Pennsylvania really took off in the 1980's through the "Johnny Appleseed" work of Steven Cord, formerly a professor at Indiana University in Pennsylvania, now director of the Center for the Study of Economics in Columbia, Maryland.

Table 1

Two-Rate Pennsylvania Cities as of 1995

Two-Rate Since Date	Land Tax Rate %	Building Tax Rate %	One-Rate %*	% of Tax on Land	Removed From Build-ings in $000's	Population
Aliquippa Schools '93	16.3	1.1	4.4	85.5	2,115	13,374
Aliquippa '88	7.9	0.7	2.3	75.9	1,001	13,374
Clairton '89	10.0	2.1	3.7	53.7	300	9,656
Coatesville '91	5.2	2.5	3.0	33.9	70	11,038
Connellsville '92	11.3	1.7	3.0	50.1	384	9,229
DuBois '91	5.1	1.3	1.9	43.9	31	8,286
Duquesne '85	8.0	3.8	4.6	34.0	134	8,845
Harrisburg '75	3.2	1.1	1.4	36.0	2,533	52,376
Lock Haven '91	3.1	1.0	1.7	61.8	117	9,230
McKeesport '80	10.0	1.9	3.6	59.0	865	26,016
New Castle '82	8.7	2.2	3.4	46.6	1,192	28,334
Oil City '89	8.5	2.7	3.8	42.5	478	11,949
Pittsburgh '13+	18.4	3.2	6.1	57.4	73,739	369,379
Scranton '13+	6.6	1.2	2.6	65.9	3,997	81,805
Titusville '90	61.3	1.5	2.0	32.9	308	6,434
Washington '85	17.7	1.8	4.8	70.4	1,495	15,791

Total amount of taxes removed from buildings: $88,767,010

* One-Rate refers to the tax rate if there were no rate differentiation between land and buildings and the tax yield was unchanged. Scranton and Pittsburgh had a land tax to building tax ratio of 2 to 1 from 1913 until 1979 when both expanded land tax rates beyond that ratio. Please note: PA property tax rates are expressed in mills, i.e. Aliquippa: 16.3% = 163 mills. Source: Center for the Study of Economics, 2000 Century Plaza, Suite 238, Columbia, MD, 21044

In 1993, legislation sponsored by state representative Sue Laughlin extended the two-rate option to school districts of the third class that had coterminous boundaries with third class cities. Only eight school districts met this qualification, but it was a beginning. Currently, HB 2093, sponsored by Representative Ronald Buxton, would extend the two-rate tax option to include all school districts.

In addition to this school district bill there are six other bills in the Pennsylvania State Legislature that would further extend the two-rate tax option. Twin bills in both the House and Senate would give the two-rate tax policy choice to the nearly 1000 boroughs of the state. Their total population is two and a half million.

Bills, which are part of Representative Joseph Gladeck's enterprise package, extend the option to first and second-class townships and cities of the first class (which applies only to Philadelphia). His "Tax Free Development Zone Act" (HB 1256) recommends that municipalities wishing to designate an area as a tax free zone use the split-rate tax as well.

Among the cities that have gone to the two-rate system there is a considerable spread between the taxes on the value of land and those on the value of buildings. For instance, the small city of Aliquippa, which led the way towards the two-rate option for school districts, taxes land 16 times more heavily than buildings. Pittsburgh's tax rate on land is nearly six times the rate of buildings; the Titusville ratio is nearly 9 to 1, while Harrisburg's ratio that has been 3 to 1 will soon change to 4 to 1.

Table 2

Land to Building Tax Ratios in Pennsylvania

Cities Using The Two-Rate Tax

Cities	Land-to-Buildings Tax Ratio (1996)
Pittsburgh	5.61 to 1
Scranton	3.90 to 1
Harrisburg	4.00 to 1
McKeesport	4.00 to 1
New Castle	1.75 to 1
Washington	4.35 to 1
Duquesne	5.61 to 1
Aliquippa	16.20 to 1
Clairton	4.76 to 1
Oil City	1.23 to 1
Titusville	8.68 to 1

Source: Center for the Study of Economics,
2000 Century Plaza, Suite 238, Columbia, MD 21044

Some Data on Consequences

Let us now consider how this has worked in Pittsburgh and Harrisburg in particular. Pittsburgh has the longest history of this approach dating back to 1913. This city has extended its land value tax since that time so that now land values are taxed six times more heavily than are building values. Pittsburgh has a more compact development pattern than many cities, with the big buildings concentrated in the downtown area, not sprawled across the land, as is the case in so many cities where land speculation forces "leapfrog" development. Pittsburgh was highlighted in a Fortune magazine story (8/8/83) entitled "Higher Taxes that Promote Development." Research conducted by Fortune's real estate editor on the first four cities to go to the two-rate system independently verified that this approach does indeed encourage economic regeneration in the urban centers.

A recent study (Table 3) by University of Maryland economists, Wallace Oates and Robert Schwab, compared average annual building permit values in Pittsburgh and 14 other eastern cities during the decade before and the decade after Pittsburgh greatly expanded its two-rate tax. Pittsburgh had a 70.4% increase in building permits while the 15 city average decreased by 14.4% of building permits issued. These findings about Pittsburgh's far superior showing are especially remarkable when it is recalled that this city's traditional basic industry - steel - was undergoing a severe crisis throughout the latter decade.

Research based on building permits issued in the three-year period before and after the implementation of the two-rate tax policy in Pennsylvania cities consistently shows significant increases in building permits issued after the policy was put in place.

Table 3

Average Annual Value of Building Permits
(Thousands of Constant 1982 Dollars)

City	1960-79	1980-89	% Change
Pittsburgh	181, 734	309,727	+70.4
Akron	134, 026	87, 907	-34.4
Allentown	48, 124	28, 801	-40.2
Buffalo	93, 749	82, 930	-11.5
Canton	40, 235	24, 251	-39.7
Cincinnati	318, 248	231, 561	-27.2
Cleveland	329, 511	224, 587	-31.8
Columbus	456, 580	527, 026	+15.4
Dayton	107, 798	92, 249	-14.4
Detroit	368, 894	277, 783	-24.7
Erie	48, 353	22, 761	-52.9
Rochester	118, 726	82, 411	-30.6
Syracuse	94, 503	53, 673	-43.2
Toledo	138, 384	93, 495	-32.4
Youngstown	33, 688	11, 120	-67.0
15-City Average	**167,503**	**143,352**	**-14.4**

Source: "Urban Land Taxation for the Economic Rejuvenation of Center Cities: The Pittsburgh Experience" by professors Wallace Oates and Robert Schwab of the University of Maryland, 1992, available from Center for the Study of Economics, 2000 CenturyPlaza, Suite 238, Columbia, MD 21044

Pennsylvania is a pioneer leading the way and this is being increasingly acknowledged. A Wall Street Journal article (3/12/85) was entitled "It's the Land Tax, by George, That Sets Pennsylvania Apart." (The reference is to Henry George who drew great public attention to these possibilities a long time ago.)

Recently the headline of an article in The Washington Post (9/24/95) simply stated "D.C. Should Learn From Pittsburgh." Stories in the Philadelphia Inquirer (6/5/95) and the

Philadelphia Weekly (7/19/95) urged the adoption of land value tax policy. The Herald Mail announced (10/8/95) "Hagerstown Council to Consider Split Tax Rate." This is a just a small sampling of the rapid increase in media attention to this policy.

To turn now to Harrisburg, which was once considered one of the most distressed cities in the nation. Harrisburg since 1982 has sustained an economic resurgence that has garnered national acclaim. It twice won the top United States community honor as All-American City, along with the top state recognition from the state Chamber of Business and Industry as Outstanding Community in Pennsylvania, all because of Harrisburg's development initiatives and progress.

Harrisburg taxes land values three times more than building values. This city's glossy promotional magazine points to its 2/3 lower property tax millage on improvements than on land as one reason why businesses should locate there.

Mayor Stephen Reed of Harrisburg sent the following letter to Patrick Toomey, businessman, civic activist, and member of the Home Rule Commission of Allentown (10/5/94):

> The City of Harrisburg continues in the view that a land value taxation system, which places a much higher tax rate on land than on improvements, is an important incentive for the highest and best use of land in already developed communities, such as cities.
>
> In our central business district, for example, our two-tiered tax rate policy has specifically encouraged vertical development, meaning highrise construction, as opposed to lowrise or horizontal development that seems to permeate suburban communities and which utilizes much more land than is necessary.
>
> With over 90% of the property owners in the City of Harrisburg, the two-tiered tax rate system actually saves money over what would otherwise be a single tax system that is currently in use in nearly all municipalities in Pennsylvania. We therefore continue to regard the two-tiered tax rate system as an important ingredient in our overall economic development activities.
>
> I should note that the City of Harrisburg was considered the second most distressed in the United States twelve years ago under the Federal distress criteria. Since then, over $1.2 billion in new investment has occurred here, reversing nearly three decades of very serious previous decline. None of this happened by accident and a variety of economic development initiatives and policies were created and utilized.
>
> The two-rate system has been and continues to be one of the key local policies that have been factored into this initial economic success here.

Here are a few of the improvements mentioned in the Harrisburg promotional literature:[2]

- The number of vacant structures, over 4200 in 1982, is today less than 500.
- With a resident population of 53,000, today there are 4,700 more city residents employed than in 1982.
- The crime rate has dropped 22.5% since 1981.
- The fire rate has dropped 51% since 1982.

These results are especially noteworthy when one considers the fact that 41% of the land and buildings of Harrisburg cannot be taxed by the city because the state or non-profit bodies own it.

Maryland and Beyond

Now on to the state of Maryland, which has had some very interesting recent developments. The Governor vetoed enabling legislation for the two-rate policy in April 1994. Immediately following the veto the Henry George Foundation of America, based in Columbia, began to research the history of the property tax in Maryland. The HGFA suspected the existence of an earlier law permitting municipalities the two-rate tax option.

After weeks of law library research HGFA found a 1916 law in the 1994 Annotated Code of Maryland that had gone through several permutations. This indicated that Maryland municipalities could go to the two-rate system.

The Attorney General of the state of Maryland was asked for an opinion and after researching the statutes, on January 25, 1995 issued Option #95-002 which confirmed the authority of municipalities (with the exception of Baltimore) to set differential property tax rates.

The small town of North Beach will probably go to the two-rate system next April and Hyattsville may soon follow. Mayor Steven Sager of Hagerstown, which has only 35% home ownership, is urging his city council to move in this direction.

Joshua Vincent of the HGFA reports that the buildings to land ratios in Maryland are "more professional, less politicized. There is no distortion of residential assessments such as that existing in Pennsylvania. As a result, upper and upper-middle class homeowners pay their fair share but the poor and the working class get a real break."

No doubt Pennsylvania could be learning more about accurate assessment practices from Maryland while Maryland is learning how best to implement the two-rate tax system based on Pennsylvania's successful experiences so far. But interest is being shown in other states and cities as well.

Last February assessments expert Ted Gwartney, Walter Rybeck of the Center for Public Dialog, and this paper's author were asked by West Virginia Delegate, Bruce Petersen, to speak to the State House of Delegates about Pennsylvania's land value tax. Delegate Petersen is writing enabling legislation for land value taxation for West Virginia.

The mayors of Wheeling and Cincinnati have stated that they would like to move their local public finance in this direction.

Detailed studies on the effects of the two-rate policy have been conducted for Washington, DC, St. Louis, Missouri, and the state of Washington. There are groups actively supporting this policy in these places as well as in nearly every state in the United States and numerous other countries as well.

The City of Amsterdam in New York has recently received permission to implement the two-rate tax policy and will serve as a pilot project for that state.

The Art of Tax Improvement

While much has been learned about the successful use of land value based local public finance in Pennsylvania, mistakes have been made. For instance, the City of Uniontown reverted back to the flat rate system after an initial experience with the two-rate approach. What happened in Uniontown? Here the two-rate shift was combined with an overall tax increase the same year. A handful of irate community residents equated the two-rate policy with the tax increase and had it rescinded.

There is a lesson here in the "art of tax improvement." It is necessary to move to the two-rate system while maintaining a revenue neutral tax base, at least initially. Another key is to move gradually. One generally accepted guideline is to shift no more than 20% of the taxes off of buildings and onto land each year for a period of five years, or 10% each year for a period of ten years, in order to fully shift all taxes off buildings and onto land values.

Such a gradual transition, combined with community education, allows the citizenry to make the adjustments required, particularly to orient away from expectations of speculative gain in real estate land price escalation and towards investment in the development of affordable housing and business activities. Obviously as buildings are taxed less their value might rise, while the value of the more heavily taxed land should fall. While more research of these types of effects is needed it would appear from the long continuation of this tax policy in areas that have tried it that it meets with voter approval.

The Need For The Public To Be Informed

With the many positive results of this policy in Pennsylvania, why have only 15 cities implemented it, when 50 cities could do so? Why is the main thrust and public discussion focused there as elsewhere on reducing reliance on property taxes and giving local municipalities options to levy sales and income taxes?

The truth is that the word has just simply not gotten out. The success so far has come from the persistent efforts of just a handful of devoted activists who have educated city council members and urged them to adopt this policy.

But the majority of state legislators, public officials, community leaders, and the public at large remain for the most part in the dark. This does appear to be gradually changing in the legislature though because of the several current land value tax bills already mentioned. Both the Pennsylvania League of Cities and Municipalities and the State Association of Boroughs have professional lobbyists following these bills.

Unfortunately at this time, few economics or government professors at the university level introduce their students to this policy. Indeed this macroeconomics approach has been taught not by mainstream academic institutions but for the most part by the devoted teachers who volunteer their time at the Henry George School of Social Science, headquartered in New York with branches in Philadelphia, Chicago, San Francisco, Los Angeles, and Santo Domingo, and by the important work of the Robert Schalkenbach Foundation, also in New York.

There is a great need for institutions like the Jerome Levy Economist Institute to come to the fore of enlightened economic education and to teach their students about public finance policies that further free market incentives while at the same time narrowing the gap between the rich and the poor.

I feel a great deal of appreciation for the Jerome Levy Economics Institute for sponsoring this "Land, Wealth, and Poverty" conference and I thank you very much for the opportunity to present this information to you today.

---

[1] David Kotz, "How Many Billionaires Are Enough?" New York Times, 19 October, 1986.

[2] "Harrisburg - An Economic Profile" available at the City Government Center, 10 N. Second Street, Harrisburg, PA 17101-1678, Tel. 717-255-3040.

20

How Pennsylvania Boroughs Attained Land Tax Option

Published in *GroundSwell* - A Bi-Monthly Publication of
Common Ground-USA, January - February 1999, Vol. 12 No. 1.

In November 1998, Pennsylvania's legislature gave the land value tax (LVT) option to the state's nearly 1,000 boroughs. This is a major breakthrough for LVT supporters. Several years of persistent effort and high drama through the twists and turns of state legislative politics preceded the bill's passage.

In 1990 I moved back to my hometown of Chambersburg, Pennsylvania from San Francisco, where I had served for several years as the Education Director of the Henry George School of Northern California. When I found that, as a borough, Chambersburg was not permitted an LVT option and that nobody was actively pushing to expand the LVT option to taxing jurisdictions other than cities, I decided to spearhead such a campaign. Consulting with Steven Cord, then director of the Center for the Study of Economics, I developed an initial game plan for LVT enabling legislation for these smaller municipalities.

During the previous 25 years, 56 bills had been submitted to the Pennsylvania legislature that attempted to amend various borough township or school district codes to offer local governments a split-rate tax. The only bill to pass permitted only eight school districts in the state to adopt LVT. The other bills had all sunk in legislative committees. Knowing that only 10% of introduced bills ever pass to become laws we nonetheless decided to make another attempt this time with the focus solely on the "Borough Bill."

Pennsylvania has six general classifications of local governments that can levy taxes - cities, boroughs, townships, towns, school districts and counties, each of which operates under separate codes. (There are also three classes of cities and two classes of townships.) There are very few towns, and they are very small. They operate by town meeting and do not have a formal elected body.

The only taxing jurisdictions with an LVT option, other than the cities and those eight school districts, were 45 boroughs and five counties that had adopted "home rule charters" none of which had opted for LVT. As of 1995, 15 cities and one school district had adopted split-rate property taxes, shifting tax rates off of buildings and onto land values.

I met with my State Representative, Jeffrey Coy, and asked him to sponsor a bill enabling boroughs to adopt LVT. Representative Coy had not heard of the split-rate tax but thought he could support it as a local tax reform option if I would get the Chambersburg borough council to pass a resolution asking for the legislation.

After I talked to Chambersburg Mayor Robert Morris, Council President Bernie Washabaugh and then Borough Manager Julio Lecuona, I was placed on the Council agenda to make a presentation and a request for a resolution. My twenty-minute presentation included a short talk, data presented with an overhead projector, supplementary written material to each council member, and a prepared resolution. After my presentation, the Council passed the following:

RESOLUTION FOR MAYOR AND TOWN COUNCIL
OCTOBER 27, 1993

AN APPEAL TO THE PENNSYLVANIA LEGISLATURE TO EXTEND TO THE BOROUGHS OF PENNSYLVANIA THE LOCAL OPTION TO IMPLEMENT A TWO-RATE PROPERTY TAX, WHEREBY SEPARATE MILLAGE RATES CAN BE LEVIED FOR BUILDINGS AND LAND VALUES.

WHEREAS, second and third class cities currently are permitted to levy different tax rates on buildings and land values,

WHEREAS, at present, fifteen cities have chosen to implement a two-rate tax,

WHEREAS, decreasing the rate on buildings and improvements encourage property owners to build on and improve their property without the fear of incurring a higher property tax bill,

WHEREAS, increasing the levy on land values discourages land speculation and encourages infill development in urban areas,

WHEREAS, the option to levy a two-rate property tax has recently been extended to school districts of the third class with a coterminous boundary with a third class city (Section 672, Act 16, 1993),

NOW THEREFORE BE IT RESOLVED on motion by Councilman G.W. Pentz seconded by Councilman T.L. Newcomer that the Mayor and Town Council of the Borough of Chambersburg in Franklin County urge the Pennsylvania legislature to pass enabling legislation that would extend the two-rate property tax option to the boroughs of the state.

With this resolution in hand, I made another appointment with Representative Coy who instructed one of his aides to prepare the legislation that he would sponsor. We subsequently found out that Representative Richard Olasz, at the request of the Borough of Homestead, a suburb of Pittsburgh, had prepared the needed legislation. Dan Sullivan of Pittsburgh had spoken to the Homestead Chamber of Commerce about land value tax, but had not spoken directly to borough council, and did not know that they had requested the land tax option. The borough council of Wilkinsburg, another Pittsburg suburb, also endorsed the Olasz bill after it was introduced.

Representative Coy became a co-sponsor of Olasz's bill along with 41 other representatives both Democrats and Republicans.

The Pennsylvania State Association of Boroughs (PSAB), a handful of other Georgists and I began to work in earnest on the passage of HB 2532. Jack Gardner, the lobbyist for PSAB, Dan Sullivan, Founder of the Pennsylvania Fair Tax Coalition, Mike Goldman and I distributed literature and spoke to as many legislators and legislative aides that we could manage to buttonhole at the Capitol. Other LVT supporters, and particularly Common Ground members, called, faxed and wrote letters supporting the bill to the state's 200 representatives. The following message, composed by Sullivan, was our primary piece of literature to educate the legislators about the bill:

Land Value Tax Option for Boroughs

Simple - Allows boroughs to split the existing property tax rate into separate rates on land and improvements, and to charge lower rates on improvements than on land. This bill is so simple we have included the entire provision on the bottom of this page.

Easy - No constitutional amendment required no loopholes to plug, no new bureaucracy to administrate.

Proven - This same option has been available to Pennsylvania cities for decades. Fifteen cities have made use of it.

No New Taxes - By splitting the rates on an existing tax, we avoid the danger of replacing a bad tax with a worse tax. This truly is property tax reform.

Revenue Neutral - The revenue limit for separate land and building rates is exactly the same as existing revenue limit for property tax.

Saves Homeowners Money - Homeowners save in almost every community, but save even more in municipalities with more deteriorated, absentee owned land. For example, they save over 25% in Pittsburgh but over 39% in Clairton.

Stimulates Development and Renovation - Land can't move, but idle landowners can clean up their acts. Pennsylvania cities that replaced property tax with land tax have consistently enjoyed increased construction and renovation.

Taxes Out-of-State Landowners - Absentee landlords tend to maintain and improve their properties less than homeowners, which is why they pay more. No other local tax can draw as much revenue form out-of-state taxpayers.

The Entire Provision - (Amending Section 1302.1 of the Borough Code so that) Boroughs may in any year levy separate and different rates of taxation for municipal purposes on all real estate classified as land, exclusive of the buildings thereon and on all real estate classified as buildings on land. When real estate tax rates are so levied, 1) the rates shall be determined by the requirements of the borough budget, 2) higher rates may be levied on land if the respective rates on land and buildings are so fixed so as not to constitute a greater levy in the aggregate than the maximum rate allowed by law on both land and buildings, and 3) the rates shall be uniform as to all real estate within the classification.

The legislation was reviewed by the Local Government Committee and sailed through the House, passing with a 2-to-1 vote in 1995. Our efforts intensified as the bill entered the Senate. A mailing, telephone messages and faxes were sent to all 50 Senators and we made visits to all the Senate offices.

The legislative session was ending that year with a short five-day Senate session - a small window of opportunity for the passage of this land value tax option for boroughs. The bill went through all required readings and was approved by the Local Government Committee. Senate leadership ruled that it did not need to go through the Finance Committee, because it was a local option bill and entailed no expenses by the state.

One day before the final session, the Senate leadership decided that it would have to go through the Finance Committee after all. PSAB's Gardner, an experienced lobbyist, assured us that the bill's passage still looked good, although the ruling to commit to Finance was discomforting.

Sullivan, Goldman, Gardner and myself stood in the Finance Committee meeting rooms on the last day of session, anticipating that HB 2532 would be reported out of the Finance Committee, put to vote and passed. We were stunned when the Finance Committee chairman concluded the meeting without even a mention of the Borough Bill, effectively killing it. To this day we do not know who objected or why the leadership decided to kill the bill.

Gardner had said all along that, because no one on the Senate side had "adopted" the bill and was committed to seeing it through to passage, and because nobody wanted controversy on the final days of the session, it was vulnerable to the slightest objection from any senator. He had suggested that we be soft-spoken and avoid ruffling feathers, which we did. Once the bill was expected to pass, we stopped promoting it and simply made ourselves available to answer any questions that might come up. Under the circumstances, it was the right strategy, but it was not enough. We would have to begin our efforts all over again with the next legislative session.

We learned from experience, and our effort in the next session was much more effective. We decided to have identical bills sponsored in both the House and the Senate. We found that Representative Joseph "Gladeck, Jr. had several land value tax provisions in a set of bills he called his "Economic Development Legislation Package." The Borough Bill was one of them so we were covered in the House.

I made an appointment with my state Senator, Terry Punt, who, like Representative Coy before him, stated that while he had not heard of it before, the split-rate tax option made sense. Punt happily agreed to sponsor a bill, which bombed in a Senate committee, but was later revived as the bill that finally passed. Senator Punt had become Chairman of the Community and Economic Development Committee and was strong and skillful in his promotion of the bill. He enlisted several other senators as co-sponsors of the bill - Afflerbach, Jubelirer, Wozniak, Thompson and Heckler. It was referred to the Local Government Committee in January 1997, giving it two full years to wend its way through the legislature.

Meanwhile I had become Co-Chair of the Housing Task Force of the Greater Chambersburg 2000 Partnership. To increase public understanding of the split-rate tax, I worked with the Task Force's Policy Development Committee in organizing a Tax Reform Forum, which was held at Shippensburg University in May. The Forum had 20 co-sponsors and featured eight speakers - Senator Terry Punt, Mayor Anthony Spossey of Washington, PA, John Gardner, Walter Rybeck, Director of the Center for Public Dialog, Ben Howells, Jr., a former councilman from Allentown, PA, Joshua Vincent, Dan Sullivan, and Mike Waters, the other Housing Task Force co-chair. I served as moderator. The event drew nearly seventy people including borough and state officials and interested local citizens. Five newspaper stories were published about the Tax Reform Forum and an excellent videotape was produced.

The only cloud now on the horizon was the Pennsylvania Farm Bureau (PFB), one of the largest and strongest lobbies in the state. The PFB was suspicious of land value taxation. They are a "statewide general farm organization with a membership of more than 25,200 farm and rural families in the Commonwealth." PFB lobbyist informed us that if just one farmer in a borough would have to pay a higher tax under a split-rate system they would oppose the bill. After considerable wrangling back and forth between Punt's office and the PFB, Punt agreed to amend the bill to exempt farmland in boroughs from the split-rate tax. This meant that the farmer would pay a conventional property tax at the equivalent overall rate.

Senator James Gerlach, Chair of the Local Government Committee, formerly amended the bill. While not what we really wanted, the amended bill was acceptable to both Gardner at the PSAB and PFB. Only a relatively small number of boroughs had farms and only a small percentage of land values were from farmland within boroughs. If this was what it would take to pass the legislation, we were willing to live with it.

SB 211 was now acceptable to all major parties and ready to be voted on. It passed the Senate unanimously by a vote of 48 to zero. We were delighted! Now on to the House, where we knew our work was cut out for us.

In early October of 1997 Representative Thomas Armstrong, the Local Government Subcommittee Chairman on Boroughs, convened a hearing on both versions of the Borough Bill - Representative Gladeck's HB 555, which had not been amended by the farmers' lobby, and Senator Punt's SB 211, which had already passed the Senate with the amendment. Testifying on behalf of the passage of the bill was PSAB's Jack Garnder; Joshua Vincent as President of the Henry George Foundation; Napoleon Saunders, Business Manager for the City of Harrisburg; Tom Scott, Legislative Counsel for the Pennsylvania Environmental Council and this writer, Alanna Hartzok, as State Coordinator of PFTC. A seven-minute videotape of Mayor Anthony Spossey, who spoke of the successful experience of the split-rate tax in the City of Washington, Pennsylvania, was also shown.

The only opposition voice was John Bell, Counsel on Governmental Affairs of the Pennsylvania Farm Bureau. Bell opposed both HB 555 and SB211 in its original form. He DID endorse the amended SB 211, saying, "We believe that Printer's Number 940 of Senate Bill 211 can achieve the objectives that boroughs wish to achieve without placing greater burdens upon farmers within boroughs." Given the opposition from the farmers' lobby during the months preceding this committee hearing I had written a paper entitled "Pennsylvania Farmers and the Split-Rate Tax" which presented strong evidence for the potential beneficial effects of land value taxation on viable farming operations in the state. This paper was later published by M.E. Sharpe, Inc. in Land Value Taxation, an anthology assembled by Kenneth Wenzer.

The paper was so convincing that Representative Armstrong was now concerned that the Farm Bureau amended SB 211 would hurt farmers by NOT permitting the split-rate tax for farms in boroughs! The subcommittee members carefully considered the pros and cons and legalities involved in both versions of the bill, SB 211 and HB 555. Eventually, their recommendation was to go with the amended and Farm Bureau approved Senate version of the bill.

The PFTC organized "Public Finance Alternatives: A Philadelphia Regional Forum" which was held in January of 1998. This Forum had 20 co-sponsors, and featured seven major speakers - Napoleon Saunders, Mayor Spossey, Jack Gardner, Jr., Joanne Denworth, President of the Pennsylvania Environmental Council; Richard Rybeck, Deputy Administrator of the Office of Policy and Planning of the Washington, DC Department of Public Works; Joshua Vincent, now Director of the Center for the Study of Economics. I was the moderator. About 80 people attended this Forum. Press coverage was excellent with favorable stories in three newspapers including the Philadelphia Inquirer and the Philadelphia Weekly. The ball was rolling. Or so it seemed.

There was no action on the Borough Bill for several months and the legislature adjourned for the long summer recess. We were told by Gardner that everything was lined up for the bill's passage in the fall and that there was really nothing more we could do. There was no other opposition in sight and the vote of the needed majority of representatives appeared certain. The fate of the bill was in the hands of the House Republican leadership. Follow-up phone calls to the House leaders assured us that passage was a "done deal."

All of us anxiously awaited for word of the passage of SB 211 by the House as the days of the final 1997-1998 legislative sessions passed into weeks and then months. Shortly before the November elections, I received word that the bill was suddenly in serious jeopardy. Apparently Senator Punt, a Republican, had shown support for Democratic incumbent, Representative Jeffrey Coy, over the Republican candidate. (Both legislators represented Franklin County where Republicans had endorsed Coy, as they were pleased with his legislative performance, and did not want to be dictated by the central state Republican committee.) But to assure a Republican majority in the House, the State Republican leadership was determined to have a Republican win Jeff Coy's district, which was within Punt's senatorial district. To punish Punt for crossing party lines, the Republican leadership had decided that his bills would not be put up to vote. Was our five years of work for passage of the Borough Bill to have no result?

Representative John M. Perzel of Philadelphia, the House Majority Leader, was in charge of placing items to be voted upon on the Agenda. I called Representative Purcell's office and said that I was quite disturbed to hear of the situation. The legislative aide first implied that I did not know what I was talking about but later in the conversation said, "Lady, do you want your bill to pass or not?" I was informed that SB 211 was being "amended" to be sponsored by a "loyal Republican senator." We do not to this day understand how they intended to do this legally, but they could certainly kill the bill so that someone else could introduce it in a subsequent session.

When I told Senator Punt's Harrisburg office of this situation his chief aide expressed outrage but not surprise to encounter such dark forces of partisan politics. She had been watching the workings of the Pennsylvania legislature for a number of years and had seen numerous backroom political power plays that she found both disturbing and disheartening. We agreed that the best interests of the people were definitely not being served by the machinations of the Republican leadership.

I was advised by several people that I should keep quiet about the inside story of Pennsylvania politics until the election was over. If I were to stir things up about the backstab to Senator Punt, then the Republican leadership might just discard SB 211 entirely. I did call the Republican candidate against Jeff Coy, who was Franklin

County Commissioner Robert Thomas. He had heard me speak about land value taxation several times during the years I served as co-chair of the Greater Chambersburg 2000 Housing Task Force.

When I told him what I had heard about Senator Punt's bill, he expressed disbelief that the Republicans in Harrisburg that were supporting him would do such a thing. He informed me that several of the Republican leaders would be speaking at his upcoming campaign breakfast and invited me to come to ask them questions. I did indeed attend this breakfast at a restaurant in Franklin County and asked Representative John Barley, House Appropriations committee Chairman, what had happened to SB 211. All he said in response was, "Why isn't Terry (Senator Punt) here? You go ask him why he isn't here with us today."

When I informed Senator Punt's aide that this was Representative Barley's response, she checked Punt's calendar and determined that he had apparently never received an invitation to the breakfast.

I was put into a very difficult position at that point. As a strong advocate of the Borough Bill, I had invested several years as a citizen activist in the legislative effort for its passage. It was in the best interest, apparently, for the bill's passage this session if I kept quiet about the inside political power play. But as a constituent of Coy's District, I was furious that the centralized state Republican Party was becoming such a strong outside force in our local governance. They were putting a substantial amount of funds into Thomas's campaign chest. The Republican Leadership in Harrisburg found it intolerable that Representative Coy, a Democrat, should continue to serve in a district where Republicans hold a 2-to-1 majority.

But both Senator Punt and Representative Coy had strong track records of serving the interests of the people of our district as they understood them, and their political affiliations were secondary. They had both attained legislative leadership roles that usually go to big city politicians rather than those from rural districts like ours. My first impulse was to write irate letters to the editors of our local papers alerting the populace to the shenanigans of the Republican central committee. But my allegiance to the passage of the Borough Bill won out. I remained silent.

The November elections came and went. Although the state Republican Party had poured more money than ever into the race for the 89th District House seat, Representative Coy retained his position with 56% of the vote - a margin of about 2,200 votes, seen by many as a victory for local control.

Shortly after the election the papers reported that Senator Punt had suffered a heart attack. Our legislative champion was in recovery in a local hospital.

What was now to become of the Borough Bill after these now six years of effort? All we could do was wait through the final remaining days of the 1998 legislative session.

The good news finally, and unexpectedly, broke. Jack Gardner called to announce that Senator Punt's Borough Bill had passed the State House by a vote of 198 for, only 2 against.

The governor's signature was the final hurdle. It is unheard of for a governor to veto a bill that had such overwhelming support, but we had been so often assured of success and then disappointed that we remained apprehensive. We finally received confirmation that the bill had been signed by Governor Thomas Ridge on November 24 as Act 108. Our efforts had finally succeeded! Now nearly 1000 boroughs with a population base of two and one half million people can choose the two-rate tax shift approach towards land value taxation.

We still do not know why Representative Perzel and the other Republican leaders decided to run Senator Punt's bill at the last moment. We have heard that their attempt to find another sponsor for the bill ran into difficulties. We suspect that there might have been some feelings of remorse after Senator Punt had the heart attack. We probably will never know the details of the discussions leading to the decision. We will chalk it up to the convolutions of politics as usual.

In any case, a special thanks goes out to members of the Pennsylvania Fair Tax Coalition who actively gave their wholehearted support to passing the Borough Bill but who were not featured in this story, especially Richard Biddle, Joan Sage, Jake Himmelstein, Judy Douty, Ed Dodson, Hanno Beck, Lou Cippoloni, and Mike Curtis.

Here are the contents of the Borough Bill:

The General Assembly of Pennsylvania,
SENATE BILL No. 211
Printer's No. 940

Introduced by Punt, Afflerbach, Jubelirer, Wozniak, Thompson and Heckler, January 29, 1997 Amended April 7, 1997, Senator Gerlach, Local Government

AN ACT

Amending the act of February 1, 1966 (1965 P.L. 1656, No. 581), known as The Borough Code, is amended by adding a section to read:

Section 1302.1. Different and Separate Tax levies.

(A) A borough may in any year levy separate and different rates of taxation for municipal purposes on all real estate classified as NONFARMLAND, exclusive of the buildings thereon, and on all real estate classified as EITHER buildings on land or FARMLAND. When real estate tax rates are so levied:

1. The rates shall be determined by the requirements of the borough budget.
2. A higher rate may be levied on real estate classified as no farmland than on real estate classified as either buildings on land or farmland if the respective rates on no farmland and on buildings or farmland are so fixed as not to constitute a greater levy in the aggregate than the levy to result from the maximum rate allowed by law on all real estate.
3. The rates shall be uniform as to all real estate within the classification.

(B) For purposes of this section:

1. "Farmland" shall include any tract of land that is actively devoted to agricultural use, including, but not limited to, the commercial production of crops, livestock and livestock products, as defined in Section 3 of the Act of June 30, 1981 (P.L.128, No. 43), known as the "Agricultural Area Security Law."
2. "Nonfarmland" shall include any tract of land that is not farmland.

(C) The provisions of this section are nonseverable. If any provision of this act or its application to any person or circumstance is held invalid, the remaining provisions or applications of this act are void.

Section 2. This act shall take effect in 60 days.

21

Pennsylvania Farmers and the Split Rate Tax

Published in *Land Value Taxation: The Equitable and Efficient Source of Public Finance*,
an anthology edited by Kenneth C. Wenzer, published by M.E. Sharpe, Inc., New York, 1999.

Introduction

Pennsylvania has been experimenting with a new approach to local tax reform which offers an entirely different angle from other current reform proposals which attempt to reduce the use of property taxes while introducing sales or income taxes. This approach, known as the "split rate" or "two tier" tax, reforms the property tax itself in a way that appears beneficial on a number of indicators.

The property tax is actually two types of taxes - one upon building values, and the other upon land values. This distinction is an important one, as these taxes have significantly different impacts on incentive motives, development results, and economic consequences.

Because buildings must be constructed and maintained in order to have value, a tax on building values is a cost of production. Such a tax results in lower production and/or higher prices.

The other part of the property tax is on the value of land. Land is most certainly not a product of human labor but a gift of Nature. A tax on land cannot be avoided by producing less land, or by moving land from one jurisdiction to another. Unlike capital items, a tax on land values is not a cost of production per se but functions as a type of user fee which has the added advantages of encouraging efficient land use while curbing land speculation.

Furthermore, since land value is enhanced by public expenditures for roads and other improvements of the infrastructure, the taxation of land values recaptures this publicly created value and places government on a firmer footing without burdening private enterprise.[1]

Pennsylvania's pioneering use of the split-rate tax makes this important distinction between land and building values. The tax is decreased on buildings, thereby giving property owners the incentive to maintain and improve their properties while the levy on land values is increased, thus encouraging good site utilization.

When considering this land value taxation policy approach, it should be kept clearly in mind that it is not proposed as an additional tax burden, but rather to be implemented in tandem with significant tax reductions on productive labor and capital.

The split-rate tax, now in place in varying degrees in 16 cities in Pennsylvania, encourages improvements and renovations, promotes a more efficient use of urban infrastructure (such as roads and sewers), and discourages land speculation and urban sprawl.[2] The split-rate tax reform provides a strong incentive for infill development as indicated by increased building permits in cities using it compared to those with the traditional property tax. This approach fosters more downtown jobs and improvements in residential and commercial buildings.

By correctly harnessing market forces and private incentives at the same time providing a solid source of financing for the public sector, the split-rate tax reform also assures a broader spread of the benefits of development to the community as a whole. Legislative efforts are now underway which would extend the split-rate tax option to the boroughs, school districts, and townships of Pennsylvania.

The possibility of extending the split-rate tax to jurisdictions that include agricultural lands raises this important question: What might be the impact of the split-rate property tax on the farmers of Pennsylvania?

To answer this question we will summarize recent research on the overall impact of property taxes on agriculture and also report on the effect that land value based taxes have had on farmers in places where similar split-rate or pure land value tax policies have been in force. Knowledge as to the precise impact of this policy approach on farmland in any particular county, township or region however, requires research and analysis as applied to that particular area.

Property Taxes in Agriculture

On average in the United States, sixty percent of the private land in the forty-eight contiguous states is in farms and ranches.[3]

Although farming and ranching cover a lot of territory, agricultural real estate represents only five percent of all real estate value in the U.S., according to the National Realty Committee. The Federal Reserve Bulletin estimates the 1994 farm business real estate at $772 billion, which is six percent of U.S. real estate value. Farm business land alone was estimated at $593 billion, which is 14% of U.S. land value. The $5 billion of agricultural real property taxes is only about three percent of total real property taxes in the U.S.[4]

As currently applied, agriculture pays a relatively small part of America's total real property taxes and thus the property tax on farmlands is not critical fiscal policy. The real property tax is more important at the local level, where such taxes constitute 76% of the tax revenue, 48% of "own revenue" and 30% of all local government revenue.[5]

The research of Gene Wunderlich[6] of the USDA Economic Research Service revealed that as currently administered, the real property tax appears to be regressive in terms of the value of holdings. Landowners whose value of farmland was $5 million or more paid one-third the rate of landowners with farmland holdings valued at less than $70 thousand. The owners whose estimated market value of farmland holdings was less than $70 thousand paid $1.45 per $100 and owners of $5 million or more paid $0.47 per $100. Holdings between these extremes graded regressively.[7]

Property tax policy, with all its partial exemptions, preferential assessments, and levels of rates and classifications, may be excessively complex, Wunderlich says. His findings lead him to recommend that before the real property tax can become an effective instrument of land policy, some of its administrative shortcomings must be addressed. Exemptions, partial and total, based on features of the owners distort the incidence of the tax. Multiple classes and rates further complicate the legal structure and administration. Reform of the real property tax to effectively support land use policy requires changes in law and management. Wunderlich's extensive research led him to the following conclusion:

Exercised differently and more vigorously than at present, the real property tax might complement other land use policies or become a strong policy instrument in its own right, but without the concerns about "takings" under eminent domain or regulation. Its influence would be reflected in land values and land prices. The value of land, therefore, is the key ingredient in tax policy pertaining to resource use.[8]

Rising Inequality and Falling Property Tax Rates

A meticulous study conducted by Dr. Mason Gaffney entitled "Rising Inequality and Falling Property Tax Rates"[9] refutes the common belief that property tax relief would be good for farmers. This research showed that property tax relief for agricultural land increases the likelihood that it will attract those looking primarily for tax shelters and speculative investments. Such nonproductive incentives ultimately inflate land values overall, making it increasingly difficult for working farmers to access and maintain acreage for viable agricultural enterprise.

Lower farm property taxes were also found to be associated with lower ratios of capital to land, and labor to land, both over time and among states. States with lower property taxes also had larger mean farm size and less equal distribution of farm sizes along with underuse and under-improvement of land.

Conversely, a positive relationship was found between higher property tax rates and more intensive use of farmland, which in turn is associated with its more equal distribution.

Gaffney's research made a clear distinction between building values and land values in agricultural holdings. This aspect of the study permits comparison with property taxes levied on buildings and land combined or separately with lower tax rates placed on buildings and higher rates on land values, as would be the case with the two-rate property tax on Pennsylvania agricultural lands.

The study showed that smaller farmers had a higher building-to-land ratio than bigger farmers. Property taxes on buildings therefore penalize the former and work to suppress improvements. The findings indicated that a property tax on land values promoted a more intensive and efficient use of agricultural land, thus supporting the overall viability of smaller farming operations.

Some specific data from Gaffney's research would be in order here. The national average of farm property tax rates peaked in 1930 at 1.32%. It fell to 0.77% in 1945, and stabilized at about that level in 1987 (0.85%). Mean acres per farm had remained fairly constant for 65 years (1870-1935) at about 155 acres. After 1935 the mean took off and had tripled to 462 acres by 1987. Real wage rates have not risen as fast as real land prices since 1955, and not at all since about 1975. This situation coupled with rising acres per farm meant that the labor-price of a farm roughly tripled, from about six years' wages (before payroll deductions) in 1954 to about 17 years' wages in 1987. Consequently, farms became unaffordable to the average person while concentration in their holdings proceeded.

In 1900 the Census Bureau began publishing farm data ranked by acres per farm. Using those data, the Gini Ratio (GR) was calculated for several decades. The GR is a measure of unequal distribution. A rise in GR means that the big got bigger and/or the small got smaller. It ranges from .00 (complete equality) to 1.00 (complete inequality).

The GR was .58 in 1900, rose only slowly, to .63 in 1930, climbed faster, to .70 by 1950, plateaued there for 15 years, then increase again to .76 by 1987. The accelerated rise since 1930 coincided with the rise of mean acres per farm; both followed the fall of property tax rates.

The GR deals only with concentration among existing farms and normally does not reflect their loss. In his research Gaffney modified the GR to combine both effects by adding the 4.5 million farms that died out between 1935 and 1988 to the lowest bracket, as farms with zero acres in 1988. Calculating the GR this way gives one a better sense of how concentration shot up after 1930-35. This increases the GR for 1988 from .76 to .92, a radical rise of inequality since 1930 (.63). "In the Great Depression (1930-41), millions of small farms provided a refuge for the jobless and homeless," states Gaffney. "Today, that refuge is closed, with explosive social consequences in urban slums."[10]

Additionally, Gaffney found that the concentration of the value of farm real estate has been growing faster than that of farm acres during most of this century, and that the Land Share of Real Estate Value (LSREV) in the top bracket (1,000 acres and over) appears to have risen faster than the building values. Higher LSREV means a higher farm price to cash flow (P/C) ratio which is another barrier to farm entry. A high P/C ratio shows a higher share of land value ($L) in farm wealth.

The common belief that high Capital Costs of Machinery and Equipment ($M&E) are the main obstacle to farm entry is therefore erroneous. At the time of this study, capital costs were only about 10% of all farm assets, much smaller than the costs of land and buildings.

To sum up these key points from this Land Ownership and Taxation in American Agriculture study:

- Rising acreages mean there are fewer farms overall.
- Rising labor prices per farm mean aspiring farmers who lack prior wealth can no longer afford to acquire farms.
- Acreage is less equally shared among a given number of farms
- The higher quality of land is moving into bigger farms
- The combination of the above factors means "the agricultural ladder has been pulled up. Entry is nearly impossible for farmers lacking outside finance."[11] Smaller farms are being forced to sell out as larger farms increase their holdings. These changes accompanied and followed a 40% drop in farm property tax rates.

This study also showed that as the concentration in both acreage and real estate value of agricultural lands proceeds, there is an increasing separation of land from capital. Large farms are for the most part lands without buildings while buildings cluster on smaller farms, many without enough land. Furthermore, the biggest landlord holdings, in dollar value, were found to be 99% pure land.[12]

Lack of buildings reveals a dearth of family labor, because so many farm buildings are operator dwellings. In 1988 operators' dwellings were 48% of farm real estate assets in the smallest acreage bracket, 16.4% for all farms, and falling steadily to 4.4% on farms 2,000 acres and over. For family-held corporate farms (of all sizes) the share is 6.3%; for other corporate farms, 3.2%.

These data support the common impression that smaller and unincorporated farms are better supplied with operator family labor. Additional statistical analysis in the Gaffney study clearly indicates that farm land values are much more concentrated than farm building values.

Such statistics suggest at least three points. First, building wealth is more equally distributed than land wealth. Second, the property tax would be more progressive if changed to a pure land tax, exempting buildings. Third, many large farms are not being used to their potential while capital on some small farms is under-complemented with land.

Yet another component of the Gaffney study bears mentioning since it concerns how the split-rate property tax might affect the farmers of Pennsylvania. It suggests "the effect of urban land speculation is toward higher concentration of landholdings...observable today around growing cities."[13]

Evidence was obtained which further supports the understanding that higher property taxes are actually to the benefit of smaller, more capital and labor-intensive farming operations. Wisconsin had the highest Building Share of Real Estate Value (BSREV) in 1988, while Florida had the lowest (.47 for WI vs. .15 for FL); yet Wisconsin's farm Property Tax Rate (PTR) exceeded Florida's 4 to 1. Wisconsin, the high tax state, led Florida 3 to 1 in farm output per dollar of farmland value, 5 to 1 in farm buildings per dollar of farmland value and 7 to 3 in machinery/livestock.

The agricultural landholdings in Florida, the low tax state, were twice as concentrated as Wisconsin according to the GR, had 5.5 more land value per farm, had more acres per farm (3 to 2), more land value per acre (4 to 1), and led in total assets (11 to 8).

Extending Gaffney's data to the eight low property tax states below Florida and to the eight above Wisconsin, he found that the differences persisted and accumulated consistently. The lower property tax states were Florida, Arizona, New Mexico, Hawaii, Montana, North Dakota, Wyoming, California and Texas. The higher property tax states were Wisconsin, Delaware, Maine, Pennsylvania, New York, New Hampshire, North Carolina, Oklahoma, and Ohio.

It was found that higher property tax rates were associated with higher building values, smaller farms (lower land values per farm and per acre) and lower GR values (which indicates a broader distribution of farm land ownership). Higher ratios of capital investment in machinery and equipment as compared to real estate, lower shared of leased land, and fuller land usage, as measured by sales per land value were also apparent. From these state comparisons, Gaffney contends that:

> The egalitarian effects of a high property tax rate seem stronger than its negative incentive effects, even though buildings are part of the tax base. These egalitarian effects would be stronger if the tax base was limited to land value only, because the land share of real estate value rises steeply with size of farm. Untaxing buildings would also eliminate negative incentive effects.[14]

Gaffney firmly concludes that large farm units are less improved and less peopled than small and medium-sized farms. They get less output per land value and are possibly being held for long-term land speculation. Large farm units appear to be, in his words:

> oversized stores of value, held first to park slack money and only secondly to produce food and fiber, and complement owner's workmanship.... If they are less efficient, heavier property tax rates will induce them to release surplus land for others.[15]

Preferential Assessments, Zoning and
Other Farmland Protection Policies

Agricultural land receives some preferential treatment in assessment in all fifty states. The level and form vary among states, but generally, the preference is in the assessment of value in current use, rather than at some higher-valued use rendered by the market. Under the pressure of residential development, for example, the assessed market value of a farmland tract might be multiples of the value for farming, but under preferential assessment law the tract would be taxed only for its value agricultural use. With some preferential assessment contracts penalties in the form of fees or taxes are charged for land use changes.[16] In Pennsylvania, for instance, the corresponding statute states that:

- Counties may covenant with owners of land in farm, forest, water supply, or open space use. Assessments reflect fair market value of land so restricted. Such agreements may be negotiated to conform to more recent provisions of preferential use assessment described below. (Title 16, Sections 11941, ff, and Title 72, Section 5490.10, Pennsylvania Statutes).
- Upon application, qualifying agricultural land, agricultural reserve, and/or forest reserve may be given preferential use assessments. Requirements include ten-acre minimum size for agricultural land, an anticipated annual gross income of $2000, and qualification for compensation under a soil conservation program for at least three years. Rollback taxes may extend for up to seven previous tax years, and include six percent interest. (Title 72, Sections 5490.1, ff., Pennsylvania Statutes).

A USDA, Economic Research Service[17] survey found that, as expected, higher taxes were levied on farmland without a preferential assessment than with a preferential assessment, but it was a very small difference. Although there is a relatively large change in taxes when a change in preferential status is made, the evidence suggests that preferential assessments, in aggregate, do not make much difference in tax rates.

For instance, in 1992, average tax per acre of agricultural land with an assessment preference was $5.12 and without assessment preference it was $5.93. In 1993, the figures were $5.39 with assessment preference and $5.94 without it.

While it is sometimes assumed that preferential assessments that lower property taxes on farmland can help keep land in agricultural use and protect it from more intensive development, a survey of the literature shows that the opposite may be true:

There is general consensus from extensive research over a twenty-year period that the economic incentive offered by lower property taxes has had minimal effect in preventing conversion of farmland to more intensive uses. In urbanizing areas, the tax reductions have not matched the profits available from subdivision and development, and in some areas may have fueled land speculation.[18]

Since most agricultural land does not encounter competition from urbanization, preferential assessments have little overall effect on land use changes. In areas that are impacted by urban pressures and land speculation, the effect of the preference is so slight, compared to value increments for more intensive uses, that it is not an effective deterrent to development. Says Wunderlich:

> Only where landowners and local government have a long term contract agreement, with severe penalties for breaking the contract, are tax preference programs likely to have some effect. A capture of all the increase in land value due to a change in land use likewise could be a deterrent to land use change.[19]   .

Preferential assessments based on agricultural use value can be highly lucrative for rural landowners and yet may not guarantee long-term retention of prime farmland. In general, the tax savings for maintaining agricultural uses are insufficient to outbid sale prices offered by developers. As a result, farmland owners often can simply take advantage of sizable tax savings while speculatively waiting for land values to appreciate. Where rollback requirements or transfer taxes are in effect, the farmland owner may simply enjoy the equivalent of a low-interest or interest-free loan while holding property for later conversion.[20] Time is simply being bought through the use of an indirect subsidy but state differential taxation laws do not assure the continuation of prime farmland in perpetuity.

Another problem for agricultural, open space and forestland is that preferential assessment usually applies only to land and not buildings and improvements. The preferential tax laws for agriculture thus favor land and penalize buildings that then must carry a larger share of the tax burden. With higher tax rates applied to capital investments such as buildings, the economic incentive is to construct and maintain them less. Yet erecting farm buildings and maintaining their value, by raising conversion costs may do more to discourage land conversion than subsidizing land values. Wunderlich concludes, "as a measure to preserve agricultural land use the real property tax is weak...the preferential assessment is shallow...and the taxes carry little or no penalty for land use change."[21] He instead recommends a shift to property taxes that would fall primarily on land values as a better way to keep land in agricultural use.

Zoning can be a bigger determinant of value than land use. If, after investigating possibilities for implementing the split-rate tax in rural areas, the community would decide to award special protection to assure the viability of farming, this measure can be effected by zoning farmland for agricultural use only, and land prices would thus reflect agricultural use only. Since this tax would rise as the value of the land increased, or would fall as it decreased, there would be no basis for speculation in land. With a policy approach that kept taxes on agricultural lands appropriate to the profits that can be realized from farming, farmers might look favorably on zoning proposals.

Shifting taxes away from labor and capital and increasing taxes on land values would help keep farm costs affordable and farming viable. Finance, which currently is invested in site costs, would be available for new technologies and practices that could improve agricultural efficiency or soil quality.

In areas with particularly high land values farmers could be granted assessment exemptions that would reduce their tax liability. For instance, they could be granted a land assessment exemption of $500 an acre, which would roughly compensate them for in-land improvements such as grading, ponding, fertilizing, or tree breaking.

Improvements in assessment practices could also reduce farmers' tax liability under this reform. Assessors could exempt not only improvements on the land (buildings, fences, etc.) but also improvements in the land, such as grading, draining, ponding, irrigation, or fertilizing. The assessor could determine in each case how much such improvements increase the selling price of the land, and then, say, for ten years, deduct from the farmer's land tax bill one/tenth of the increase (plus interest on the unpaid balance). By thus recompensing him for his improvements which have become part of the taxable land value, the farmer would receive a legitimate reduction in his land value tax bill -- many farmers would be paying less taxes as the result of a shift to the split-rate tax.[22]

Yet another way to support and protect farmers for the risks of their occupation would be to make land value tax payments conditional on crop price and production, in which case they would be insured against occasional failure in the yield.[23] Certain forms of tax abatements could be offered. For example, any tax increases resulting from the shift to the split-rate tax could be left unpaid, to accrue against the eventual transfer of the farm by either sale or death; when the transfer is made, then the government can collect its back taxes from the new owner. With these concessions to the farmer, any inconvenience caused by a more effective property tax system would seem to be very minor indeed.

When implementing zoning policies and other contracts between government and landowners, principles of justice and fairness must be uppermost. The "Agricultural Reserves" prevalent in areas of California, such as Orange County, which went into bankruptcy a few years ago, have something to teach us in this regard. Many thousands of acres of this rich county were placed in such reserves, which means that it is only taxed for its use as farmland, although oil refining, food processing and vacant land were also approved as "agricultural uses." These agricultural preserve contracts between Orange County and a few gigantic landowners clearly benefited the few at the expense of the many.

The Impact of Urban Sprawl on Farmland Prices

Low-density, discontinuous land development, known as "sprawl," contributes to many of the ills that plague our society.[24] Sprawl negates the positive purpose of cities, which is to let people live and work close together so as to utilize and enjoy the maximum efficiency of community facilities and enterprises.

Suburban sprawl results from owners holding out for high capital gains on acreage cheaply obtained years ago. Evidence suggests that the split-rate property tax reform can create economic incentives to reverse this trend, thereby conserving open space and decreasing the pressures of development that absorb agricultural land.

Sprawl inhibits the use of transit, which thus necessitates auto travel, which in turn contributes to air pollution. Energy and time are wasted in traffic jams, reducing productivity and increasing stress. Health is endangered from pollution and automobile accidents. Per capita infrastructure costs are high because roads, sewers, and other public must be extended through sparsely occupied areas. Pockets of undeveloped areas are often too small and too scattered to support meaningful conservation uses or agriculture.

Sprawl penalizes farmers who want to raise crops instead of speculate and it discourages farm improvements on fringe land around cities. Sprawl also drives up the price of land in rural areas. This fuels land speculation while making it increasingly difficult to secure access to affordable land for farming operations.

The economic incentives promoting sprawl can be partially explained by the second of two ways in which landowners earn money. Either a land owner can make money by developing a site and renting or selling it to someone who will use that development, or a landowner can wait for population increases, wage increases, or public infrastructure improvements to impart value to a site, which he can appropriate through a higher rent or sales price.

All too often, land near public infrastructure (like a subway station or major road intersection) remains vacant or grossly underutilized because a landowner is waiting for a price in excess of what space users will pay today. This phenomenon forces developers to seek cheaper sites that are farther away from public infrastructure.

Once this cheaper land is developed and inhabited, the occupants of this area create political pressure to extend the infrastructure to it. When this process occurs, land prices rise, choking off development there, (even though additional capacity exists) and again drives developers and users even farther into the hinterland.

Landowners who underutilize valuable land sites with speculative intent thus contribute to sprawl and the costly, inefficient use of infrastructure. Perhaps the most effective way to counteract the negative effects of sprawl is to implement policies which encourage the development of housing in close proximity to jobs, schools, recreation, and shopping.

A significant amount of vacant and underutilized land exists within most urban areas. By encouraging development within the existing urbanized areas the two-rate property tax counteracts sprawl and land speculation, thus decreasing development pressures and land price escalation on nearby farmlands and other rural areas.

Taking the above facts into consideration, to minimize any possible negative impact on efficiently managed farms located in the path of urban development, the two-rate tax should probably first be implemented within boroughs and cities which are near these farms before the tax is extended to the rural areas. With the resultant decrease in development and speculative pressures on rural lands, farmland prices should remain affordable for working farmers while their tax liabilities would in most cases be the same or less than is currently the case when the two-rate tax will be implemented rurally.

Once farmlands are no longer plagued by sprawl, land speculation and the resultant land price inflation would be minimized. The two-rate property tax reform could be extended to townships and school districts that include farms without concern that it would have a negative impact on genuine farming operations.

Land Speculation and Land Tenure

A "Berry's World" cartoon shows a politician, in a suit and tie with a briefcase by his side, sitting in a barn alongside a dejected looking farmer. With his hand on the farmer's shoulder, the politician says, "We in Washington see prosperity just around the corner for the family farm. All you have to do is survive until the suburbs reach you, and you'll make a fortune in real estate!"

The average value per acre (land and buildings) of Pennsylvania farmland was $373 in 1970 but and had risen to $2,339 by 1995. Rent per acre of cropland went from $15.30 to $38.80 and for pasture from $8.30 to $29.80.[25] Rents and land costs are clearly rising faster than the return farmers receive for their labor.

Considering the well-being of society as a whole, is it better to reward farmers and other workers and working capitalists for their contributions in providing life's basic necessities or to permit speculation and profiteering in our land and resource base? A very high LVT rate might lower land prices, but that would benefit young entering farmers; the current property tax benefits land-speculating older farmers who are looking to leave farming. Do we want to encourage land speculation in our farmlands or new farming opportunities? Taxing farm buildings and farmers' income is quite literally a burden on the shoulders of those who labor. Removing such a burden would contribute to the overall well-being of farmers and their families.

Increasing the tax on land values would curb land speculation, thus maintaining land price affordability for viable farming operations. "Land hoarding, another deleterious consequence of land speculation, can be reduced by site value taxation."[26] To the landowner, taxes are an expense. To the public through government, the tax is a return. Whatever the division between public and private portions of value, the quantity of land and the full value remains unchanged.

But the taxation of land values does have a significant effect on market price and the functioning of society as a whole. Lowering the tax on land values raises market price, which means the public gets less in taxes while the individual seeking access to land must pay more. Raising the tax on land values lowers the market price of land. The public thus gets more in tax revenue, and the individual seeking access to land finds that the market price is more affordable.[27]

Urban sprawl and land price escalation turns farmers into land speculators and creates arid belts around cities. Land value taxation instead "would restrain the urbanization of valuable and productive farmland, but would negatively affect those farmers who have more of an eye to land speculation than farming."[28] Eliminating the non-productive drain of land speculation while allowing farmers to keep full profits from their labor would establish the economic base on principles of market freedom and efficiency as well as fairness and equity.

There is yet another important reason to eliminate the scourge of land speculation and private profiteering in land price escalation. Widely dispersed private ownership of land and affordable land access is fundamental to a well-functioning democratic system of governance. When land becomes owned by a relatively few and unaffordable to the many, produced wealth itself becomes concentrated, the rich/poor gap increases, and the democratic process itself is eventually undermined.

There is some cause for alarm as regards landownership in the USA. Overall concentration of landownership is far more extensive than many realize.[29] For example, 1.3 billion acres, or about 58 per cent of the total landmass, is in private hands. The broadest distribution of landownership among individuals is residential but this accounts for only two per cent (26.3 million acres) of private land. Another three per cent of the U.S. population owns 55 per cent of all the land and 95 per cent of private land. Furthermore, 568 companies control 301.7 million acres of the USA or eleven per cent of the total land area or 23 per cent of all private land. These same companies control 2 billion acres worldwide - an area larger than that of Europe.[30]

Interestingly enough, nonfarmers own 40% of all private farmland in the U.S. Between 1945 and 1970 the amount of farmland remained almost constant but the number of farmers who owned their land decreased by 62 per cent.[31] Working farmers who must rent land face an unfair disadvantage. In certain areas, landlord crop shares run 50% or more. Those who simply "own" land profit without labor.

We as a society surely must reverse this alarming trend so that working farmers can afford direct access to land.

The land speculation and land tenure problems are part of the same picture and their impact on agriculture is profound. For example, between 1950 and 1970 New York State lost 5.8 million acres of farmland but its urban area grew by only about 600,000 acres.[32] "The problem is a land shortage, not in the literal but in the economic sense, and its cause is primarily land speculation,"[33] says Peddle.

From such a perspective it can be understood that fundamental reforms of our system of taxation is essential if we are to reward productive labor rather than land speculation and efficiencies of scale and careful stewardship rather than impersonal big farm consolidations.

Tax Loss Farming

A 1996 study found that annual farm losses New York State exceeded farm income. Statistics support the argument for eliminating the farm income item from the State income tax for "by exempting farm income, you automatically exempt farm losses, thereby raising tax revenue by about $10 million per year."[34]

How could eliminating farm income tax actually increase the tax base, one might ask? The answer is in a deeper analysis that distinguishes "real" farmers from "pseudo-farmers." Pseudo-farmers include those who lose more money farming than they earn over the long run. Such a list may include:

- **Losers**: Bonefide farmers who intend to earn income by farming, but just happen to be failures and who will eventually be forced to stop farming,
- **Lifestyle Choice Farmers:** Those who enjoy farming or living on a farm and are willing to pay for the privilege,
- **Tax Farmers:** Those who own farms to reap an assortment of tax and other government benefits targeted to farmers,
- **Real Estate Farmers:** Some of these include real estate speculators who receive special farm tax benefits while waiting to sell the land as building sites,
- **Political Farmers:** Politicians who own farms to impress their farming constituents.

In 1993, there were about 35,000 taxpayers in New York who reported either positive or negative farm income as reported on federal Schedule-F forms. Of these, 14,000 had an income and 21,000 had a loss. Total farm income in New York was more than offset by the losses of farms owned by households with over $60,000 in non-farm income.

The data gives some indication of where the pseudo-farmers are located on the income distribution. Of households earning over $100,000 per year in non-farm income, 84% had farm losses. Of households earning $25,000 per year in non-farm income, only 30% had farm losses. Out of the 468 farm households, which earned between $100,000 and $200,000 in non-farm income, every one reported a farm loss in 1993. By contrast, for farm households earning under $5,000 in non-farm income, only 1 in 5 reported a farm loss. While families with $50,000 and less of non-farm income generated more farm income than loss, families with over $50,000 in non-farm income had net losses of over $11 million.

The New York study further noted that despite their motivation for unprofitable farming, pseudo-farmers still competed with real farmers. The extra output might benefit consumers in the short run, by driving down prices of local produce, but there was concern that in the long run such tax-loss farming operations "may lead to scarcity as real farmers are driven out of business and pseudo-farmers sell off for land development." This study in New York concluded that:

> "Real" farmers, i.e., those who have income exceeding losses over the long run, and who farm as their principle occupation, would benefit from the proposal to exempt farm income and loss from the calculation of adjusted gross income under the personal income tax. The provision would increase the financial rewards for farming, yet give the state a revenue gain because "pseudo" farmers could no longer use income losses from farming as a way to decrease their tax liabilities from other sources of income. [35]

Similar studies should be conducted in Pennsylvania and elsewhere as it is likely that the situation may resemble that in New York to some degree. If so, it would indicate that an increase in taxes on land values should be combined not only with a reduction or elimination of taxes on buildings and other capital improvements, but also with the exemption of farm income and loss from the calculation of adjusted gross income under the personal income tax. Such a policy approach would:

- Encourage and support efficient, profitable farming operations.
- Keep farmland prices at levels affordable for entry-level farmers.
- Discourage the purchase of farms for real estate speculation and tax shelter opportunities.
- Enhance the ability of the state and local tax base to provide necessary community services and infrastructure maintenance.

Considerations Concerning Subsidies

The number of U.S. farms decreased 45% from 1960 to 1989; average farm size increased 54% during the same period. In 1990, U.S. farmers received16% of their total income from direct federal payments; 62% of that money went to only 15% of the farmers - those whose sales exceeded $100,000 a year![36]

Since then farm subsidy programs have continued to benefit relatively few recipients. In 1994 the USDA spent $15 billion on farm programs, $10.3 billion of which covered subsidies, export and related programs, (An additional $37 billion was spent on non-farm food programs such as school lunches, food stamps, and child nutrition.) Nearly one-third of the $472 million funneled to Pennsylvanians from 1985 - 94 went to just 2% of the recipients.[37] Mike Mihalke, a spokesman for Senate Agriculture Committee member Rick Santorum, said that this data "is a resounding confirmation of our philosophy that the current farm system is actually working against small and mid-sized farmers in Pennsylvania and across the nation."[38]

In Pennsylvania's Franklin County farmers received $3,340,223 in federal farm subsidies from 1985-94. The top two percent of those recipients received 21.9% of the government money. The County's Consolidated Farm Service Agency handles four subsidy programs and paid $664,315 in 1994. That money went to about a quarter of the county's farms, a total of 336.

While some might argue that larger farms get more money because they have larger operations, other farmers believe subsidies keep inefficient farmers in business. For instance, John Stoner, one of six brothers who own a 1,700-acre dairy farm with 500 milking cows in Franklin County, says that even though his farm has benefited from subsidies, he supports gradually cutting the programs. He said, "We ought to allow the chips to fall where they may."[39]

But compared to other commodities receiving federal support, such as wheat at $1,730.5 million and cotton at $1,539.5 million per annum, supports for other major Pennsylvania agricultural commodities are considerably less with corn at $692.7 million and dairy at $158.1 million.

Instead of wasted subsidies, it might make more sense and be more equitable if the federal or state government could make low-cost loans available to farmers to provide them with the necessary capital to develop their farms properly and to tax exempt all farm improvements.

Pennsylvania Studies

While research on the potential effect of the split-rate tax on farmers in Pennsylvania has not been extensive, the studies that have been conducted indicate that a shift to land value based property taxes would not have a negative impact on most farmers. Since boroughs may soon receive permission by the state to use the split-rate tax, let us first explore the possible effect on farms within boroughs.

A 1995 study of Dauphin County[40] shows that the actual impact of a two-rate property tax on agriculturally assessed property is small when the percentage share of assessed value in a borough is analyzed.

In Dauphin County there are 16 boroughs. The presence of agricultural activity, while strong countywide, is rare or absent in boroughs. Analysis of the 16 boroughs showed that eight had no Assessed Agricultural Value (AAV). Of the eight that had farms only two had an AAV over five percent of the total borough assessment. Of these eight boroughs, four had an AAV of less than one percent of the total borough assessment.

The study concludes that farmland exists, as a general rule, outside the limits of cities and boroughs. Since farmland already enjoys protections that do not exist for other types of property both in zoning and tax policy (see Farmland Protection Policies), unwarranted concern for farmland within boroughs would deny the many benefits of the two-rate property tax option to the vast majority of citizens. If citizens of a borough should want to preserve farmland within their jurisdiction, then voter referendums could establish special urban agriculture land assessment districts or tax rebates.

Dauphin County, which contains Pennsylvania's capitol of Harrisburg, a city which taxes land values four times more than buildings, has a mix of urban, suburban, and rural land. Another 1995 study prepared by the Center for the Study of Economics for the Dauphin County board of commissioners found that farmers and clearly defined rural segments made up only 4.88% of the total taxable assessed value of the county. The average tax bill for a farm with buildings was $610 for that year. With the usual two-rate shift (tax on buildings 80% of current property tax rate) the farmer would pay $729, a difference of $119.[41]

Considering the overall benefits to society of this tax shift, and the fact that future farm improvements would be taxed at a lower rate while land speculation and thus land price inflation would be curbed, this small tax increase in rapidly developing Dauphin County should not prove prohibitive to viable farming operations. There is a lot of dispersed urban value in rapidly developing counties like Dauphin. More purely rural counties would have much less land value per acre and thus the land value tax would be that much less.

With this study as well, we have to consider the boost in land values created by farm subsidies. Minus artificial price supports, combined with decreased speculative pressures, agricultural land values would be less and thus the land value tax would most likely be lighter on working farmers then this study indicates.

A 1973 study[42] of rural Indiana County which is located about 55 miles northeast of Pittsburgh with a population of 75,000 (The largest city is Indiana with a population of 13,000) showed that the impact of the split-rate tax would vary according to the level of development of the individual tract or parcel. The county has considerable coal mining and about 55% of the area was in woodland and 33% in crop and pasture. Dairying was the chief farm activity.

The researcher took a representative sample of 60 farms out of the approximately 1200 on the tax books. He determined how each of them would be affected by a 25 per cent reduction in the building tax rate and a corresponding increase in the land tax rate which would be necessary to yield the same revenue to the county's school districts as under the present uniform rate system. He also determined the possible affects if all improvements would be exempted.

The study found that only two properties would receive considerable tax changes. One farm, quite near to town and fronting a main highway, had been developed to include a motel, rest home, apartments, and dairy store. This property would receive a reduction of $681.90 if its buildings were 25 percent tax exempt, or $2727.60 if they were totally untaxed.

The other property in Indiana County significantly impacted was a multi-million dollar corporation with an estimated value of holdings of $7 million. This corporation used some of its land for growing Christmas trees and landscaping shrubbery, but most of its land was waste, woodland or brush. With a 25 percent tax exemption for buildings, the tax increase under the split-rate system would be $2,988.40 and with buildings totally exempt it would increase to $11,953.60. While Christmas tree farms in Indiana County would tend to pay more taxes under this system, properties which would experience tax decreases would be the more highly developed ones; dairy farms tended to be in this group.

With 25 percent buildings tax exemption, half the sample of 60 farms would receive tax increases of less than $50 at the end of the first year, or $200 if improvements were completely exempted. Another quarter of the sample would receive tax increases or decreases within the $50-$100 range with the 25 percent improvements exemption, or $200-$400 range if improvements were altogether exempt. Tax changes of this magnitude would generally be considered quite moderate.

The researcher concludes that the majority of Indiana farms would not pay substantially higher taxes as a result of the shift to two-rate and would be benefited by improvements in the county's total economy which would likely be stimulated by the change.

The economic growth thus encouraged could create opportunities not only for the farmer himself, but could create jobs for his children who might otherwise have to migrate to distant cities in search for them, as an increasing number of farmers' children are forced to do these days. This might be of far greater importance to the farmer than small changes in his property tax.[43]

If particular properties have building-to-land ratios higher than the citywide average, then a split-rate property tax would impose a lower tax on them. In other words, with a revenue neutral shift to split-rate, they would save more compared to the usual one-rate property tax. If they have a lower ratio, they would pay more; if the same then there is no change.

A 1988 survey of Altoona assessments found only a handful of agricultural properties on the books. These parcels would save because it was determined that their building-to-land assessment ratios (7.6467:1)were higher than the citywide average (6.8084:1)[44] A similar study in Coatesville determined that the building:land ratio was 4.3:1, while the ratio for agricultural properties was 5.9:1 Thus it was shown that farmers most decidedly had saved.[45]

Other States

California passed the Wright Act in 1887 that allowed communities to vote to create irrigation districts for the building of dams and canals and to pay for them by taxing the increase in land value. Once irrigated, land was too valuable for grazing and too costly for hoarding. So cattlemen sold fields to farmers at prices the farmers could afford. In ten years the Central Valley was transformed into over 7,000 independent farms. Over the next few decades, vast tracts of treeless, semi-arid plains became the "bread basket of America" and one of the most productive areas on earth. It is a prime example of how land value taxation can promote and enhance the viability of both an efficient and equitable agricultural base.

In a 1987 study of farms in Ohio County in the northern panhandle of West Virginia researchers asked a farmland assessor to pick three average farms, three excellent farms, and three poor ones. The study clearly indicates that the best farms, (the ones with the highest value amount in buildings and improvements), benefited positively from this tax reform; average farms paid a somewhat higher percentage (but modest dollar amount) of taxes; while the biggest percentage changes (but still modest dollar amounts) fell on poorer farms.[46]

This policy approach is an incentive for good land use not only to urban but also to rural areas. On further consideration, the researchers also conclude that a broad application of the land value tax, which would include non-farm properties and the much greater land values in urban areas, would automatically affect a significant reduction of tax burdens throughout the entire farm sector.

While land value taxation would inhibit agricultural land speculation and promote more efficient and intensive use of farmland, it is not necessarily detrimental to large-scale agricultural pursuits if carried out efficiently.

A 1995 report on property tax valuation in the State of Hawaii shows that 65% of the property tax revenue comes from land assessments. Since 1990 the island of Kauai has shifted its taxes more towards land. For example, in 1990 agricultural land was taxed at 1.05 times the improvement rate. In 1995 it was taxed at 1.87 times the improvement rate.[47] For Kauai agricultural and conservation properties, assessment appeals were only 6.6% of the total number, but in Maui, which maintains the same property tax rate on buildings as on land values, they were 9.6%. Thus, it would seem that a two-rate property tax reduces, not increases, assessment appeals.[48]

Other Countries

Farmers have been a prime force behind the use of the split-rate tax in Australia, New Zealand, and Denmark, indicating that they benefit from it financially. In the Canadian province of British Columbia farm buildings and dwellings in rural areas are completely exempt for general purposes. Farmers' dwellings are taxable for school purposes while other buildings and structures are taxable only on aggregate assessed value over $50,000.

Historically, "site rating," as land value taxation is called in Australia, was applied first to farming districts. This policy was extended to towns and cities only after its suitability for, and acceptance by farmers had been demonstrated. Site rating was first applied to the shires of Queensland in 1887 specifically to ease the position of genuine farmers, who were finding that under the system of the time they were paying more than their own share of municipal costs to make up for the token payments from other owners of vast, undeveloped property. The situation was the same in New South Wales, where site rating was also applied first to the shires, then later on to urban areas.

In Western Australia, site rating was first used in the rural districts in 1902. Only in 1948 were the 21 urban councils given optional powers to use it. Site rating has since developed to become the dominant system in Australia where it is used in approximately two-thirds of all local government councils. The councils using site value comprise more than 92% of the municipalized area of Australia. The fact that the remaining eight percent have not changed shows site rating's appeal has been primarily to farmers. The rural parts of Victoria, which still tax buildings and farm improvements, are among the eight percent. Significantly, there is no public demand in other states to change back to what they now regard as an outdated system of taxing buildings.

The states of Queensland, New South Wales, and Western Australia apply site rating universally to farming properties. In South Australia, Victoria, and Tasmania, its application is not universal. Historically, in comparisons of development between these two groups of states, it has been shown that farmers generally have been in a sounder position in the ones that have taxed potential land value, rather than the actual development itself.

In the depression years of 1930 to 1939, total acreage farmed in the site-rated states increased by 21%. Those not rating site value, decreased by eight percent. Similarly, in the post war years, 1947 to 1959, acreage cultivated in the site-rated areas increased by 35%. Other areas not site rated decreased by one percent.

Two historical examples can help display what "genuine farmers" think of site rating. The term "genuine farmer" is important. The term "farmer" is often used loosely to describe anyone who owns rural property. It is important however, to distinguish between the genuine farmer, who lives and works on the farm, and the owner who holds rural property under developed as an investment. The effects upon the two, as far as rating is concerned, are not the same. It is the interests of resident farmers that are more important for the development of Australian agriculture. Australian farmers pay less with LVT in comparison to other tax systems. For example, 81% in Keilor Shire paid less, 77% in Eltham Shire, and 55% in Frankston and Hastings Shires (all in Victoria.)

The rural shires of Rosedale and Yea have used site rating since 1921. Reversion polls were taken in 1953 and 1959 to determine whether farmers wanted to retain site value or go back to taxing improvements. The vote left no doubt that farmers prefer site value after experiencing both systems. In Rosedale Shire 84% of the registered voters voted for site rating in 1953. In Yea Shire 68% voted in favor of site rating. While the voters in the town areas of Rosedale and Yea strongly favored site rating, the farmers did so even more.

Resident farmers benefit by lower rates under site value in the majority of cases, just as householders similarly do in the towns. Such was found to be the case for farmers in the old Keilor Shire, Eltham Shire, and Frankston and Mulgrave Shires. These areas are now mostly suburban but changed to site rating when the shires were once regarded as rural. This principle still holds for today's farming districts closest to Melbourne.

It is in the interests of all Victorians to ensure farmers that they have every incentive to produce - rating land value does exactly that. Genuine farmers understand this, and have always chosen site rating as their preference once given the opportunity. Genuine farmers have recognized the better balance of development for rural areas that site rating brings: more opportunities for their children in industry, building, transport, and trade. Site rating enabled better educational facilities and a whole host of other amenities to help stop, at least to some extent, the drift to the city.

The Danes, by old tradition, believe that the land belongs to the people.[49] The rapid industrialization and land enclosures of the 18th and 19th centuries saw this tradition come under growing attacks. Farmers in Denmark were hard-pressed in the second half of the 19th century. Many of them found support in the ideas contained in a newly released book Progress and Poverty, by Henry George. As the economic situation became even tougher for small farmers the Henry George Union was founded in 1902 and cooperated with other philosophic groups and public leaders to work for land value taxation as the basis for government expenses, instead of levying taxes on income and capital.

Eventually the Justice Party was formed on this platform. Their economic policy was simple - to collect the economic rent of land and abolish all taxes on labor and capital.

For a new political party, their results were astonishing. Progress was quick and in 1952, they won 12 seats out of a possible 179. They were instrumental in the creation of a government commission for ground rent in Denmark, which wrote its report clearly advocating the benefits of site revenue. In 1957 the Justice Party, together with other political groups formed what was to become the most prosperous Danish Government based on the principles of ground rent collection (land value taxation), liberalization of trade, and a tax freeze.

It was generally expected that after the formation of the government, some kind of land value taxation would be introduced, so land speculation ceased immediately. Legislation on taxation of increased land value was prepared, presented to parliament, and subsequently passed. The economic effects of the cessation of land speculation were astounding and aroused much attention. On October 2, 1960, the New York Times headlined, "Big Lesson from a Small Nation" and noted the many improvements in Denmark's economic situation.

Prior to the election of 1957, Denmark had a sizable deficit on her balance of payments, was considerably in debt abroad, and burdened with a relatively high interest rate, large unemployment figures, and an annual rate of inflation of approximately five percent. From 1957 to 1960, however, the following improvements took place:

- The enormous deficit on the balance of payments was turned into surplus.
- Denmark's total foreign debts of 1,600 million kr. were reduced to one quarter of this, about 400 million kr.
- The rate of interest, and hence mortgage levels went down.
- Unemployment was soon replaced by almost full employment, together with considerable increases in production and wages.
- Inflation was brought to a standstill. All wage increases were real wage increases, the highest in Denmark's history.
- The time was free of strikes, industrial production went up 32%, and investment rose 135%
- Savings increased immensely, since it again became profitable to accumulate savings.
- After three years with land value tax in force, Denmark had no foreign debt, no inflation, and an unemployment level of one percent, considered full employment.

So why is this not continuing? A number of factors were at play, too complex to document for the purposes of this paper. Essentially, lack of broad-based public understanding concerning the basic principles of this policy approach led to its demise after 1964 and Denmark again experienced a number of social and economic problems to the detriment of most farmers, other workers, and business owners.

Reflections on the Potential for Revival of
Sustainable Agriculture in Pennsylvania

The high price of land means that the modern food and agriculture system provides no options for those who cannot find a paying job other than subsistence on charity or government supports. Those with minimum wage incomes are finding it increasingly difficult to afford decent housing. These social problems and pressures are bound to increase with the cut-off of welfare and other government subsidies to the poor.

In Pennsylvania in 1991, 6.9% of the children were living in severely distressed neighborhoods.[50] The state ranked 23rd in a study of the fifty states (the national average is 6.2%). Lancaster County, known for its lush farmland, has some of the state's poorest areas. "When people think of Lancaster County...it's an idyllic scene," said Ron Sell, executive director of Pennsylvania Partnerships for Children. "The reality is there is the same poverty...and unemployment happening within the city of Lancaster as the city of Philadelphia."[51]

Now more than ever before there is the need to optimize the use of land resources to meet the food, fiber, and livelihood needs of people in an environmentally sustainable way.

The effects of the split-rate tax on future land use can only be conjectured, but it is likely that the selling price of currently marginal waste, wooded and brush land would fall noticeably because they would be taxed at a higher rate. These now more affordably priced rural lands could become magnets for land reclamation and new sustainable farming projects.

Intensively managed small farms producing a diverse range of food, fiber, livestock, and energy products for local markets are the order of the day. Bio-intensive farming methods depending on renewable energy sources - including animal power and biogas - can yield both social and environmental stability.[52] The establishment of labor and bio-intensive small farming operations can be greatly furthered by land value tax policies that remove taxes on labor and productive capital while promoting affordable land access.

Conclusions

While determining the potential impact of a shift from the traditional property tax to the split-rate tax on Pennsylvania farmers is a complex subject, in summary, there is a basis, in both theory and practice, for the following conclusions:

- Overall, as currently administered in most states, the property tax appears to be regressive since farm owners with larger amounts of land value pay disproportionately less in taxes than those with less valuable holdings.

- The excessive complexity of the property tax is an administrative short-coming and must be remedied before the real property tax can become an effective instrument of land use policy.

- Smaller farms tend to have more buildings than larger ones but pay more because of these improvements under the current system.

- Overtaxing buildings and undertaxing land favors large farming operations that are not necessarily the most efficient.

- Lower property tax rates coincide with greater concentration of farm ownership and higher land costs, which is a barrier to entry-level farmers.

- The property tax would be more progressive if changed to a pure land tax that exempts buildings.

- The greater the shift of property taxes from buildings and onto land values the more likely that the surplus land of larger, less efficient farms or speculative holdings would be released for affordable purchase by entry-level farmers.

- While preferential assessments and farm subsidies may not be helpful in preserving farmland and, as currently administered, may be inequitable, zoning, tax abatements, and improvements in assessment practices could work in tandem with the split-rate tax shift, especially in urbanizing areas with high land values.

- Urban sprawl and land speculation contribute to land price inflation, which is a major barrier to entry-level farming. By encouraging infill-development and redevelopment within already urbanized areas the split-rate tax could decrease land cost pressures on farmers.

- Concentration in farm ownership has proceeded at an alarming pace for the past several decades, making it essential to fundamentally reform our system of taxation - then we can reward productive labor rather than land speculation, efficiencies of scale and careful stewardship rather than im-personal big farm consolidations.

- Most farmers in rural areas of the state and particularly those with propor-tionately higher building-to-land ratios will save with a shift to the split-rate tax.

- Although some farms near urban areas may pay more with this tax re-form, it may not be significantly more, and the overall improvements in the economic climate of the locality which would result would be of bene-fit to the farming sector as well.

- Substantially shifting taxes from buildings and productivity and onto land values could be a major stimulus for the revival of sustainable agriculture in Pennsylvania and thus could help to alleviate poverty and other social problems.

- Farmers in other parts of the world have actively supported Land value based property taxes.

Stated succinctly, the split-rate tax is likely to impact Pennsylvania farmers and farmland as follows:

- Discourage speculation in land
- Reduce the price of land to equate with its value for production
- Enable new entrants to more easily obtain land
- Limit farm sizes to those of the most productive units
- Enable the reduction of taxation on earnings and capital
- Reduce interest rates as land became more affordable
- Prevent rural depopulation
- Discourage urban sprawl on farm land
- Encourage owner-occupation rather than absentee ownership
- Promote more responsible use of land.

Our evidence thus suggests that the split-rate tax policy approach, especially with a heavy reduction of millage rate on building values, would significantly enhance incentives for the continuation and expansion of a viable, efficient, and sustainable agriculture in Pennsylvania and anywhere else if used.

---

[1] Dr. C. Lowell Harriss, "The Economic Effects of Today's Property Tax," Encylopaedia Britannica, 15th Edition (1974).

[2] Alanna Hartzok, "Pennsylvania's Success with Local Property Tax Reform: The Split Rate Tax," American   Journal of Economics and Sociology, vol. 56 no.2 (April, 1997):205.

[3] US. Department of Agriculture, Economic Research Service, "Major Land Uses in the United States" 1992.

[4] Economic Research Service, US. Dept. of Agriculture, Agricultural Real Estate Taxes, AREI Update No. 9, 1995.

[5] "Own revenue" is taxes, fees, charges generated within the fiscal unit, that is, no funds transferred from other jurisdictions. Advisory Commission on Intergovernmental Relations, Significant Features of Fiscal Federalism, Vol. 2 (1994): 66, 67.

[6] Gene Wunderlich, "Land Taxes in Agriculture: Preferential Rates and Assessment Effects," The American Journal of Economics and Sociology, vol. 56 no. 2 (April, 1997): 220.

[7] Gene Wunderlich and John Blackledge, "Taxing Farmland in the United States," USDA Economic Research Service Agr. Econ. Report #679, (March 1994)

[8] Gene Wunderlich, "Land Taxes in Agriculture," 218-219.

[9] Mason Gaffney, "Rising Inequality and Falling Property Tax Rates," published in Land Ownership and Taxation in American Agriculture, edited by Gene Wunderlich, (San Francisco: 1992 Westview Press) 119.

[10] Gaffney, "Rising Inequality," 120.

[11] *Ibid.*, 123.

[12] *Ibid.*, 125.

[13] *Ibid.*, 128.

[14] *Ibid.*, 131.

[15] *Ibid.*

[16] See: David Aiken, State Farmland Preferential Assessment Statutes, Univ of Nebraska RB 310, September 1989.

[17] "Agricultural Real Estate Taxes," USDA , Economic Research Service, AREI update no. 9 (1995)

[18] Jane Malme, Preferential Property Tax Treatment of Land, (Cambridge: Lincoln Institute of Land Policy, 1993) 22.

[19] Wunderlich, "Land Taxes in Agriculture," 5.

[20] Justin R. Ward, F. Kaid Benfield, and Anne E. Kinsinger, "Reaping the Revenue Code: Why We Need Sensible Tax Reform for Sustainable Agriculture," Natural Resources Defense Council, New York (1989): 73-74.

[21] *Ibid.*, 7.

[22] Steven Cord, " Impact of a Graded Tax on a Rural Area," The American Journal of Economics and Sociology, vo. 35 no. 1 (January 1976) 74.

[23] Incentive Taxation, October 1994 , Henry George Foundation of America, 2000 Century Plaza Suite #238, Columbia, MD, 21044.

[24] Rick Rybeck, "Tax Reform Motivates Sustainable Development," American Institute of Architects/DC News, (Dec. 1995/Jan. 1996) 4-5.

[25] "Statistical Summary Annual Report," National Agricultural Statistics Service, USDA/Pennsylvania Department of Agriculture, PASS-119 (1995-1996) 88.

[26] Francis K. Peddle, Cities and Greed: Taxes, Inflation and Land Speculation, Canadian Research Committee on Taxation, Ottawa, Ontario, Canada (1994) 180.

[27] For a discussion of "market price" as distinct from "full value" see Gene Wunderlich, "Land Taxes in Agriculture," op.cit. 6.

[28] Peddle, op.cit., 223.

[29] Peter Meyer, "Land Rush - A Survey of America's Land," Harper's Magazine, January 1979, 49.

[30] Meyer, op.cit., 50.

[31] Peddle, 57.

[32] Meyer, 63.

[33] Peddle, 58

[34] As reported in 6/5/96 memorandum to the Senate Minority Finance Committee Staff with data from Tax Free Farm Income, 3/20/96, 2.

[35] *Ibid.*, 2.

[36] US News & World Report, (March 25, 1991) 19, citing USDA.

[37] As reported in "Farm Subsidies Fair?" Public Opinion, Chambersburg, PA 9/9/95, 3A.

[38] *Ibid.*

[39] *Ibid.*

[40] Available from the Center for the Study of Economics, 2000 Center Plaza, #238, Columbia, MD, 21044.

[41] Available from the Center for the Study of Economics, 2000 Center Plaza, #238, Columbia, MD, 21044.

[42] Steven Cord, "Impact of a Graded Tax on a Rural Area," The American Journal of Economics and Sociology, vol. 35 no. 1 (January 1976): 71-75.

[43] *Ibid.*, 4.

[44] Steven Cord, "Survey of Altoona Assessments," October 1988, available from the Center for the Study of Economics; see footnote no.37.

[45] The Coatesville study was also conducted by Steven Cord and is available from CSE.

[46] Walter Rybeck, Center for Public Dialogue, 10615 Bruswick Ave, Kensington, MD, 20895.

[47] Property Taxation in Hawaii, research from SRD Group, 247 Flinders Land, Melbourne, 3000, Australia, 1995.

[48] Incentive Taxation Bulletin, Henry George Foundation of America, May 1995. Tax information provided by Gary Kiyota, Tax Administrator for the County of Hawaii.

[49] Viggo Starcke, Triumph or Fiasco, SV Press A/S (Stig Vendelkers Forlag), Denmark , (1972).

[50] Kids Count Data Book, a study paid for by the Annie E. Casey Foundation, as reported in "A rough go for Pa. kids" Public Opinion, Chambersburg, PA, 4/25/94

[51] *Ibid.*

[52] David C. Korten, "Civic Engagement to Create Just and Sustainable Societies for the 21st Century," The People-Centered Development Forum, (New York, NY, 1/10/96)

These organic apples, grown at the Aradhana eco-homestead, headquarters for Earth Rights Institute's East Coast office, won first place in the Franklin County Fair, Pennsylvania, on August 21, 2001.

22

Lunch and Lecture with Ralph Nader

Green presidential candidate Ralph Nader was in Philadelphia on Wednesday, March 8th for lunch with a number of land value taxation advocates at the famous White Dog Cafe on Sansom Street near the University of Pennsylvania. Attending the luncheon gathering, which raised $1000 for Nader's presidential campaign chest, were Melanie Douty, Richard Biddle, Joan Sage, Bradley Keach and Herb Lubowitz, all members of the Philadelphia based Henry George School of Social Science, Jake Himmelstein, Treasurer of the Council of Georgist Organizations, Paul Johnson, former Board President of the Henry George School of Northern California, Rebecca Hicks, editor of Green Revolution, a publication of the School of Living, Anne Goeke, Green Party leader and activist from Lancaster, Ted Gwartney, Director of the New York City based Robert Schalkenbach Foundation, and Alanna Hartzok, United Nations NGO Representative, International Union for Land Value Taxation, who ad worked with Green Party organizer Dan Kinney to make arrangements for the gathering.

Nader, already familiar with basic ideas of Henry George, requested and was given a brief update on the movement for land value taxation. He gratefully received an information packet containing Alan Durning's book *Tax Shift* and other relevant material. When shown *The New Economics of Sustainable Development*, James Robertson's latest book (published by the European Commission) that makes the case for eco-tax reform, land value taxation and citizen dividends, he requested and received this as well.

Stating that there is a huge problem with media access for third party candidates, Nader realizes that a major obstacle to getting his campaign issues out to the broad public is that not enough time is given for depth consideration of issues. He was looking to us for sound bites to get our message across and was given several suggestions such as "tax waste, not work" and "tax bads, not goods." The Nader campaign will be approaching a dozen major civic groups to invite them to co-host a debate that the media would want to cover.

Very articulate about the problem of wealth maldistribution and how our democracy has been compromised and undermined by the concentration of economic power, Nader is clearly looking for powerful solutions to add to his arsenal of proposals for change. He very much likes the Tobin Tax, a proposed tax on global financial exchanges of 1% or less which would raise billions of dollars from currency exchange and speculation. The impact that our discussion made on him was immediately apparent, as he proposed that there be public debates about the merits of land value taxation and the economics of Henry George in his talk to several hundred students and Green Party members in the Steinberg-Dietrich Hall at the Wharton School immediately following our lunch with him.

Nader is running a serious campaign for President under the Green Party ticket, intent on winning 5% of the vote, which would give several millions of dollars of funding for Green Party efforts. He is running "To escalate people's expectations of what is possible," stating that there are "huge capabilities being obstructed by the concentration of power."

When asked about taking votes away from Democrats, Nader responds with a question, "Are you satisfied with the Democrats?" He reports getting four Republican votes for every six Democratic votes in California for his previous run for President to show that there is definitely room for a third party force that can cross both major party lines of the "duopoly."

He says "they have you hostage if you do not particularly like the Democrats but accept them as the least bad choice. Most of you are taxpayers, consumers, workers and voters. Do you want more power for all those roles?"

Nader views our government as rule by the few, with the entrenchment of power and wealth defeating the advance of democracy. He states that Thomas Jefferson, Abraham Lincoln, and Teddy Roosevelt all warned of the excesses of monied interests.

"These are booming times according to GDP and executive stock, and news reports that things could not be better, but there is a huge disconnect between this and the majority of people," says Nader. "Anyone who controls the yardstick controls the agenda."

He points out that with the nine trillion dollar plus GDP there is massive consumer debt and the US has 20 percent child poverty, the highest of any Western nation. The majority of workers are making less today when adjusted for inflation then in 1979. More and more family members are trying to eek out a middle class living, spending 163 hours more a year working for less than 20 years ago. Fifty million Americans try to make ends meet on less than $10 an hour. Bill Gates wealth equals that of 120 million Americans, while vast numbers of Americans are broke with no net wealth at all or deeply in debt. Public works, transportation, schools, drinking water quality and other infrastructure is crumbling while stadiums and arenas are being built for the enrichment of a few, like the Roman stadiums of past ages.

Here are other themes that Nader touched on:

- We now have a plutocracy - rule by the rich and powerful, where decisions are made by the few not the many.
- Industries use government funds - corporate socialism produces a corporate state.
- Government policy entrenches fossil fuel and nuclear, not clean technology.
- Corporations need to internalize their costs instead of turning our air and water into sewers.
- The military budget is twisted into a grotesque excess.
- The National Security state vendors take $80 billion to defend prosperous countries. Funds for F20 fighters and B2 bombers are more than combined federal budgets allocated for social needs.

Nader asks of the American people, "Do you really want this?" He told the story of Granny D, an 85 year old from New Hampshire who walked 3100 miles across the country and asked at her news media gathering at the Arlington National Cemetery, "Did those brave men give up their lives for this?" referring to the sorry state of democracy in America.

"American people have lost their taste for self government," says Nader. He says we have been living in a state of increasing demoralization and that it is time for another populist progressive movement. We have to move beyond even participatory democracy to "initiatory democracy" where people are not simply following a movement, but they themselves become leaders who are putting forth and implementing ideas to create a better political and economic system.

Quoting the Roman statesman and philosopher Cicero who said that "Freedom is participation in power," Nader is calling for strengthening the roots of a democratic society. He says:

> We can have democracy or concentration of wealth in the hands of the few - not both. The two major parties are like fossils, they have no grassroots. They raise huge amounts of money for electronic combat and no longer have storefronts or any real loyal supporters. It is one corporate party with two heads wearing different makeup.

Speaking to concerns of the students against sweatshops movement who helped organize his talk at the Wharton School, Nader spoke about the "corporatization of universities." He suggests that the University of Pennsylvania website list all corporate contributions so that graduate students working on projects will know if their professor is a corporate consultant.

Nader further urged that research universities should have annual meetings with their Boards of Trustees - a "meet your rulers day" with all the corporate sponsors and trustees on an auditorium stage to answer questions from students for at least three hours every year.

He urged students to become part of statewide PIRGs (Public Interest Research Groups) noting that New York State has 100 staff and 14 offices. He told us that in 1976 when 26,000 Penn State students signed a petition for PIRG funding, the students lost two to one on the panel, which was two-thirds industrial and agribusiness representatives. "They knew that if they allowed PIRG the students would go after those companies," he said.

Nader is optimistic about the ripple affect of the student anti-sweatshop movement:

> They have learned more about corporate abuse than they ever would in the classroom and realized their power as students to join together and use the libraries, newspapers, and campus media, all to create a movement without having to go begging a TV station for 30 seconds in the evening news.

Nader says that the big injustices in the world are not being dealt with in the college curricula or in the media, which is 90% entertainment and ads. "We are losing control of our children to hucksters and videos." He would like to see an end to the trivialization of the media and urges citizens to "take control of what we own as a people" meaning the airwaves and broadcast bands.

He called taxation a "nightmare of inequity and inefficiency" stating that:

> We need a big debate on different kinds of taxation; to talk about how corporations are freeloading on public services and getting tax breaks while taxes are falling on workers and smaller businesses. We need to open a debate about land taxation and Henry George, to tax bad things not good things, and not tax people who go to work everyday.

Addressing growing concerns about the World Trade Organization (WTO) and IMF and World Bank policies, he advocates trade agreements which do not impinge on consumer, labor and environmental issues or make them vulnerable to trade restrictions, stating that we need to pull up not pull down standards for trade agreements. He explains the problem with the WTO by bringing the issues close to home, asking

> What if the state of Georgia had no minimum wage, no environmental or workers safety laws, and so could produce cheaper goods and thus control the market, which is what the WTO wants worldwide. Global markets without global democracy is a big problem.

Ralph Nader intends to ignite a small progressive movement and turn it into a major political force. He is drawing the line in the sand for us. Dare we step across?

23

Diary of an Outreach Activist

Published in *Land & Liberty*, Winter 1999.

Bangkok, Thailand -- Member of a delegation working with the Millennium Peoples Assembly Network (MPAN) to establish a permanent Global Peoples Assembly to serve as "inclusive voice of the world's people." My particular focus is to affirm the importance of the ground rent of the earth's land, water, and air as the proper and just funding source for global governance institutions.

The Dhammakaya Foundation, our host, is a Buddhist organization working for world peace through inner peace. In 30 years it has become the largest Buddhist group in Thailand. We met for discussions and gala dinners and outings with our hosts of the Dhammakaya MPAN committee many times during our weeklong visit. The topic I presented was "Financing Planet Management - Sovereignty, World Order, and the Earth Rights Imperative."

We were given a special place of honour at the Lights of Peace Day ceremonies at the nearly completed Dhammakaya peace pilgrimage site, which is being built to serve one million meditators. Nearly 200,000 people gathered for meditation and spiritual teachings around the golden domed cettiya, or stupa, upon which sat 10,000 orange robed monks.

As the full moon rose high above and the monks chanted, the Abbot lit a torch that was taken by a runner down to our platform. With a long silver lighting stick, we lit a torch that then lit 100 smaller torches and then the lamp in a huge urn. Spreading from there, within moments, the lights of 100,000 other torches were lit in dozens of concentric circles around the stupa and among the people, giving a spectacular and magical display of the Lights of Peace as a choir of children sang songs of jubilation.

The Hague, Netherlands -- Participating in the The Hague Appeal for Peace conference with nearly 8000 activists from all over the world. This was the largest peace conference ever held on earth. Plenary speakers included UN Secretary General Koffi Annan and Archbishop Tutu. As Co-Chair of the Peoples Agenda

Committee, I had helped to compile sections on land tenure and taxation policy that advocate land value taxation. Rob Wheeler, Coordinator of MPAN, and I had several occasions to play our guitars and lead the MPAN participants in songs of peace and justice. Closing the final meeting, former UN Assistant Secretary General Robert Muller, now a beloved "Peoples Ambassador" joined us on his harmonica.

New York City -- The UN Department of Public Information's 52nd Annual Non-Governmental Organizations Conference at the UN. I organized and chaired a noonday workshop entitled Financing Local-to-Global Public Goods: An Integrated Perspective. The workshop description follows:

> World stability and human security require that we re-think the logic of globalization, including the best ways to finance public goods such as health, education, infrastructure, environmental sustainability and efforts for peace and conflict resolution.

Workshop presenters addressed these concerns, discussed successful public finance practices and work-in-progress on "green tax shift" policies which harness incentives for both efficient and equitable wealth production and distribution AND sustainable economic and social development.

Workshop presenters were Ted Gwartney, Executive Director, Robert Schalkenbach Foundation; Gina Erickson, State Program Director, Centre for a Sustainable Economy; Joshua Vincent, Executive Director, Centre for the Study of Economics, and Rashmi Mayur, Special Adviser, MPAN.

Oaxaca, Mexico -- Milenio Verde (the Green Millennium), a conference on the Global Effort for the Conservation of the Planet was hosted by the Mexican Green Party in this colorful multi-cultured city six hours drive south of Mexico City. Jeff Smith, President of the Geonomy Society, and I communicated the Georgist economics paradigm to nearly 300 Green Party activists from 30 countries. Simultaneous translation into French, Spanish, and English facilitated the exchange. Interspersed with the highly intellectual content of the week's proceedings were joyous dance performances, beautiful handcraft displays, and chocolate drinking ceremonies presented by local people.

Speaking on the panel on Urban and Rural Development, I presented an overview of green tax shifting which included the work with land value taxation in cities in Pennsylvania. Jeff Smith, on a panel on Sustainability, outlined the basics of geonomics and the citizen's dividend.

I moderated a panel on Electoral and Governmental Experience of the Green Force which included Green leaders form Africa (Senegal), France, and Mexico's Green Party Presidential candidate Jorge Gonzalez Torres.

The last day of Milenio Verde found us atop Monte Alban, a central mountain ringed by the Oaxaca Valley that in turn is encircled by a ring of mountains. Two hundred of us formed a silent circle in the ceremonial center of this Mayan temple complex. As the full moon rose, silhouetting the magnificent pyramids, a shaman performed an earth healing ritual and brightly clothed indigenous people danced and drummed.

The Great Cetiya at The Dhammakaya Foundation World Headquarters near Bangkok, Thailand. Built to last 1000 years, there are grounds for one million people to meditate together for world peace. The author stands on the far left of the group in the middle. The photo was taken on the Light of Peace Day, March 1st, 1999.

24

IMF and World Bank Protest Journal

This is the author's personal experience of the history-making Mobilization for Global Justice movement that brought more than 50,000 activists to the streets, churches, synagogues, and universities of Washington, D.C. from April 8 – 17, 2000.

I arrived in Washington early Friday afternoon, April 14, after a short trek from my home in south central Pennsylvania. Sierra Club pack on my back and yellow and green protest sign in hand, I checked in first at the Mobilization Convergence Center on Florida Avenue to pick-up the latest events listings among the tables full of flyers and announcements. Members of dozens of environmental, labor, student and social justice organizations were taking part in the actions. Signs, slogans, banners and buttons were everywhere. Several hundred people milled about outside enjoying a vegetarian lunch prepared by the meal crew at the Center.

I had to decide among numerous teach-ins and rallies being held that day and the next, which included:

- Teach-In on the Devastating Effects of the IMF and the World Bank
- Latin America Solidarity Conference
- Keep Space for Peace
- Sweatshops: Globalizing the Resistance
- National Student Day of Action to Lift the Economic Sanctions on Iraq
- Issues forums at American University, University of the District of Columbia, All Soul's Church and the Convergence Center on Disarmament, Corporate Globalization, Narmada Valley, Climate Change
- Impacts of Globalization on the Environment and Human Rights
- Justice in Health Care
- A demonstration at the Treasury Department and the White House addressing the enormous waste of our tax dollars on Star Wars Development
- A protest at the Mexican Embassy against Mexico's military policy against autonomous indigenous communities in Chiapas and to support the Zapatista challenge to World Bank/IMF land policies.

I headed off for the Foundry United Methodist Church for the International Forum on Globalization (IFG) Teach-In but found the church already filled to capacity. Buying the half-price ticket, I joined the over-spill crowd in a church down the street where the speakers were being viewed on a big video screen. The event had begun at 9:00 am and would continue on until 10:30 that night. Every one of the speakers I heard was dynamic and highly informative. The line-up of 30 speakers that day at just the IFG venue included:

- Maude Barlow, Council of Canadians, Canada
- Walden Bello, Focus on the South, Thailand
- Catherine Caufield, Author
- John Cavanagh, Institute for Policy Studies
- Herman Daly, University of Maryland
- Kevin Danaher, Global Exchange
- Oronto Douglas, Environmental Rights, Nigeria
- Susan George, Transnational Institute, France
- Martin Khor, Third World Network, Malaysia
- Andrew Kimbrell, Center for Technology Assessment
- David Korten, People-Centered Development Forum
- Jerry Mander, International Forum on Globalization
- Robert McChesney, University of Illinois
- Anuradha Mittal, Food First
- Njoki Njehu, 50 Years is Enough, Kenya
- Vandana Shiva, Research Foundation for Science & Ecology, India
- Lori Wallach, Public Citizen

Strolling in front of the White House after leaving the IFG Forum at about 6:00 pm, I struck up a conversation with a DC policeman sitting in his squad car. He was genuinely interested in what the protests were all about, listening carefully as I described concerns for the worldwide maldistribution of wealth, the burdensome debt and structural adjustment programs imposed by the IMF and World Bank and the kind of people/planet finance system that could replace those institutions. Tears came to his eyes as he said he wished he could be doing something more meaningful with his life. I urged him to organize talks and discussions on these issues with his fellow police officers. He graciously took my information packet, said he would be in touch with me by email to learn more, and cautioned me to be careful.

Arriving at the tail end of the kick-off for Ralph Nader's Presidential Candidacy, a drinks and snacks fundraiser with Ralph at the Luna Grill on Connecticut Avenue, I chatted tax policy issues with Green Party and Jubilee Justice activists before continuing a few steps further to Othellos. A room had been reserved there for DC land value tax advocates and interested others to discuss together how we could better organize so our message could be heard in this mass movement. Those around the table included:

- Deb Katz, director of the Washington Regional Network for Livable Communities
- Cheryl Cort, president of the Washington Regional Network for Livable Communities
- Anne Goeke, local-to-global Green Party and Women in Black leader
- Adamou Garba from Nigeria who serves as President of the African Federation of Green Parties
- June Lang, originally from Zimbabwe, now a peace and justice activist from Lancaster
- Jeff Hammond, formerly with Redefining Progress and editor of the book Tax Waste Not Work, now a congressional aide
- Sam Husseini, Communications Director for the Institute for Public Accuracy
- Jim Schulman, Director of Sustainable Community Initiatives
- Joshua Vincent, Director of the Center for Economic Studies
- Walt Rybeck, Director of Center for Public Dialog and wife Erica
- Rick Rybeck, with the Washington Planning Department and wife Ellen
- Alanna Hartzok, your reporter and UN NGO Representative for the International Union for Land Value Taxation

Over Italian food and red wine, this "table of people who are working to save the world," as the waiters called us, networked and discussed the relevance that a shift to land and resource based taxes had to the Jubilee 2000 movement and the establishment of equitable public finance systems in DC and worldwide. After a good nights sleep at the comfortable home of Washington friends, I bid farewell to my gracious hosts and headed off for my teach-in choice of the day, the Latin America Solidarity Conference at St. Steven of the Incarnation Episcopal Church. Soon six or seven hundred people had arrived to attend this daylong educational event.

The morning session began with an announcement that at 8:45 a.m. fire wardens had declared that the Mobilization's Convergence Center on Florida Avenue had unsafe electrical wiring and thus was a fire hazard. Their pronouncement was backed up by 200 police officers that closed the Center down, confiscating the big street theatre puppets, signs, food and the three food trucks. As closing doors were locking out hundreds, a few who spoke up against search and seizure without warrants were arrested. Some pondered why response by officials to similar conditions concerning public safety in the housing units of poor neighborhoods was so rare in comparison.

The morning good news was that a group of 25 people, 20 of whom were from 11 countries from the global south, had arrived at 6:30 a.m. at the doorstep of the home of World Bank President James Wolfensohn. Displaying "Wake Up World Bank" signs, this delegation sang songs of peace and justice under the watchful eyes of police and plainsclothes security officers and a bevy of media. Wolfensohn appeared and cautiously approached the protestors. Dr. Vineeta Gupta, who has documented numerous examples of human and environmental exploitation resulting from World Bank policies, presented him with a letter. Wolfensohn said he would read it later. This small and brave Indian woman said, "No, I will tell you what it says NOW!" and proceeded to do so.

We continued on with the Latin American Solidarity Teach-In. Organizers put before us a feast of 24 workshops and plenary session speakers that included:

- Kevin Danaher, Co-Founder of Global Exchange and Editor of Corporations are Gonna Get Your Mama and 50 Years is Enough
- Bertha Lujan, Frente Autentico del Trabajo, Mexico
- Camille Chalmers, Haitian Platform to Advocate Alternative Development
- Peter Mott, Interconnect
- Jennifer Harbury, Global Exchange
- Artruro Griffiths, Center for Community change
- Chuck Kauffman, Nicaragua Network

To give you a further impression of the vast range of issues of concern discussed in just this one teach-in of the April 15 day at the Mobilization, here are some of the topics of the 24 workshops presented at the Latin American Solidarity Teach-In:

- Fair Trade/Alternatives
- The CIA in Latin America
- Environmental Challenges in Latin America
- New Visions and Challenges to Democracy
- Workers Resisting Privatization, Downsizing and Union-Busting
- The Drug War in Latin America
- Sweatshops without Walls (U.S. Farmworkers)
- Indigenous Struggles in Latin America
- Labor Organizing in Defiance of Corporate Control
- Land and Peasant Issues
- US-Cuban Relations
- North American Free Trade Agreement/WTO
- Women and Globalization: The Brunt of the Burden, the Force for Change
- IMF/World Bank
- International Campaign for Human Rights
- Immigration
- Human Rights: The Violations Continue
- Militarization

- Haiti
- Debt
- Fighting the Global Sweatshop
- Non-Violence Training
- Hot Spot: Bolivia

In the workshops I attended, I learned about the vision of democracy of the Zapatista and Pro-Democracy Movements in Mexico and Peru, land struggles in Central and South America, the plan of the World Bank to give loans for the poor to purchase land (with interest of course, any way to make a buck), and the Cochabamba Federation of Factory Workers of Bolivia. The latter, led by Oscar Olivera, were among the groups of workers and church leaders who successfully rallied against water-price hikes and privatization. Oscar was forced into hiding, escaping detention hours before President Hugo Banzer imposed a state of emergency and rounded up protest leaders. After four days of hopping between safe houses, Olivera emerged on April 12 after verbal assurances he would not be arrested and traveled the next day to the Mobilization in Washington.

At the Bolivia workshop, I linked up with Georgeane Potter who is also in the middle of the struggles there. Georgeane leads the Jubilee 2000 movement in Bolivia, was schooled at George Washington University and has written two books on the IMF/World Bank. We got in her car and headed downtown for the scheduled Press Conference with Olivera. In this very fluid Mobilization, the press was instead trailing the crowd who were protesting against the U.S. prison-industrial complex and in support of a retrial of Mumia Abu Jamal. On a corner just down from the IMF and World Bank buildings, we waited on alert amidst chants of "Whose Streets? Our Streets!" Word passed our way that the police had corralled a number of protestors. Neither Georgeane nor I intended to be arrested for civil disobedience, so when numbers of protestors started pressing towards us we thought it was a good time to get back to the car. On the news that evening we learned that 600 had been arrested shortly thereafter and carted off to jail.

After the two-hour wrap-up strategy discussion back at the Latin American Solidarity Conference, I returned again to my friend's warm hospitality for a pleasant nights rest. The next day was to be the Big One.

Some of the early-bird protestors were out at the perimeter at 6:30 a.m., necessitating the arrival of some IMF/World Bank officials by buses and vans at an even earlier hour, or having to find ways to get to their meeting rooms through tunnels connecting the buildings. This was quite a departure from their normally unimpeded routine of arriving by limousine.

Georgeane picked me up around 10:00 on Sunday morning, April 16. We decided to drive as far as we could towards the Rally Against the IMF/WB at the Ellipse between the White House and the Mall. After parking the car, we scouted around a while, observing protest scenes at every intersection around the perimeter established by the police as a shield around the IMF/WB buildings where meetings were being held Sunday and Monday. The "Old Grannies" of the Women's International League for Peace and Freedom were out doing their funny but serious songs, protest banners were unfurled hither and yon, and numerous groups were performing skits or chanting and drumming. I talked with members of Black Family Farmers about the problems of that were forcing them off their farms and into low-wage jobs. I learned about their lawsuit and protests of the USDA, that black owned farms were going out of business at a rate five times that of white farmers in 1990, and that Black farmers, who are less than 1% of U.S. farmers and owning less than one million acres, are now on the verge of extinction.

Heading off to for the epicenter at the Ellipse, we found ourselves on a corner with David and Fran Korten (When Corporations Rule the World, YES Magazine) and Vandana Shiva, a powerful Indian leader, the Gandhi of our times. Although I had met both David and Vandana several times before, these luminaries were considerably more interested in Georgiane than in me, Bolivia news being hot as it is at the moment and all. But as they walked and talked along I held high my brightly colored "The Earth Belongs to Everyone - People/Planet Finance" sign, with its Earth People picture from an embroidery by a women's craft cooperative in El Salvador. As it worked out, several people took pictures of my sign that day and I did two radio interviews.

Among the throngs of this Festival of Resistance, we wound our way up to the fence right in front of the speakers and performers platforms on the Ellipse. Michael Moore had just started, and we all chuckled about the threat to the established order posed by the "dangerous" puppets that were confiscated the day before.

A few yards away I noticed the Kensington Welfare Rights Union folks in their black "Up and Out of Poverty in Pennsylvania" tee-shirts that I had last seen at the Hague Appeal for Peace Conference last May. Sure enough, Cherie Honkala, one of the leaders of this Philadelphia based movement, was there in the middle of them.

Walking over, I told Cherie I had been trying to catch up with her to have a talk for four years. Last time she had cancelled because of a HUD boarded-up housing take-over the day of our scheduled meeting. I told her I had finally figured out a way to get to talk with her, which would be to join her in a squat. She laughed and gave me a hug saying, *that will work!* I figure it is either meet with her in jail for an illegal housing takeover for the homeless or become a police officer and book her, as Cherie has been arrested for non-violent civil disobedience more often than anyone else that I know.

One of the speakers that day was a woman from Ghana who had come to the USA to be a domestic worker for a World Bank official. She told of working as a slave and being treated like an animal from early in the morning until late at night.

Not allowed to leave the house and without pay for four months, she was taken to the airport and told she would be paid once she was on the plane back to Ghana. Knowing she would never be paid, she managed to escape the airport and eventually made her way to a domestic workers support organization.

When she contacted her mother in Ghana, her mother told her the family there was being harassed by the World Bank because she was speaking out about the abuse she had experienced in the US. This woman thankfully now has lawyers working on her case. Her story is just one example of the kinds of slavery and exploitation we are hearing about now, and yet another reflection of the arrogance and domination that working people the world over are experiencing from those heading up these global financial institutions.

Still hanging with Georgeane after hearing the Ghana lady and other labor union and environmental activists speak to the crowd of now tens of thousands (estimates ran as high as 50,000 on this sunny Sunday), we decided to scout about the scenes around the perimeter. While Georgeane was telling me about how she happened to be in Berlin when they took the Wall apart with small hammers and screwdrivers, I spotted a giant cardboard Trojan Horse with the words IMF/World Bank scrawled on its sides, piloted underneath by shopping cart pushers. Nearby a huge pink pig was chowing down on an earth globe. Around the next corner appeared a giant set of teeth powered by a conglomerated contraption calling itself the IMF/WB pulverizer.

Passing a street intersection now covered with a huge woven multicolored yarn spiderweb and a group of hoola-hoopers, Georgiane expressed her concern that it all looked perhaps a bit too frivolous and playful. Her protest movement in Bolivia used barbed wire blockades rather than yarn and plastic toys and soap bubbles. But she grew less concerned about that when we smelled a bit of tear gas or pepper spray now and then.

Shortly thereafter we paused with a group sitting on a little grassy oasis dabbling their feet in the basin of a water fountain. We were sharing my one remaining peanut butter and jelly tortilla when we struck up a conversation with a group of young people from Montana wearing nose rings and buffalo tee shirts. After talking a bit about the connections between the shooting of national park escaped buffaloes to preserve grazing land for cattle and corporate control and IMF/WB policy (they admitted the connections were a bit of a stretch, but the bottom line was greed for profits above all else), we noticed that one of the buffalo nose-ringer kids had his hand wrapped in bandages and a finger splint. He told us that a policeman had beaten his hand with a baton as he was grabbing onto a metal barrier that morning. The Mobilization medics had applied the bandages.

The perimeter barriers were the areas of the most intense confrontation throughout the days of the protest. The perimeter barriers and blockades were also the focal points of important dialog between police and protestors, and occasionally IMF/WB officials, protestors and the media. We were near one such scene when cameras started running as protestors surrounded two men trying to get into the meetings. One official began a speech announcing his rights to move freely. Protestors shouted back, asking if he had the right to freely put in place policies that were increasing poverty, human misery and displacement all over the world. After shouts back and forth, the suited men retreated as the barrier held.

I caught up with one of them who informed me he was from Liberia and that the people inside the IMF/WB buildings were not corrupt like his own government. A few steps later someone put a microphone in his face and he stated that his people needed money to get out of poverty. When I shouted "but you just said your own government was corrupt" he walked away in frustration.

Georgiane left for her car shortly thereafter, needing to conserve some energy for her participation the next day. I joined the march with my sign and my flute and got a bit of a chant going of "Whose Earth? Our Earth!" Many blocks long, the tens of thousands of colorful, playful, serious and determined Festival of Resistance protestors flowed back down into the Ellipse. I collapsed for a rest under a shade tree on the grassy lawn, now playing my flute along with the drumbeats of an African brother sitting on the other side of the same tree.

The beautifully painted mural was still standing, a visual focus for the many well-informed, socially concerned, compassionate and dynamic speakers who had come from all over the world to sound their voices against institutions of inequity and exploitation and for a world that works for everyone. The mural showed two large hands, each with metal cuffs and chains, outstretched towards the earth. On the left handcuff were the words World Bank/IMF and on the side, Break the Bank. On the right handcuff the words Corporate Colonialism and on that side, Dump the Fund.

As musicians and singers with global justice theme songs performed on the stage in front of the mural, I took some time to jot down some of the messages on the signs and tee shirts passing all around me. My favorite one, near a giant green turtle, was Turtles and Teamsters United at Last. Here are some of the others:

- Make the Global Economy Work for Working Families
- Stop Washington's War on the Worlds Poor
- Mobilize for Justice
- More World Less Bank
- Down with the Babylon System
- Real Men Do Not Abuse Women and Children
- Drop the Debt and the Bondage
- Workers of the World, Unite and Fight
- Morally Bankrupt
- Organize, Demand Justice for All
- Close School of the Americas
- Jobs with Justice

- Stop Corporate Greed
- End Exploitation of Domestic Workers
- This Is What Democracy Looks Like*

Walking into a Metro station with Rita Jane Leasure, president of the School of Living, a land trust friend I had spotted dancing on the Ellipse at the end of the day, a security guard told me I was not allowed to carry my sign on into the subway because it had a stick. He told me the stick was dangerous. He said that was the rule. So I broke the stick off over my knee, but he said that the four inches remaining was still a stick. So I broke that off with my hand and he said, "that is good enough for me" and allowed me to pass into the Metro.

I think it is a rather strange world, when my taxpayer dollars pay for bombs and attack Apache helicopters and fighter planes and police batons and tear gas, but the stick on my little pretty protest sign that says "The Earth Belongs to Everyone" is considered a threat to public safety.

Arriving home late Sunday evening, I slept in a bit and took a hot relaxing bath in the morning. After feeding our two cats, ten biodiverse free-range happy hens, and Snowflake the goat, I was ready to watch the Monday, April 17, Mobilization for Global Justice action from a distance. There on C-Span, giving press interviews at the Carnegie Institute and elsewhere, were a number of wonderful global citizen activists, several of whom I had met or heard speak during the past three days:

- Njoki Njehu from Kenya. Director of the 50 Years is Enough
- Trevor Nwgane, a political leader and veteran of the anti-apartheid movement from Johannesburg, South Africa
- Walden Bello, author and activist from Thailand and the Philippines
- Robert Weissman, Co-Director, Essential Action
- Mark Weisbrot, Co-Director, Center for Economic and Policy Research
- Jonah Goka, Chair, Zimbabwe Coalition on Debt and Development
- Tony Mazzocchi, Labor Party National Organizer
- Oronto Douglas, Environmental Rights Action, Nigeria
- Chris Clement, a Howard University student
- Tanya Margolin, a George Washington University student
- Maitet Pascual, President of the Freedom from Debt Coalition, Philippines
- Steve Kretzman, Mobilization for Global Justice
- Celia Olario, Independent Media Center
- Dr. Vineeta Gupta, the social justice researcher from India
- Actors Susan Sarandon and Tim Robbins

All spoke with dignity, fervor and knowledge, from a place of heartfelt compassion and concern. All spoke with determination to bring an end to hunger, homelessness, poverty and exploitation everywhere. All spoke with courage to build a world that works for everyone.

One of the reporters asked, "How can you use us to help you, now that we have awakened? There is clearly a deep, deep flaw in Western civilization."

The philosopher Joseph Campbell once said that there is a new myth arising, a new story around which people everywhere will rally. This is the story of the one earth and the one human family. A beautiful introduction to this story unfolded this week in Washington.

A lone figure dressed in orange with a black hood protests the abuse of prisoners of war in front of the White House in Washington, D.C.

25

D.C. Protest Provides New Insights

Published as a guest editorial in *Public Opinion*, Chambersburg, PA, April 21, 2000.

This week in Washington, Mobilization for Global Justice protestors and the D.C. Police Department pioneered a breakthrough in peaceful civil disobedience and the non-violent strategy spawned by Mahatma Gandhi and Martin Luther King. Carrying flowers given to them by the protestors, Police Chief Charles Ramsey and Assistant Police Chief Terry Gainer kept the calm and were open to dialog.

"It is important for all of us to look at this from different perspectives," said Ramsey in a C-Span interview on Monday, April 17. "There is a lot to be learned."

At the 20th Street and Pennsylvania Avenue perimeter barrier, established by the police to keep protestors away from the International Monetary Fund and World Bank buildings where bank officials had assembled for their annual meeting, protestors explained to police why they were there and why they were prepared to be arrested for their concerns. They also talked about the role of the police in a democracy at a time of massive protest. By negotiating a diplomatic zone for protestors and police to dialog, a potentially violent confrontation was avoided.

Protestors and police then agreed upon an opening of the barrier, through which protestors could walk into the closed-off zone behind the line, and the actions that would be taken by both police and protestors after the crossing.

Four hundred protestors then proceeded behind the lines for what was termed "voluntary arrest" where they were then calmly handcuffed and taken into detention. Protestors were thus able to demonstrate their determined resistance to institutions they believe to be unjust and inequitable, but without damage to either persons or property.

My experience with the tens of thousands of others who participated in the Mobilization for Global Justice was profound and life changing. Dozens of teach-ins and educational events were held in the streets, churches, synagogues, and universities of Washington, D.C. from April 8 - 17. Hundreds of speakers from all over the world spoke with dignity, fervor and knowledge. All spoke with determination, compassion and concern to bring an end to hunger, homelessness, poverty and exploitation everywhere. All spoke with courage to build a world that works for everyone.

At a Mobilization press conference one of the reporters asked, "How can you use us to help you, now that we have awakened? There is clearly a deep, deep flaw in Western civilization."

As I was leaving the Ellipse at the end of the Sunday rally, a security guard told me I was not allowed to carry my sign into the subway because it had a stick. He told me the stick was dangerous. He said that was the rule. So I broke the stick off over my knee, but he said that the four inches remaining was still a stick. So I broke that off with my hand and he said, "that's good enough for me" and allowed me to pass into the Metro.

I think it is a rather strange world, when my tax dollars pay for bombs and attack Apache helicopters and fighter planes and police batons and tear gas, but the stick on my little pretty protest sign which says "The Earth Belongs to Everyone" is considered a threat to public safety.

The philosopher Joseph Campbell once said that there is a new myth arising, a new story around which people everywhere will rally. This is the story of the one earth and the one human family. A beautiful introduction to this story unfolded this week in Washington.

The author's
grandson
Aidan Hartzok
holding
The Sign.

26

Professional Superhero

An interview with Alanna Hartzok, United Nations NGO Representative for the
International Union for Land Value Taxation, by Adam Monroe as
published in IN Magazine, Vol. xiv, No. 1, 1997.

INsider - Who are the United Nations NGOs (Non-Governmental Organizations)
and what influence do they have?

Alanna - UN/NGOs are concerned with human rights, the environment, disarmament, spiritual development, food, health, and a great array of humanitarian not-
for-profit activities. Some universities have also established their linkage to the UN
in this way.

The influence and organizing capacity of UN/NGOs has been growing. The
concerns of UN/NGOs are usually global and transcend the interests of any particular nation state. So in some ways they are freer to work for the good of the
world's people as a whole than are official UN nation state representatives, who are
beholden to the interests of their particular country. If the world is going to work
for any of us, it has to work for all of us.

I was fortunate to attend Habitat II in Turkey, the most recent UN sponsored
global conference. (It was) such a natural high to be with people from around the
globe who were deeply concerned about how to create a better world. For my
NGO, I organized and conducted six seminars at Habitat II on this theme: "The
Earth is the Birthright of All People." John McConnell, Equinox Earth Day founder, spoke at one of these and presented his Earth Trustee ideas - that the earth's
land and resources are humanity's common heritage and a percentage of the value
of earth resources should be distributed as dividends to people rather than having
the earth used for private profit through land speculation.

INsider - Tell us more about the organization you represent.

Alanna - I represent the International Union for Land Value Taxation. We work to
establish democratic rights to the earth. The earth is the birthright of all people, or
certainly should be. The site or market value, called ground rent, of land and re-

sources should be collected for the benefit of the community as a whole rather than funneled as private profit into the hands of a few. This is the proper source of funding for community needs.

Sixteen cities in the state of Pennsylvania are now practicing a local tax reform based on this approach and it has revitalized the local economies. For instance, Mayor Steven Reed of Harrisburg says this has been the key policy that helped his city go from being the second most distressed municipality in the US to being one of the highest quality of life cities on several indicators. Thousands of boarded-up buildings were fixed up, good jobs were created, and the crime and fire rates dropped significantly. The newly formed Greater Municipality of Cape Town in South Africa plans to go entirely to this system during the next few years. We need to keep an eye on Brazil as well because land rights activists there have applied so much pressure that the government has promised to put in place a land value taxation system there, too.

Some of these common heritage resource funds could also be distributed as "earthshare dividends" directly to individuals. They do this in Alaska where citizens receive dividend checks of $1000 a year for state oil resources. Public finance policies based on this approach are a practical method of achieving democratic rights to the earth. Meanwhile, taxes on workers need to be relieved so that people can have economic freedom.

Understanding the tax system is extremely important so that we can use our political democratic rights to vote for economic democracy. Our democracy is in danger because of the maldistribution of wealth problem due to the concentration of wealth into the hands of the few. Democracy has been political but not economic. America brought over the system that damaged old Europe and once the frontier closed, it began wreaking the same problems here.

The problem is we treat land and natural resources as commodities for private profit and speculation. Relatively few now quite literally own and control the earth. The words of Thomas Paine that were not heeded are these: "Men did not make the earth... it is the value of the improvement only, and not the earth itself, that is individual property... Every proprietor owes to the community a ground rent for the land which he holds."

Thomas Jefferson said: "The earth is given as a common stock... Wherever in any country there are idle lands and unemployed poor, it is clear that the laws of property have been so far extended as to violate natural right."

People should share equal ownership of and access to land. The end-point of democratic economics will be the real beginning of human liberation.

INsider - Should the United Nations be reorganized to give more influence to other member nations than the few who sit on the Security Council?

Alanna - You have certainly done your homework. There are many UN reform proposals being put forth at this time. Currently very tiny nations as well as giant superpowers have equal representation at the UN, although the Security Council members have the largest degree of power. The World Federalist Association wants a world government that will supercede national interests as such, but because they have not thought through the kinds of economic issues we have been discussing, that would be dangerous at this time. Other efforts include the Constitution for the Federation of Earth, which would scrap the UN and nation state system entirely.

INsider - What is the relationship between the UN and the other "world government" taking shape around the WTO (World Trade Organization)?

Alanna - There are indications that at this time the UN and the corporate elite that have major control of the WTO are in bed together. But then again, we are all in this together, are we not?

Many people sincerely believe that current capitalist arrangements really will solve civilization's problems. With the demise of Marxism and state bureaucratic socialism, many are at a loss for a viable alternative. It may be more a problem of bad ideas rather than bad people. Each of us has to consider if we are part of the problem or part of the solution.

But we have only to look at the growing pockets of third world conditions growing under our noses within first world nations to see that the present type of capitalist system is not working.

INsider - Will the UN endorse the MAI (Multilateral Agreement on Investment)?

Alanna - As things now stand I would say that the MA would likely be supported by the powers in control. But the MAI would override local and national democracies to such a degree that surely the people will not tolerate it. MAI is one of the best things the elites could be promoting right now in order to provoke popular resistance to elite control. As Princess Leia said in Star Wars regarding the designs of the Evil Emperor, "The tighter he closes his fists the faster star systems fly between his fingers."

The spirit of Gandhi's *satyagraha* or truth force is the correct approach. Gandhi strongly criticized and worked against unjust institutions but always respected people as individuals.

Be proactive in creating the new rather than simply reactive in attacking the old. Let the old fall of its own dead weight.

There is, of course, an out-of-control system of power that is well documented in David Korten's book, *When Corporations Rule the World*, a highly recommended read, and in the writings of Vandana Shiva on "biopiracy." The result, as my associate Trent Schroyer, a TOES (The Other Economic Summit) organizer puts it, (the corporate culture) "eats out the substance of human community by reducing us to economic individuals or information processing cyborgs of the system."

Nevertheless, I am somewhat concerned about the anti-corporation emphasis to be found in many of the progressive movements. There ARE hardworking business people and political leaders who really are trying to make things work better for everyone.

I think what's really happening is that under the guise of neoliberal economics, the power elite are trying to take over the world, while those with greater vision and compassion are trying to transform it to a higher dimension.

INsider - So, what do you do when you are not saving the world?

Alanna - I live in a modest home on a few acres of land with my two teenagers in rural Pennsylvania. This year our homestead's organic garden is filled with peas, beans, beets, radishes, tomatoes, potatoes, corn, chard, carrots, okra, onions, peppers, cucumbers, and lovely statice and strawflowers. Our pygmy goat and the cats are playful and the two horses are a luxury. Sometimes I celebrate life by playing guitar or piano and singing.

INsider - What is your best advice for America's next generation?

Alanna - Be kind to yourself, and your family members, friends and neighbors. Without getting too fanatical, be conscious about the food you eat and the things you use in terms of their impact on your body, mind, and spirit, the earth and other people and life forms of the earth.

Work cooperatively with each other to establish right livelihoods so that your creative abilities are freed to fulfill the greater purpose of your lives. Link hearts and hands in your own communities and across the globe to transform the system.

* Note: Since the time of this interview, the two old horses died and were replaced by three sheep. The sheep kept crawling under the fence and running around the neighborhood, so they were replaced by another two beloved horses that are residing on the "Aradhana" eco-homestead as of year 2007.

OH SAY CAN YOU SEE
A Perspective on the Current Crisis

Presented at the Books Not Bombs/Stop Iraq War Forum organized
by students at Shippenburg University, Pennsylvania on March 5, 2003.

The unjust and inequitable ownership and control of vast amounts of the land
and natural resource wealth of our planet is a root cause of the great majority
of local-to-global conflicts and wars. Our current form of democratic governance is
severely limited in its capacity to negotiate peaceful means of resolving resource
inequities and disputes, whether over oil and other minerals or over land for housing and livelihoods.

Neither the market system as currently structured nor the force of military
might have provided a democratic means to equitably share the gifts of nature. This
fatal flaw of democracy can be most clearly seen upon review of some of the 3,000
major and 10,000 minor CIA covert operations during the past several decades.
This Third World War - the war on the people of the third war - has slaughtered at
least six million people in the third world since World War II, as determined by
former CIA chief John Stockwell and others.[1]

Taking control of Iraq has been a long-running strategic design of the oligarchy
that has come to rule the United States. An article headlined "Seizing Arab Oil"
which appeared in Harper's magazine in 1975 outlined "how we could solve all
our economic and political problems by taking over the Arab oil fields (and) bringing in Texans and Oklahomans to operate them."[2]

Similar stories appeared in other magazines and newspapers at the time. Today, there are 41 members of the Bush administration with direct links to the oil
industry. Many of them have held high office in the military-industrial complex that
President Dwight D. Eisenhower warned us about many years ago when he said:

> In the councils of government, we must guard against the acquisition of unwar-
> ranted influence, whether sought or unsought, by the military industrial complex.
> The potential for the disastrous rise of misplaced power exists and will persist.[3]

In the words of Dr. Michael Klare, professor of peace and world security studies at Hampshire College and author of *Resource Wars,* "Controlling Iraq is about oil as power, rather than oil as fuel. Control over the Persian Gulf translates into control over Europe, Japan, and China. It's having our hand on the spigot."[4]

Dr. Stephen Pelletiere, author of *Iraq and the International Oil System: Why America Went to War in the Persian Gulf,* was the CIA senior political analyst on Iraq during the Iran-Iraq war and a professor at the US Army War College in Carlisle, PA for 12 years (1988-2000). He made this statement during the Carlisle Peace College Forum on Iraq on October 19, 2002:

> The only way, if we are saying to go into Iraq and change the regime, for us to change the regime is for us to stay in Iraq, and effectively take over the oil wells and to hand them back to the same companies - Exxon/Mobil, British Petroleum, Royal Dutch - which originally exploited the oil when the cartel ruled the Gulf. That is imperialism. That is a classic case of imperialism. You cannot put any other face on it. As soon as a country invades another country with the intention of ac- quiring the assets of that country to exploit for its own aggrandizement, that is im- perialism. That is, I think, the only accurate way to look at what is happening there.
>
> The US, in an incredibly rapid space of time, is going through a tremendous trans- formation in which we are ceasing to be a republic and are in the process of be- coming an empire and no one seems to be aware of this transformation, at least you are not getting any of this from the media... The media is going through its own transition. It is behaving in a way I have never seen it. The administration is ly- ing and the media is simply reporting what it is told. I see over and over again statements made by our media that are flat out lies, like the story of Iraq gassing its own people.

The vast build-up of US military forces in preparation for a unilateral preemptive "shock and awe" attack on Iraq is immoral and illegal. It demonstrates a truly shocking disregard for the steps that humanity has made since WWII to build global institutions based on law and peaceful resolution of conflicts. If this situation were a case of domestic abuse, the Bush administration would be guilty of making terrorist threats and issued a restraining order by the legal authorities. If home- grown terrorists based in Los Angeles had organized a hijacking of airliners to fly into the twin towers, would we have surrounded California with the full force of our military in order to launch an all out attack?

The current situation has nothing to do with saving the people of Iraq from a ma- levolent dictator, eliminating a source of terrorism in the world, or providing for the security of the United States. The current situation has everything to do with a small clique of cunning and super wealthy men with a focused group intent to grab geopoliti- cal control of Eurasia and "full spectrum dominance"[5] of the globe. This clique of men is not the true representative of an enlightened democracy - rather they are truly the representatives of the military-industrial complex and of several multi-national corporations. This moment - March 2003 - is their *carpe diem* - their time to seize rule of the world in a crescendo of voracious desire for wealth and power.

First, foremost and most immediately we must stop this maniacal and diabolical war in the heart of Eurasia. We must first, foremost and most immediately stop this war because we know that, in the words of Starhawk, "gorilla chest-beating does not constitute diplomacy, having the world's largest collection of phallic projectile weapons does not constitute moral authority, and invasion and penetration are not acts of liberation."

We must support and strengthen international law and the mechanisms to enforce it. International law is the just and civilized way for human beings to deal with individuals who are guilty of crimes against humanity. We here in the United States must turn our fast growing forces for peace and justice on earth towards the reinstatement of the United States in the Anti-Ballistic Missile Treaty to stop nuclear proliferation. North Korea would not be acting as it is if we had not pulled out of the ABM Treaty and put them on the Axis of Evil list. We need to sign on to the International Criminal Court, the Kyoto Treaty to curb climate change, the Treaty to Ban Land Mines, the Convention on the Rights of the Child, and the Convention on Equal Rights for Women.

The use and enforcement of these institutions of global governance will move us far along the path towards the abolition of war and the elimination of weapons of mass destruction worldwide including the elimination of weapons of mass destruction from the homeland of the superpower called the United States of America. The strength and good will of the other superpower - we, the citizens of the world - can bring these goals to fruition.

We hereby pledge our patriotic duty, "our lives, fortunes and sacred honor" NOT to a Pax Americana but to a Pax Gaia - an order of peace and justice on earth whereby the wealth of the world will shift away from the production of weapons of mass slaughter and towards the healing of the planet and the people. We, the people of the world, will now build a new global order to shift the wealth of the world out of the control of the World Trade Organization, the International Monetary Fund, the World Bank and other private bank accounts of the less than 300 multi-billionaires who now have as much wealth as three billion people.

We need to take a giant step forward to a new form of democracy. We, the people of the world, must now direct the wealth of the world towards the building of local-to-global economic democracies in order to meet the needs for food, shelter, healthcare, and education for all. This is not a pale, pallid plea for charitable contributions to the begging bowls of the poor. This is a pronouncement upon a criminally unjust system of global exploitation and a prescription for the curing of the worldwide crisis of person/planet pain.

The task before us is that of building a global order based on the full honoring of our common humanity with profound recognition and respect for the dignity of each and every child, woman and man.

A new democratic mandate, which we might call "earth rights democracy," recognizes that the gifts of nature - the land, oil, minerals, other natural resources and a substantial amount of the monetary value accruing to their use - rightly belong to the people of the world as a whole. The earth is our birthright and our common heritage. What we make from our mental and physical labor can rightfully be held as individual property but the profit of the earth should be shared by all and for all.

The cure for economic and war crimes against humanity is to declare once again, yes, RIGHT NOW, a new order of the ages, *novus ordo seclorum*, to form a more perfect union of people and planet fully awakened to the realization that though we are many, we are in truth one humanity, *epluribus unum*, out of many one.

O say can you see[6], our common humanity, sprung from the earth our mother and seeded from the sun, we are in truth, children of the universe, and no less than the trees and the stars,[7] you and I have the equal right to be here now and to claim this planet and its land and resources as our full, fair and natural birthright.

The current crisis is now the time to pledge allegiance to the earth, and all the life which it supports, One Planet, in our care, irreplaceable, with sustenance and respect for all.[8]

Right now this pledge means **NO WAR ON IRAQ!**

---

[1] John Stockwell, former CIA Station Chief in Angola in 1976 working for then Director of the CIA, George Bush, spent 13 years in the Agency. This information is from his speech available on video by email to fdorrel@hotmail.com

[2] Robert Dreyfuss, "The Thirty-Year Itch," *Mother Jones*, March/April, 2003, p. 41.

[3] "Military-Industrial Complex Speech," Dwight D. Eisenhower, 1961 (Public Papers of the Presidents, 1035-1040), Robert Dreyfuss, op.cit., 41.

[4] Michael Klare, *Resource Wars*.

[5] Suggest Google search for "full spectrum dominance" as dimension of current U.S. foreign policy.

[6] From The Star-Spangled Banner, a poem by Francis Scott Key dating to the War of 1812 between the US and Great Britain. Sung with the melody of a popular 1700 era English tune which celebrated wine, women and song, Congress declared it the US National Anthem in 1931.

[7] Phrases from the *Desiderata*.

[8] From artwork by Janina Lamb, artist; Lamb & Lion Studio (cards, posters, prints bumper stickers) Box 298, Tamworth, NH 03886 USA, Tel: 603-323-7539 Fax: 603-323-8842.

– 28 –

Letter to a Church

Written on March 14, 2005, this letter was published as a guest editorial in the *Public Opinion*, a Gannett newspaper in Chambersburg, Pennsylvania.

To the Minister(s) at Mt. Pleasant Church,

Thank you for the Happy Easter card and jellybeans and previous invitations to attend services at your church.

I grew up regularly attending King Street United Brethren Church and after leaving the Chambersburg area, was on a 25-year vision quest for truth. During that time, living in different countries and major world cities, I found answers to my big questions about psychological and spiritual realities and political and economic justice issues. I gained a big picture understanding of world affairs and some profound perspectives concerning what is happening to the planet and humanity in these times, including what needs to be done to build a world that works for everyone.

So please tell me, is your church a "blessed are the peacemakers" church or are you a "Rambo Jesus" church? Are people there deeply searching for how they can be peacemakers, or are they gung-ho for the imperialist policy of "full spectrum dominance' that is now the guiding principle of U.S. foreign policy?

Are the church members concerned about the fact that less than 300 multi-billionaires now have as much wealth as half the people on the planet, three billion of us? That in the U.S. the top 1% of the people now has two trillion dollars more wealth than the bottom 90%? Are they deeply aware that 30,000 people die of hunger each day, needlessly?

Are they concerned to hear that our government keeps trying to depose democratically elected President Chavez of Venezuela because he has been enacting land reform and capturing more oil funds to distribute in goods and services to the poorest people of his country? Is your church working for peace and justice on earth or are you among those caught up in the ridiculous belief about the "rapture"?

The above are the issues and concerns central to my life, along with pathways of emotional healing in my work as a mental health counselor. If these are not concerns of your church, then believe me, you would not want me as a member. I would make everyone too uncomfortable.

Sincerely,

Alanna Hartzok

The author speaking at the Federation of World Peace and Love
celebration in New York City, 2002.

29

A Friend of Mine Bombed a Friend of Mine

This guest essay was published in the Public Opinion, Chambersburg, Pennsylvania, November 1, 2004. The original title was "War in Iraq touches many lives near and far."

I first met Ali Shabou over the Internet. He is a warm, caring, competent and intelligent person who was on the planning team for one of the great global conferences of the 1990s. Ali and I were coordinating arrangements for Harrisburg Mayor Stephen Reed to participate in the Mayors Conference in Amman, Jordan in 1995. Although Mayor Reed had to cancel out with short notice due to the crisis flooding of Harrisburg during the days preceding the conference, I had the opportunity to meet Ali in person in Istanbul in 1996 at the UN Habitat conference of representatives of all 160 UN member states. I was there to lead several sessions at the NGO Forum attended by 15,000 high-minded people from all over the world.

Ali was a UN Habitat official and so he was deeply involved with the nation state proceedings during the long days of the conference, but a small group of us would meet with him in the late evenings for dinner and discussions. At one point when the United States and delegates from some of the Arab states were having a particularly difficult time reaching consensus on a section of the Action Agenda, which was to be the major outcome of the conference, Ali was called in to mediate. His intervention was successful and the nations of the world were able to agree on important guidelines for ways to work together to secure shelter for all.

Recently Ali was appointed by the UN Habitat Agency to work for the reconstruction of his country, Iraq. Ali went to Baghdad a few months ago to investigate the situation. My colleague who works with Ali at the UN Habitat headquarters in Nairobi told me that when he returned, he gave his report with tears flowing down his face. Ali told them that he never could have imagined the horrific conditions of his homeland and of the massive destruction and suffering of the people he had seen everywhere.

There is a connection between Ali and someone I met recently. Air Force Lt. Col. Matt McKeon was my host during the weeklong National Security Seminar at the US Army War College last June. Flying the radar-evading F-117 "Nighthawk"

Matt was the Eighth Fighter Squadron's commander of the first bombing raid on Ali's homeland with instructions to strike against Saddam Hussein's bunker at the beginning of the so-called "shock and awe" attack on Baghdad.

I sometimes try to imagine how I would introduce my friend Ali to my friend Matt. Would I say, "Ali, meet Matt, who dropped megatons of bombs on your hometown"? How would Ali respond to meeting Matt face to face? How would Matt respond if he could grasp the enormous amount of pain, suffering, despair and worry about his family that Ali has experienced during the past 18 months? Had these men met two years ago, they would have assuredly liked each other.

Martin Luther King once said that we have learned how to fly in the air like birds, and how to swim in the sea like fish, but we have not yet learned to walk together on the earth like brothers and sisters. May we find a way to take down the walls that are dividing us at this sad and sorrowful time. Humanity is one family.

National Security Seminar Number One
U.S. Army War College, Carlisle, Pennsylvania, June 7-10, 2004
The author is second from the left in the front row.

30

Economics of War and Peace

Presented in summary form on February 23, 2007 on the Economists for Peace and Security panel at the Eastern Economics Association 33rd Annual Conference in New York, Economics of War and Peace was later posted on the EPS website.

Summary: This paper builds a narrative around a series of four graphs. Part One describes a simple economy where basic needs are secured given access to land and natural resources. Parts Two and Three articulate the root injustice built into the current economic paradigm and how this leads to the private appropriation of great wealth by an elite few. These sections describe how the military-industrial-financial complex and an imperialistic U.S. foreign policy grow from a base of economic injustice. Part Four depicts a new role for democratic governance – the creation of "earth rights democracy" that recovers the economic surplus of land and natural resource "rent" for the benefit of the people as a whole while simultaneously lifting taxes from those who use their physical and mental labor to produce needed goods and services. The last section presents several working examples of this economic policy.

The First Graph

Essentials of Economic Rent and a War Economy

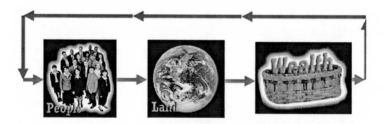

In a naturally just and harmonious society,
everyone has fair access to the gifts of nature
in order to procure their livelihood.

A Peaceful Flow of Goods

The first graph represents a simple economy based on equitable direct access to the gifts of nature. In such societies wealth is fairly distributed and there are often rules and ceremonies to ensure that no one group or family accumulates wealth while others lack the basic necessities. There is no hoarding while others go hungry. There are no homeless as all have access to raw materials to build shelter. There are no prisons in land-based cultures, as the severest form of punishment is usually banishment from the group. Designated wise ones or elders mediate conflicts.

Jeffersonian democracy envisioned broad ownership of land worked by independent family farmers. Early American society was in large part Jeffersonian in character. The frontier image of the log cabin and the highly self-sufficient homestead was a reality for many. Wage labor was looked down upon as lacking in individual freedom. Thomas had a firm understanding that political democracy must be based on fundamental economic democracy. He said, "The earth is given as a common stock for men to labor and live on."

Abraham Lincoln clearly articulated this perspective when he said:

> The land, the earth God gave to man for his home, sustenance, and support, should never be the possession of any man, corporation, society, or unfriendly government, any more than the air or water, if as much. An individual, company, or enterprise should hold no more than is required for their home and sustenance. All that is not used should be held for the free use of every family to make homesteads, and to hold them as long as they are so occupied.

The burning issue of the Reconstruction period immediately after the Civil War was that of land reform of the southern plantations. Thaddeus Stevens and the other Reconstructionists pushed to distribute the plantation lands to the former slaves and other poor landless people who were to receive "forty acres and a mule." Northern industrialists, fearing a loss of their labor pool if northern workers were also to assert their right to land, rejected this proposal. Millions of people in the United States have suffered the vicissitudes of poverty ever since.

The US economy became ever more complex, urbanized and centralized over the ensuing years. Yet the allure of "the simple life" of rural homesteading emerged once again in the twentieth century, especially during the Depression and periods of war. Scott Nearing, an economist and college professor who had lost his position because of his pacifist beliefs and anti-war activism, and his musician wife Helen became well known from their books about their homesteading experiences which spanned more than five decades. They produced most all of their food, shelter and energy while living a lifestyle balancing manual and intellectual or creative work and play.

Bob Swan, Chuck Matthei, Ralph Borsodi and Mildred Loomis launched the community land trust movement and were leading voices urging thousands to try homesteading through the publications and activities of the Institute for Community Economics and the School of Living. Their vision continued through the back-to-the-land movement of the sixties and seventies and is kept very much alive today with several rural land trust communities, the Federation of Equalitarian Communities, the E.F. Schumacher Society and many other similar associations.

Harvey Baumgartner, who describes himself as a "sixty-year-old subsistence farmer from Wisconsin" tells us in a recent issue of *Mother Earth News* how he built a fully functioning homestead in just a few years after leaving his structured employment. He began by planting a large garden and building a simple home of logs, sod, cob, and hay bales, then added a chicken coop, root cellar, clay oven, barn for his goats and horse, and a sauna. He loves this way of living and greatly enjoys visits from his grandchildren.

He says:

> I am interested in reviving strong rural communities... Bringing back the way we used to interact and rely on each other seems like something worth working toward. With my neighbors, it has been easy to start the process by exchanging items we need.... Each new day is an adventure here on my hilltop homestead. I eat fresher foods now and always have plenty. No longer is my focus on making money. I now concentrate my energy on the quality of my life, and I'm discovering true wealth. ... I live in harmony with the natural world and its cycles...Until recently, I felt I was a steward of this land but since I've been living here I've come to feel that I am only a guest. I am just here as one of many participants, and my aim is not to dominate the land, but to live in harmony with it. And so I treat this land with the reverence and love it deserves.

Harvey did not have much money when he started his homestead. But he had come to own a twelve acre hayfield. His is a very personal story that reminds us that human beings can live joyous and meaningful lives of self-reliance and cooperation beginning with the most basic of all needs - access to land.

Given the option of a secure place to be on this planet, no doubt multimillions of people who now live miserable lives of degrading poverty, hunger, and exploitation would chose this simple way of life in harmony with nature over that of the daily grind and struggle required to pay rent to live in our towns and cities. With secure access to land, most all human beings everywhere on earth can acquire the skills to provide for their own basic needs.

The Second Graph

Privilege Fund Grows

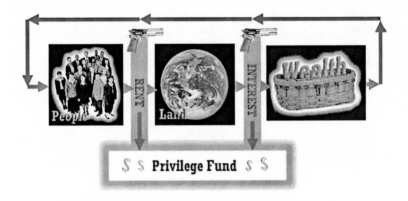

When people must pay rent for access to land, exploitation of labor begins.
Because of the Rent Leak, people cannot get capital without borrowing
from the Privikege Fund lending system, and paying interest.

We have reached the deplorable circumstance where in large measure a very powerful few
are in possession of the earth's resources, the land and all its riches, and all the franchises and
other privileges that yield a return. These monopolistic positions are kept by a handful of
men who are maintained virtually without taxation . . . we are yielding up sovereignty.
– Agnes de Mille (1905-1993)

G raph 2 indicates that structural violence - the wealth gap and conditions of economic injustice - begins at the point where a few gain control of most of the land and natural resources of the earth, thus excluding others from the gifts of nature. As the economy develops and land values increase, a Privilege Fund grows as a result of the private capture of land rent. Privilege Funders' excessive accumulation of this unearned income gives them a great capacity to make loans to others, thereby capturing enormous amounts of interest as well as other types of economic rent (the excess of price over the necessary cost of production). The gun images situated above the terms "rent" and "interest" indicate that these are initial points of structural injustice.

The Classicals and the Law of Rent

Let us now define our terms as enunciated by Adam Smith and other classical economists. Land, Labor and Capital are the three primary economic factors of production in the analysis of classical economists, who described their field of focus as the study of "the production and distribution of wealth." The term Land indicates "all nature-given resources." The term Capital means "wealth used to produce more wealth" and refers to tangible items of tools and machinery, not financial instruments. By "distribution" the classicals did not mean carting apples off to sell in markets but rather how the overall wealth pie was divided between the three factors. The return to Land they termed Rent; the return to Labor is the usual meaning of Wages; and the term used to describe the return to Capital was Interest.

The Graph 2 illustration requires explanation of one of the most fundamental laws of political economics - the Law of Rent. "Rent" is the term used by the classical economists to define the payment that must be made for access to "Land" (natural resources). "Rent" is unearned by the landholder, who has the privilege of holding title to "Land." John Stuart Mill and other 19th-century economists called land rent and land price gain the "unearned increment." Classical economist David Ricardo refined the Law of Rent in his *Principles of Political Economy and Taxation* (1817). He said "without a knowledge of [the theory of rent], it is impossible to understand the effect of the progress of wealth on profits and wages, or to trace satisfactorily the influence of taxation on different classes of the community."

The Law of Rent is among the most important and firmly established principles of economics. The Law of Rent states that the rent of a land site is equal to the economic advantage obtained by using the site in its most productive use, relative to the advantage obtained by using marginal (i.e., the best rent-free) land for the same purpose, given the same inputs of labor and capital. This law has a number of important implications, perhaps the most important being its implication for wages. The Law of Rent implies that wages bear no systematic relationship to the productivity of labor and are instead determined solely by the productivity of labor "on marginal land."

Surface land and extractive resources have no production costs, having been produced by nature. The value of surface land sites increases as the community grows and develops. Surface land values are highest in the cities – the centers of production and exchange of wealth. Cities grew in locations of some natural advantage, such as a harbor or the confluence of rivers, or at the foot of trails through mountain passes. As settlements grew and had need for public infrastructure and services, systems of taxation were established to pay for schools, libraries, transportation systems, water and irrigation systems, etc. These public amenities further increase the desirability of these locations, which results in an increase of the land values of serviced sites. Land value is thus a reflection of the labor and activities of the entire community of people. No one individual creates land value. Similarly the market value of finite extractive resources increases, as there is more demand for the utilization of such resources.

The classical economists who turned their attention to the problem of poverty and questions concerning root causes of the rich/poor gap came to the realization that Land Rent represents a social surplus and belongs by rights to the community as a whole and thus should not be privately appropriately by land title holders. A fair economy would capture land rent for the benefit of the entire community. (Further explanation of this is the focus of Graph 4 in this article.)

Unfortunately, the truths brought forth by the classical economists have been obfuscated, a truth elaborated by Mason Gaffney in *The Corruption of Economics*. The reality of our present neoclassical economic system is that most people must pay increasing amounts of *rent* for access to land either to other titleholders or to banks in the form of mortgage payments. Thus begins the exploitation (note the gun images on the graph) of those who have only their labor to bring to the process of wealth creation. Because of the "rent leak" most people cannot secure capital (homes included) without borrowing from the "privilege fund lending system" and paying interest. As the privilege fund grows, so does the wealth gap between the super rich and the rest of us.

Under our current property-in-land laws, land is treated as a market commodity. Whoever holds title to valuable natural resources and desirable land sites reaps the land rent as individual profit. Land speculation adds fuel to the fire of increasing land values. We are all familiar with the phrase "make a killing in real estate."

Our Western form of land tenure has deep historical roots. The land of Europe was once held as a commons. There were well-established community rules of use rights to the forests, fields, and streams. However, after several hundred years of the enclosure or privatization of the common lands in Europe, which began with the Statute of Merton of 1235, most of the people were mired in poverty and abhorrent living conditions. Some of those who managed to make a living for themselves in the emerging cash economy gradually were able to acquire land once again, this time by purchase. Land then became a market commodity with a sale price. All three factors of production - land, labor, and capital - could now be bought and sold.

Fast-forwarding to our own times we see that those who once had access to common lands, the common people, now are viewed by Privilege Funders to reside in a "labor pool." Most of us commoners *sans* commons are currently drowning in a sea of debt. The reality of burgeoning numbers of people in prison in the United States today shows a similar result to how the economy was structured during times of the debtors' prisons of the Middle Ages. Most of us of social concern are quite aware that people of color and poor white people, those who had no previous capacity to stake claim to land and natural resources, disproportionately populate our prisons. The Bureau of Justice Statistics reported as of June 30, 2007 (note update since this paper was given):

- 2,299,116 prisoners were held in federal or state prisons or in local jails – an increase of 1.8% from yearend 2006, less than the average annual growth of 2.6% from 2000-2006.
- 1,528,041 sentenced prisoners were under state or federal jurisdiction.
- There were an estimated 509 sentenced prisoners per 100,000 U.S. residents – up from 501 at yearend 2006.
- The number of women under the jurisdiction of state or federal prison authorities increased 2.5% from yearend 2006, reaching 115,308, and the number of men rose 1.5%, totaling 1,479,726.
- At midyear 2007 there were 4,618 black male sentenced prisoners per 100,000 black males in the United States, compared to 1,747 Hispanic male sentenced prisoners per 100,000 Hispanic males and 773 white male sentenced prisoners per 100,000 white males.
- In 2004 there were an estimated 633,700 State prisoners serving time for a violent offense. State prisons also held an estimated 265,600 property offenders and 249,400 drug offenders.

Wealth Concentration and the Boom/Bust Housing Market

Everywhere in the world where land is treated as a market commodity land prices are inexorably and relentlessly increasing. People are working longer and harder to make payments for land access, either as apartment rentals or mortgage payments. With improved technology and enhanced productive capacity, wealth increases as development proceeds. However, land prices, and thus housing costs, increase more rapidly than the wages of those who work for a living. This reality is one example of the workings of the Law of Rent.

Shelter is a basic necessity of life. Lifelong renters pay as much as ten times the cost of their rental unit in the course of their lifetime. Others do everything they can to find a way to purchase a home. Since wages do not keep up with the ever-increasing price of land and thus the cost of a house, those who work for a living must borrow if they wish to own a home. An ever-greater amount of their wages is then taken from them via mortgage interest payments. Not long ago a one-income family could afford home purchase. Today, two income families are struggling to make the mortgage payments.

If suddenly a new continent were to be discovered and people could flee to it to gain free access to land, the rent of land in the "old continent" would decrease and the wages of workers in the "old continent" would increase as a proportion of total wealth produced. Those who could directly work the land on the new continent could keep all of what they produced with no need to pay either land rent or mortgage interest. However, if the property rights laws of the new continent were essentially the same as that of the old, the Law of Rent would gradually take effect and the people of the new continent would eventually be ground down to economic insecurity and poverty as had happened previously on the old continent. This is what is happening now to increasing numbers of the people of the United States. They are being ground down to subsistence levels and below. And there are no new continents to discover.

"The burden of housing costs in nearly every part of the country grew sharply from 2000 - 2005, according to new Census Bureau data.... The numbers vividly illustrate the impact, often distributed unevenly, of the crushing combination of escalating real estate prices and largely stagnant incomes." Thus began an October 3, 2006 *New York Times* article, "Across Nation, Housing Costs Rise as Burden" by Janny Scott and Randal C. Archibold, who also tell us that:

- Housing prices have been rising faster than household incomes and in many parts of the country, real estate prices have escalated sharply in recent years. In New York City, more than half of all renters spend at least 30 percent of their gross income on housing, a percentage figure commonly seen as a limit of affordability.
- The places with the highest overall percentages of people carrying a heavy housing burden were in fast-growing areas of California, Colorado and Texas. Boulder, Colorado and College Station, Texas had the highest number of renters spending nearly 50 percent of their income on housing.
- The percentage of mortgage holders spending at least 50 percent of their income on housing rose as well. For instance, in Clifton, New Jersey, 12

percent of mortgage holders spent at least 50% of their income on housing in 2000, rising to 27 percent by 2005.

- Poorer communities well located to employment opportunities and close to public transportation had the highest overall percentages of homeowners spending 30 percent or more of their income on mortgage payments.

Stephen Ohlemacher, in an AP story out of Washington on October 4, 2006, tells a similar story headlined "More Americans Find Themselves 'House Poor'." Among the Census Bureau statistics that Ohlemacher highlights is that California has the most expensive housing costs among the states. "We are really reaching the outer edge of the envelope of what people can manage," said Cynthia Kroll, senior regional economist at the University of California at Berkeley.

Note that California has the sixth largest economy in the world. With a gross state product (GSP) of about $1.4 trillion, its economy is surpassed only by the economies of the United States, Japan, Germany, the United Kingdom and France. But the average worker's paycheck has been shrinking compared to the increases in apartment rents and mortgage costs increase.

The above examples illustrate the workings of the Law of Rent, namely, (1) land prices and hence housing costs rise faster than wages; (2) land with locational advantages such as proximity to employment and transportation generate the highest land rents; (3) higher wages that might be generated in these areas are more than offset by the higher rents and mortgage payments extracted from workers who live there; (4) over time, no matter the degree of progress and development, workers gradually lose their stakes in the economic game as wealth concentrates in the hands of the few who are positioned to capture rent and interest.

Privilege Funders invest the rent and interest they receive in the development of large-scale capital industries – corporations - which they control and monopolize. Wages are further driven down when machines replace people. Tools become labor enslaving rather than labor saving. Asset prices soar for real estate, stocks and bonds. Wages and living standards decrease.

Since the 1980s, mortgage lenders and the financial sector in general have backed real estate interests in lobbying to shift taxes off property. Along with the Federal Reserve's easy-credit policy lowering short-term interest rates from 20 percent in 1980 to just 1 percent in 2004, tax cuts for property have spurred asset-price inflation. Former Federal Reserve Chairman Alan Greenspan has characterized this policy approach as promoting "wealth creation" but others call it "debt creation" because bank credit has fueled the rise in real estate (read "land rent") and other assets.

Most families have gone deep into debt to afford housing leaving many workers "one paycheck away from homelessness" as the popular phrase puts it. If one of the two-wage earners of the typical American middle-income family loses their job, there is a high likelihood that they will miss their mortgage payment. As Michael Hudson and others have pointed out, due to heavy mortgage debt workers are afraid they might miss their mortgage payment and lose their homes if they strike or even to stand up against being forced to work overtime without pay.

A Center on Budget and Policy Priorities analysis of Census Bureau data discovered that between 2001 and 2005 the median income for non-elderly households - working US families - fell 3.7 percent, or $2000. Tax cuts for the wealthy and for businesses combined with low-interest-rate policies yielded booming real estate markets. But with the boom comes the bust and now housing prices are falling. Many wage earners who bought homes, lured by lower mortgage interest rates the past few years, will be paying for an asset which will be worth less than it cost. If one of the two wage earners is faced with unemployment in a time of recession, many will lose their homes and equity.

Many families in the United States and other developed countries have made more money in recent years from the rising price of their homes than from their salaries. But to realize this price gain, they have to borrow against it. This means that as their major asset – their home – has risen in price, so has their debt. Figures compiled by US mortgage behemoth Freddie Mac show that Americans withdrew $727.4 billion in equity from their homes during the years 2000 – 2005.

> This borrowing has pushed the savings rate into negative territory for the first time since the beginning if the Great Depression. As a result of this massive borrowing, the ratio of mortgage debt to home values has never been higher. With home prices falling, millions of homeowners will soon lose the ability to borrow against their homes. This will force people to curtail their consumption. Tens of millions of families bought homes at bubble inflated prices and now face the prospect of seeing their life savings disappear in the housing crash. In many cases, it will cause people to lose their homes, as they will not be able to maintain their mortgage payments.
> – Dean Baker, "After the Housing Bubble Bursts," Truthout, October 24, 2006

Meanwhile, the concentration of wealth in the hands of the few is proceeding at an alarming pace. As of year 2006, the wealthiest 20 percent of households were earning 50.4 percent of the nation's gross income; the poorest 20 percent were earning just 3.4 percent. Total wealth accumulated is significantly more concentrated than income. The top one percent of the US population now has more than one trillion dollars more wealth than the bottom 90 percent or viewed as a percentage, the top one percent holds 38% of all wealth.

"The bottom 20 percent basically has zero wealth. They either have no assets, or their debt equals or exceeds their assets. The bottom 20 percent has typically accumulated no savings," says wealth gap expert Edward Wolff in a recent Multinational Monitor interview on "The Wealth Divide - The Growing Gap in the US Between the Rich and the Rest."

Wolff's analysis tells us that the top one percent of families hold half of all non-home wealth. While the major assets of the middle class are their home, checking and savings accounts, certificates of deposits, money market funds and pension accounts, in other words, labor income derived assets, the richest 10 percent of families own about 85 percent of all stocks and financial securities, 90 percent of all business assets. These financial assets and business equity are even more concentrated than total wealth.

"The United States has rising levels of poverty and inequality not found in other rich democracies. It also has less mobility out of poverty," says Holly Sklar in "Growing Gulf Between Rich and Rest of US." She tells us that since 2000, America's billionaire club has gained 76 more members while the typical household has lost income and the poverty count has grown by more than 5 million people.

The extant of poverty and inequality in the United States is seldom seen or reported on television. "The infant mortality rate in the United States compares with that in Malaysia -- a country with a quarter the income," according to the 2005 Human Development Report which also tells us that the "infant death rates are higher for [black] children in Washington, D.C., than for children in Kerala, India." Kerala is a relatively poor state where basic needs are nonetheless being met due to a significantly higher degree of fairness in wealth distribution then can be found in other states and countries.

Forbes magazine has been publishing an annual list of America's 400 richest people since 1982. That first year *Forbes* found that 13 of these people were billionaires. Year 2006 Forbes finds all 400 of the richest people in America are billionaires. Their total net worth is $1.25 trillion. In 2004, the most current year with stats available, the 56 million American families who make up the poorer half of America's wealth distribution had a total combined net worth of just $1.29 trillion, as reported in the weekly e-newsletter Too Much, the September 25, 2006 edition.

Taking a global look, *Forbes* finds that the income of the world's 500 richest people exceeds that of the poorest 416 million. The Human Development Report finds that the average income of the top 20 percent of the world's population is 50 times the average income of the bottom 20 percent.

Addressing the situation of dire inequality with which we are now confronted, newly elected Senator Jim Webb had this to say in "Class Struggle" article published in the November 15, 2006 edition of *The Wall Street Journal*:

> The most important--and unfortunately the least debated--issue in politics today is our society's steady drift toward a class-based system, the likes of which we have not seen since the 19th century. America's top tier has grown infinitely richer and more removed over the past 25 years. It is not unfair to say that they are literally living in a different country. Few among them send their children to public schools;

fewer still send their loved ones to fight our wars…. Trickle down economics didn't happen.

A troubling arrogance is in the air among the nation's most fortunate. Some shrug off large-scale economic and social dislocations as the inevitable byproducts of the "rough road of capitalism." Others claim that it's the fault of the worker or the public education system, that the average American is simply not up to the international challenge, that our education system fails us, or that our workers have become spoiled by old notions of corporate paternalism…. Most Americans reject such notions. But the true challenge is for everyone to understand that the current economic divisions in society are harmful to our future. It should be the first order of business for the new Congress to begin addressing these divisions, and to work to bring true fairness back to economic life…. Our government leaders have no greater duty than to confront the growing unfairness in this age of globalization.

Homelessness and Hunger in the United States

Much of the homeless problem can be attributed to increases in the number of the poor in the 1980s and declines or rough constancy in the number of low-rent rental units; the number of homeless has grown since 1983, despite economic recovery, with the number of homeless families growing especially rapidly, so says Richard B. Freeman and Brian Hall in "Permanent homelessness in America?"

The National Low Income Housing Coalition's 2006 "Out of Reach" report on housing affordability tells us that the cost of affordable rental housing continues to grow, outpacing the wages of those who need it most. The NLIHC national two-bedroom Housing Wage - defined, as the hourly wage a full time worker must earn in order to afford a two-bedroom rental unit - climbed to $16.31 for 2006, up from $15.78 from 2005. Yet in 2005, the most recent year for which data on median hourly wage are available, the median hourly wage for all workers was $14 and the estimated average renter wage was $12.64. The report found that the problem is particularly stark for the lowest wage earners, including those who earn just the minimum wage, even in states that have higher minimum wages than the federal minimum wage, which has been stalled at $5.15 since 1997.

"Minimum wage earners are unable to afford even a one-bedroom home anywhere in the country, and 88 percent of renters in cities live in areas where the FMR (Fair Market Rent) for a two-bedroom rental is not affordable even with two minimum wage jobs," state the authors of "Out of Reach."

The Urban Institute reported in the year 2000 that even in a booming economy, at least 2.3 million adults and children, or nearly one percent of the U.S. population, are likely to experience a period of homelessness at least once during a year. For people living in poverty, the likelihood grows to 6.4 percent. For recent years surveyed the estimates of the number of people likely to be homeless at least once in a given year is between 2.3 and 3.5 million. Children are nearly 25% to nearly 40% of those who are homeless and using homeless services.

"Housing costs are on the rise in metropolitan areas, while extreme poverty and other vulnerabilities are facts of life for millions of people, homeless and otherwise. Preventing homelessness in a booming economy is an ongoing challenge," says Martha Burt, a researcher at the Urban Institute.

The U.S. Conference of Mayors and Sodexho, Inc. 2006 Hunger and Homelessness Survey says that during the previous year, requests for emergency shelter increased in the survey cities by an average of nine percent. Requests for shelter by homeless families alone increased by five percent. An average of 23 percent of the requests for emergency shelter by homeless people overall and 29 percent of the requests by homeless families alone are estimated to have gone unmet during the last year with emergency shelters in most of the survey cities having to turn away homeless families due to lack of resources. Survey cities reported that over the last year, people remained homeless an average of eight months.

A Second Harvest survey found that while 89 percent of U.S. households were food secure throughout the entire year of 2005, the remaining households - 11% or 35 million people, including 12.4 million children – were not. In the category of "very low food security" were at 3.9 percent of households – 4.4 million people. Overall, households with children had nearly twice the rate of food insecurity as those without children. In households with very low food security, eating patterns of one or more household members were disrupted and their food intake was reduced at times during the year because the household lacked money and other resources for food.

Ninety-five percent of city officials included in the Sodexho report expect that requests for emergency food assistance by families with children will increase during 2007. Seventy-five percent expect that requests by homeless families will increase during 2007. Along with unemployment and other employment related problems city officials cite other causes of hunger, in order of frequency, include high housing costs, poverty or lack of income, medical or health costs, substance abuse, utility costs, transportation costs, and the lack of education.

The U.S. government has been returning less rather than more of received tax funds back to the people during the past several decades. Although neoliberalism pushes for the reduction of state intervention in other parts of the world, in the U.S. taxes have steadily been reduced for the higher income levels but raised for the majority of the population. Most of these funds have been spent as subsidies to the agricultural, military, aerospace and biomedical sectors. Thus, the income of those at the top increases to the detriment of everyone else.

Sodexho USA Chief Operating Officer Richard Macedonia, said … it is disheartening and disturbing to learn that so many of our fellow Americans are in desperate need of shelter, food, clothing and the other basic necessities of life - and that in nearly every major US city, the problem of hunger and homelessness is steadily growing.

Others made these statements during the press conference when the Sodexho Survey was released:

- As mayors of cities in the richest and most powerful nation in the world, we cannot simply stand by as our residents – families with children – continue to suffer. – Douglas H. Palmer, U.S. Conference of Mayors President and Mayor of Trenton

- The results of this report shed light on a very real challenge facing this nation. All of us, as Americans should ask ourselves, are we willing to confront the difficult issues of hunger and homelessness and identify the causes? - T.M. Franklin Cownie, Des Moines Mayor and Co-Chair of the U.S. Conference of Mayors Task Force on Hunger and Homelessness

- Hunger and homelessness are not simply part of the 'natural order of things'. They represent inexcusable failures of political will and human imagination. All of us – at all levels of government and throughout society – must rededicate ourselves to addressing the needs of ALL Americans. - Congressman Jim McGovern.

Middle Class Stress

In the United States, not only are the poor people becoming poorer, sicker, and hungrier each year, the middle class is also increasingly stressed and distressed. In "The Middle Class on the Precipice: Rising financial risks for American families," Elizabeth Warren tells us that middle-class families are being "threatened on every front.... Even with two paychecks, family finances are stretched so tightly that a very small misstep can leave them in crisis.... Incomes are less dependable today. Layoffs, outsourcing and other workplace changes have trebled the odds of a significant interruption in a single generation."

Warren's analysis leads her to conclude that the security of middle-class American families has vanished. "The new reality is millions of families whose grip on the good life can be shaken loose in an instant," she says. Economic pressures have caused more middle-class families to turn to credit cards and mortgage refinancing just to make ends meet. Debt is now greater than savings. Yet, as previously noted, mortgage refinancing is becoming less of an option for many.

The Higher Debt of Higher Education

Sandra Block in "Students Suffocate under Tens of Thousands in Loans," a *USA Today* story published February 22, 2006, paints a glum picture of the price of higher education. The average college graduate owes $19,000 but many undergrads have debt exceeding $40,000. "The weight of debt is forcing many to put off savings for retirement, getting married, buying homes and putting aside money for their own children's educations," says Block. "It's a real crisis," says Diana Cantor, director of the Virginia College Savings Plan. "You're strapped before you get started."

Block goes on to report that the average debt for a college graduate has risen 50% in the past decade, after inflation. Tuition has soared much faster than pay for the kinds of low-wage jobs that students tend to hold, thus it is difficult to avoid going into debt to pay for college. The option to extend their payment periods for up to 30 years sharply boosts the interest to pay. For example, a borrower who takes 30 years to pay off a $20,000 loan at 6.8% will pay about $27,000 in interest. That compares with $7,619 on a loan paid off in 10 years.

If many people will be 55 or 60 years old before their student loans are paid off, how will they be able to help pay for their own children's college education?

Health Insurance and Drug Profits

Rather than caring about anyone's health, insurance companies are in it for the money. Jim Hightower tells us in his "Insurance Giants Take Stock in Tobacco" that a number of insurance companies are doing a good bit more than providing insurance. Hightower says:

> The four major insurance companies now own Health Maintenance Organizations and are major owners of tobacco companies. These are what I call Full-Service companies: they profit by selling you health insurance, then profit by selling you cigarettes to give you diseases, then profit again by selling you medical service for your diseases.

Uninsured people file for bankruptcy every year because they cannot pay their medical bills. Others cannot afford the high cost of prescription medicine or simply cannot get health insurance. Yet in 2004, the 13 largest drug companies netted profits of $62 billion, and U.S. hospitals posted $26.3 billion in profits. While 46 million Americans — including 8 million children — go without health insurance, the top 12 HMO executives earned $222.6 million this year.

In 2004, the 13 largest drug companies netted profits of $62 billion and U.S. hospitals posted $26.3 billion in profits. While 46 million Americans - including 8 million children - went without health insurance, the top 12 HMO executives earned $222.6 million this year.

Inequality has broad societal consequences and effects physical health as well. Despite varying degrees of health care and expenditure, research and analysis of the past several years reveals that countries with the greatest economic inequality have the most people suffering from poor health. Thus in addition to eliminating poverty we must solve this problem of the vast gap between the super-rich and the rest if we are improve overall physical and mental health.

Worldwide Wealth Gap

Inequality is widening worldwide. The World Institute for Development Economics Research of the United Nations University reported in 2000 that the top 1% of the world's population — some 37 million adults with a net worth of at least $515,000 — accounted for about 40% of the world's total net worth. The bottom half of the population owned merely 1.1% of the globe's wealth. The net worth of the world's typical person — whose wealth was above that of half the world's population and below that of the other half — was under $2,200.

"Developed countries have pulled ahead of the rest of the world," says Edward N. Wolff, a professor of economics at New York University who is a co-author of the new study. "With the notable exception of China and India, the third world has drifted behind."

The U.S. accounted for 4.7% of the world's population but 32.6% of the world's wealth. Nearly 4 out of every 10 people in the wealthiest 1% of the global population were American. The average American had a net worth of nearly $144,000, losing only to the average Japanese, who had $180,000, at market exchange rates; the average person in Luxembourg, who had $183,000; and the average Swiss, who had $171,000. By contrast, in 2000 the average Chinese had a net worth of roughly $2,600, at the official exchange rate. China, home to more than a fifth of the world's population, had only 2.6% of the world's wealth. And India, with 16.8% of the world's people, accounted for only 0.9% of the world's wealth.

When discussing and studying inequality it is important to make a clear distinction between inequality of income and inequality of wealth. A recent study by Emmanuel Saez of the University of California, Berkeley, and Thomas Piketty of the École Normale Supérieure in Paris, found that in 2004 the top 1% of Americans earned a higher share of the nation's income than at any time since the 1920s. Still, that share was only 16%. But even as income inequality has reached near record levels in many countries, the distribution of the world's wealth — things like stocks, bonds or physical assets like land — has become even more narrowly concentrated than income.

Among Americans, wealth is distributed about as unequally as it is around the globe. The study cited data from the Federal Reserve's Survey of Consumer Finances, which found that the richest 1% of Americans held 32% of the nation's wealth in 2001. This tops the inequality in every country but Switzerland among the 20 nations that measure these wealth disparities and are cited in the report. Wealth inequality vastly outstrips the inequality in the distribution of income.

The Human Development Report for 2005 tells us that the ration of the poorest 10% of the population to the richest 10% for the world as a whole is 1 to 103. Absolute income inequality between rich and poor countries is increasing. The incomes of the richest 20% of the world's people are approximately 140 times those of the poorest 20%. As one example, in 1990 the average American was 38 times richer than the average Tanzanian. Today the average American is 61 times richer, according to the most recent HDR.

However, "average" is a relative concept. As discussed previously, the wealth is fast flowing to the top in the United States. What is crystal clear is that both "developed" and "developing" countries share the same very serious problem - the growing wealth divide, with the wealth of the world now concentrated in the hands of a very few.

At least one capitalist publication is well aware of this state of affairs: "The three richest people in the world have more money than the poorest 48 nations combined," says Thomas Kostigen in *MarketWatch*, December 12, 2006. David Korten, in "The Limits of the Earth" (*The Nation*, July 15/22, 1996) tells us "the world now has more than 350 billionaires whose combined net worth equals the annual income of the poorest 45% of the world's population."

Vincent Navarro, the director of the Public Policy Program at John Hopkins University, said in his article, "The Worldwide Class Struggle" that "the primary conflict in today's world is not between North and South but between an alliance of the dominant classes of North and South against dominated classes of North and South."

Susan George thinks that this conflict might have something to do with "the land problem." She says, "The most pressing cause of the abject poverty which millions of people in the world endure is that a mere 2.5% of landowners with more than 100 hectares control nearly three-quarters of all the land in the world, with the top 0.23% controlling over half. " (Susan George, *How the Other Half Dies*, Penguin Books, 1976, p. 24.)

The Land Problem

In understanding the land and land rent problem we come to grasp how it is that despite doctrines of human rights and democratic governance we live on a planet where a few hundred multi-billionaires now have accumulated as much wealth as that of half of the world's population of six billion people. The fact of the matter is that the land problem is a worldwide problem, and the "law of rent" functions universally and currently for the benefit of the few and to the detriment of the many.

Anne Christendom, in her article published in the New York Times on September 12, 1992, about Bangladesh, the poorest country in the world, states her view that the root of the problem of persistent malnutrition in the midst of relative plenty is the unequal distribution of land ownership. She says:

> The wealthiest 16% of the rural population had come to control two thirds of the land while almost 60% of the population had less than one acre. Bangladesh is classed as a democracy but great numbers of children die of hunger and malnutrition. Not surprisingly landowners dominate the government. Even when Bangladesh shows high economic growth this is due primarily to exports on the world market. The extensive poverty of the majority is untouched.

An example of this primary structural injustice from an earlier time was what happened in Ireland, whose elite landowners were profiting from exporting food while millions starved during the "potato famine." With land concentrated in the hands of a few and while huge amounts of food was being exported as cash crops to

England, between 1841 and 1851 at least 2.5 million people died of starvation, about one quarter of the population

Addressing now the root cause of the concentration of the world's wealth and the persistence of poverty amidst abundance, let us look at some bottom line (meaning the earth) numbers:

- "At best, a generous interpretation would suggest that about 3% of the population owns 95% of the privately held land in the USA." (Peter Meyer, " Land Rush - A Survey of America's Land - Who Owns It, Who Controls It, How much is Left" in *Harpers*, January 1979.)
- 568 companies control 22% of private land in the USA, a land mass the size of Spain. Those same companies land interests worldwide comprise a total area larger than that of Europe - almost 2 billion acres.

In order to show that there was no need for land reform in Central America because our land in the USA is even more concentrated in ownership than Central America, Senator Jesse Helms read these facts into the Congressional Record in 1981:

- In Florida, 1% owns 77% of the land. Other states where the top 1% own over two-thirds of the land are Maine, Arizona, California, Nevada, New Mexico, and Oregon.
- A United Nations study of 83 countries showed that less than 5% of rural landowners control three-quarters of the land.

In specific countries we see these numbers (for these and other statistics go to Geodata section of www.earthrights.net):

- 86% of South Africa is still owned by the white minority population
- 60% of El Salvador is owned by the richest 2% of the population
- 80% of Pakistan is owned by the richest 3% of the population
- 74% of Great Britain is owned by the richest 2% of the population
- 84% of Scotland is owned by the richest 7% of the population.
- In Venezuela, 77% of the farmland is owned by 3% of the people.
- According to a 1985 government report, 2% of landowners hold 60% of the arable land in Brazil while close to 70% of rural households have little or none. Just 342 farm properties in Brazil cover 183,397 square miles - an area larger than California (Worldwatch, Oct. 1988)
- In Spain, 70 per cent of the land is owned by 0.2 per cent of the people.

- In Britain, 69 per cent of the land is owned by 0.6 per cent of the population. Just 158,000 families own 41 million acres of land while 24 million families live on four million acres.

With so few people owning and controlling so much of the land of the planet, including the prime locations, it is easy to understand how these same few are in position to capture land rent, deposit most of this unearned income into their banks, then receive interest payments from the funds they loan. Some researchers estimate that at least as much as one third of most countries GDP is rent.

Further exacerbating the problem, the FIRE sector – finance, insurance and real estate – channels much of their profits (about 70 percent in the United States and Britain) into real estate, according to economist and former Wall Street analyst Michael Hudson, who says:

> Most of the remaining credit is extended to institutional speculators in the stock and bond markets – whose greatest gains are in the public-sector assets being sold at such low prices that great capital gains are guaranteed," says Hudson. "Unprecedented underwriting fees to investment bankers have been supplemented by more fees for mergers and acquisitions, enriching the financial sector at the expense of the rest of the economy. So we are brought back to the fact that what is being planned by today's wave of privatizations is the creation of power elites whose families are likely to dominate their societies for centuries to come, much as feudal European conquerors shaped subsequent development.

At the other end of the extreme is the reality that members of poor families are being captured, forced or sold into slavery. After journeying across five continents to investigate the issue, David Batstone reports in his book *Not for Sale: The Return of the Global Slave Trade and How We Can Stop It*, that human trafficking generates $31 billion annually and enslaves 27 million people around the globe, half of them children under the age of eighteen. Batstone profiles the new generation of abolitionists who are leading the struggle to end this appalling epidemic.

Joseph E. Stiglitz, former Chief Economist with the World Bank and one of three winners of the 2001 Nobel Prize in economics, shared his insights on the land problem in an interview with Greg Palast, a writer for *The Observer* (London). Stiglitz described in detail the four-step plan used by the international banking institutions to extract wealth from around the world. In his view the process leads to financial barbarism, pillage and plunder and has resulted in immense suffering, starvation and destruction. "It has condemned people to death," Stiglitz said bluntly in the interview.

When Palast asked Stiglitz what he would do to help developing nations, Stiglitz proposed radical land reform and an attack at the heart of "landlordism" including excessive rents charged by the propertied oligarchies worldwide. When

Palast asked why the World Bank didn't follow his advice, Stiglitz answered, "If you challenged it (property rights in land), that would be a change in the power of the elites. That's not high on their agenda."

Graph 3 will focus on how the military-industrial-financial complex and an imperialistic U.S. foreign policy have grown out of this concentration of wealth and power in the hands of so few.

The Third Graph

Privilege Fund Enables War System

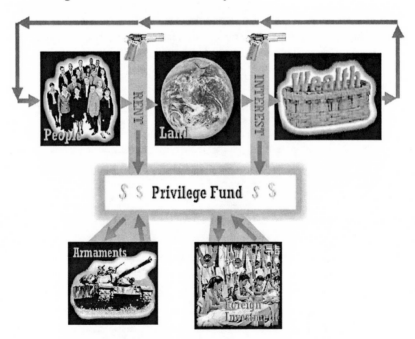

Collectors of the Privilege Fund invest in land and resources in "underdeveloped" countries.

To quell protests, investors call for military intervention.

Privilege Fund Enables War System

> He who joyfully marches to music in rank and file has already earned my
> contempt. He has been given a large brain by mistake, since for him the
> spinal cord would fully suffice. This disgrace to civilization should be done
> away with at once. Heroism at command, senseless brutality, deplorable
> love-of-country stance, how violently I hate all this, how despicable and
> ignorable war is; I would rather be torn to shreds than be a part of so base
> an action! It is my conviction that killing under the cloak of war is nothing
> but an act of murder. – Albert Einstein (1879 – 1955)

Graph 3 indicates that Privilege Funders, with their enormous capacity to accumulate
and control wealth and power, invest in land and resources in "underdeveloped" countries. To quell protests, investors call for military intervention. Privilege Funders play a
strong role in developing US foreign policy in ways that further their own interests. A
large share of the taxes of working people pay for elite wars of aggression fought in the
name of human rights and democracy but in reality for the expansion of Privilege Funder control of land, natural resources and key locations. A disproportionate number of
poor people give their lives in these wars.

Mason Gaffney in "Rent-Seeking and Global Conflict" contends that national
governments originate historically to acquire, hold and police land. "Other functions are assumed later, but sovereignty over land is always the first business. Private parties hold land from the sovereign; every chain of title goes back to a grantor
who originally seized the land," says Gaffney who suggests we keep in mind that
rent seeking in its original form is land grabbing.

Arguing that conventional economists are wrong when they submit, "national
defense is a public good," Gaffney reveals that what is defended behind the defense wall is land previously seized, as was native lands in the Americas. "Every
land title in the world goes back to a taking by force," he says. Furthermore:

> The Lords and Barons have much at stake; the serfs and vagrants very little. Rent is
> what is being defended, along with, no doubt, traditional feelings of machismo and
> some local folkways and mores.…. But it is outside the defense wall of the nation
> proper that rent seeking is most dynamic and destabilizing. Military force (often in
> tandem with finance) is used to project sovereignty into foreign nations, and over
> no-man's-lands like the oceans, polar regions, radio spectrum and outer space.

Gaffney identifies two general kinds of offshore rent-seekers:

- *Caciques*, a generic term for local cooperating rulers from the native population,
  are drawn from the matrix of the local landholding oligarchy which imperial
  powers work through in a kind of control symbiosis. Although turnover

among individual caciques may be high, the local oligarchy remains stable often thanks to the support of imperial power elites.

- Rent-seekers of the second kind are U.S. or allied multinational interests, mostly corporations. The cacique is expected to assign to them, or be complaisant in their taking concessions and resources like minerals, transportation routes, communications, bank charters, plantations, exploration, over flights, and navigation rights. Native elites normally control more of the traditional resources like farmland.

"Both these groups have major influence on U.S. policies and often manage to direct large discretionary government funds to their own interests," says Gaffney. His analysis shows how rivalry to appropriate limited rent-yielding resources leads to conflict:

> The biggest gains to rent-seekers come from buying in on the ground floor, cheap, when tenures are precarious or uncertain. Then one invokes the U.S. armed forces and the sanctions of ancillary statecraft to raise the value of one's acquisition. The three main concerns are to firm up precarious tenures (as by supporting the government that granted them); to hold down taxes on their holdings; and to avoid pure competition (as by giving preferential access to the U.S. market, or Pentagon procurers). Profits to be made are more the products of statecraft and force then of capital inputs proper.

Graph 3 shows the development of the "iron triangle" of the military industrial complex (MIC) - the close and symbiotic relationship between a nation's armed forces, its arms industry, and associated political and commercial interests. In such a system, the military is dependent on industry to supply material and other support, while the defense industry depends on government for a steady revenue stream. President Dwight David Eisenhower coined the term in his farewell presidential address to the nation wherein he warned of the dangers of "a permanent arms industry of vast proportions." In this speech he said that the agenda of those who profit from war is counter to the survival of democracy:

> In the councils of government, we must guard against the acquisition of unwarranted influence, whether sought or unsought, by the military-industrial complex. The potential for the disastrous rise of misplaced power exists and will persist.

As pejorative terms, the MIC refers to an institutionalized collusion among defense contractors (industry), The Pentagon (military), and the United States government (Congress, Executive branch), as a cartel that works against the public interest, whose motivation is profiteering. Taxes on working people subsidize the MIC to such a degree that the United States has developed a permanent war economy. Members of Congress go to Washington to grab funds for their back-home arms industry in the name of providing local employment.

The MIC, to which we will now add the letter F – Military-Industrial-Financial Complex or MIFC - goes hand in hand with U.S. foreign policy which we have previously described as largely dominated by rent-and-interest seeking Privilege Funders, mostly corporations, banks, a handful of billionaires, and their allied local elites, the caciques or vassals. Altogether the forces of these players have brought us to the current official U.S. foreign policy of "full spectrum dominance" of the world and its resources. But the roots of U.S. foreign policy can be found in the distant past.

Roots of Imperialism

John Mohawk says in his essay "The Problem of the Modern World":

> When land became a 'commodity' and lost its status as provider and sustainer of life, Western civilization began its history of subjugation and exploitation of the earth and earth based cultures. For nearly five centuries people have been coerced from their landholdings. The problem, in the English-speaking world, has its roots in the sixteenth century.

Mohawk is talking about the Enclosure Period. This is the time of violent direct suppression of the indigenous people of Europe. Between the thirteenth and seventeenth centuries, masses of peasants were evicted from their holdings or saw their common lands fenced off for sheep.

The Enclosures began after the signing of the Magna Carta in 1215. This was the great charter that King John was forced by the English barons to grant. Traditionally interpreted as guaranteeing certain civil and political liberties, the right to land for the common people was not among them. The first legal act to enforce enclosures was the Statute of Merton of 1235, which spoke of the need to "approve (meaning improve) the land in order to extract greater rent." The land barons were of course extracting rent from those who formerly had free access to the fields, forests, streams and meadows of the commons.

The Enclosures redefined land as "private property" and thereby gave it the status of a commodity, tradable within an expanding market system. Since the majority of people were denied access to the land and were forced to become wage laborers, labor also became a tradable commodity. The Enclosures were justified by its perpetrators as necessary in order to make "improvements." Whole villages were being pulled down to make way for the more profitable industry of sheep farming and families were turned adrift onto the roads. Those who did not starve became "displaced persons" and "internal refugees" – and soon paupers, prisoners, servants or soldiers.

The word "privilege" derives from "private law." Private property-in-land laws of Enclosure appropriated the Commons for the privileged few to the exclusion of the vast majority of the people of England, Ireland, and Wales and much of Europe.

Over several hundred years 4,000 Private Acts of Enclosure were passed covering some 7,000,000 acres. Probably the same sized area was enclosed without application to Parliament. About two thirds involved open fields belonging to cottagers while one third involved commons such as woodland and heath. In the census of 1086, more than half the arable land belonged to the villagers. By 1876, only 2,225 people owned most of the agricultural land in England and Wales. As newer agricultural methods and technologies were applied, landowners could raise the rents of their lands by phenomenal amounts. As the cash economy developed, the rent money accumulated into the hands of the landholders and the plight of the people worsened. To survive, they often were forced to borrow money from the landholders at high rates of interest.

The forerunner of this state of affairs goes all the way back to Roman law which developed the ownership concept that legitimized the accumulation of wealth by a few at the expense and impoverishment of the many. The Roman land law of *dominium* legalized the usurper's claim to land originally obtained by conquest and plunder. Early Christian leaders had dealt with the question of ownership and Roman law and railed against the *dominium* concept of ownership as "an exclusive and unlimited right to dispose of a thing, to the exclusion of all others."

The original Judeo-Christian land ethic was that of *koinonia* - land was God's gift to the community as a whole for the *autarkeia* or self-sufficient livelihood of all. The early Christian prophets lost out to the proponents of plunder and privilege when Christianity became the "official" religion of Rome at the Council of Nicaea, convened in 325 by the Roman Emperor Constantine I. This Council of around 300 male bishops, convened after most of the radical followers of Jesus had been hung, burned or thrown to the lions, was more concerned with establishing orthodox doctrines and creeds than with bringing a vision of peace and justice down to earth.

U.S. Land Grabs and Usurpations

Bill Moyers, in his recent lecture on The Meaning of Freedom delivered at West Point on November 15, 2006, gave a sobering sequence of United States "foreign" policy reminding the freshly minted cadets of the many years during which the army's chief engagement was "wiping out the last vestiges of Indian resistance to their dispossession and subjugation. One People's advance became another's annihilation and one of the most shameful episodes of our history." Let us review these fights:

The **Mexican–American War** was a land grab conflict fought between the United States and Mexico from 1846 to 1848. Mexico had not recognized the secession of Texas in 1836 and when it was annexed by the U.S. in 1845 Mexico announced its intention to take back what it considered a rebel province. As a result of this war the Mexican territories of California and New Mexico were ceded to the United States.

The **Spanish-American War**, fought from April through August 1898, was a conflict between the Kingdom of Spain and the United States of America that took place from April to August 1898. The war ended in victory for the United States and the end of the Spanish Empire in the Caribbean and Pacific. Representatives of Spain and the United States signed a peace treaty in Paris on December 10, 1898, which established the independence of Cuba, ceded Puerto Rico and Guam to the United States, and allowed the victorious power to purchase the Philippines Islands from Spain for $20 million. Moyers reminded the West Point graduates that after its "liberation" the island of Cuba was made a "virtual protectorate, ruled by a corrupt dictator."

The **Philippine-American War** (1899-1902) was America's first true colonial war as a world power. Though the Philippines had been "purchased" from Spain, the Filipinos had been fighting a bloody revolution against Spain since 1896 and had no intention of becoming a colony of another imperialist power. In February of 1899, fighting broke out between the occupying American Army and the Filipino forces.

The Anti-Imperialist League was formed in the United States against the annexation of the Philippines and in an attempt to thwart those who wanted to gain a "foothold" in the markets of Asia. Among the writers of that time was Mark Twain, vice president of the League from 1901 until his death in 1910. Of the Philippine-American War Twain said:

> We were only playing the American Game (democracy and human rights) in public — in private it was European.…. What we wanted, in the interest of Progress and Civilization, was the Archipelago, unencumbered by patriots struggling for independence.

General Smedley Butler became aware of the form and shape of U.S. imperialism in the early decades of the twentieth century. After serving thirty-years in the Marine Corps he was the most decorated U.S. military officer of his day. Butler's powerful writings clearly articulate his agony and anguish upon fully perceiving the end goals of his military ventures. Speaking of his time in the military in his 1934 book, *War is a Racket*, Smedley wrote:

> I spent most of my time being a high-class muscle man for Big Business, for Wall Street and for the Bankers. In short, I was a racketeer, a gangster for capitalism.... I helped make Mexico, especially Tampico, safe for American oil interests in 1914. I helped make Haiti and Cuba a decent place for the National City Bank boys to collect revenues in. I helped in the raping of half a dozen Central American republics for the benefits of Wall Street. The record of racketeering is long. I helped purify Nicaragua for the international banking house of Brown Brothers in 1909-1912. I

brought light to the Dominican Republic for American sugar interests in 1916. In China I helped to see to it that Standard Oil went its way unmolested.

During those years, I had, as the boys in the back room would say, a swell racket. Looking back on it, I feel that I could have given Al Capone a few hints. The best he could do was to operate his racket in three districts. I operated on three continents.

War is just a racket. A racket is best described, I believe, as something that is not what it seems to the majority of people. Only a small inside group knows what it is about. It is conducted for the benefit of the very few at the expense of the masses.…. The trouble with America is tat when the dollar only earns 6 percent over here, then it gets restless and goes overseas to get 100 percent. Then the flag follows the dollar and the soldiers follow the flag. I wouldn't go to war again as I have done to protect some lousy investment of the Bankers.

Out of war nations acquire additional territory, if they are victorious. They just take it. This newly acquired territory promptly is exploited by the few – the selfsame few who wrung dollars out of blood in the war. The general public shoulders the bill. Ad what is this bill? This bill engenders a horrible accounting. Newly placed gravestones. Mangled bodies. Shattered minds. Broken hearts and homes. Economic instability. Depression and all its attendant miseries. Back-breaking taxation for generations and generations.

John Stockwell, self-described as "CIA, Marine Corp, three CIA Secret Wars, a position in the National Security Council in 1975 as the Chief of the Angola Task Force running the Secret War in Angola, the third CIA Secret War I was part of" has given us his overview of the decades of U.S. wars of aggression, starting where Smedley Butler left off. Stockwell's statement below and the following ones by Daniel Sheehan and Peter Dale Scott are all to be found on a video compilation by Frank Dorrel -- What I Learned about U.S. Foreign Policy -- which can be viewed in its entirety at: www.addictedtowar.com

Trying to summarize this Third World War that the CIA, the U.S. National Security Complex with the military all interwoven in it in many different ways, has been waging, let me just put it this way, the best heads that I coordinate with studying this thing, we count at least minimum figure six million people who've been killed in this long 40-year war that we have waged against the people of the Third World.…

They are people of countries like the Congo, Vietnam, Kampuchea, Indonesia, Nicaragua, where conspicuously, they nor their governments, do not have the capability of doing any physical hurt to the United States. They don't have ICBM's; they don't have armies or navies. They could not hurt us if they wanted to. There has rarely been any evidence that they really wanted to.…. Cheap shots, if you will, killing people of other countries of the world who cannot defend themselves under the guise of secrecy and under the rubric of national security.

Senator Church said in the 14 years before he did his investigation that he found that they (the CIA) had run 900 major operations and 3000 minor operations. And if you extrapolate that over the whole period of the 40 odd years that we've had a CIA you come up with 3000 major operations and over 10,000 minor operations. Every one of them illegal. Every one of them disruptive of the lives and societies of other peoples and all of them bloody and gory beyond comprehension. . ...

Daniel Sheehan, formerly Chief Legal Counsel for the Christic Institute, says:

There exists in operation now a secret team of some two dozen men, former CIA covert operatives, former U.S. Pentagon arms suppliers, who have joined together in private enterprise outside of the control of the American government, either the Congress or the President, who are mounting their personal wars around the world. . . And that's the group we are dealing with right here – who're making war around the world for their own personal profit.

And from Peter Dale Scott, Professor at the University of California at Berkeley who has conducted extensive research on covert action and CIA activities:

To think of the democratic governments that have been overthrown in the last 30 years by military coups, it is almost like giving a capsule history of CIA covert operations in the last 30 years. I mean there was the overthrow of Prime Minister Mosaddeq in Iran in 1953; there was the overthrow of Arbenz in Guatemala in 1954; there was the overthrow of the Brazilian government in 1964; there was the overthrow of the Ghana government in 1996. A lot of the governments I just mentioned got into trouble with international oil companies because they tried to assert their national prerogatives over their own resources. Time after time the CIA has come in on behalf of those multi-national companies.

The Federation of American Scientists, which counts more than three dozen Nobel laureates in science on their board of sponsors, has catalogued some two hundred military incursions since 1945 in which the U.S. has been the aggressor. Many of these operations have deodorant-sweet names, perhaps to better shield us from the gross reality of intent to slaughter: Desert Spring, Provide Comfort, Shining Hope, Open Arms, Golden Pheasant, Greensweep, Green Clover, Silent Promise, Safe Harbor, Sea Angel, Desert Calm, New Life, Garden Plot, Operation Freedom Train.

Gore Vidal, in his 2002 book *Dreaming War*, states that these "recorded military unilateral strikes that the U.S. has made against Second and Third World countries is a great scandal not discussed in our Media or known to our taxpayers." Vidal is appalled by those:

. . .forty years of mindless wars, which created a debt of $5 trillion that hugely benefited aerospace and firms like General Electric. This while median household income was reduced by 7 percent. The federal income tax started out as a nibble on the rich, leaped on us like a lion in 1943, and continues to devour pounds of flesh from those who work for a living while the cost of living soars.

Historian William Blum in his books *Killing Hope* and *Rogue State: A Guide to the World's Only Superpower* has compiled a shockingly long list of more than 70 countries where the U.S. has intervened, sometimes more than once, militarily or through covert operations, sanctions, embargoes, and/or assassinations since World War II. On the list with specific details are China, Marshall Islands, Italy, Greece, Philippines, Korea, Albania, East Germany, Iran, Guatemala, Costa Rica, Indonesia, Haiti, Guyana, Iraq, Vietnam, Cambodia, Laos, Thailand, Ecuador, The Congo/Zaire, France/Algeria, Brazil, Peru, Dominican Republic, Cuba, Ghana, Uruguay, Chile, Greece, South Africa, Bolivia, Australia, Portugal, East Timor, Angola, Jamaica, Honduras, Nicaragua, Seychelles, South Yemen, South Korea, Chad, Grenada, Suriname, Libya, Fiji, Panama, Afghanistan, El Salvador, Haiti, Bulgaria, Albania, Somalia, Peru, Mexico, Yugoslavia, Afghanistan, Iraq.

General Owoye Azazi, Nigeria Chief of Defense Staff and Francis Kabiowei Udisi discussing ways and means to bring permanent peace to the Niger Delta region.

Blum's view is that "The engine of American foreign policy has been fueled not by a devotion to any kind of morality, but rather by the necessity to serve other imperatives" which he summarizes as follows:

- Making the world safe for American corporations;
- Enhancing the financial statements of defense contractors at home who have contributed generously to members of congress;
- Preventing the rise of any society that might serve as a successful example of an alternative to the capitalist model;
- Extending political and economic hegemony over as wide an area as possible, as befits a "great power."

In his article "Unleashing Armageddon in the Middle East" Dr. Elias Akleh tells us that in the mid-1970s the American Power Elite (what we are herein calling Privilege Funders) drew a "Grand Plan" to control and to monopolize global oil and nuclear energy resources, for "he who controls energy resources determines the fate of nations." Akleh says that:

> The base of this Grand Plan is the invasion of energy rich countries to directly control their resources, and to create subservient governments that would exploit their own people as cheap labor to harvest energy for the United States.

President Jimmy Carter's administration had pledged itself to non-intervention in the Third World, to a sincere commitment to arms control, and to work for worldwide human rights. President Carter accomplished much along these lines in the beginning of his term in office, but in the end he reversed himself and fell victim to Cold War fever. Following the Soviet invasion of Afghanistan in 1980 Carter issued his famous statement to a joint session of Congress in which he said:

> An attempt by any outside force to gain control of the Persian Gulf region will be regarded as an assault on the vital interests of the United States of America (and) will be repelled by any means necessary, including military force.

Michael T. Klare, professor of peace and world security studies at Hampshire College, describes in his book, *Resource Wars: The New Landscape of Global Conflict*, how the United States began a military build-up in the Persian Gulf area at that time which has continued to this day. The Carter Doctrine was invoked during the Iran-Iraq war of 1980 - 88 and again in August 1990 when Iraqi forces occupied Kuwait. "Controlling Iraq is about oil as power, rather than oil as fuel. Control over the Persian Gulf translates into control over Europe, Japan, and China. It's having our hand on the spigot," says Klare.

When Iran's democratically elected Prime Minister Mohammad Mossadegh nationalized his country's oil industry in order to benefit the Iranian people rather than the multinational oil corporations he was deposed in a 1953 coup orchestrated by Kermit Roosevelt, grandson of President Theodore Roosevelt.

In the name of democracy, but in reality at the behest of the MIFC, many democratically elected leaders have met similar fates when they attempted to put in
place economic democracies in order to improve the living conditions of their
people. When the Chilean people elected Salvador Allende as their president and
promised to nationalize their copper and other resources the U.S. CIA used covert
actions to overthrow him resulting in the deaths of more than 3,000 and the tor-
tures of tens of thousands. We know now that the U.S. sent advisers to help with
the killings and torture.

In 1961, democratically elected leader of the Congo, Patrice Lumumba,
planned to claim the resources of the Congo for the people of the Congo. His
stand for economic sovereignty resulted in his murder, again with U.S. complicity
and the backing of the Eisenhower administration. The mass murderer and tor-
turer Jonas Savimbi was then installed.

Zbigniew Brzezinski, former US National Security Advisor, describes "superpower politics" and the "American global system" in his 1997 book, *The Grand
Chessboard - American Primacy and Its Geostrategic Imperatives*. Brzezinski presents the
strange viewpoint that in order to provide the basis for global cooperation in the
distant future, US foreign policy must be based on global dominance in the present. It is a bit like providing a rational for a husband dominating his wife so that in
the future they can have a respectfully cordial relationship. The focal point of the
chessboard is Eurasia - the "globe's most important paying field" where the US
must maintain control as "the central basis for global primacy." After laying out his
three-step formula to "offset, co-opt, and/or control the geopolitical critical Eura-
sian states" Brzezinski says:

> In a terminology that hearkens back to the more brutal age of ancient empires, the
> three grand imperatives of imperial geostrategy are to prevent collusion and main-
> tain security dependence among the vassals, to keep tributaries pliant and protected,
> and to keep the barbarians from coming together.…. Competition based on terri-
> tory still dominates world affairs.

John Perkins' book *Confessions of an Economic Hit Man* has been praised by Harvard
Professor John E. Mack as a revelation of the inner workings of "our deeply en-
trenched governmental/corporate imperialist structure." Covertly recruited by the
National Security Agency but working as a consultant with private firms, Perkins'
job was to convince governments of countries including Indonesia, Panama, Ecuador, Columbia, Saudi Arabia, Iran and others to implement policies and programs that promoted U.S. based banks and corporations.

Perkins describes the mechanisms of imperial control behind several major
world events such as the fall of the Shah of Iran, the deaths of Panamanian president Omar Torrijos and Ecuador's Jaime Roldas, and the U.S. invasions of Iraq.
Perkins had come to like and respect Torrijos and Roldas, but his "day job" was

not in their interests as they had insisted on retaining control of their country's resources. Both were killed.

Perkins says it took him many years to garner the courage to write this book because it reveals that he was one of the "highly paid professionals who cheat countries around the globe out of trillions of dollars" and whose tools included "fraudulent financial reports, rigged elections, payoffs, extortion, sex and murder." All of his "case studies" fit into the pattern of the numerous other overt and covert wars of aggression that the U.S. has supported or directly waged against people of many countries of the world on behalf of Privilege Funders' ideas of law and order.

Andrew Bacevich, in his book *The New Militarism: How Americans Are Seduced by War*, describes the propaganda methods that keep up the illusion that certain foreign nations constitute a threat to the US, thereby maintaining a permanent level of international tension. He identifies elements of "messianism embodied in American civic nationalism, with its quasi-religious belief in the universal and timeless validity of its own democratic system, and in its right and duty to spread that system to the rest of the world."

Bacevich describes how U.S. militarism has been built around a set of glaring contradictions, for example, the contradiction between the military coercion of other nations and the belief in the spreading of "freedom and democracy. This combination is historically coterminous with Western imperialism," says Bacevich. "Reaching 'freedom' at the point of an American rifle as no less morally and intellectually absurd."

Soldiers Sickened and Abused

What about those holding the American rifles? *Foreign Policy in Focus* columnist Conn Hallinan describes the "shafting of vets":

> Modern battlefields are toxic nightmares, filled with depleted uranium ammunition, exotic explosives, and deadly. The soldiers are shot up with experimental vaccines that can have dangerous side effects from additives like squalene. Soldiers are not only under fire; they are assaulted by their own weapons systems and medical procedures. Upwards of 20,000 Americans have been wounded in Iraq, some of those so grotesquely that medicine has invented a new term to describe them - polytrauma. An estimated 7,000 vets have severe brain and spinal injuries and have required amputation.

Bill Moyers told the West Point students "the chicken hawks are failing you" and described to them contents of the October (2006) issue of the magazine of the California Nurses Association, which contains a long report on *The Battle at Home*. In veterans' hospitals across the country - and in a growing number of ill-prepared, under-funded psych and primary care clinics as well - the report says that nurses "have witnessed the guilt, rage, emotional numbness, and tormented flashbacks of GIs just back from

Iraq." Yet a returning vet must wait an average of 165 days for a VA decision on initial disability benefits, and an appeal can take up to three years. Just in the first quarter of this year (2006) the VA treated 20,638 Iraq veterans for post-traumatic stress disorder, and faces a backlog of 400,000 cases. According to a 1994 Congressional report (as stated by William Blum in "Johnny Got His Gun, *The Anti-Empire Report*, January 12, 2007):

Approximately 60,000 military personnel were used as human subjects in the 1940s to test two chemical agents, mustard gas and lewisite (blister gas). Most of these subjects were not informed of the nature of the experiments and never received medical follow-up after their participation in the research. Some of these human subjects were threatened with imprisonment at Fort Leavenworth if they discussed theses experiments with anyone, including their wives, parents, and family doctors. For decades, the Pentagon denied that the research had taken place, resulting in decades of suffering for many veterans who became ill after the secret testing.

In the decades between the 1940s and 1990s a number of government programs used soldiers as guinea pigs - marched to nuclear explosion sites, pilots sent through the mushroom clouds; chemical and biological weapons and radiation experiments; behavior modification experiments; widespread exposure to the highly toxic dioxin of Agent Orange in Korea and Vietnam. There were reported millions of experimental subjects.

In the 1990s many thousands of American soldiers came home from the Gulf War with unusual, debilitating ailments. Exposure to harmful chemical or biological agents was suspected but the Pentagon denied that this had occurred. As years went by the veterans suffered from neurological problems, chronic fatigue, skin problems, scarred lungs, memory loss, muscle and joint pain, severe headaches, personality changes, passing out, and other disorders. Eventually the Pentagon began to own up to the fact that these soldiers were indeed in the vicinity of poisonous gas releases; an estimated nearly 100,000 U.S. soldiers could have been exposed to trace amounts of sarin gas.

Soldiers have been forced to take vaccines against anthrax and nerve gas not approved by the FDA as safe and effective and punished, sometimes treated like criminals, if they refused. (During WW II soldiers were forced to take a yellow fever vaccine, with the result that some 330,000 of them were infected with the hepatitis B virus.)

Through all the recent wars countless soldiers have been put in close proximity to the radioactive dust of exploded depleted uranium-tipped shells and missiles on the battlefield. DU has been associated with a long list of rare and terrible illnesses and birth defects. It poisons the air, the soil, the water, the lungs, the blood, and the genes.

Troops serving in Iraq or their families have reported purchasing with their own funds bullet-proof vests, better armor for their vehicles, medical supplies, and global positioning devices, all for their own safety, which were not provided to them by the army. There are frequent complaints by service women of sexual assault and rape and the hands of their ale counterparts. Numerous injured and disabled vets from all wars have to engage in an ongoing struggle to get the medical care they were promised.

A New York Times article published May 12, 2006 – "Army Acts to Curb Abuses of Injured Recruits" – describes accounts of the callous, bordering on sadistic, treatment of soldiers in bases in the U.S. Repeated tours of duty fracture family a life and increase the chance not only of death and injury but also of post-traumatic stress disorder. National Public Radio's "All Things Considered" on December 4, 2006 and other days ran a series on Army mistreatment of soldiers home from Iraq and suffering serious PTSD. At Colorado's Ft. Carson these afflicted soldiers were receiving a variety of abuse and punishment much more than the help they need, as officers harassed and punished them for being "emotionally weak."

It is as General Smedley Butler said of war: "The general public shoulders the bill. And what is this bill? Newly placed gravestones. Mangled bodies. Shattered minds. Broken hearts and homes. Economic instability. Depression and all its attendant miseries."

Nuclear Bombs

The malefic vision for the planet that the Privilege Funders and their institutions have spawned has reached an absurd and horrifying crescendo under the Bush administration's doctrine of "preemptive nuclear war." After the 2002 Nuclear Posture Review the 2003 Senate decided that the new generation of "low yield mini-nukes," which have up to six times the explosive capacity of the Hiroshima bomb, were "safe for civilians" as the explosions are (if they bang according to design) underground.

The United States is apparently going head with its plan to build the country's first nuclear warheads in nearly 20 years. The effort will require a huge refurbishment of the nation's complex for nuclear design and manufacturing, with the overall bill estimated at over 100 billion dollars.

Michel Chossudovsky, Professor of Economics at the University of Ottawa, Director of the Center for Research on Globalization, and author of *Globalization of Poverty*, is a clear-sighted analyst who is alarmed that use of these bombs is now on the table. Chossudovsky says:

> In an utterly twisted logic, nuclear weapons are presented as a means to building peace and preventing "collateral damage"… Even at the low end of its 0.3-300 kiloton yield range the nuclear blast will simply blow out a huge crater of radioactive material, creating a lethal gamma-radiation field over a large area.

We cannot minimize the possibilities of a nuclear holocaust. The US Strategic Command Headquarters in Nebraska, in coalition with US allies, is responsible for overseeing a global strike plan and has created a new command unit, the Joint Functional Component Command Space and Global Strike, mandated to oversee the launch of a nuclear attack against not on "rogue states" but also China and Russia.

Russia aims most of its 8,200 strategic nuclear warheads at U.S. and Canadian targets. The U.S. aims most of its 7,000 on Russian missile silos and command centers. Each of these thermonuclear warheads has roughly 20 times the destructive power of the bomb dropped on Hiroshima, according to a report on nuclear weapons by the National Resources Defense Council. According to the Center for Defense Information, if an attack is suspected the commander of the U.S. Strategic air Command has only three minutes to decide if a nuclear attack warning is valid, ten minutes to locate the president for a 30-second briefing to decide whether or not to attack and if so, to consider which pre-set targeting plan to use. Once launched, the missiles would take 10 to 30 minutes to reach their Russian target.

Some would say that a nuclear holocaust is already underway, albeit less dramatically than all-out nuclear war. The US nuclear industry has produced 1.2 billion pounds of depleted uranium waste which is being recycled into DU munitions. Under international law, DU meets the definition of a weapon of mass destruction and violates US military law as well as the Geneva and Hague conventions.

Leuren Moret, a radiation scientist, and Doug Rokke former U.S. Army Depleted Uranium Project director, are certain that there has been a cover-up by three administrations of the health problems and cancers cause by DU. The Veterans Administration reports that well over 500,000 Persian Gulf veterans have gone on medical disability since 1991. Moret, Rokke and others attribute many of these disabilities to DU exposure.

The Arms Trade and Military-Industrial Profits

Bryan Brender, in his article "US is top purveyor on weapons sales list" *(Globe Staff*, November 13, 2006) writes that the United States last year provided nearly half of the weapons sold to militaries in the developing world. Major arms sales to the most unstable regions – many already engaged in conflict – grew to the highest level in eight years. According to the annual assessment, the United States supplied $8.1 billion worth of weapons to developing countries in 2005 – 45.8 percent of the total and far more than second-ranked Russia with 15 percent and Britain with a little more than 13 percent.

In addition to weapons already delivered, new contracts for future weapons deliveries topped $44 billion last year – the highest overall since 1998, according to the report. Nearly 70 percent of them were designated for developing nations.

Arms control specialists said the figures underscore how the largely unchecked arms trade to the developing world has become a major staple of the American weapons industry, even though introducing many of the weapons risks fueling conflicts rather than aiding long-term US interests.

"We are at a point in history where many of these sales are not essential for the self-defense of these countries and the arms being sold continue to fuel conflicts and tensions in unstable areas," writes Daryl G. Kimball, executive director of the nonpartisan Arms Control Association in Washington.

One startling example of arms sales involves that of surplus F-14 parts to Iran. Democratic Senator Ron Wyden wants to cut off all Pentagon sales of these parts, which are used for the Tomcat fighter jets made famous in the 1986 Tom Cruise movie, Top Gun. The U.S. retired its F-14s last fall leaving only Iran - which bought these jets in the 1970s when it was a U.S. ally - flying the planes. Wyden has put forth the Stop Arming Iran Act.

"It just defies common sense to be making this kind of equipment available to the Iranians with all that they have done that is against our interests," says Wyden in an *Associated Press* interview by Sharon Theimer, published January 29, 2007.

While selling fighter jet spare parts to Iran may defy one sort of common sense, it makes total sense when hung together with the profit motives of a government entwined military-industrial-financial complex. Iran and Iraq have been taking alternate turns as "ally" and "enemy" of America, like plucking "hate me, hate me not" daisy petals. The dissembling can now be seen in truth as Great Game manipulations for power and control.

The Military-Industrial Complex and Iraq's Oil

In the mid 1990s Saddam Hussein was preparing to establish lucrative agreements with French, Russian, Chinese and other oil companies (estimated to be worth $1.1 trillion), excluding US and British companies and thus realigning the global energy industry. Months after the U.S. invasion of Iraq it was revealed that control of Iraq's oil fields was one of the chief issues discussed in Vice President Dick Cheney's Energy Task Force meeting with oil executives in 2001. Among the items released under court order were maps of Iraq's oil fields pipelines and refineries.

As of this writing the Iraqi government is about to pass a law giving Western oil companies the right to the country's massive oil resources. A January 7, 2007 article – "Blood and oil: How the West will profit from Iraq's most precious commodity" - published by *The Independent* says:

> Production-sharing agreements (PSAs) would enable oil majors such as BP and Shell in the UK and Exxon and Chevron in the US to sign deals of up to 30 years to extract Iraq's oil. The legislation was drafted with the assistance of an American consultancy firm hired by the US government, major oil companies and the International Monetary Fund with little or no input from Iraqi members of parliament.

So much for Tony Blair's proposal that the "oil revenues, which people falsely claim that we want to seize, should be put in a trust fund for the Iraqi people administered through the UN" or then US Secretary of State Colin Powell's solemn promise that "the oil of the Iraqi people belongs to the Iraqi people; it is their wealth, it will be used for their benefit."

According to the US-based Center for Public Integrity, 150-plus US companies have won contracts in Iraq worth over $50 billion. There remains no doubt that Iraq has been shattered and hundreds of thousands killed in a war for oil and profit, power and plunder, and maybe in some very warped minds, just for the sheer hell of it.

The Costs of Imperialism

Empire monitoring and control requires vast numbers of US foreign bases, more than 700 in about 130 countries. These are staggering numbers but the 2003 *Base Status Report* fails to mention garrisons in Kosovo, Afghanistan, Iraq, Israel, Kuwait, Kyrgyzstan, Qatar and Uzbekistan established in the two-and-a-half years since 9/11.

The Pentagon similarly fails to note all of the $5-billion-worth of military and espionage installations in Britain, which have long been conveniently disguised as Royal Air Force bases. If there were an honest county, the actual size of our military empire would probably top 1,000 different bases in other people's countries but no one – possibly not even the Pentagon – knows the exact number for sure, although it has been distinctly on the rise in recent years, according to a January 15, 2004 article at TomDispatch.com.

Discussing America's empire of bases, Chalmers Johnson says:

> Once upon a time, you could trace the spread of imperialism by counting up colonies. America's version of the colony is the military base. By following the changing politics of global basing, one can learn much about our ever-larger imperial stance and the militarism that grows with it. Militarism and imperialism are Siamese twins joined at the hip. Each thrives off the other. Already highly advanced in our country, they are both on the verge of a quantum leap that will almost surely stretch our military beyond its capabilities, bringing about fiscal insolvency and very possibly doing mortal damage to our republican institutions.

The Center for Defense Information, founded by former top-ranking admirals and generals, reports that overall defense spending will rise to more than $550 billion. Compare that to the $20 billion that the United Nations and all of its agencies and funds spend each year on all of its programs to make this a safer and more livable world. According to United Nations calculations a $40 billion increase in funding could feed, clothe, and educate the entire globe. Economists Allied for Arms Reduction has calculated that for less than two-thirds the cost of the $1.2 trillion dollars that would be the lifetime costs of a proposed multi-layered Ballistic Missile Defense system, the entire *Millennium Development Goals* for poverty eradication worldwide could be fully funded.

A recent study by Nobel prize-winning economist Joseph E. Stiglitz and Harvard University's Linda Bilmes estimates the true cost of the Iraq misadventure at $2.267 trillion projected to the year of 2010.

"The big prize here for Bush's foreign policy is not the acquisition of natural resources or the enhancement of U.S. security, but rather the lining of the pockets of the defense contractors, the merchants of death who mine our treasury," says Robert Scheer in "Ike Was Right" posted at Truthdig.com, December 26, 2006.

The U.S. now spends more on empire than at any time since World War II and more than the combined military budgets of rest of the world.

The federal government is not able to accurately track the amount of money being spent on the wars in Iraq and Afghanistan. Nor does Congress seem to know how much it appropriated for these wars. *The Defense Monitor* reported in September/October 2006 that "outlays for the war are impossible to track; DOD mixes those records with outlays for non-war costs, making it impossible to determine if the money was spent as DOD, or Congress, intended." It would appear that the federal government has become hopelessly complex, or maybe too corrupt, to meet basic standards and expectations of government accountability.

Military Contractors, Mercenaries and Militias

Thus it should not surprise that Army investigators have opened up to 50 criminal probes involving battlefield contractors in operations in Iraq, Afghanistan and Kuwait. Senior contracting officials, government employees, residents of other countries and U.S. military personnel have been implicated in millions of dollars of fraud allegations according to a January 27, 2007 Associated Press story, "Army Probes War Contractor Fraud."

The Pentagon has viewed outsourcing a wide variety of military tasks as much more efficient but the GAO reported in December 2006 that the military has been losing millions of dollars because it cannot monitor industry workers in far-flung locations. Some 60,000 contractors have been supporting the Army in Southwest Asia, which includes Iraq, compared with 9,200 contractors in the 1991 Persian Gulf War. Commanders are often unsure how many contractors use their bases and require food housing and protection.

One Army official said the service estimates they are losing about $43 million each year on free meals provided to contractors who also get a food allowance. Tod Robberson discusses the "contractor's war role debate" In The Dallas Morning News, November 28, 2006. The target contractor is DynCorp International in Irving, Texas. With more than 5,000 employees in and around Iraq and Afghanistan, DynCorp's paramilitary workforce deploys alongside the U.S. military. Its active and pending federal contracts have a current value of $5.7 billion. Taxpayers provide 97% of DynCorp's revenue. Its biggest contracts involve training foreign police and other security services and drug-crop eradication.

Rep. Janice Schakowsky has been monitoring DynCorp's activities but says that she has been repeatedly thwarted in efforts to review U.S. government audit reports on the company's contracts because, according to the State Department. The need to protect DynCorp's commercial secrets supersedes the public's right to know. "There seems to be no real interest in overseeing or reporting or holding accountable any of these contractors. And we're talking about billions of dollars of taxpayer money," she says.

Robberson reports that human rights groups have been particularly critical of the free license DynCorp and other security contractors seem to enjoy when their paramilitary units deploy in world trouble spots such as Iraq, Afghanistan, Sudan or Colombia. Iraq's ambassador to Washington echoed those concerns in an interview, labeling such units "imported militias."

Contractors currently rank as the second-largest foreign force, behind the U.S. military, serving in Iraq. Blackwater USA was formed in 1997 to provide additional support to military and law enforcement organizations. It was one over sixty private security firms employed following the U.S. invasions of Afghanistan and Iraq.

Blackwater consists of nine companies. Company literature claims the company runs "the largest privately owned firearms training facility in the nation." The facility, located in North Carolina, is composed of several ranges, indoor, outdoor, urban reproductions and has over 7000 acres of land spanning Camden and Currituck counties. In November 2006 Blackwater announced it recently acquired an 80-acre facility 150 miles west of Chicago, in Mount Carroll, Illinois to be called Blackwater North.

Iraq for Sale: The War Profiteers, a documentary film, suggests that the company may have been partially responsible for the Abu Ghraib scandal.

Blackwater employees all have military experience, but in order to join this new breed of warriors - private security contractors - they must pass an eight-week course for which they must pay $20,000. One of their lessons is on how to break a man's arm with your bare hands, as reported in "Blackwater: Inside America's Private Army" by Joanne Kimberlin and Bill Sizemore, The Virginian-Pilot, July 23, 2006.

An investigation by The Chicago Tribune revealed some ugly truth about the subcontractors that are paid to do the menial work for the bigger U.S. and other military contractors. An international network of such companies has apparently brought thousands of laborers to Iraq. The Tribune reporters found that "subcontractors and brokers routinely seized workers' passports, deceived them about their safety or contract terms and, in at least one case, allegedly tried to force terrified men into Iraq under the threat of cutting off their food and water."

The U.S. military has confirmed that laws banning human trafficking have been violated and has ordered contractors "to return passports that have been illegally confiscated from laborers on U.S. bases." Zia Mian, Foreign Policy in Focus, January 2007 reported this in "The Three U.S. Armies in Iraq".

"Not one contractor of the entire military industry in Iraq has been charged with any crime over the last three and a half years, let alone prosecuted or punished. Given the numbers of contractors, let alone the incidents we know about, it boggles the mind," says Peter Singer, an expert on U.S. private military contractors.

International Financial Institutions and Multi-National Corporations Trounce on Peoples Right to Land

International financial institutions (IFIs), purportedly established to alleviate poverty in developing countries, have instead furthered the aims of the MIFC. For example, *Economic Justice News* (September, 2006) reports that the World Bank's private sector lending arm, the International Finance Corporation (IFC) was set up in 1956 with the goal of lending to small and medium-sized businesses in developing countries to stimulate broad based economic growth. But the loan beneficiaries are often large multinational corporations. Large infrastructure projects as well as oil, mining and gas projects accounted for 13.6% of spending in 2005, and just 1.4% went to education and healthcare combined. This is despite World Bank reports that show that large infrastructure and extractive industries projects create poverty by displacing communities and detaching them from their traditional means of livelihood.

More than 50,000 people participated in the World Social Forum held in Nairobi from January 20-25, 2007. In her article about the Forum – "Debt, the Illegitimate Legacy of Africa's Dictators" - Joyce Mulama writes that most of the debts that hurt the economies of the world's poor countries are illegitimate and that the debt burdens are increasing. Jubilee South, a global alliance of anti-debt movements, estimates that over 60 countries will fail to realize the anti-poverty Millennium Development Goals by 2015 if their debts are not fully cancelled.

Joel Varado, a Filipino member of the House of Representatives who spoke at the WSF, said his country's debt had increased from 599 million dollars in 1965 to 60.1 billion dollars at present. The current debt is 48 percent of the GDP.

According to Moussa Demba, coordinator of the African chapter of Jubilee South, sub-Saharan Africa's total debt burden is about 210 billion dollars, which is 85 percent of GDP. Kenya's total debt burden is about 10 billion dollars with debt servicing costs of about 22 percent of the country's budget. There is now a movement in Kenya to pressure through their legislators a new law calling for the suspension of repayment of Kenya's illegitimate debt.

"It is no secret that a number of the loans were given to many dictatorial, unaccountable and irresponsible leaders in Africa and elsewhere, and the money never benefited those that it was meant for," said Nobel Peace laureate Wangari Maathai in her speech to the WSF for which she received a standing ovation.

There are many examples of how the International Monetary Fund has forced weak nations to open their borders to subsidized food from abroad, destroying their own farming industries and, perhaps most importantly, preventing state spending on land reform. Given fair access to land and natural resources, the people of every country of the world could develop to meet their basic needs without external funding. But the IFIs in various combinations with the military-industrial-financial complex have colluded to prevent ordinary people of the non-elite classes from securing rights to land and natural resources.

For example, George Monbiot investigated land expropriations on the Basotu Plains of Tanzania, funded by Canada whose chemical and machinery companies, world leaders in wheat technology, benefited when that crop was planted rather than corn, beans or cassava. Dispossessed were 40,000 members of the Barabaig tribe, who were beaten, imprisoned and tortured when they tried to return.

In India, a much bigger scheme being funded by the UK will dispossess some 20 million people from their lands in the state of Andhra Pradesh. As neo-liberal economic structures of the privilege funders have clawed their way deeper into Africa, over the past ten years, the number of people in sub-Saharan Africa living on less than a dollar a day has risen from 242 million to 300 million.

Land distribution is the key determinant of food security. Small farms are up to 10 times as productive as large ones, as they tend to be cultivated more intensively. Small farmers are more likely to supply local people with staple crops. But governments dominated by first world elites don't like land reform, which hurts big farmers, and the companies that supply them.

Mike Whitney pointed his finger in the right direction about one important outcome of recent war in Lebanon. Writing in Information Clearing House Blog – "Why Fisk is wrong about Lebanon," January 28, 2007 – he states that "the real purpose of the $7.6 billion in loans is to shackle Lebanon to the international lending institutions that are demanding additional taxes on the poor, more privatization of state-run industries, and restructuring the economy to meet the requirements of the global banking elite."

Whitney called the World Bank loan "Phase 2 of the assault on Lebanese sovereignty." Echoing similar insights of Smedley Butler of decades ago, Whitney says:

> The US military is just the left hand of the banking establishment. One hand washes another. It's the perfect system; the US-Israeli war machine flattens an entire country and then their buddies in the corporate-banking business rake in the profits from loans and reconstruction contracts. At the same time, they insist that the *New Lebanon* be rebuilt according to the neoliberal model; the same economic model that has kept Latin America and Africa in abject poverty for two decades.

The global system of elite, Privilege Funder control of the land and natural resources of the planet, financed by deficit spending and the tax dollars of working people, may be on the verge of collapse along with the public infrastructure of the United States. Non-defense discretionary spending declined 38 percent between 1980 and 1999 as a share of GDP, from 2.5 percent to only 1.5 percent. The National Education Association tells us that the nation's school facilities need $268 billion to put facilities into good condition so that the children are physically safe.

In 2005, the American Society of Civil Engineers calculated that poor road infrastructure cost motorists $54 billion a year in repairs and operating costs and the 3.5 billion hours per year that Americans are stuck in traffic costs the economy more than $67 billion annually in lost productivity and wasted fuel. The report showed a decline of 1 percent in maintenance spending for the country's power grid since 1992, while demand rose 2.4 percent annually over the same time period.

Agonizing over the shift from the American dream to the American nightmare, Bill Moyers in his America 101 lecture given to the Council of Great City Schools on October 27, 2006, had this to say:

> Democracy has been made subservient to capitalism, and the great ideals of the American Revolution as articulated in the Preamble to the Constitution are being sacrificed to the Gospel of Wealth. . . . . The simple proposition of the common good that might balance the influence of organized wealth with the interests of ordinary people - the most basic assumption of all political teaching since ancient Greece - is written out of Washington life.

In "A National Intelligence Estimate on the United States," *Harper's*, November 17, 2007, Chalmers Johnson warns us that the United States "faces a violent contradiction between its long republican tradition and its more recent imperial ambitions." He sees that our economy is now based on a form of "military Keynesianism" whereby the flow of the nation's wealth - from taxpayers and (increasingly) foreign lenders through the government to military contractors and (decreasingly) back to taxpayers - requires sustained military ambition in order to avoid recession or collapse. Johnson says:

> Military Keynesianism may be economic development by other means, but it does very often lead to real war, or, if not real war, then a significantly warlike political environment. This creates a feedback loop: American presidents know that military Keynesianism tends to concentrate power in the executive branch, and so presidents who seek greater power have a natural inducement to encourage further growth of the military-industrial complex. As the phenomena feed on each other, the usual outcome is a real war, based not on needs of national defense but rather on the domestic political logic of military Keynesianism.

As U.S. Senator Robert La Follette Sr. observed, "In times of peace, the war party insists on making preparation for war. As soon as prepared for war, it insists on making war."

The Unitary Presidency

George W. Bush has taken the political and economic dynamics of military Keynesianism to a never before experienced extreme in the doctrine of The Unitary Presidency. Vice President Cheney complained in 2002 that he had seen a significant erosion in post-Watergate power with the passage of reforms such as the War Powers Act, the Budget and Impoundment Control Act, the Freedom of Information Act, Executive Order 11905, which outlawed political assassination, and the Intelligence Oversight Act. Cheney said that these reforms were "unwise" because they "weaken the presidency and the vice presidency." Bush has claimed that he is "the commander" and "the decider" and that therefore he does "not owe anybody an explanation" for anything.

From Bill Moyers message to West Point, November 29, 2006 quoting James Madison:

> In no part of the Constitution is more wisdom to be found, than in the clause which confides the question of war and peace to the legislature, and not to the executive department. Beside the objection to such a mixture to heterogeneous powers, the trust and the temptation would be too great for any one man.

The United States Military Commissions Act of 2006, enacting Chapter 47A of title 10 of the United States Code, is an Act of Congress (Senate Bill 3930) signed by President George W. Bush on October 17, 2006. The Act's stated purpose is to "facilitate bringing to justice terrorists and other unlawful enemy combatants through full and fair trials by military commissions, and for other purposes."

Signed into law by President Bush on October 17, 2006, the Military Commissions Act suspends the right of habeas corpus to persons "determined by the United States" to be an "enemy combatant" in the Global War on Terror. An "enemy combatant" is anyone who has "purposefully and materially supported hostilities against the United States." The law has drawn severe criticism for its failure to specifically designate who in the United States will determine who is and who is not an "enemy combatant."

After passage of the Act, Jonathan Turley, professor of constitutional law at George Washington University said, "What, really, a time of shame this is for the American system. What the Congress did and what the president signed today essentially revokes over 200 years of American principles and values."

William Rivers Pitt notes that:

> This administration has proven itself to be astonishingly impatient with criticism of any kind. The broad powers given to Bush by this legislation allow him to capture, indefinitely detain, and refuse a hearing to any American citizen who speaks out against Iraq or any other part of the so-called War on Terror. If you write a letter to the editor attacking Bush you could be deemed as purposefully and materially supporting hostilities against the United States. If you organize or join a public demonstration against Iraq, or against the administration, the same designation could befall you. ("In Case I Disappear," Truthout Perpective, September 29, 2006.)

The Military Commissions Act was drafted in the wake of the Supreme Court's decision on Hamdan v. Rumsfeld in which the Court held that military commissions set up by the Bush administration to try detainees at Guantanamo Bay "violate both the Uniform Code of Military Justice and the four Geneva Conventions." On June 29, 2006, the Court issued a 5-3 decision holding that it had jurisdiction, that the federal government did not have authority to set up these particular military commissions, and that the military commissions were illegal.

Hamdan's defense attorney, Lieutenant Commander Charles Swift, was named one of the 100 most influential lawyers in America by the *National Law*

Journal just days before this Court decision. The following October, the Navy announced plans to dismiss him under its "up or out" promotion policy.

Death Throes of Democracy

The line has been crossed. The Republic lost. Johnson oppines:

Congress has forfeited the power to declare war, the Courts have failed to restrain presidential ambition, and the Military at lower levels is too intimidated and at higher levels too well paid to take back democracy in the name of the people.

Johnson thinks that it is unlikely that the People could restore constitutional democracy via a grass roots movement to break the hold of the MIFC and establish public financing of elections because of the conglomerate control of the mass media and the difficulties of mobilizing the United States' large and diffuse population.

The only truly possible scenario that could check presidential, imperial power would be, in Johnson's viewpoint, the:

...economic failure that is the inevitable consequence of military Keynesianism.... With no political check, debt accrues until it reaches a crisis point. The writing is on the wall with projected Iraq War costs of $1 trillion (American Enterprise Institute) to $2 trillion (Stiglitz and Bilmes), the enormous U.S. trade deficit of $213 billion to China and $350 billion worth of U.S. Treasury bills held by China.

The U.S. Department of Commerce reported in "Trade Picture" -- Economic Policy Institute, February 10, 2006 – that the international deficit in goods and services trade reached a record level of $726 billion in 2005, an 18% increase over 2004's $655 billion level which was an 8% increase since the previous year.

Based on several substantial studies, Matt Crenson recently reported for *The Associated Press* that if the US government conducts business as usual over the next few decades, a national debt that is already $8.5 trillion could reach $46 trillion or more, almost as much as the total net worth of every person in America. There have been three tax cuts on the richest of the rich. In 2001 alone the richest 1% received tax relief that will amount to $479 billion over ten years.

And so we hear again the voice of General Smedley Butler alerting us to this line item on the bill of war: "Back-breaking taxation for generations and generations."

Johnson predicts that bankruptcy will "open the way for an unexpected restoration of the American system, or for military rule, revolution, or simply some new development we cannot yet imagine."

As this article nears completion there is a fever pitch of preparation for what is likely to be the most destructive and horrific war the world has ever known. There are ominous signs that Iran is in the crosshairs of attack. Dr. Elias Akleh gives us alarming details in an article titled "Unleashing Armageddon in the Middle East," online at Information Clearing House, November 10, 2006:

US and NATO countries have now amassed the largest military armada in the Middle East, consisting of Carrier Strike Group 12 led by nuclear powered aircraft carrier USS Enterprise, the Eisenhower Strike Group, which is another nuclear powered aircraft carrier with accompanied military vessels and submarines, the Expeditionary Strike Group 5 with multiple attack vessels led by aircraft carrier USS Boxer, the Iwo Jima Expeditionary Strike Group and the US Coast Guard. Canada has sent its anti-submarine HMCS Ottawa frigate to join the American Armada in the Persian Gulf. On October 1st the USS Enterprise Striking Group had crossed the Suez Canal to join NATO armada at the eastern shores of the Mediterranean Sea. The NATO force is composed of troops and naval vessels from several countries and is lead by Germany. It includes German command naval forces, Italian navy, 2 Spanish warships, 3 Danish warships, 10 Green warships, 2 Netherlands warships, and French, Belgium, Turkish and Bulgarian troops in South Lebanon. This is the largest mass ever of military power in the region, and it is gathering for a reason.

Albert Einstein once said, "I know now with what weapons World War III will be fought, but World War IV will be fought with sticks and stones."

Other brilliant and astute minds are expressing great alarm concerning our current reality. The playwright Harold Pinter raged against American foreign policy in his Nobel Prize acceptance speech saying that the United States had not only lied to justify waging war against Iraq but had also "supported and in many cases engendered every right-wing military dictatorship in the last 50 years." He said:

> The crimes of the United States have been systematic, constant, vicious, remorseless, but very few people have actually talked about them. You have to hand it to America. It has exercised a quite clinical manipulation of power worldwide while masquerading as a force for universal good. It's a brilliant, even witty, highly successful act of hypnosis.

In Frank Dorrel's "What I Learned About U.S. Foreign Policy" video compilation former U.S. Attorney General Ramsey Clark says:

> We have a war party in this country and we've had it all along! And you can call it Democrat for a while, you can call it Republican for a while, but it has been the special economic interest in this society that's governed us from the time that we founded our governments on this continent. And the people have never controlled those governments.
>
> We call ourselves the world's greatest democracy – we are absolutely a plutocracy! It's the most obvious thing in the world! Wealth governs this country! And wealth uses military violence to control the rest of the world as best it can. And we're responsible! And we will pay the price for it!
>
> If we don't control our violence, if we don't control the effect of the symbol of our glorification of violence, on our children and on the rest of the planet, then this human species is going to be the first to destroy itself completely. And that's the road the United States government has put us on.

Martin Luther King, Jr. made this profoundly disturbing statement in his famous "Beyond Vietnam" speech at the Riverside Church in New York City on April 4th, 1967, exactly one year before he was assassinated on April 4th 1968:

The greatest purveyor of violence on earth is my own government.

Here ends the Graph Three description of the political-economic system of the Privilege Funders who have brought us to the brink of annihilation of the human species on planet earth.

What are we going to do about it?

The Fourth Graph

Transforming the Privilege Fund

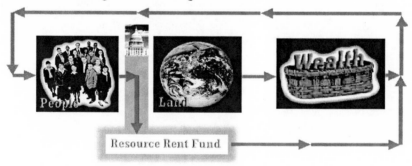

**Man did not make the earth, and, though he had a natural right
to "occupy" it, he had no right to "locate as his property" in perpetuity any part of it; neither did the Creator of the earth open a
land-office, from whence the first title-deeds should issue. It is
the value of the improvement, only, and not the earth itself, that
is individual property. Every proprietor, therefore, ... owes to
the community "ground-rent" for the land which he holds. -
Thomas Paine (1737-1809)**

Preliminary to Description of Graph Four

Before getting to the heart of the matter of Graph 4, let us consider fundamental
values, basic human needs, and what might be reasonable expectations for the end
goals of a fair and functional economic system. For this we will draw upon the vision of a newly emerging political-economic framework called PROUT (Progressive Utilization Theory), some of the Millennium Development Goals as agreed to
by all UN Member States and human rights declarations.

PROUT envisions a world wherein all life forms – plant, animal and human – are
evolving in an integrated manner and expressing the full flowering of physical, psychic and
spiritual potentialities. According to this philosophy, every human being has three fundamental desires: (1) the desire to physically survive; (2) the desire to expand one's horizons and
realize one's maximum potential; and (3) the desire for an inner spiritual peace. The fulfillment of these desires brings happiness. Their frustration brings sorrow.

PROUT includes food, clothing, housing, medical care and education as basic
necessities that must be available to all people through full employment and adequate purchasing power.

All UN Member States have pledged to achieve several Millennium Development Goals by the year 2015, among them: (1) reduce by half the proportion of
people living on less than a dollar a day; (2) reduce by half the proportion of people
who suffer from hunger; and (3) achieve significant improvement in the lives of at
least 100 million slum dwellers.

The basic framework for these goals was set forth in the Universal Declaration of
Human Rights, adopted by the UN General Assembly on December 10, 1948. Article
I states: "All human beings are born free and equal in dignity and rights." Article 25 says:

> Everyone has the right to a standard of living adequate for the health and
> well-being of himself and of his family, including food, clothing, housing
> and medical care and necessary social services, and the right to security in
> the event of unemployment, sickness, disability, widowhood, old age or
> other lack of livelihood in circumstances beyond his control.

The UN Habitat II Action Agenda, adopted by all UN member states in 1996, states:

> Access to land and legal security of tenure are strategic prerequisites for the provision of adequate shelter for all and for the development of sustainable human settlements affecting both urban and rural areas. It is also one way of breaking the vicious circle of poverty. Every Government must ....strive to remove all possible obstacles that may hamper equitable access to land and ensure that equal rights of women and men related to land and property are protected under the law. The failure to adopt, at all levels, appropriate rural and urban land policies and land management practices remains a primary cause of inequity and poverty.

This Action Agenda recommends "land value capture" and "land based taxes" as important approaches to addressing these challenges.

The International Declaration on Individual and Common Rights to Earth declares:

> The earth is the common heritage of all and that people have natural and equal rights to the land of the planet. By the term "land" is meant all natural resources. This Declaration affirms that individuals do have the right to secure and exclusive occupation of land as long as (1) it is not used in such a manner as to destroy or impair the common heritage; and (2) there is a condition upon private and exclusive right to land and that is payment of the "rent" – the annual value attaching to the land alone apart from any improvements thereon – to the community as a whole.

> To allow this value (rent) to be appropriated by individuals enables land to be used not only for the production of wealth but as an instrument of oppression of human by human leading to severe social consequences which are everywhere evident.... Denying the existence of common rights in land creates a condition of society wherein the exercise of individual rights becomes impossible for the great mass of people.

Linking these several perspectives, the realization dawns that to secure economic human rights and to maximize human happiness we need to put in place policies based on an ethic of equal rights to the earth.

GRAPH 4 – A NEW ROLE FOR GOVERNANCE

Graph 4 indicates the profoundly important role that governance must play if we are to establish economic democracy and "earth rights." This graph shows the Privilege Fund converted to a Resource Rent Fund utilized for the public good. Workers, with their just economic opportunities restored, can now accumulate capital through their own savings. Economic justice, abundance and peace are thereby restored.

Prior to the intentional corruption of economics and the resulting travesty of the neoclassical distortion, classical economists had begun to catch the wave of this way forward. Michael Hudson, author of *Super Imperialism: The Economic Strategy of American Empire* and other works, tells us that the "rent tax" is what classical economics was all about. "Adam Smith, David Ricardo, and Alfred Marshall explained the basic logic for taxing windfall gains to land values," says Hudson. Here are some quotes that Hudson has assembled, beginning with Adam Smith who stated in the *Wealth of Nations*:

> (The rent of land) is a species of revenue which the owner, in many cases, enjoys without any care or attention of his own. Though a part of this revenue should be taken from him in order to defray the expenses of the state, no discouragement will thereby be given to any sort of industry. The annual produce of the land and labour of the society, the real wealth and revenue of the great body of the people, might be the same after such a tax as before. Ground rents, and the ordinary rent of land, are, therefore, perhaps, the species of revenue which can best bear to have a peculiar tax imposed upon them.

The French Physiocrats, advisors to Kings Louis XV and XVI, coined the term *laissez faire*. Some also credit them for first use of the word "capitalist" as they wanted to transform the countryside away from the land monopoly of the aristocracy to peasant entrepreneurial activities. Towards this end, and to avoid what they perceived to be a looming bloody revolution, they urged the King to place a tax on land, the *impot unique*. Their advice was not taken and the French Revolution erupted.

Thomas Paine was in communication with the Physiocrats, as is apparent by his statement: "Every landholder owes to the community a ground rent for the land which he holds."

David Ricardo developed the Law of Rent in 1815-1817. In his *Principles of Political Economy and Taxation* he explained "without a knowledge of (the theory of rent), it is impossible to understand the effect of the progress of wealth on profits and wages, or to trace satisfactorily the influence of taxation on different classes of the community."

Alfred Marshall in *Principles of Economics* (1898) based his price theory on the principle that land rent is:

> a surplus in the sense in which the earnings from other agents are not a surplus ... there is this difference between land and other agents of production, that from a social point of view land yields a permanent surplus, while perishable things made by man do not.

Marshall explained that economic growth "tends on the whole to raise the value of land."

Over a hundred years ago Simon Patten, the first Professor of Economics at the Wharton School at the University of Pennsylvania held that rather than funding military industries and financing wars, tax dollars should finance public infrastructure via progressive taxation as a key to building an economics of peace. "If a state is military in character and passive in its [economic development] policy," Patten said, "it is a consumer of wealth and not a producer." Properly funded (from rent capture) public infrastructure investment would "promote general prosperity" and build a "pleasure" economy of abundance.

Graph 4 portrays a new role and *raison d'etre* for the state. This new mandate for governance is to establish a world of peace and prosperity for all based upon principles and policies of earth rights democracy. Without earth rights policies in place, governments succumb to the plays of power, profit, privilege and plunder.

Graph 4 indicates this role of governance with the color GREEN - a reminder that human interaction with the earth to secure basic human needs must be within the capacity of the planet's ability to sustain life for future generations of humans and other life forms.

Here is a proposed "Earth Rights Amendment" that can be adopted by municipal charters or state and national constitutions:

People have a right to the earth, sustained in a healthy condition. Therefore,

1. Government shall enforce the liability of persons – corporate or real – who damage the carrying capacity of the earth.
2. People have a common heritage right to "rent" – the economic value of land sites and natural resources that can be used to meet human needs.
3. Their agent – government – is obliged to effect this sharing by:
4. Collecting resource rent via taxes, leases, use fees, dues, or other means and then
5. Disbursing the recovered rent via provision of government services and/or dividends that benefit all members of society equally.

The constitutions of several countries and commonwealth governments claim the land and natural resources on behalf of the people as a whole. Presently, however, natural resource rent largely escapes taxation, going instead to a few individual or corporate resource owners rather than by rights to all citizens. Various methods of land value capture for public benefit have been developed which can be utilized to secure these common ownership rights. Thus there is now a great potential for the emergence of citizen movements to realize and enforce their "rights to rent" by establishing land value capture and taxation systems.

An emerging new perspective on tax reform, based on the "earth rights democracy" framework, holds that capturing rent for public benefit can yield several positive results including:

- Fair distribution of wealth
- Environmental protection

- Wealth production
- Provision of adequate government services
- Peaceful resolution of territorial conflicts.

This public finance approach <u>removes</u> taxes from privately created wealth including:

- Income, especially from wages, payroll
- Capital, especially of durable quality and non-polluting
- Sales, especially for basic necessities
- Homes and other buildings.

The full rent for private use of our common heritage resources should be collected from:

- Surface land sites according to land value
- Public lands for timber, grazing, mining
- Electromagnetic spectrum
- Geo-orbital zones
- Oil and minerals
- Fish in the ocean
- Water resources
- Emissions into air, water, or soil.

There are numerous examples, past and present, of attempts to base tax policy on this prescription, to capture rent and remove taxes on labor and productive capital. Several examples follow.

Surface Land Value Capture

In New York City after World War I there was an acute housing shortage with high crime and unrest in slums. Construction of housing had halted during the war and was still stalled. Industry blamed the crisis on shortage of investment capital and excessive labor costs. The state legislature determined that high taxes on buildings were the true impediment and passed legislation enabling the city to exempt taxes for ten years on new buildings used only for dwellings. The land beneath such exempted new buildings continued to be taxed. A building boom commenced. No public expenditures were involved in this program. The literature tells us that the "construction industry revived, the dwelling shortage ended, civic panic subsided, and municipal revenues rose."

Unfortunately, the exemptions were rescinded instead of being incorporated into permanent housing legislation. There were two reasons for this. First, when the housing crisis ended, the real estate industry (read big land interests) contended that government should stop interfering with the free market. Since the building tax exemption was a market correction, not an interference, this was a self-serving argument by land speculators and those who counted on housing shortages to allow them to charge high rents. The neoliberal economic paradigm, which neglects the importance of land and land rent, supported these interests as opposed to the public good.

In the state of Pennsylvania twenty municipalities, including Harrisburg, the state capital, have gradually shifted their local property tax systems away from taxes on buildings and instead capture increasing amounts of land rent via taxes based on land values. In all cases studied, building permits increased in those municipalities compared to others of similar size nearby.

Buildings formerly vacated and boarded up were repaired when owners realized it was better to have productive, serviceable properties than to speculate on future rises in land values, especially as they had now to pay taxes on their unused or underused land. With little or no grants or loans, these cities increasingly have been able to fund their needs for roads, fire and police protection and other services including environmental remediation.

In most cases the decision to implement this form of land value capture was made by city officials. In the case of Allentown, the state's third largest city, it was the citizens who pushed for this tax reform by means of a home-rule charter initiative. They voted for a municipal charter that froze or eliminated all other taxes and permitted tax increases on land values only for a period of twelve years. This city now experiences self-sufficient economic revitalization, the logical and expected result of this kind of tax shift. Allentown's new construction and renovation grew by 82% in dollar value in the three years after the system began. This was 54% more than that of Bethlehem, a nearby city of similar size, despite the latter's receipt of a significant amount of federal grant money.

A Virginia Polytechnical University study of Pennsylvania's land value tax (rent capture) cities found that the combination of lowering taxes on buildings and raising them on land values results in a measurable, significant increase in building values generated. The stronger the shift, the more the built environment improved.

Other significant changes detected in similar studies of this policy indicate that:

- Taxes on the majority of owner-occupied and rental homes are reduced
- Construction and rehabilitation of residential and commercial buildings are stimulated
- The serious escalation of housing prices and housing rent experienced by most United States cities was averted in these Pennsylvania cities because housing stock expanded.

- Central business districts were revitalized because they attracted greater private investment.
- More efficient land use resulted as a city's idle lots and underused buildings were put into productive use; this in turn reduced the pressure for costly and environmentally harmful urban sprawl.

Hong Kong's use of a land lease method of capturing land values has been a significant boost to this Asian city. The government owns all the land. Assessment is basically an annual value system, which to a significant degree captures land values for the public, with relatively low tax burdens on industry and labor. A large, subsidized public housing sector is made possible partly because the government already owns the land needed for such dwellings. In addition, the government further subsidizes this housing through grants and loans, at concessionary interest rates, to its housing authority.

Road Usage Rent Capture

Taxation of motor vehicle ownership and usage also involves land values, although this is often unrecognized. To the extent that road usage rights represent rights to use of a land-related resource, taxing that right is completely in line with land value capture policy. In Singapore, where road space is a valuable resource road usage pricing has been implemented since 1975 and has significantly reduced traffic congestion. At the same time, tax rates on income and productive enterprise have been steadily reduced.

To avoid overcrowding and wasting fuel as vehicles idle in traffic jams, London recently introduced land value capture through traffic congestion pricing based on heavy or light use time of day. The number of vehicles in central London has been dramatically reduced, and traffic flows better.

Rent Capture by Obeying the Law

Substantial increases in the amount of land rent captured for public benefit can be gained simply by complying with assessment laws already in place. For example, the U.S. city of Southfield, Michigan found to be out of compliance with a state law that all taxable properties were to be appraised at market value. In Southfield buildings were assessed at 70-80% of market value, but land at only 5-10%. When a Southfield citizen ran for mayor urging compliance, the city stopped exaggerating the value of new construction and renovations, and appraised all land according to highest and best use. James Clarkson was elected to four terms as mayor, each time winning on the issue of fair assessments. Taxes on average homeowners were significantly reduced. The tax base, enhanced by land rent capture, rose by 20% a year during that time, affording many benefits to Southfield's citizens.

Special Benefit Districts

Special benefit assessment districts have often utilized land value capture as the mechanism to pay for new or better public works projects. Upon determining a need for infrastructure benefits, such as paved streets, sidewalks, utilities extensions, or other amenities, a governing jurisdiction designates a district embracing all bene-fiting properties according to the relative land values of the affected properties served by or adjacent to the facility. A land levy is then put in place that pays for the improvements via the capture of the land values, which increase due to the benefits received to the sites because of the new infrastructure.

If such land value capture mechanisms are not in place then holders of vacant land or blighted properties often receive an unearned windfall as their properties increase in value at public expense.

Land value capture benefit assessments districts have the following advantages: Citizens find them to be fair, as those receiving benefits bare the costs; others, who do not benefit, are not expected to pay; orderly urban growth is fostered as local government have more control over where infrastructure is to be extended; benefit districts tend to be democratic and efficient in that projects go forward only if af-fected owners approve; waste is minimized as those who have to pay take pains to confirm that facilities will be worth their cost.

One example of this type of special benefit assessment district was put in place in Ohio, which, after catastrophic floods, inaugurated a flood control system paid for by land value capture. Approximately 77,000 parcels along 110 miles of river valley were individually assessed within two years and land value taxes were levied. The total calculated benefits to properties of the flood control system exceeded $100 million, more than three times the cost of the flood protection project, dem-onstrating that infrastructure can be self-supporting under a land value capture sys-tem.

California's Wright Act allowed communities to vote to create irrigation dis-tricts that could issue bonds to be repaid by taxing the increase in land value. Once irrigated, land was too valuable for grazing and too costly for hoarding. So cattle-men sold fields to farmers at prices the farmers could afford. In ten years the Cen-tral Valley was transformed into over 7,000 independent farms.

Over the next few decades, vast tracts of treeless, semi-arid plains became the breadbasket of America and one of the most productive areas on earth. It is a prime example of how land value taxation can promote and enhance the viability of both an efficient and equitable agricultural base.

This land value capture system brought prosperity and healthy, thriving com-munities. The value of town sites also were enhanced due to the higher productiv-ity of the surrounding farms, yielding higher tax proceeds to local jurisdictions. The irrigation districts became multi-purpose, providing electric power, reclamation, and recreation, as well as water. Some five million acres turned green under this tax reform, which one analyst called "an extraordinarily potent engine for the creation of wealth."

Unfortunately, a large private banking institution disliked the Wright Act because it mandated that the local irrigation districts held the first lien on land for unpaid land value taxes. Banks were relegated to second place as lien holders. One large private bank initiated lawsuits against the enabling legislation and after several tries the Supreme Court dismembered the Wright Act. Now large agribusiness corporations farm the Central Valley using taxpayer-subsidized irrigation.

As more people come to understand the importance of and need for earth rights policies, along with grasping the confluence of the land and land speculator interests with the mortgage and banking interests, there should be fewer setbacks like this in the future. As we keep in mind the two guns above the "rent" and "interest" sections of the graphs, the task ahead for "we the people" becomes clear.

Banks, Rent and Interest

Michael Hudson has it right. Explaining the importance of a rent capture approach to public finance in his paper to the government of Latvia he points out that:

> The motto of real estate speculators is that "rent is for paying interest." Whatever property rent, or monopoly rent, is not taxed is available to be pledged as interest to banks. Buyers borrow the money to obtain real estate or entire companies, including the natural monopolies being privatized. They increase their revenue (and hence, their ability to pay interest on yet larger loans) by raising prices while avoiding taxation by "watered costs" that are tax deductible, headed by interest payments. Bankers and bondholders end up with the economic rent, while owners and managers get capital gains from asset-price inflation.

Hudson has noticed that the more intensely real estate, stock and bond speculation grows, and the more tax subsidies are given to run into debt, then even more money is diverted to speculation and privatization rather than capital formation and employment. Hudson sees a simple and direct solution to the rent/interest problem:

> Under international law sovereign countries have the alternative of simply annulling their debts and taxing their rent-yielding property and capital gains... What is called for is government revenue to build up basic infrastructure. There are two sources of revenue: taxes and Treasury credit creation... If credit is to be created, certainly the national Treasury can create it as efficiently as private banks.

Rent Capture for Solving Humanitarian Crises and Territorial Conflicts

In "The Root Causes of Humanitarian Emergencies," Frances Stewart reports that over the twentieth century an estimated 169 million people were killed in large-scale collective violence, including seventeen individual episodes where more than one million people were killed.

After extensive research into the origination of this massive collective violence, Stewart concluded "The causes are to be found in the interactions of power-seeking with group identity and inequalities".

R. Vayrynen writing in "Weak States and Humanitarian Emergencies: Failure, Predation and Rent-Seeking" urges conflict resolution workers to acknowledge fundamental realities regarding politics and economics by which the state generates and sometimes escalates and prolongs violent conflict through state predatory and rent-seeking activities. Vayrynen's key hypothesis is that:

> Humanitarian crises occur in societies in which the state is weak and elites greedy in pursuing their own interests. In the post-colonial neo-patrimonial state, a strong leader stands at the top of the power pyramid and supports a network of cronies in civilian and military bureaucracies.... The net result is state plunder, exploitation and anarchic, anaemic or failed state systems and increased reliance on force, coercion, and the possibility of organized state sponsored violence against opposition forces.
>
> When the coercive power of the state and the exchange power of the market have been subverted by corrupt politicians and bureaucrats it makes the prospects for sustainable peace extremely unlikely. Trying to harness the integrative power of the community in such a situation by working in and through other civil society institutions, (families, religious, educational, heath, and others) may be helpful in terms of emergency relief and humanitarian assistance. However, it will not yield sustainable peace in either the medium or long term.... These good initiatives will always be subverted by actions of corrupt governments, and the increasing criminalization of politics.

Paul Collier, Mats Berdal, David Malone and others argue strongly that many conflicts can be explained in terms of a competition for control of the production and distribution of natural resources, including land. ... "Conflict diamonds" and the often-illegal exploitation of other natural resources such as timber and oil in Sierra Leone, Angola, the Congo and Sudan point towards resource wars being a significant feature in future conflict transformation work.

Clearly there is an utmost necessity to redefine the role of governance as capturing rent for the many rather than surrendering its powers to the plunder of the few if we are to build a world of peace and justice. Developing strong institutions for this purpose is the task before us, and there are models and guidelines emerging to this end.

Oil and Other Resource Rent Funds

"Experiences with Oil Funds: Institutional and Financial Aspects" is an ESMAP report issued June 2006 which analyzed about a dozen oil and other natural resource rent funds currently in place. Fred Foldvary in "Peace through Confederal Democracy and Economic Justice" has applied the concept of establishing resource rent funds for public benefit as a way to address several areas of violent conflict in the world. There is much to be learned regarding the strengths and weaknesses of various pioneering approaches to these emerging institutions.

The Alaska Permanent Fund, established in 1980, is an excellent model of a transparent and accountable institution that captures resource rent to finance a number of public benefits as well as via direct citizen dividend payments. Under this state's constitution, the people as a whole legally own natural resources. The APF captures rent via oil royalty payments, and then places these moneys in an investment fund that generates dividends paid annually to all individuals, including children, resident in the state for at least one year. More than $27,000 per person has been distributed in this way during the past 28 years. Overall, the dividend program has dispersed more than $10 billion into the Alaskan economy. Alaska is the only state in the United States where the wealth gap has decreased during this period.

New proposals for the establishment of government rent funds are also coming to the fore. One such is the Bayelsa State Oil Fund Commission Bill that would remedy conflicts over oil revenue and environmental degradation in the Niger Delta of Nigeria.

Another indication of the growing interest in capturing rent for public purposes is a measure before the U.S. Senate Appropriations Committee that would recoup $10 billion in lost royalties from oil companies who had been drilling in waters owned by all Americans without paying for those rights under leases awarded in 1998 and 1999.

The United Nations Habitat Agency's newly launched Global Land Tool Network is in an initial phase of development of a program for land value taxation and capture which will be useful for cities and countries who want to implement this approach to poverty eradication and the establishment of fair and sufficient sources of public finance.

Call for a Global Resource Agency

In that many significant sources of actual and potential natural resource rent lies outside of nation state boundaries in the global commons, there is an urgent, rational ethical and democratic imperative for the creation of some type of Global Resource Agency that would be responsible for:

- Monitoring the global commons,
- Determining rules for access to transnational resources,
- Issuing use permits, and
- Collecting and distributing transnational resource rents and revenues.

A Global Resource Agency would have charge of traffic on the seas; over food resources in the ocean; of mineral resources of the ocean floor; over air traffic and use of the electromagnetic spectrum and satellite orbital zones; and all other transnational resources. It would share with local and regional governing authorities jurisdiction over mineral ores, oil and natural gas under land and water.

Other significant global revenue sources are taxes or fees based on the polluter-pay principle such as carbon dioxide emissions, international flights or aviation fuel, international shipping or dumping at sea (if such is to be permitted at all), and air pollution due to industrial activities.

A primary duty of the Global Resource Agency would be to accurately assess and collect these resource rent and user fees and equitably distribute the funds worldwide as calculated by formulas based on population, development criteria and currency purchasing capacity.

Revenues raised from access fees for the use of global commons could fund sustainable development programs, environmental restoration, peacekeeping activities, or low interest loans for poverty eradication. Funds are also needed on the global level to finance justice institutions such as the World Court and the International Criminal Court and to facilitate policy convergence in areas such as trade, currency exchange, and human rights.

Local communities can and should deal with local surface sites such as for farms, residences, businesses, and community benefit or services; regional authorities can best administer regional systems and areas such as watersheds, rivers, ports, forests, grasslands, parks, etc. However, a global authority is needed to regulate, administer, and see to the equitable use of, and profit from the high seas, air, shared water bodies, mineral deposits, etc.

Rather than fight wars over control of transnational resources, the Global Resource Agency would resolve such matters through the use and application of international regulations and law. Such a body could also assume substantial authority for levying fines and penalties for the abuse of common heritage resources. Punitive action would be brought against individual violators of such laws, as well as against government agencies and jurisdictions.

The royalties from the use of such resources would constitute an independent revenue stream adequate to enable the Global Resource Agency to administer its tasks: accurately and fairly assessing the value of transnational resources; collecting resource rents and royalties; patrolling and policing the transnational territory; seeing to the restoration, protection, and sustainable use of such resources; checking violations and maintaining courts before which those accused of violations could be tried; and equitably distributing the funds for worldwide poverty eradication.

Thus the Global Resource Agency would be based upon the pooling of sovereignty over the seas, the air, and the mineral resources of the earth - through recognizing and declaring these to be the common heritage of all the people of the earth. Any person or corporation extracting raw materials from the earth or dumping anything into the global commons would thus be licensed by the Trustees of the Global Resource Agency, and required to pay full resource rents and user fees. The charge would need to be enough to protect the resource, to use it sustainably and in the case of non-renewable resources to build a fund for the gradual replacement by renewable resources. These fees would both support and maintain our systems of global governance and be equitably shared to promote peace, poverty eradication and sustainable development worldwide.

A number of national governments would likely be willing to support the establishment of a Global Resource Agency if it were truly capable of promoting stability and economic human rights for their people. The push for its creation could come from a unity of these countries plus a powerful network of non-governmental organizations. Lead organizations would need to be recruited to promote and develop the plan and to talk with potential governments that might be interested. Places to look for components of a Global Resource Agency include the Law of the Seas Treaty, the Moon Treaty, the UN Commission on the Limits of the Continental Shelf and the Committee on Energy and Natural Resources for Development.

Information Technology for Rent Capture

The powerful tools of information technology can well serve our work in securing the earth as our birthright. Cities and towns are putting property values and tax information into computer databases and onto the web, where this information is transparent and easily accessible. Geographic information systems (GIS) are computer maps containing detailed data. These new technologies are now being utilized in the development of ways to easily, simply and effectively implement land value capture policies.

"Google Earth" types of information technology will be of great assistance to us in finding answers to these important questions: Who owns the earth? How much do they profit? How much land rent do they pay into the common fund?" LANDSAT satellite technology can help us determine if land, water and air resources are being polluted or destroyed. Those indicators can serve as red flags indicating the need to levy pollution taxes or fines. All of these concerns can be monitored by the masses via computer technology. Safeguarding the planet and capturing rent for the people could become "the best game on earth."

Conclusion

"We are not aliens. We are from the same planet."

These are the words on a placard carried by two women among the fifteen thousand people marching for peace and human rights in San Francisco, as shown in a photo from the June 2006 edition of PeaceWork, a publication of the New England Regional Office of the American Friends Service Committee.

U.S. Congressman Dennis Kucinich, a current candidate for President, spoke elegantly the ultimate truth of where we come from in his "Spirit and Stardust" speech given at the Praxis Peace Institute Conference held at Dubrovnik Croatia on June 9, 2002:

> We need to remember where we came from: to know that we are one. To understand that we are of an undivided whole: race, color, nationality, creed, gender are beams of light, refracted through one great prism.
>
> As we aspire to universal brotherhood and sisterhood, we harken to the cry from the heart of the world and respond affirmatively to address through thought, word and deed conditions which give rise to conflict: Economic exploitation, empire building, political oppression, religious intolerance, poverty, disease, famine, homelessness, struggles over control of water, land, minerals, and oil.

This series of graphs has traced inequalities and root causes of wars to the most fundamental flaw in the "person/planet" relationship – the private appropriation of most of the riches of the earth by a few individuals, corporations and banks. Graph 4 has shown us a way forward with several examples of capturing rent for the benefit of the people of the world from the local to the global level.

The very first image in each of the graphs portrays a group of humans as representing humanity as a whole. The identity of each and every one of us as full-fledged and equal members of the human race is the sine qua non – the essential identity – from which to claim our fair share rights to planet Earth.

Exclusive territorial rights to land and natural resources can no longer be based primarily on discovery or prior claim, on conquest or military force, or by financial or legal mechanisms.

The only rational, supportable, moral, just and ethical basis upon which to assert a private claim to the resources of the earth is by birthright to the gifts of nature. The claim by birthright can only be legitimate if it is acknowledged that all other human beings have an equal claim to the gifts of nature. The deepest ethical dimension of territorial rights recognizes that humanity is one and indivisible in its fundamental right to the planet.

We now have many keys in the form of earth rights policies that our governments can use to unlock the riches of the commons in order to meet the basic needs of all those now living while at the same time these common resources can be held in trust for future generations. We are ready to establish earth rights democracy.

If we are to move from warfare to earthshare we must grasp the profound interconnectedness of all life on our small and wondrous world. How we hold the earth is how we hold each other. The rules and laws of governance, of how we choose to live together on the planet, need to reflect this most fundamental truth:

The Earth Belongs to Everyone

About Earth Rights Institute

Alanna Hartzok and Anne Goeke are the Co-Founders and Co-Directors of Earth Rights Institute. Our main offices are in Pennsylvania and California. Earth Rights Institute is dedicated to securing a culture of peace and justice by establishing dynamic worldwide networks of persons of goodwill and special skill, promoting policies and programs which further democratic rights to common heritage resources, and building ecological communities.

Earth Rights Institute initiates and supports programs to reduce poverty and improve the quality of life in distressed rural and urban communities. Our major program areas are earth rights policies, ecological community development, humanitarian aid and building a culture of peace. At this time our primary African partners are in Nigeria, the Democratic Republic of Congo, and Cote d'Ivoire where we have recently opened an office under the directorship of Dr. Toure Dramane.

Our vision and view is that another world is possible and is emerging – a decentralized yet global society where basic needs are met for all, the earth is protected and conserved, and healthy, happy humans live in sustainable communities. Earth Rights Institute collaborates with many individuals, as well as businesses, governments and other non-governmental organizations to achieve our mission.

We welcome your interest, collaboration and support. You may sign-up for our announcements and newsletters, to be a volunteer or intern, and/or make financial contributions to support our work on our website at www.earthrights.net.

Included on our website is an invitation to enroll in our free online course on Land Rights and Land Value Capture. You will receive an Earth Rights Institute certificate upon course completion along with an invitation to collaborate on earth rights implementation projects.

You may also contact us via email or phone.

Alanna Hartzok in Pennsylvania
Alanna@earthrights.net
717-264-0957

Anne Goeke in California
Annie@earthrights.net
310-881-726

About the Author

Alanna Hartzok is an educator, activist, consultant and lecturer in the areas of economic democracy, land rights, financing sustainable development, and public finance policy reform. She is co-director of Earth Rights Institute, a civil society organization working for economic justice and peaceful resolution of conflicts, a United Nations NGO representative for the International Union for Land Value Taxation, a board member of United for a Fair Economy, and on the Advisory Council of the Prout Research Institute of Venezuela.

She recently (2008) completed development work on the Land Rights and Land Value Capture Program of the UN Habitat's newly launched Global Land Tool Network. This program, intended to address the UN Millennium Development Goal of improving the lives of 100,000,000 slum dwellers by the year 2020, describes the what, why, and how of this earth rights policy in preparation for worldwide implementation projects.

In 2004, she was with the team that launched the first ecovillage, a living model of sustainability, in Nigeria in the Niger Delta town of Odi. In 2001, she was a candidate for Congress in the Ninth District of Pennsylvania. In 1993, she initiated tax reform legislation and worked with state legislators to guide it through government hearings to nearly unanimous passage of Senate Bill 211, signed by Governor Thomas Ridge as Act 108 in November of 1998.

Her published articles on tax reform have been useful to legislators in the states of Pennsylvania, Maryland, New Jersey and New York. Her articles are referenced in the literature of the Association of Bay Area Governments in California, in a recent issue of the Federal Reserve Bank of St. Louis Review, in Dialogues, a publication of the Canada West Foundation, and in several books, including The *Natural Wealth of Nations*, a Worldwatch Institute book by David Roodman. She is one of several people featured in *Planet Champions: Adventures in Saving the World* by Jack Yost.

She has given lectures and presented papers on alternatives to neoliberal economics, the land problem, green tax and land value tax policy at numerous venues including the Congressional Black Caucus Forum on Energy in West Africa, UN Habitat World Urban Forums, E. F. Schumacher Society, Chautauqua Institution and the Eastern Economics Association.

In addition to her work with Earth Rights Institute, Alanna maintains a psycho-spiritual counseling practice. A mother of two and grandmother of one, she enjoys permaculture gardening at her eco-homestead in south central Pennsylvania and playing guitar, piano and Native American flute.

BIBLIOGRAPHY

Agarwal, Anil & Sunita Narain. "The Sharing of Environmental Space on a Global Basis" in *Sharing the World: Sustainable Living & Global Equity in the 21st Century* by Michael Carley & Philippe Spapens, London: Earthscan Publications Ltd., 1998.

"Agricultural Real Estate Taxes," USDA , Economic Research Service, AREI update no. 9, 1995.

Aiken, David. "State Farmland Preferential Assessment Statutes," Univ. of Nebraska, RB 310, September 1989.

Akleh, Elias. "Unleashing Armageddon in the Middle East," Countercurrents.org, November 9, 2006.

Alaska Permanent Fund, www.apfc.org

Andersen, Al. "An Educational Challenge Designed to Achieve Economic Justice Worldwide," at www.csf.colorado.edu/sustainable-justice

Avila, Charles. *Ownership: Early Christian Teachings.* Maryknoll, NY. Orbis Books/Maryknoll, 1983.

Bacevich, Andrew. *The New American Militarism: How Americans Are Seduced by War.* New York: Oxford University Press, 2005.

Bacon, Robert and Silvana Tordo. *Experiences with Oil Funds: Institutional and Financial Aspects.* Energy Management Assistance Program (ESMAP), The World Bank Group, Report 321, June 2006.

Baker, Dean. "After the Housing Bubble Bursts," *Truthout/Perspective*, October 24, 2006.

Barlow, Maude. "Water Privatization and the Threat to the World's Most Precious Resource: Is Water a Commodity or a Human Right?" *International Forum on Globalization Bulletin*, Summer, 2001.

Barnes, Peter "The Pollution Dividend," *The American Prospect*, #44, May-June 1999.

Barnaby, Frank. edit. *Building a More Democratic United Nations.* London: Frank Cass & Co. Ltd. 1991.

Barnet, Richard J. "Stateless Corporations: Lords of the Global Economy," *The Nation*, December 19, 1994.

Batstone, David. *Not for Sale: The Return of the Global Slave Trade and How We Can Fight It.* Harper Collins, 2007.

Baumgarter, Harvey. "Grandpa's Hobbit House," *Mother Earth News*, Issue #218, October/November, 2006.

Beck, Hanno T. "Ecological Tax Reform," in *Land Value Taxation*, Kenneth C. Wenzer, ed. New York: M.E. Sharpe, 1999.

_____, Brian Dunkiel and Gawain Kripke, "A Citizens Guide to Environmental Tax Shifting" Friends of the Earth, 1999.

Bender, Bryan. "US is Top Purveyor on Weapons Sales List," *Globe Staff*, November 13, 2006.

Berry, Thomas. "The Spirituality of the Earth" in *Toward a Global Spirituality.* The Whole Earth Papers #16. East Orange, NJ: Global Education Associates, 1982.

Block, Sandra. "Students Struggle under Tens of Thousands in Loans," *USA Today*, Feb. 22, 2006.

Blum, William. *Killing Hope: U.S. Military and CIA Interventions Since World War II.* Common Courage Press, 2004.

_____. *Rogue State: A Guide to the World's Only Superpower. Common Courage Press*, 2000.

_____. "Johnny Got His Gun," *The Anti-Empire Report.* January 12, 2007.

Borsodi, Ralph. *Seventeen Problems of Man and Society.* India: R.C. Patel, 1968.

Brauer, David, "The Eagle Dies on Friday," *Utne Reader*, September-October, 1998.

Brock, Richard. "Farmland Prices EXPLODE," *The Corn and Soybean Digest*, Mar 1, 2004.

Brueggeman, Walter. "Land: The Foundation of Humanness," *The Whole Earth Papers* #17, Global Education Associates, 1982.

Brzezinski, Zbigniew. *The Grand Chessboard - American Primacy and Its Geostrategic Imperatives.* New York: Basic Books/Perseus Books Group, 1997.

Bureau of Justice Statistics, http://www.ojp.usdoj.gov/bjs/prisons.htm.

Butler, Smedley. *War is a Racket*. New York: Round Table Press, 1935.

Cairns, Earle Edwin. *The Christian in Society*. Chicago: Moody Press, 1973.

Carley, Michael & Philippe Spapens, *Sharing the World: Sustainable Living & Global Equity in the 21st Century*. London: Earthscan Publications Ltd., 1998.

Chossudovsky, Michel. *The Globalisation of Poverty: Impacts of IMF and World Bank Reforms*. London: Zed Books, 1998.

Cobb, Clifford et. al., "Fiscal Policy for a Sustainable California," San Francisco, CA: Redefining Progress, 1995.

Cohen, Solomon Solis. "The Land Question in the Talmud," a pamphlet available from the Robert Schalkenbach Foundation, New York.

Collins, Chuck and John Miller, "Tax Reform Follies," *Dollars and Sense*, March/April, 1999.

Cord, Steven. " Impact of a Graded Tax on a Rural Area," *The American Journal of Economics and Sociology*, vol. 35, no. 1, January, 1976.

Dorrel, Frank. "What I Learned About U.S. Foreign Policy," a video documentary available at http://www.addictedtowar.com/dorrel.html. (highly recommended)

Dreyfuss, Robert."The Thirty-Year Itch," *Mother Jones*, March/April, 2003..

Dunkley, Godfrey. "Good news as Cape Town Chooses SVR," *Land & Liberty*, Winter 1997.

Durning, Alan Thein and Yoram Bauman. *Tax Shift*. Seattle: Northwest Environment Watch, 1998.

Earth Ethics quotes: http://www.earthethics.com/archive_of_ quotes.htm

Edwards, David. *Burning All Illusions*. South End Press, 1996.

Eisenhower, Dwight D. "Military-Industrial Complex Speech," Public Papers of the Presidents, 1035-1040, Robert Dreyfuss.

Elkins, Stanley and Eric McKitrick. "Thaddeus Stevens: Confiscation and Reconstruction." *The Hofstadter Aegis: A Memorial*. New York: Alfred A. Knopf, 1974.

"Farm Subsidies Fair?" *Public Opinion*, Chambersburg, PA September 9, 1995.

Ferrell, John. "This Land Was Made for You and Me." *Rain Magazine*, June 1982.

Foner, Philip, ed. *The Complete Works of Thomas Paine*. New York: Citadel Press, 1945.

Fraser, C. Gerald."United Nations Development Programme at Crossroads" *Earth Times*, May 16 - 31, 1999. www.earthtimes.org

Freeman, Gerene L. "What About My 40 Acres & A Mule?" *Emerging Minds Archives*, http://www.emergingminds.org/nov03/diduknow.html

Freeman, Richard B. and Brian Hall in "Permanent homelessness in America?" *Social Science Research Network*, March 1988, http://papers.ssrn.com/sol3/papers.cfm?abstract_id=344808.

Gaffney, Mason and Fred Harrison. *The Corruption of Economics*, Shepheard-Walwyn, 1994.

Gaffney, Mason. "Rising Inequality and Falling Property Tax Rates," published in *Land Ownership and Taxation in American Agriculture*, edited by Gene Wunderlich, San Francisco: Westview Press, 1992.

_____. *Henry George, Edward McGlynn & Pope Leo XIII*. NY: Robert Schalkenbach Fdn., 2000.

_____. "Rent-Seeking and Global Conflict," Paper presented to University of California Seminar on Global Conflict and Cooperation, Laguna Beach, Feb. 1988. (www.masongaffney.org).

Gary, Ian. "Oil for us; hope for them: U.S. trade with Africa should stress value of human rights," *Philadelphia Inquirer*, July 9, 2001.

Gates, Jeff. *The Ownership Solution*, Addison Wesley, 1998.

George, Henry. *Progress and Poverty*. New York: Robert Schalkenbach Foundation, 1992. First published 1879.

_____. *Social Problems*. New York: Robert Schalkenbach Foundation, 1996. First published 1883.

_____. "Ode to Liberty" a speech delivered in San Francisco on July 4, 1877, pamphlet available from the Robert Schalkenbach Fdn.

_____. *The Science of Political Economy*. New York: Robert Schalkenbach Fdn., 1992. First published 1898.

George, Susan. *How the Other Half Dies*, Penquin Books, 1986.

Global Institute for Taxation. *Taxation Alternatives for the 21st Century*. Proceedings of the 1999 conference.

Goldman, Michael. *Privatizing Nature: Political Struggles for the Global Commons*. London: Pluto Press, 1998.

Hamilton, Leonard, ed. *Gerrard Winstanley: Selections from His Works*. London: The Cresset Press, 1994.

Hamond, Jeff M. edit. *Tax Waste, Not Work: How Changing What We Tax Can Lead to a Stronger Economy and a Cleaner Environment*. San Francisco: Redefining Progress,1997.

Harrison, Fred. *The Losses of Nations*. London: Othila Press, 1998.

Harriss, C. Lowell."The Economic Effects of Today's Property Tax," Encylopaedia Britannica, 15th Edition, 1974.

Hartzok, Alanna. "Democracy, Earth Rights, and the Next Economy," E.F. Schumacher Lecture published in pamphlet form, 2002.

_____. "Financing Local to Global Public Goods: An Integrated Green Tax Shift Perspective." Global Institute for Taxation, Conference on Fundamental Tax Reform. New York, September 30, 1999.

_____. "Financing Planet Management: Sovereignty, World Order and the Earth Rights Imperative." New York: Robert Schalkenbach Foundation, 1995.

_____. "Pennsylvania's Success with Local Property Tax Reform: The Split Rate Tax," *American Journal of Economics and Sociology*, vol. 56 no.2, April, 1997.

_____. "The Alaska Permanent Fund: A Model of Resource Rents for Public Investment and Citizen Dividends." *Geophilos*, a publication of the Centre for Land Policy Studies, London, Spring 2002.

_____. "Pennsylvania Farmers and the Split Rate Tax " in *Land Value Taxation: The Equitable and Efficient Source of Public Finance*, an anthology edited by K. C. Wenzer, New York: M.E. Sharpe, 1999.

Hallinan, Conn. "Shafting the Vets," *Foreign Policy in Focus*, November 10, 2006.

Heilprin, John. "Army Probes War Contractor Fraud," *The Washington Post*, January 27, 2007.

Hightower, Jim. "Insurance Giants Take Stock in Tobacco," *Alternet*, April 26, 2000.

Hoerner, J. Andrew."Harnessing the Tax Code for Environmental Protection: A Survey of State Initiatives" in State Tax Notes, Special Supplement, Tax Analysts, April 20, 1998.

"Household Food Security in the United States," *Economic Research Services*, USDA, 2002.

Howells, Benjamin, William Kells and Steven Cord. "Allentown Research Results," *Incentive Taxation*, July, 2000.

Huddle, Norie. Best Game on Earth. www.bestgame.org.

Hudson, Michael with G.J. Miller and Kris Feder. *A Philosophy for a Fair Society*. London: Shepheard-Walwyn, 1994.

_____. *Superimperialism: The Economic Strategy of American Empire*, 2nd edition. London: Pluto Press, 2003.

Human Development Report, 2005.

Johnson, Chalmers. *The Sorrows of Empire: Militarism, Secrecy, and the End of the Republic*. New York: Owl Books/Henry Holt, 2005.

_____. "A National Intelligence Estimate on the United States," *Harper's Magazine*, January 17, 2007.

"Kids Count Data Book." *Public Opinion*, Chambersburg, PA, April 25, 1994.

Kimberlin, Joanne and Bill Sizemore. "Blackwater: Inside America's Private Army," *The Virginian-Pilot*, July 23, 2006.

King, Martin Luther, Jr. "Beyond Vietnam: A Time to Break Silence." A speech delivered on April 4, 1967, at a meeting of Clergy and Laity Concerned at Riverside Church in New York City.

Klare, Michael T. *Resource Wars: The New Landscape of Global Conflict*. New York: Henry Holt, 2001.

Kohr, Leopold. *The Breakdown of Nations*. New York: E.P. Dutton, 1978.

Kostigen, Thomas. "The Three Richest People in the World," *Market Watch*, December 12, 2006.

Korten, David C. *When Corporations Rule the World*. Co-published in USA by Kumarian Press and Berrett-Koehler Publishers, 1995.

_____. "Civic Engagement to Create Just and Sustainable Societies for the 21st Century," The People-Centered Development Forum, New York, NY, January 10, 1996.

_____. "The Limits of the Earth," *The Nation*, July 15/22, 1996.

Kotz, David. "How Many Billionaires Are Enough?" *New York Times*, October 19, 1986.

Kucinich, Congressman Dennis. "Spirit and Stardust," speech given at the Praxis Peace Institute Conference, Dubrovnik, Croatia, June 9, 2002.

Land and Liberty. A periodical published by the Henry George Foundation, UK.

Locke, John. *Second Treatise on Civil Government*. 1690. at: http://www.constitution.org/jl/2ndtreat.htm

Maheshvaranda, Dada. *After Capitalism: Prout's Vision for a New World*. Proutist Universal Publications, 2002.

Malme, Jane. "Preferential Property Tax Treatment of Land," Lincoln Institute of Land Policy, 1993.

Meyer, Peter. "Land Rush - A Survey of America's Land - Who Owns It, Who Controls It, How much is Left," *Harpers*, January 1979.

Mian, Zia. "The Three U.S. Armies in Iraq," *Foreign Policy in Focus*, January, 2007.

Mische, Patricia. "Spirituality and World Order," published in Toward a Global Spirituality: The Whole Earth Papers #16, Global Education Associates, 1982.

Mohawk, John. *The Problem of the Modern World*, CREATION, May/June, 1982.

Mora, Barbara and Monic Sjoo. *The Great Cosmic Mother: Rediscovering the Religion of the Earth*. San Francisco: Harper Collins, 1991.

Moyers, Bill. "Message to West Point," November 29, 2006.

Nafziger, Wayne, Frances Stewart and Raimo Vayrynen. *War, Hunger, and Displacement: The Origins of Humanitarian Emergencies*. Oxford University Press, 2000.

National Coalition for the Homeless. "Why are People Homeless?" Fact Sheet #1, September 2002, http://www.nationalhomeless.org/causes.html

National Student Campaign Against Hunger and Homelessness http://www.nscahh.org/hunger.asp?id2=8802

Newcomb, Steven T. *Pagans in the Promised Land*. Eugene, OR: Indigenous Law Institute, 1992.

Noyes, Richard, *Now the Synthesis: Capitalism, Socialism, and the New Social Contract*. New York: Homes & Meier, London: Shepheard-Walwyn, 1991.

Oates, Wallace and Robert Schwab. "Urban Land Taxation for the Economic Rejuvenation of Center Cities: The Pittsburgh Experience," *Incentive Taxation*, October, 1992.

Palast, Greg. "IMF's Four Steps to Damnation," *Observer*, April 29, 2001.

Paul, Leslie Allen. *Sir Thomas More*. New York: Roy Publishers, 1959.

Peddle, Francis K. *Cities and Greed: Taxes, Inflation and Land Speculation*. Canadian Research Committee on Taxation, Ottawa, Ontario, Canada, 1994.

Pelletier, Stephen. *Iraq and the International Oil System: Why America Went to War in the Gulf*. Praeger Publishers, 2001.

Pennsylvania Department of Agriculture, "Statistical Summary Annual Report," National Agricultural Statistics Service, PASS-119, 1995-1996.

Perkins, John. *Confessions of an Economic Hit Man*. San Francisco: Berrett-Koehler, 2004.

Petrarolpha, Fabio L.S. "Brazil: The Meek Want the Earth Now," *Bulletin of the Atomic Scientists*, November/December, 1996.

Pitt, William Rivers. "In Case I Disappear," *Truthout Perspective*, September 29, 2006.

Ricardo, David. *On the Principles of Political Economy and Taxation*. London: John Murray, 1821. (available on the internet).

Robberson, Tod. "The Contractors' War Role Debate," *The Dallas Morning News*, Nov. 28, 2006.

Robertson, James. *Future Wealth: New Economics for the 21st Century*. New York: Bootstrap Press, 1990.

Roodman, David Malin. *The Natural Wealth of Nations: Harnessing the Market for the Environment*, New York: W. W. Norton & Company/World Watch, 1998.

_____. "Paying the Piper: Subsidies, Politics, and the Environment," *Worldwatch* Paper #133, 1996.

Rybeck, Rick. "Tax Reform Motivates Sustainable Development," *American Institute of Architects/DC News*, Dec. 1995/Jan. 1996.

Schroyer, Trent. edit. *A World That Works: Building Blocks for a Just and Sustainable Society*. New York: Bootstrap Press, 1997.

_____. and Tom Golodik, editors. *Creating a Sustainable World: Past Experience/ Future Struggle*. Apex Press, 2006.

Scott, Janny and Randal C. Archibold. "Across Nation, Housing Costs Rise as Burden," *New York Times*, October 3, 2006.

Siegel, Eli. "Ownership: Some Moments." *The Right of Aesthetic Realism to Be Known*, Periodical of the Aesthetic Realism Foundation, May 5, 1999.

_____. "Self and World." *The Right of Aesthetic Realism to Be Known*, Dec. 22, 1999.

"Significant Features of Fiscal Federalism," Advisory Commission on Intergovernmental Relations, Vol. 2 (1994).

Sjoo, Monida and Barbara Mor, *The Great Cosmic Mother: Rediscovering the Religion of the Earth*. San Francisco: Harper & Row, 1987.

Sklar, Holly. "Growing Gulf between Rich and Rest of US," *Information Clearing House*, October 3, 2005.

Smiley, David. "Third World Intervention: A New Analysis,"Redfern, Australia: New South Wales Henry George Foundation, 1998.

Smith, Gaddis. *Morality, Reason, and Power: American Diplomacy in the Carter Years*. New York: Hill and Wang, 1986.

Smith, J.W. *Economic Democracy: The Political Struggle of the Twenty-First Century*, 2nd edition, Institute for Economic Democracy Press, 2006.

_____. *Money: A Mirror Image of the Economy*. Institute for Economic Democracy Press, 2006.

Starcke, Viggo. "Triumph or Fiasco," Stig Vendelkers Forlag Press, Denmark,1972.

Stiglitz, Joseph E. *Globalization and Its Discontents*. New York: W.W.Norton, 2003.

The Gemara, Baba Bathra, (122, A) http://www.come-and-hear.com/bababathra/bababathra_122.html

The Quotes Center. http://teachers.sduhsd.k12.ca.us/gstimson/quotes.htm

Tideman, Nicolaus and Florenz Plassman. "A Markov Chain Monte Carlo Analysis of the Effect of Two-Rate Property Taxes on Construction," *Journal of Urban Economics*, Vol. 47, March 2000.

_____. "Taxed Out of Work and Wealth: The Costs of Taxing Labor and Capital," pp. 146-74 in F. Harrison (ed.), *The Losses of Nations: Deadweight Politics vs. Public Rent Dividends*, London: Othila Press, 1998.

Tully, Shawn "Is the Housing Boom Over?" *Fortune*, September 27, 2004.

U.S. Department of Agriculture, Economic Research Service, "Major Land Uses in the United States" 1992.

UN Habitat II Action Agenda , June 15, 1996, go to www.uno.org for this and other UN documents.

"America's Real Estate," Urban Land Institute, 1997.

Vallianatos, Evaggelos. *This Land is Their Land: How Corporate Farms Threaten the World*. Common Courage Press, 2006.

_____. "Why Small Farmers are Essential to Democracy," *The Progressive Populist*, August 1-15, 2002.

Vidal, Gore. *Dreaming War*. New York: Thunder's Mouth Press/Nation Books, 2002.

_____. *Perpetual War for Perpetual Peace: How We Got to be So Hated*. New York: Thunder's Mouth Press/Nation Books, 2002.

Ward, Justin R. with F. Kaid Benfield, and Anne E. Kinsinger, "Reaping the Revenue Code: Why We Need Sensible Tax Reform for Sustainable Agriculture," Natural Resources Defense Council, New York, 1989.

Webb, James. "Class Struggle," *Wall Street Journal*, November 15, 2006.

Wenzer, Kenneth C. editor, *Land Value Taxation: The Equitable and Efficient Source of Public Finance*. New York: M.E. Sharpe, 1999.

Whitney, Mike. "Why Fisk is Wrong about Lebanon," *Information Clearing House*, January 28, 2007.

"Whose Common Future?" A Special Issue of *The Ecologist*, July/August, 1992.

Wolff, Edward N. *Recent Trends in Wealth Ownership,* 1983-98. Calculations based on 1998 Survey of Consumer Finances conducted by the Federal Reserve Bank.

_____. "The Wealth Divide: The Growing Gap in the US Between the Rich and the Rest," *Multinational Monitor,* May, 2003.

World Institute for Development Economics Research, United Nations University, 2000.

World Peace News, a quarterly publication, November, 1993.

Wunderlich, Gene."Land Taxes in Agriculture: Preferential Rates and Assessment Effects," *The American Journal of Economics and Sociology,* vol. 56 no. 2, April, 1997.

_____. and John Blackledge. "Taxing Farmland in the United States," USDA Economic Research Service Agricultural Economics Report #679, March 1994.

Yost, Jack. *Planet Champions, Adventures in Saving the World.* Portland: Bridge City Books, 1999.

PHOTOGRAPH AND ILLUSTRATION CREDITS

Title page, Earth image, open source

p. 25, 107, 220, 246, 264, 340, from Alanna Hartzok photo collection

p. 50, courtesy of E. F. Schumacher Society, www.schumachersociety.org

p. 55, Earth in shopping cart, from Organic Mall, www.organicmall.com

p. 59, mskzalameda, with interesting commentary
http://hubpages.com/hub/earth_for_sale

p. 66, Wangari Maathai, courtesy of Green Belt Movement,
www.greenbeltmovement.org

p. 68, Canyon de Chellys, courtesy of Lorene Willis, www.jicarilla.net

p. 82, Child in Jakarta slum garbage dump, 2004 Reuters Fdn., Alert Net,
www.alertnet.org

p. 83, Pie diagrams, as found in *Tax Shift*

p. 88, North Mountain West Virginia Care website, www.northmountain.org

p. 108, courtesy of Francis Udisi

p. 144, Communications Coordination Committee of the United Nations,
www.cccun.org

p. 150, courtesy of Gordon Abiama

P.155, Courtesy of Annie Goeke

p. 174, from website of Alaska Permanent Fund Dividend Division,
www.apfc.org

p. 186, courtesy of Gordon Abiama

p. 193, Refugees in transit, UNHCR, the UN Refugee Agency, www.unhcr.org

p. 253, courtesy of The Dhammakaya Foundation, www.dhammakaya.or.th

p. 266, courtesy of Abram Hartzok

p. 276, courtesy of Federation of World Peace and Love, www.fowpal.org

p. 278, courtesy of U.S. Army War College Foundation, www.awcfoundation.org

p. 279, 282, 298, 324, four charts original design by Mildred Loomis, circa1954,
graphics design upgrade 2004 by Lindy Davies, director, Henry George Institute, www.henrygeorge.org

p. 306, courtesy of Francis Udisi

INDEX

Other books published by The Institute for Economic Democracy Press

Economic Democracy: A Grand Strategy for World Peace and Prosperity, 2nd edition, J.W. Smith, 2008

Money: A Mirror Image of the Economy, 2nd edition, J.W. Smith, 2008

The Emperor's God: Imperial Misunderstandings of Christianity, Michael Rivage-Seul, 2008

Emerging World Law, Editors Eugenia Almand and Glen T. Martin, 2008

Ascent to Freedom: The Philosophical Foundations of Democratic World Law, Glen T. Martin, 2008

Twenty-First Century Democratic Renaissance: From Plato to Neoliberalism to Planetary Democracy, Errol E. Harris, 2008

World Revolution Through World Law: Basic Documents of the Emerging Earth Federation, Glen T. Martin, 2005

Millennium Dawn: The Philosophy of Planetary Crisis and Human Liberation, Glen T. Martin, 2005

A Constitution for the Federation of Earth, Editor Glen T. Martin, 2008
Earth Federation Now! Tomorrow is Too Late, Errol E. Harris, 2005

WHY: The Deeper History of the September 11th Terrorist Attack on America, 3rd edition, J.W. Smith, 2005

Cooperative Capitalism: A Blueprint for Global Peace and Prosperity, 2nd edition, J.W. Smith, 2005